Business Studies

Susan Hammond

Longman Group UK Limited,
Longman House, Burnt Mill, Harlow,
Essex CM20 2JE, England
and Associated Companies throughout the world.

First published 1988
This edition 1991
Fifth impression 1992

Set in 10/12pt Palatino, Linotron 100/300
Produced by Longman Singapore Publications Pte Ltd
Printed in Singapore

The publisher's policy is to use paper manufactured from
sustainable forests.

Acknowledgements

We are grateful to the following for permission to reproduce copyright material:

Associated Examining Board for questions from past examination papers and an adapted
extract 'Assessment Objectives' from the *AEB Business Studies – 655 Syllabus – Advanced Level,
1991 Examination*; University of Cambridge Local Examinations Syndicate for questions
from past examination papers; The Economist Publications Ltd for the article 'Fax and
Fiction: Tokyo' from *The Economist* 22.8.88 and an adapted extract from the article 'Business
Brief' from *The Economist* 29.10.83; The Liverpool Daily Post and Echo Ltd for an extract from
Liverpool Echo 8.8.90; Merseyside Development Corporation for an extract from the
advertisement 'Investment Thrives On Our Banks'; the Department of Trade and Industry
for the Assisted Areas Map © Crown copyright, reproduced from Industrial Development
Act Annual Report; Computerland Europe for an advertisement.

Cover: New York Stock Exchange, USA.
Photo: Pictor International, London.

Contents

Introduction: to the student

Teachers do not find it easy to write textbooks. They have knowledge relating to the subject – and what they do not have they can research. They will have experience of the examinations the students may face. They may even have the ability to write clear accessible prose.

All teachers will acknowledge that their approach to the subject will differ from that of their colleagues. Their approach will also differ from group to group, depending on the interests, experience and ability of the group being taught. That is where a textbook differs. Once the words have been written and the type set, the textbook is fixed until it finally falls to pieces in the hands of the student. The book needs to cope with a wide variety of abilities and interests simultaneously.

The way in which you use this book will depend on the type of person you are, the situation in which you are learning, and your previous experience. The following sections are only suggestions on the ways in which you might proceed.

The lone student

If you have already taken a course in business studies, or in a related subject like economics or commerce, you should read Chapters 1, 2 and 3 to refresh your memory.

If you have never studied these subjects before, you should read these chapters carefully. They introduce ideas and terms frequently used in writing about business, and unless you have some knowledge of them you will find your further reading hampered.

In a class

Your approach to the subject will be decided by your class teacher. This loss of freedom is compensated for by the fact that you will have the support of a person who can explain unfamiliar terms and direct your studies according to your progress.

1   Begin with one of the suggested activities at the end of each chapter. You do not need any knowledge of business to investigate the marketing or production of a company. You pose the questions 'Why?', 'Where?', 'When?', 'How?', 'At what cost?' and 'To whom?'. The answers will give you your first insight into the behaviour of business. You can then use the chapters of the book to put your new-found knowledge into context.

2   Study the chapters in turn, and test your knowledge before you begin to experience the wide range of practice prevalent in the world of business. The discoveries you make may shake your confidence in this book. They should not do so. Business, like the world in which it exists, is changing all the time. A textbook can only provide you with the tools to observe and then interpret what you see.

Some of you may be experiencing a teaching strategy known as supported self study. The essentials of this approach are:

    ☐   A regular meeting between student and tutor to discuss the work to be done, timing and methods.

    ☐   Combined student–tutor assessment of achievement.

The first edition of this book was successfully used to prepare students for A-level using this strategy. As a result of this experience, this new edition includes learning objectives for each chapter and a larger number of self-assessment questions.

Studying at advanced level

You should not interpret the words 'advanced level' as meaning 'the same as before only more of it'! This is a mistake many students make. They see progression from one course to another as automatic, and success in GCSE, BTEC General, CPVE or similar courses as a good predictor of success as they move on. Advanced level means what it says. It demands a higher level of intellectual skill. When students find this difficult, they tend to excuse themselves by saying they lack the intelligence required. That is the easy way out. Some people do find it easier than others, but experience suggests that it is lack of commitment to the course, lack of understanding about what is required and lack of confidence that are the root of failure, rather than lack of ability.

What are intellectual skills?

All human activity demands the use of the mind and the body. It is the way we are made. The dressmaker has to make decisions about design (related to the person who will wear the dress), suitable material, quantity required, pattern layout, costs, etc., before scissors are put near material. A plumber may have to plan the rerouting of pipes before installing an appliance. People involved in practical work are at one end of a range of experience. They have the advantage of seeing a physical result to their work and spotting the mistakes they have made. Their manual skills are there for all to see. Many reach advanced level. They have perfected their skills and gone on to acquire more difficult ones.

Intellectual skills have a great deal in common with this. You are setting out on a course that will develop your ability to analyse problems more rapidly, see connections with other problems, and judge the validity of your conclusions before you use expensive materials. You will learn to plan and to put plans into action. You will think faster and more clearly than people who have not had your training and you will get things done.

Levels of skill

A plumber can repair a burst pipe, but some can also plan the water and waste disposal system for a house. The latter is a higher skill. It is usual in our society to grade people by the skill level they have reached. Intellectual skills are no different. You will see this more clearly if we look at the assessment objectives for the examination.

Assessment objectives

The assessment objectives of the various A- and A/S-level examinations are laid down in the published syllabuses. Students should be constantly aware of these objectives when preparing the different forms of assessment set by their tutors. Several of the GCSE syllabuses (for

Assessment objectives

1   Knowledge

Candidates should have knowledge of:

- the terminology of business.

- specific facts relating to business.

- the methods of enquiry into business problems.

- the nature and purpose of business activity.

2   Comprehension

Candidates should have the ability to:

- understand and interpret information presented in written or numerical form.

- translate such information from one form to another.

- recognise errors and fallacies in given information.

- apply basic principles to routine situations.

3   Application

Candidates should be able to:

- select and apply given principles in unfamiliar situations.

- select the appropriate method for the solution of a problem.

- apply procedures appropriate to a situation.

4   Analysis

Candidates should be able to:

- recognise unstated assumptions.

- distinguish between statements based on fact and those based on hypothesis.

- examine the implications of complex and changing business situations.

5   Synthesis and evaluation

Candidates should be able to:

- make deductions from the material presented.

- examine the implications of a situation.

- make valid generalisations about given business situations.

- weigh the reliability and value of evidence drawn from a variety of sources.

- check that the conclusions that have been drawn are consistent with the evidence presented.

6   Expression

Some of you may believe that it is what you say that counts, rather than how you say it. Try to banish this idea from your minds. As a chief examiner, I read numerous scripts in which I could not award marks because the candidates lacked the ability to express their ideas in a clear and logical manner and were therefore unable to communicate their understanding of the complexities of the situation. Since that time I have read the reports of other chief examiners, and can see in them the same concern. Remember:

- Marks are awarded for the structure of diagrams. The correct labelling of axes, for example, will be credited.

- Examinations are, in themselves, unfamiliar situations. No matter how many 'model answers' you prepare during your course, you will face questions which are unfamiliar in the examination itself. You must have the ability to plan and present your information in a clear and logical manner.

Plainly put, you cannot demonstrate the skills demanded by the assessment objectives at A-level if your expression and presentation are poor.

example NEA Business Studies Syllabus B) contain profiles that can be usefully adapted for advanced level, and which can provide tutor and student with an instrument for review or target setting. Student awareness of the demands of the A-level syllabus often has the effect of lowering resistance to work demanded by increased participation in the planning of courses of study and a consequent increase in control.

The assessment objectives given on page vi have been adapted from the AEB A-level Business Studies Syllabus. They are, however, sufficiently broad based to form a useful framework for any A-level course.

Assessment methods

Advanced level business studies syllabuses vary in their methods of assessment (see pages viii and ix). You should remember that the method chosen is the one judged most suitable to allow you, the candidate, to demonstrate to the full the skills you have acquired during the course. The mark allocations are there to help you judge the amount of information you need to give and the importance you should attach to that question or part of a question.

Coursework in Business Studies and Commerce: a student guide by Diane Wallace (Causeway Press) is intended for GCSE students. It provides a good starting point for advanced level students, and emphasises good practice that you may have forgotten.

The projects suggested at the end of each chapter in this book should be seen as no more than suggestions. All have been used in an A-level business studies course, but they were selected after discussion with local employers and managers.

Studying at advanced level

If the examination requirements seem overwhelming it is worth looking more closely at your study techniques. Your tutors may impress you with the speed with which they read and assimilate information and the clarity with which they analyse a problem. Do not assume that this is inherited ability. Years of practising these skills have made them more able to apply them. Like all skills, there are accepted methods that can make this process easier. If you are new to studying you might find the structured approach outlined in such books as *Strategies for Studying* by Coles and White (Collins) useful. Specialist textbooks will obviously treat different aspects of business in more depth than is possible in this book. There is a selection at the end of this book ('Booklist' page 405). The shelves of a good library will hold a great many more. The financial pages of national newspapers such as *The Guardian, The Times, The Independent, The Daily Telegraph* and *The Financial Times*, or their Sunday equivalents, will give many examples of the way in which changes in society affect business and the way in which individual businesses respond to these. *Management Today*, published by the British Institute of Management, contains excellent articles on individual businesses and industries, while publications such as *Marketing*, designed for marketing professionals, give revealing insights into the problems associated with different business functions. Trade union journals offer a different, but no less valid, perspective on the business world, as do political articles.

Conclusion

If this Introduction has made you despair of business studies, you may be consoled by the thought that every experience in your life will give you useful material to help you understand business. After all it is the people who make the business and people are all around you. Very few of the examples and quotations given in this book are pure invention. They all have a solid grounding in the experience of a local community concerned with earning a living. That knowledge is available to you through your family, friends and experience, including work experience.

This book can help you make sense of this world by offering a body of knowledge in, hopefully, a coherent and logical order. But of course that knowledge is always changing, and no book can give you the skills you need. You can only acquire them for yourself.

Assessment methods

1   Short answer questions

(AEB Paper 1, Section A)
These questions place emphasis on knowledge and understanding. They should be answered as accurately and concisely as possible. You should make a habit of learning as you go through the course, not simply to gain marks in this section, but because it is difficult to practise skills of analysis, synthesis and evaluation if you are always trying to remember the basic information on which your argument is based.

2   Data response questions

(AEB Paper 1, Section B; CLES Paper 1)
Data response questions provide you with data presented in statistical, diagrammatic or verbal form and ask for your interpretation of that data in a series of questions. Some of these questions will be based on the information given. As a general principle you should assume that you will get no marks if you simply copy down the information given. Look carefully at the mark allocation to help you decide on the amount of time and effort you should give to each part of the question.

3   Structured questions

Data response questions are structured in that they are divided into parts and the level of skill required rises as you work your way through the question. Remember your assessment objectives when tackling a structured essay. The following is my analysis of a question taken from the CLES Paper 2 of 1987:

a The government has decided to privatise public libraries. How might this decision be implemented? (10 marks)
Knowledge and understanding of different methods of privatisation. Some analysis of the particular problems that might be involved in privatising libraries. Judgment as to which would be the best method to use in this instance.

b As the chief librarian of a public library, write a report to the local member of parliament either supporting or condemning this proposal. (15 marks)
Analysis, synthesis and evaluation of the arguments for and against privatisation. Whichever point of view you decide to take you must have a good knowledge of the opposition's arguments so that you can counter them. You should also remember that this is a business studies question, and uncritical repetition of media reports will not be viewed favourably.

4   Essays

The open-ended essay is one of the more difficult skills required for A-level. You will find it useful to remember all the basic rules that teachers of English have tried to instil in you over the years:

□   Analyse the question set. The answer you provide must relate to the question set – not the question you wished had been set!

□   Plan your answer carefully, organising your arguments logically, so that one point in the argument follows naturally from the one given before.

□   Sentences and paragraphs should be

kept short. This provides you with a disciplined framework and limits the tendency to irrelevance. Check frequently to make sure that you have not drifted away from the main line of your argument.

The open-ended essay is one in which there is no right answer. The examiner is testing your ability to construct and present a logical argument or logical solution to a business problem. This demands skills of knowledge, understanding, application and analysis. The marking scheme is usually heavily weighted towards analysis, synthesis and evaluation. You should always be aware of the fact that there are few right answers. Changes in circumstances will influence the course of action. Phrases such as 'On the other hand, if ...' can remind you that you are supposed to give weight to the arguments you present. The business studies student who thinks that there is a right answer has not made full use of the time spent studying.

5   Case studies

A case study puts you into a business situation and, through the questions set, guides you through an analysis of the situation. It then asks you to offer ideas for the solution of the problem. The mark allocation will indicate the importance of each part. The initial steps will test some of the basic information required. You will be expected to analyse the problem, suggest solutions and evaluate the solutions you have suggested. Before coming to a final decision you must be able to outline the pros and cons of each course of action and argue forcefully for the one you have selected as best.

6   Projects

(CLES Advanced Level Paper 4. A/S-level and advanced level, modular, research assignment.)

Personal investigation into the circumstances and/or problems of a business provides valuable experience, not least in developing the ability to collect original data through observation and interview, organise the information into a coherent report, draw conclusions from the evidence and present recommendations with confidence. The examinations board offers guidelines on the formation and presentation of research assignments. The following are some basic principles to bear in mind:

☐   The report on your research assignment will need to demonstrate the skills required by the assessment objectives of the examination. A mass of factual information will give you no opportunity to do this.

☐   Start with a question that you must answer, or a hypothesis to test.

☐   Decide what information you are going to need.

☐   Where will you find this information?

☐   How will you collect the information?

☐   Plan your timetable carefully.

☐   Organise your filing system before you start collecting your information. Bits of paper have a nasty habit of disappearing.

☐   Evaluate your information as you collect it. Is it reliable? If not, why not?

☐   Outline your report and check that it is logically presented.

☐   Write your report. If you are trying to answer a question, then you will need to draw conclusions from the evidence you have collected, and make recommendations on a course of action. If you are testing a hypothesis then you will need to provide evidence in support of the hypothesis or against it. Whichever it is, the final sections of your report should be supported by the evidence you have collected.

Part 1   The business environment

1   What is business studies?

When you have studied this chapter you should be able to:

□   Define a business.

□   Appreciate the importance of business activity in our lives.

□   Appreciate the wide variety of activities of the business community.

□   Understand the ways in which all businesses resemble each other.

□   Identify and define the different methods of classifying business activity.

□   Appreciate the uses of classification.

□   Distinguish between the different forms of business ownership.

□   Understand the need for different forms of business ownership.

□   Apply your knowledge to given situations.

□   Identify the type of business organisation most suited to a described business.

□   Identify the themes in the study of business.

What is a business?

The human body requires a minimum of food, drink and protection from the extremes of climate in order to survive. People co-operate in order to satisfy these basic needs, with the family as the most basic economic group. In some societies the amount produced is just enough to keep people alive. These are known as *subsistence economies*. Other people are more fortunate and are able to produce a surplus in some goods. This surplus may be stored as an insurance against future hardship or traded for goods and services which the society cannot produce for itself.

Very early in human history it was realised that individuals possessed different talents, and that if they concentrated their efforts on the activities in which they excelled the standard of living of the whole community would improve. This specialisation also implied that trade would have to take place. The weaver might have had a higher standard of living by concentrating all effort on making cloth. She/He also needed food and shelter which would be provided by other individuals or groups of individuals. The activities in which people engaged were no longer directed towards the satisfaction of all their own needs – and luxuries if they were fortunate – but were concentrated on a relatively narrow range of goods and services which they would exchange with other people. People began to be described by the work they did, a development which is reflected in some British family names, e.g. Cartwright, Weaver, Thatcher, Butcher, Farmer, Smith, etc.

The word 'busy' is used to describe a person who is engaged in action, i.e. occupied. We tend to be selective in the way we use it. You seldom hear people describe themselves as being busy if they are doing a hobby. The word is used to describe activities people regard as being important to their survival or comfort. Look at the following list of activities. Imagine that you are engaged in each of them in turn and somebody asks for your help. In which of these situations are you more likely to make the response 'I'm busy'?

- ☐   cooking the evening meal for the family.

- ☐   watching television.

- ☐   writing an essay which has to be handed in the next day.

- ☐   writing a letter.

- ☐   getting ready to go out.

- ☐   cleaning the tools of your trade so they will be ready for use the next day.

A reasonable response might be that it would depend on the request for help. If you thought it was trivial you might make the response 'I'm busy' in all of the above situations. If the request was urgent enough you might not make that response in any of them. Most people would make the response 'I'm busy' in the first, third and last situations described. In the fourth situation the type of letter being written would help decide your answer. The purpose of this discussion is to emphasise the fact that we use the word 'busy' to describe actions that we consider important.

In developed economies very few people attempt to satisfy the full range of their needs and wants by their own direct work. Most people sell their skills as carpenter, teacher, plumber, manager, accountant or lawyer to other people, and use the money they get in return to buy the goods and services they need to live. The activities necessary to provide us with the goods and services we want are carried out in factories, mines, workshops, foundries, shops and offices, where a group of people with different skills can co-operate to produce goods and services for sale to other people. Some people, of course, continue to work from home for a variety of reasons. It may be cheaper, or more convenient, or the amount of work undertaken may not justify a separate workshop or office.

A business may be simply defined as *a person or group of people buying in goods and services in order to produce other goods and services for the purpose of sale at a profit.*

This definition leaves a problem. What about the people employed in state education, the health service, defence and other central and local government activities? They are excluded by this definition. The problem lies in the way we use the word 'business' – that is, to describe organisations that buy and sell for a profit. However, central and local government organisations share many of the same problems and use the same techniques as commercial enterprises. You will find examples drawn from these areas in a number of chapters in this book. These organisations can also provide useful topics of study for coursework and projects for A- and AS-level examinations.

1 Define:
  a a business
  b specialisation.
2 What is the main purpose of all business activity?
3 What is the difference between the NHS and Unilever?
4 List five activities you undertake in the course of the day. Which activities deserve the response 'I'm busy' if you are interrupted while carrying them out? Why?
5 In what ways does a school resemble a business?

The diverse nature of business

In a wealthy society business is not just concerned with the satisfaction of basic needs. From our definition we can see that the existence of a business community in a society means that surpluses have been generated. The wealthier the society, the more advanced the technology and the wider the range of goods and services available. Take an author as an example. She/He works in a small room at home.

☐ The shelves were erected by a local joiner. The joiner employs one person and takes on another if there are sufficient orders.

☐ The desk was purchased from a shop specialising in the sale of second-hand office furniture. It was made by a business specialising in the manufacture of office furniture.

☐ The carpet and curtains were manufactured by companies with a *turnover* (that is the total amount of money the business has received from sales) of several million pounds a year.

☐ The computer was manufactured by a British business employing less than a thousand people.

☐ The computer monitor was manufactured by a Japanese business with several very large factories in a number of countries. This type of business is called a *multinational enterprise*.

☐ The telephone service is supplied by British Telecom, which has a virtual *monopoly* (that is it is the only producer of that good or service) on telecommunications in the UK.

Then there are the publishers responsible for the books, the manufacturers of filing cabinets, paper clips, paper, wastepaper baskets and so on.

This long – and incomplete – list of the business activity needed to satisfy just one part of the author's wants could be discouraging for a potential student. To acquire knowledge, analyse it, form opinions and make judgments on such a wide range of activities must seem an impossible task in the comparatively short period of time available.

It would be an impossible task if we attempted to take each separate business activity and study it in detail. Instead our aim is to develop a broad understanding of the way in which all businesses work. We shall do this by:

- ☐   concentrating on the activities and experiences they have in common.

- ☐   grouping businesses according to characteristics they share, when this will add to our understanding of their behaviour. This process is called *classification*.

There are six main elements that are common to all business activity:

- ☐   objectives;

- ☐   the resources used by the business;

- ☐   the functions undertaken by the business;

- ☐   the constraints on achieving the objectives;

- ☐   the functions of management;

- ☐   integrating themes.

The objectives of business

A company is required by law to state the type of business activity it intends to undertake before it can begin trading. In addition to these stated aims the managers of a business will have a number of long-term objectives that they will attempt to achieve. These will include profitability, survival, prestige, growth and social objectives.

Profitability

The word 'profit' should be approached with caution. It has a number of meanings which will vary according to the context in which it is used.

1   To an economist profit is the reward for risk-taking. The person who takes the risk of organising resources to produce a new product or to provide a new service is sometimes referred to as an *entrepreneur*. A person mortgages a house to raise money to start a business. She/He is risking a major personal capital investment in this enterprise and is putting more into it than just labour. Profit is seen as the reward for this extra commitment.

2   An accountant would define profit as the difference between *revenue* and *expenditure*; that is the difference between the money received as a result of the activities of the business (the revenue), and the costs associated with those activities (the expenditure). If it costs £100 000 to produce a certain number of goods which bring in a revenue of £125 000 when sold, a profit of £25 000 has been made.

3   In political terms a profit can be elevated to the most important drive in the economy of a country, encouraging people to work productively and to take risks, which will lead to greater wealth for all. Other people see profit as the result of employers using their power to take an unfair advantage of the people they employ and of the people they sell to. Profit, in this case, is believed to exist because wages and salaries have been unfairly depressed and/or prices have been unfairly high (*exploitation*).

Again, in stating the objectives of a business, economists assume that each business will attempt to *maximise* its profit, that is to continue to expand production until it has made the greatest amount of profit it is capable of. In practice it is more likely that a business will *satisfice.* This unpleasant word means simply that the business will decide on a profit level it considers to be satisfactory taking into account the amount of capital employed, the general profit level of the industry it is operating in, the profits it has achieved in previous years, the personal ambitions of its owners and managers and the overall objectives of the business.

The idea that businesses aim for a satisfactory level of profit rather than the maximum possible profit suggests complacency on the part of management and owners. In setting profit targets businesses are limited by:

☐   the funds the business has at its disposal. Achieving maximum profit may require further investment which the business cannot afford.

☐   the complexity of the decisions to be made. If there are a large number of decisions it becomes increasingly difficult to judge the effect each separate decision will have on the final outcome – particularly as the outcomes of one decision may have unforeseen effects on the outcomes of other decisions.

☐   the quantity and quality of the information available to management when making the decisions.

Research suggests that management places a very high level of importance on achieving profit objectives, especially long-term objectives. This implies that the profit targets set as satisfactory are in fact the best possible targets the management believes the business is capable of. You should remember that long-term rather than short-term profit objectives tend to be regarded as the more important when considering the importance of profit in relation to the other objectives of a business.

The following examples will give you some insight into the way in which the importance of profitability can vary according to the circumstances in which a business finds itself.

1   The owner of a small business deliberately decides against acquiring more assets because she/he wishes the business to stay small. Expansion might bring higher profits, but the additional responsibility would interfere with the private life of the owner.

2   A very large business with factories in a number of countries deliberately selects a very low price for a new product in a particular national market. In the short term it sacrifices profits. In the long term it drives its competitors out of business and is therefore in a position to make higher profits.

3   A business is running at a loss. It can remain in operation for two years. There is reason to believe that within the next twelve months more people will buy the goods it sells and within eighteen months it will make a profit once more. A decision is made that it should accept the present losses and stay in operation, rather than sell the business and re-invest the proceeds of the sale in a more profitable venture.

The examples given above were designed to show that the profit motive, although essential for the survival of a business, can appear to be superseded in the short term if other objectives are seen to be more desirable. The small business owner in the first example was satisficing. There was enough profit to finance a satisfactory lifestyle and no desire to sacrifice personal objectives to make more money. The sacrifice to be made in terms of leisure was greater than the satisfaction to be gained from additional income and greater personal prestige. In other words the *opportunity cost* of expanding the business was too great.

Profit, as a *surplus of revenue over expenditure*, is the most important objective of any business.

1   It provides money to buy raw materials, employ labour and pay for the services needed to keep the business in operation.

2   It provides a reserve for future investment. The small business owner who refuses to expand to achieve greater profit might find a valued lifestyle threatened if a change in technology lowers the price of competitors' goods but the business has insufficient reserves, generated by profits, to buy the new machines.

3   It can make it easier for a business to raise capital from outside sources. People are more willing to buy a share of a business that is making a good profit than one that is making a low profit compared with the rest of the business community.

4   Profit can act as a measure of the success of a business. We will examine this more closely in Chapter 6. Here it is sufficient to say that people tend to judge their success or failure compared with other people. It is, for example, one of the problems of a teacher or lecturer that if the whole class achieves low grades on an exercise the students are likely to blame the marking rather than their individual achievement, and will still see themselves as top if they manage 19 marks out of 100. In other words, they are judging themselves by the achievements of their fellow students rather than by the standard which they might expect to achieve.

5   Profit can act as an incentive to greater effort. In Chapters 12, 13 and 14 we will examine the role of money in persuading people to work more productively. For some people money is a *motivator* – something which has a powerful effect on the way people behave – for others money is relatively unimportant.

Because profit allows a business to continue in existence and is essential for future investment, it is usually regarded as the prime objective of all businesses owned by private individuals, as opposed to those owned by the state.

Survival
This must be as important an objective for a business as it is for individuals. We saw earlier how the need to survive can override the profit motive in the short term. The *divorce of ownership and control* – where a business is owned by one group of people and managed or controlled by another – can lead to a conflict of objectives. The management might be more interested in survival strategies to secure their jobs. Survival can be a short-term objective to achieve future profits. It can also be seen as a subversive, unrecognised objective arising out of the personal experience and objectives of the people employed. The desire to protect their employment can lead to a reluctance to take necessary risks. When it is the latter it can be described as *sabotage* – an action designed to hinder the achievement of a stated objective.

Prestige
The desire for prestige, i.e. to be held in high regard by other people whose opinions you value, does not seem at first sight to contribute a great deal to either the profit motive or survival. It can, however, contribute to both, and some businesses actively seek to enhance their prestige in order to increase sales. Businesses might seek prestige from high quality products, from care for the environment, from the use of the latest technology or from care

for its employees. Essentially it is attempting to build up an image for excellence in one area of its operations that will attract potential customers, or present a more favourable impression of its operations to the world. If customers believe that the activities of a business, undertaken to acquire profit, are in some way dishonourable, they may withdraw their custom from that business.

The pursuit of prestige could lead to lower profits in the short term when money might be spent on advertising, improving quality control or the provision of better employee services. In the long term a company with prestige can expect to find a better quality of applicants for any jobs they advertise, an increase in sales and, potentially, an increase in profits.

Growth

The objective of growth might be rationally based on the fact that if the business grows larger the cost of each item it produces will fall (*economies of scale*). It might also be the result of a personal desire on the part of the owner for more power or it might be a desire to take over and eliminate competitors so that there will be more scope for greater profit. In the first and last cases the profit motive dominates. In the second case it is an example of personal motives subordinating purely business motives.

Society

A business can be defined as a person or group of people who offer goods and services to the rest of the community in return for payment. From our analysis of business objectives we could add 'for a profit' to this definition. Profit can be seen as an advantage derived from an action, not necessarily expressed in monetary terms. The social benefits derived from a nationalised industry, such as cheap transport services or lower fuel costs, can be interpreted as a 'profit' to the community. A nationalised industry may run at a loss over a number of years and receive payments from the Treasury to cover the losses (*subsidies*). The extent of this is a political decision.

SELF ASSESSMENT

1 Distinguish between an accountant's and an economist's definition of profit.
2 Give two circumstances in which other objectives might be more important than profit.
3 How would you distinguish between the short term and the long term in a business context?
4 Give two arguments to support the view that profit is the most important long-term objective of a business enterprise.
5 Why might a business be prepared to accept a reduction in short-term profits to achieve objectives relating to prestige and social approval?

The resources of business

For ease of reference it is usual to divide the resources used by business into *land, labour* and *capital*. These are known as the *factors of production*.

1 *Land* is used to describe all natural resources – including those obtained from the sea! – such as minerals, wood, water and the land itself.

2 *Labour* describes the physical and mental skills of the population who are able to work.

3 *Capital* is used to describe all manufactured things which are used to produce other goods and services. This implies that at some time in the past people have sacrificed the opportunity to use some goods immediately (*consume* them) in return for a higher standard of living in the future.

4 Some economists would add *enterprise* (the ability and willingness to risk the loss of capital) to this list.

The classification of resources given above is a convenient shorthand for the very wide range of materials, machinery, skills and information a business imports from its environment. These are also known as *inputs*.

Of course not all businesses will require the same type of resource in the same quantities and at the same time. Some businesses need a small number of highly skilled people whilst others need large numbers of unskilled people. The generation of electricity on a scale demanded by modern society requires a great deal of capital, e.g. a hydro-electric scheme could require a capital investment of £450m. The joiner mentioned in the list of businesses at the beginning of this chapter runs a business on a very small amount of capital. Electricity generation uses large quantities of oil and coal, the joiner uses small quantities of wood. Despite these differences all the businesses mentioned need the factors of production. This they have in common.

SELF ASSESSMENT

1 Group the following inputs into a business in terms of land, labour, capital and enterprise:
  wood   computer   typist   factory   paper   manager   van   plastic   lathe
  food
2 How long do you think each input might stay in the business? Give reasons for your answer.
3 Give three ways in which a retail store would differ from a factory in the type of resources it requires.

The functions of business

All businesses, irrespective of size, product or the technology used, have several functions in common, including production, marketing, finance, control and people.

Production
The production function relates to all activities concerned with the creation or making of the goods or services the business intends to sell. This will include the purchase of raw materials, the location of the business, the organisation of the work process and the control of quality. Methods of production will vary according to the product of the business, its size, the size of the market and the technology available to it.

Marketing
The marketing function includes researching the market, product planning, packaging, pricing, advertising, sales promotion and the distribution of the product to the final consumer. These activities are known as the *marketing mix*. They are the ingredients in any marketing plan, but their relative importance will vary according to the type of product, the customers (either consumers or other firms) and the objectives of the business itself.

Finance

Every business needs money to start up and to remain in operation. The management of money is, therefore, essential for business survival.

Control

A business has its objectives, and all its activities should be directed towards achieving those objectives. It needs to establish ways of testing whether or not this is happening and to adapt its methods accordingly. To do this it will use a variety of methods, many based on statistical and accounting techniques.

People

All businesses need to manage people. Even the smallest business in which the owner is the only person concerned has this function. The owner has to manage him/herself! If you do not believe this, think about how often your own ability to achieve your objectives depends on such apparently trivial things as getting out of bed early enough in the morning, organising a study programme or simply remembering to make a list of the things you need to do. Managing yourself is probably the most difficult task in people management!

Constraints

A *constraint* is a restriction placed on an individual or a group which prevents them achieving their objectives. Constraints can be *internal* (availability of finance, available skills in the workforce, existing plant, organisation), or *external* (the state of the economy, legal requirements, the behaviour of competitors and customers, social and political attitudes).

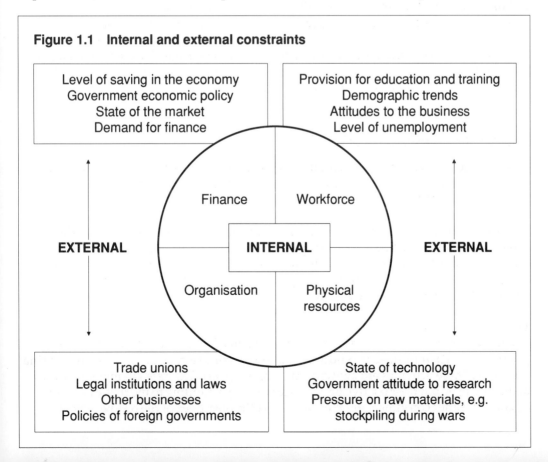

Figure 1.1 Internal and external constraints

Level of saving in the economy
Government economic policy
State of the market
Demand for finance

Provision for education and training
Demographic trends
Attitudes to the business
Level of unemployment

EXTERNAL

INTERNAL

Finance

Workforce

Organisation

Physical resources

EXTERNAL

Trade unions
Legal institutions and laws
Other businesses
Policies of foreign governments

State of technology
Government attitude to research
Pressure on raw materials, e.g. stockpiling during wars

SELF ASSESSMENT

1 From the information given in the text explain why the design of a new product is the concern of all the business functions.
2 Distinguish between internal and external constraints.
3 From your own experience give examples of how the constraints listed on page 9 can affect decisions you have to make.
4 Your objective is to achieve a high grade in A-level business studies. What methods of control are available to you to check whether or not you are on course for this target?
5 Sally Jones is the production manager for an engineering business. The new sales manager has increased orders for one of the products by 25 per cent over the period of a year. Explain simply the effects this might have on Sally's job.

Managing

The term *management* describes all the activities required to acquire and organise all the resources a business needs in order to produce goods and services.

The need for management is not limited to businesses. All organisations – the civil service, schools, hospitals, the armed forces – need to acquire and organise resources in order to achieve their objectives. It can be the quality of the management that determines whether or not a business will be a success and achieve, in full, the objectives it has set for itself. If you do not believe this think of some activities in which you have been involved. How often have you been dissatisfied because you did not have the resources you needed or people were not working together?

The smallest business requires managing. Look at the following example.

Maggie Drew runs a small catering business. Her contracts range from wedding receptions, through business lunches to dinner parties and small receptions in private houses.

Maggie prides herself on offering her clients imaginative menus featuring fresh food in season. A trained chef and confectioner, Maggie produces very high quality food – and charges accordingly.

Clients who pay high prices expect a good standard of service. Early in her enterprise Maggie decided that she could not afford to employ a permanent staff. Over five years she has built up a network of contacts that range from suppliers to waiting, bar and kitchen staff.

In July 1989 Maggie accepted a contract to cater for a wedding reception for fifty people in a private house. The menu included a number of elaborate gateaux, an exotic centrepiece of fruit and a wedding cake on the theme of the West Indian island where the bride and groom met.

What is Maggie's management function? To answer that question in detail you would need to know a great deal about her business. It is possible to give an outline of the things she would have to do:

☐ decide what materials she needed and where she could buy them;

☐ decide how many staff she would need, who they would be, what they would do and when they would do it;

- discover what facilities were available in the house and how this would affect her organisation;

- keep an eye on the clock to make sure everything would be ready in time;

- make sure that she was not spending too much money and that the food produced was of the quality her clients expected from her.

Maggie is acquiring and organising the resources she needs to produce the service (including goods) which she sells at a profit.

Maggie Drew is typical of the owner/manager. She not only takes part in the process of production, she also manages the business. This was the most common pattern of business until a hundred years ago. As businesses grew in size and became more complex it became difficult for one person to carry out all the management functions. This led to the rise of professional managers. These are people whose expertise in handling complex problems has been developed by education and experience. Figure 1.2 shows the different levels of management.

Figure 1.2   Levels of management

SENIOR MANAGEMENT
Develops long-term plans
Reviews achievement
Evaluates departmental performance
Appraises senior and middle management for performance and promotion

MIDDLE MANAGEMENT
Develops intermediate range plans
Appraises staff for performance and promotion
Establishes departmental objectives and targets
Evaluates departmental performance

SUPERVISORY MANAGEMENT
Supervises day-to-day tasks
Makes day-to-day plans
Assigns tasks to operatives and junior supervisors
Appraises junior supervisors and operatives for performance and promotion

---

Management functions

1   *Planning*   This involves identifying trends, anticipating what is likely to happen and deciding on the best course of action to enable the business to reach its objectives.

2   *Organisation*   This is the activity which brings together people, materials and equipment in such a way that the work gets done. This involves:

     ❏   deciding what needs to be done;

     ❏   putting the tasks in a logical order;

     ❏   giving specific tasks to people to perform.

3   Successful organisation also requires *co-ordination* – making sure that all the activities required to achieve the objectives of a business work together.

4   *Direction* An organisation will not run on its own. People need an explanation of what is required of them and mistakes need to be corrected. The activities of issuing directions, explaining and motivating are important elements in this management function.

5   *Control* No business works perfectly. Circumstances, both internal and external, change and the business has to change to meet them. The control function of management is concerned with assessing how the business is performing and whether

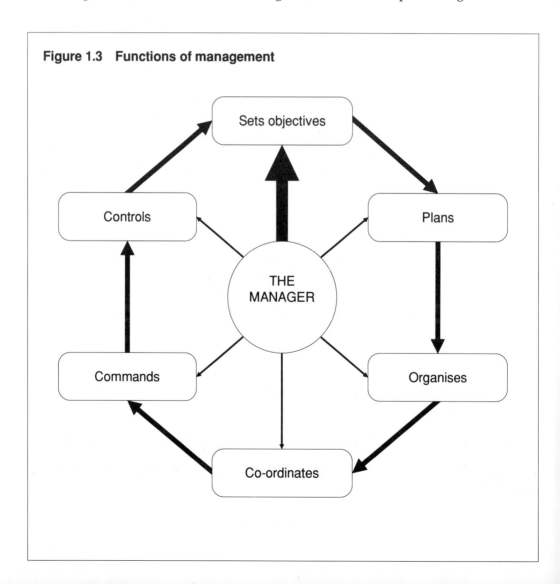

Figure 1.3 Functions of management

or not it is achieving its objectives. The information gathered from the control function can then be used as a foundation for future planning and organisation.

The functions of management are illustrated in Figure 1.3.

Common themes in business studies

As you study business you will become aware of recurring problems that are in the background of all business decisions. They can be seen as additional constraints on decision makers. Sometimes the decision makers may not be fully aware of their existence. Read the following passage.

> Joe Webb is a toolmaker and a good one. He has a great deal of pride in his job and has always enjoyed his work. Joe has worked for the same business since he began his apprenticeship thirty years ago. In his opinion, the 'boss' has always treated him well so he never bothered to join a trade union.
>
> Three years ago the business began to run into trouble. An important raw material used in production was in short supply. The price rocketed. As if that was not enough major competitors re-equipped with new technology that economised on the use of this material and reduced the need for skilled workers like toolmakers. Joe did not worry too much at first. He began to get concerned when the redundancy notices started to go out.

Joe's situation illustrates four of the main themes in all business decisions.

1 *Conflict* There is a conflict between Joe's objectives and those of the business he works for. Joe wants security, a job and a reasonable income. The business wants to survive and make a profit.

2 *Change* The introduction of new technology and a change in the supply and price of the raw material meant that the business had to change to survive.

3 *Interdependence* The behaviour of other businesses in introducing new technology affected both the decisions made by Joe's employer and Joe's life.

4 *Scarcity* The important raw material was in short supply – that was why the price went up.

We could add two more themes.

5 *Ethics* Was the business right to make people redundant? What effect would it have on the local community?

6 *Size* If Joe had worked for a larger business it might have been able to retrain him.

As you encounter different business problems during your course you will find these themes in all of them.

SELF ASSESSMENT

1 In what ways might being a member of a trade union have helped Joe?
2 Explain how scarcity and ethics could play a part in a business's decision to retrain workers rather than make them redundant.

This section has been concerned with the experiences and problems shared by all businesses. This is summarised in Figure 1.4. In the next section we will be looking at the ways in which we can group businesses. This makes it easier to deal with the differences that exist between them. It also makes it possible to examine the common problems of similar types of business.

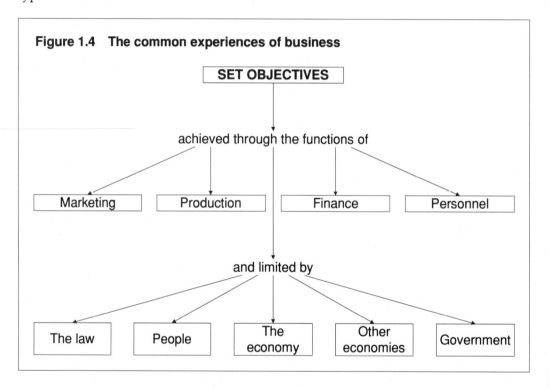

Figure 1.4   The common experiences of business

SET OBJECTIVES

achieved through the functions of

Marketing   Production   Finance   Personnel

and limited by

The law   People   The economy   Other economies   Government

Describing the difference

The first part of this chapter has been concerned with the *common experience* of all business enterprise. Even a superficial reading of the section should have made you realise that, at any one time, no two businesses have precisely the same 'mix' of objectives, resources, functions or constraints. Products differ, and resource requirements will vary in both size and type. A business whose customers finance their purchases of its product by borrowing money will experience a sharper and more immediate drop in sales when interest rates rise than a business making a relatively cheap product.

Businesses which appear very different may have certain characteristics in common that have a significant effect on their behaviour in certain situations. For example the size of a business will determine the financial resources it has at its disposal. When studying business it can be useful to group together all businesses that share a particular characteristic in order to gain an insight into the problems they face or the advantages they enjoy as a result. This grouping is known as *classification*. Figure 1.5 illustrates ten possible classifications. You should remember that grouping disparate items into classes for ease of reference is normal practice. Classes in schools and colleges are good examples. 'The business studies group' is a convenient term of reference for staff in some situations. The list of potential classifications in business is not limited to ten.

Classification by size

Businesses are generally classified as being small, medium or large – a simple statement that disguises a number of problems of definition. The terms of reference of the Bolton Committee, set up in 1968 to inquire into the role of small firms in the British economy, defined small firms as those with not more than two hundred employees. This proved to be inadequate. How would you classify a business with less than one hundred employees but with a high value product and a turnover of £1m per annum? There are of course some businesses that clearly fall into one category or another. Nobody would dispute that Ford (UK), ICI

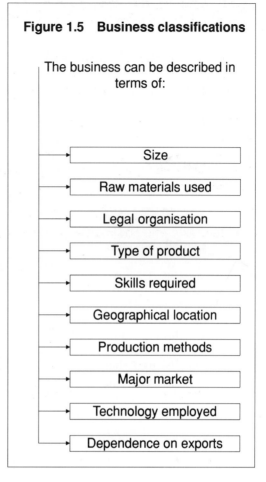

Figure 1.5   Business classifications

The business can be described in terms of:

- Size
- Raw materials used
- Legal organisation
- Type of product
- Skills required
- Geographical location
- Production methods
- Major market
- Technology employed
- Dependence on exports

and Unilever are very large businesses. Equally the one person corner shop is a very small business. The classification of businesses by size can be done according to the following criteria.

1 *The size of its market share*   The market share of a business is its total sales expressed as a percentage of the total sales of the industry in which it operates. We will examine the importance of this in Chapter 3, 'Markets'. In this chapter it is sufficient to point out that if a business employs less than one hundred people, but has a 90 per cent share of the market in which it operates, the influence it exerts on that market will be greater than the influence exerted on its market by a business employing thousands, whose market share is 20 per cent.

2 *Annual sales (turnover)*   A high-cost product can generate more sales per employee than a low-cost product.

3 *The amount of capital employed*   A business which uses advanced technology is likely to have relatively few employees. Automation will intensify this trend.

4 *The way in which it is organised*   The Bolton Committee argued that personal management by the owners of a business was a characteristic of a small firm. As

Figure 1.6   Small and medium-sized companies

If, over a period of **two years**:

£2m	**Turnover** is equal to or less than:	£8m
£975 000	**Assets** are equal to or less than:	£3.9m
50	Average weekly **employees** are equal to or less than:	250
it is a **small** company.		it is a **medium**-sized company.

businesses increase in size the work load becomes too great for a small group of people, managers are employed and the control exercised by the owners decreases. We shall look at this in more detail when we discuss classification by ownership below.

5   The *law* distinguishes between small and medium-sized companies. The criteria on which it does this is summarised in the chart in Figure 1.6.

Classification by size is an introduction to the importance of scale in business. The word 'scale' indicates the way in which you should think of the size of a business. It is not the *absolute* size which is important but the size of a business *in relation to* the size of other businesses. Throughout this book the theme of scale will constantly recur.

SELF ASSESSMENT

1   Explain briefly why there are a number of ways of classifying a business by size.
2   A friend who has been offered a job by a business tells you that it must be larger than the small factory next door to your college because it employs 3000 people and the business that owns the factory employs only 300. Is this necessarily right? Explain your answer.

Classification by ownership

The major distinction is between businesses owned by central or local government, i.e. the *public sector* of the economy, and businesses owned by individuals or groups of individuals, i.e. the *private sector* of the economy. This classification is useful when speaking in general terms.

'The Government has set a limit of 3 per cent on all wage increases for public sector employees.'
'It is difficult to estimate the effect of the cutback in Government spending on the private sector.'

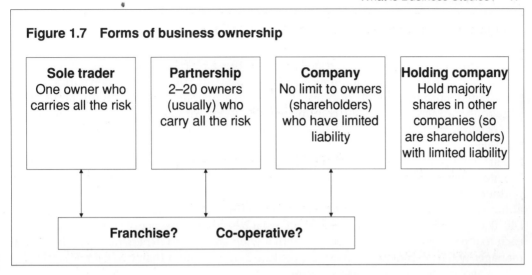

Figure 1.7   Forms of business ownership

Sole trader	Partnership	Company	Holding company
One owner who carries all the risk	2–20 owners (usually) who carry all the risk	No limit to owners (shareholders) who have limited liability	Hold majority shares in other companies (so are shareholders) with limited liability

Franchise?   Co-operative?

Neither the public nor the private sectors are *homogeneous* (that is of identical structure) in terms of ownership, and when discussing the problems associated with different types of ownership it is important that we specify which type we are talking about. These are outlined in Figure 1.7.

Forms of private ownership – the sole trader
This term is used to describe a business wholly owned by *one* person, although there may be a number of people employed in running the business. Businesses owned by one person are often, but not necessarily, small. Their growth is limited by the amount of capital available and this in turn is limited by the personal resources of the founders and their success in trading.

Sole traders are accountable only to themselves and this can make this form of business ownership very attractive to people who have strong ideas on the way in which they want their business to be run. Added to this there are very few legal restrictions on the formation of a one person business, which increases its flexibility. The owner of the business does not have to consult other people before making decisions which can improve the speed with which the business responds to changing conditions.

The lack of specific business skills on the part of the owner is often considered a drawback but this can be overcome by employing people with these skills or by using the professional services offered by other businesses, e.g. accountants, solicitors, and marketing and advertising agencies.

The sole trader is entirely responsible for the debts of the business. Should it fail and there is insufficient money to pay the debts of the business the owner can be declared bankrupt through legal process. All the property of the business and the personal property of the owner will then be sold to pay the debts and, should the money realised by the sale prove to be insufficient for this purpose, the court will have a claim on the income of the bankrupt until all the debts have been paid. The sole trader is thus said to have *unlimited liability* for the debts and conduct of the business.

Partnerships
Partnerships are groups of people who contribute capital and management expertise to the same business enterprise and accept joint responsibility for the operation of the business. The minimum number of partners is, of course, two. The maximum number in most cases is

twenty. Like the sole trader, partners are liable for all the debts and conduct of their business, and because several people share responsibility and the actions of one partner could have serious consequences for the rest, there are legal restrictions on the responsibilities of the partners to each other. These are defined by the *Partnership Act* of 1890. Amongst other things this Act states that partners should receive an equal share of the profits. When partners have contributed varying amounts of capital this is unreasonable. To deal with this and similar situations, partners can vary the conditions of the Act by drawing up a legal document – a *deed of partnership* – which sets out the conditions under which they agree to do business together.

Partnerships can benefit from having more capital and expertise than the sole trader. A solicitor with experience in conveyancing (the transfer of property rights) might seek partners with experience of the legal problems of business and divorce. These are not automatic benefits of a partnership. The person setting up business as a sole trader with £40 000 in capital will have a stronger financial base than three people contributing £5000 each to a partnership. Again, a person with a wide and varied experience as an industrial manager will have more expertise for a venture as a sole trader than two friends setting up as partners in their first business venture.

Limited companies

As the size of business enterprises increased in the nineteenth century, the amount of capital required increased and the ability of sole traders and partners to accumulate the necessary finance declined. Many people were willing to lend small amounts of money to a business but they had no control over the way in which it was used. They were at the mercy of the owners of the business. The solution to this problem was sought in law.

1   Companies – that is groups of people who collectively own a business under certain legal conditions – were established as *separate legal entities* from the people who owned them. This meant that the company would be treated as a separate person in law from its owners. The company could sue and be sued, own property and survive the death of its owners.

2   The company was granted *limited liability*. This can be seen as a logical extension of the fact that the company is a separate legal entity. The company is responsible for its own debts and conduct of business. If, at any time, the company cannot pay its debts it may be forced to sell all its assets in order to do so. The company goes into *involuntary liquidation*. This process is also known as *winding up*. Shareholders will lose the money they have invested in the business but other assets they possess cannot be touched.

3   Legal restrictions were placed on the formation of companies to ensure that the privileges given above were not abused.

The first instance of limited liability being granted to a restricted range of businesses was in 1662. General limited liability was extended to all *registered* companies by the *Limited Liability Act* of 1855. The conditions under which a company can register with the *registrar of companies* (a civil service function) are defined by the Companies Acts. The first of these Acts was passed in 1844 but the formation of modern companies is regulated by the Acts of 1948, 1967, 1976, 1980, 1981 and 1983. These Acts were consolidated by the Companies Act of 1985. British company law is constrained by EC directives. The 1981 Act, for example, dealing with the format of accounts and the disclosure of accounts to the public, was the result of an EC directive of 1978.

Registration of a limited company

The first stage in the formation of a limited company is taking the decision. The person, persons or business which takes this decision and puts into operation the necessary steps for the formation of a company are the *promoters*. Promoters:

- issue the *prospectus*. This document is required by law if the shares in the company are going to be offered to the public generally. It includes the information a prospective shareholder or lender might require to make an informed decision about the investment, for example the financial position of the business and the rights of shareholders.

- organise the preparation of the documents required for registration.

- buy any property the business will need.

- find directors for the company.

- procure capital for the company.

Promoters are held to be in a position of trust in relation to the company. It is illegal for a promoter to make a secret profit out of the formation of the company. In order to register a company the promoters must deliver the following documents to the registrar of companies:

- the *memorandum of association*. This states the objects of the company, the amount of share capital and the way in which the share capital will be divided, for example £500 000 divided into 500 000 shares with a par value of £1 each.

- the *articles of association*. These cover such matters as the rules dealing with the transfer of shares, the holding of shareholders' meetings, the powers of the directors and the issuing of dividends.

- the *names of the directors* and the secretary of the company.

- a *statement of capital*.

- a signed statement that the provisions of the Companies Acts have been satisfied.

If the registrar is satisfied that the proposed company fulfils all legal requirements and the necessary fees have been paid, then the certificate of incorporation will be issued. There are several advantages of a registered company:

1 It is a separate legal entity and therefore:

- the debts are the debts of the company. Members of the company are not personally liable for the debts apart from the money they have invested in the business.

- the company remains in existence and is not affected by the death or misfortunes of its members. If a major shareholder in a company is declared bankrupt, that person's shares will be sold to pay her/his debts, but the company will not necessarily be affected by this.

- it can sue and be sued.

- it can own property. This means that the property owned by the company will not change with a change in ownership of the company.

- [ ] taxation on companies is on a flat rate basis, that is companies pay tax on a fixed proportion of their profits. Sole traders pay tax on a graduated scale; the higher their income, the greater the percentage of their income they pay in tax.

2   Shareholders benefit from limited liability.

3   There is no limit to the number of shareholders in a registered company. This increases the opportunity for raising capital.

Registering a business as a company does have some disadvantages:

- [ ] the legal process is time-consuming and expensive.
- [ ] the accounts of a registered company are open to the public.
- [ ] a company is limited in the type of business it can undertake by its memorandum of association.
- [ ] the legal requirements covering the running of a registered company, for example in the way in which it raises capital, are more stringent than for other forms of business ownership.

Public and private companies

A registered company is a private company; the name includes the abbreviation 'Ltd', unless it satisfies the three legal requirements necessary for a public company:

- [ ] the name must include the words 'public limited company' or the abbreviation 'plc'. This statement must also be included in the memorandum of association.
- [ ] the memorandum must comply with the requirements of the Companies Act.
- [ ] the company must have a minimum share capital of £50 000.

The minimum number of shareholders in both public and private companies is two. Private companies cannot advertise their shares for sale and cannot be listed on the Stock Exchange, whereas public companies can do so. This is the major disadvantage attached to private companies.

Co-operatives

The most common forms of co-operative in the United Kingdom are the Co-operative Retail Societies and the Co-operative Wholesale Society, the modern successors of the co-operative movement founded in Rochdale in 1844. In recent years there has been a revival of interest in worker or producer co-operatives. The basic principles of co-operative organisation are:

- [ ] the business is owned by the workforce.
- [ ] the workforce controls the objectives and management of the business.
- [ ] there is a voting system so that the workforce can make their wishes known about decisions.
- [ ] profits are divided amongst the members according to the work done rather than the amount of capital invested.

Businesses can register as co-operative societies under the Industrial and Provident Societies Acts of 1965–1975. The Co-operative Development Agency (CDA) and the Industrial Common Ownership Movement (ICOM) assist with the setting up of co-operatives, for example by providing model rules.

SELF ASSESSMENT

1 Define the term 'unlimited liability' and state two types of business organisations it applies to.
2 Give two advantages of the company as opposed to the sole trader as a form of business ownership.
3 Distinguish between the memorandum of association and the articles of association.
4 What is the major function of the registrar of companies?
5 Give one reason why a private company might decide to register as a public company.

Public enterprise

The public sector of the economy offers many goods and services to the consumer, some of which are financed entirely by money the government obtains from taxes or by borrowing and which are offered to the consumer free of direct charge at the point of use. Other goods and services are offered in return for payment. Usually the state owns the capital and land required for production, employing the necessary labour. Sometimes the state rents land and borrows money. In general these resources are used to produce goods and services that it is believed the private sector cannot or will not produce efficiently. This is discussed in more detail in Chapter 2. The state can be involved in business in a number of ways:

☐ by owning shares in a public or private company. In this case the business will be funded and operated according to normal commercial criteria.

☐ by providing services such as health, policing, defence, social security and advice to trade and industry. The finance for these services comes from taxation, the community charge, the business rate and government borrowing.

☐ by establishing, by Act of Parliament, a public corporation.

Public corporations

Like registered companies, a public corporation is a separate legal entity. It has been incorporated. British Rail is the type of public corporation usually referred to as a nationalised industry. Others, such as the water authorities, are sometimes called public utilities. Each nationalised industry was established by an Act of Parliament. However, there are basic similarities in their legal organisation.

1 A government minister is responsible for establishing the policy of the industry. Overall objectives are likely to be decided by the government. A company will have profit, marketing, social and other objectives decided by its board of directors. The profit objective may not be the most important for a nationalised industry. When many of them were first set up in the 1940s they were not required to make a profit but to break even, taking one year with another. This simply meant that if the industry made a loss in 1952 then it should make sufficient profit in 1953 to cover the loss it made the year before. Nationalised industries have now been given a target to reach. This is expressed as a

percentage return on capital employed. In a year they are expected to cover costs and make a 'profit'.

2   Each public corporation has a board. This is a group of people appointed by the minister responsible for the industry and drawn from the industry itself, the private sector and trade unions. The board interprets the general policy guidelines laid down by the minister.

3   There is a consumer organisation which looks after the interests of the customers. Nationalised industries are monopolies. That is they are the sole providers of a good or service. The customer has no alternative but to use that business, therefore the customer needs protection.

The debate as to whether or not nationalised industries are good or bad for the economy and people tends to be fought on political grounds.

SELF ASSESSMENT

1   State two differences between the public and private sectors of industry.
2   Give one reason why it is useful to distinguish between the public and private sectors.
3   In what ways would a business in the public sector resemble an enterprise in the private sector?
4   Why does the fact that nationalised industries are monopolies cause some concern?

Classification by activity

Another way of describing the types of business in an economy is by grouping all businesses according to the type of product that they produce, whether goods or services. The broadest definition is in terms of primary, secondary and tertiary sectors.

1   The *primary sector* refers to all businesses engaged in mining, quarrying, farming, fishing and drilling. These are sometimes known as *extractive industries*.

2   The *secondary sector* includes manufacturing, assembly, construction, the nationalised industries and the supply of gas, electricity and water.

3   The *tertiary sector* includes public and private service industries: banking, insurance, retailing, health services, and education are some examples.

These main divisions of business activity can be broken down into sub-divisions. An article discussing the effects of government policy on agriculture might distinguish between its impact on arable and on livestock farming, and might further sub-divide those two categories into cereal and non-cereal producers and dairy and beef cattle farmers.

SELF ASSESSMENT

1   Distinguish between the primary, secondary and tertiary sectors of the economy.
2   Give two advantages of classifying industry in this way.

Conclusion

We began this chapter by stressing the diversity of business activity and developed the idea that it was possible to study very different organisations by concentrating on the characteristics they have in common and also by grouping similar businesses together. In the next chapter we will treat all businesses as if they were identical. This will allow us to look more closely at the role business plays in society.

REVIEW

1 Read each of the following statements and decide which of the possible business objectives they refer to.
  a 'We need to increase sales by 50 per cent if we are to remain comparable with our nearest rivals.'
  b 'Taking over Baxen Ltd will double our production.'
  c 'The potential profits might be excellent but we cannot afford the risk.'
2 Classify the following business activities into primary, secondary and tertiary sectors. State also whether or not you would consider them to belong to the public or to the private sector.
  a An independent transport business, organised as a private limited company and employed mainly in carrying agricultural produce.
  b Two people who jointly own a small pottery.
  c A bottle reclamation plant owned by a local authority.
  d A football club whose first team plays in the first division in England and Wales.
  e A multinational company which manufactures cars.
  f A small independently owned fishing boat giving tourists fishing trips.
  g Britoil before privatisation.
3 In 1986 Jenny Hart bought an empty shop and started a business as a general grocer, newsagent and tobacconist. She was a good businesswoman, with a clear idea of her customers' needs. By 1989 the shop was thriving, with a turnover that compared favourably with similar businesses.

It had not been easy. In the first year Jenny had worked from five in the morning to ten in the evening. She paid herself basic wages by the hour but took no profit. Any surplus funds generated were immediately put back into the business in increased stock or improved equipment. By the end of 1987 Jenny felt confident enough to employ part-time staff and life became a little easier. Although profits were impressive, Jenny was not sure she wanted to carry on with the business. She had very little time for a social life – and very little energy for one either. On the other hand she did enjoy being her own boss, making decisions and getting results.

A friend suggested she took a partner. Jenny thought about the idea for some time. It had its attractions but there were disadvantages. She thought she would need to know somebody very well before she would consider them as a partner.
  a From the information given above classify the resources Jenny used in her business:
    i in 1986–87.
    ii in 1987–88.
  b What method did Jenny use to increase the level of resources used in her business?
  c From the evidence given in the passage list Jenny's objectives in order of importance. Give a brief explanation to justify your decisions.
  d Give one reason why Jenny would:

    i find a partnership a good idea.

    ii hesitate about taking on a partner.

4 In 1973 Jason Balshaw and his brother John went into partnership as building contractors. Jason had recently been made redundant and was able to invest £5000 in the new business. The maximum amount John could contribute to the investment was £3000. Jason insisted they had a deed of partnership drawn up.

    For the first four years the business did well. In 1977 the brothers were invited to tender for a contract worth £60 000. Jason was reluctant to get involved. John was enthusiastic.

    'Look Jas, we can go on as we are or we can start to grow. This is our big chance. We have got the skills, the capital and the contacts. What more do we need?'

    Jason shook his head. 'It's not as easy as that, lad. We've never taken on a job as big as this before. We would have to employ more people, keep a check on things, buy in the supplies. This woman wants some fancy tiling. Do you know where to get it? I don't. No, it needs thinking about.'

    John shook his head. When it came to taking risks Jason was always the cautious one. He needed careful handling. 'Well, while you think about it why don't we just get some advice? Only we can't leave it too long. The tender has to go in before a fortnight Thursday.'

  a Explain the term 'deed of partnership'.

  b Why was it sensible for the Balshaws to have a deed of partnership drawn up?

  c Outline the skills the Balshaws would need to manage a big job and explain why each is necessary.

  d Give a brief explanation of the way in which the following themes are acting as constraints upon the Balshaws' decision.

    i size.

    ii conflict.

    iii change.

    iv interdependence.

  e Suggest reasons why Jason might be more cautious than John.

5 Darley's Ltd was incorporated in England in 1977. The memorandum of association submitted for registration stated that the purpose of the company was to manufacture children's toys. The company was successful.

    In 1989 the directors of the company were concerned about the state of the toy market. They wanted to diversify. With the permission of their shareholders they applied for re-registration as a public limited company.

  a Explain the term 'memorandum of association'.

  b Outline the process of company registration.

  c Explain briefly why Darley's needed to apply for re-registration as a public limited company.

  d What distinguishes a public limited company from a private limited company?

  e Give two advantages to Darley's of becoming a public limited company.

Activities

1 Conduct a survey of:

  a a local high street shopping centre.

  b a transept of a city centre.

  c an industrial estate.

  In each case:

    i classify the type of business you find.

    ii explain the logic of their location in that area.

2 Interview several small business owners. You are interested in:
   a their motives in setting up a business.
   b the satisfactions they gain from running their own business.
   c their ambitions for the future.
   As a group compare the answers you were given, noting any similarities and differences.
3 Visit several business organisations, preferably one from each of the primary, secondary and tertiary sectors. You should find out the answers to the questions given below and any other questions that interest you:
   a What is the name of the business?
   b When was it formed?
   c What is the legal organisation of the business?
   d Is this its only location? If not, how many other factories does it have:
      i in the UK?
      ii in the world?
   e Where is its headquarters?
   f Is the business organised into departments? If so, what are they?
   g What is the product of the business?
   h What goods and services does it buy in?
   i Who does it sell its products to?
   The purpose of these visits is to familiarise you with the diversity of business enterprise. If you have studied business before you may already be aware of this. Those of you who have not should write a formal report in a suitable format drawing attention to the points of similarity you have noticed and the extent to which the businesses differ.

Suggested projects
1 Should a business register as a limited company?
2 Make a critical comparison of the business objectives and strategies of two businesses.

Essay questions
1 Comment on the factors a business should take into account when assessing the advisability of becoming a public limited company.
2 Analyse the possible effects on the private sector of an increase in state control of business.
3 Evaluate the contribution made by the small business sector to the economy of the UK.
4 The practice of classifying business enterprises is a useful analytical tool provided that the limitations of a particular classification are recognised. Discuss this statement, illustrating your answer with reference to the business community.

2   The business as a system

When you have studied this chapter you should be able to:

□   Define a system.

□   List the major elements in a system.

□   Distinguish between an open and a closed system.

□   Analyse a simple system.

□   Appreciate the value of a systems approach in understanding business organisations.

□   Distinguish between different types of economic systems.

□   Appreciate the strengths and weaknesses of different economic systems.

□   Appreciate the similarities and differences in the experience of business organisations in different economic systems.

□   List the major elements in the monetary system.

□   Outline the contribution each element makes to the working of the monetary system.

□   Appreciate the interface between business and the political, social and ecological systems.

In Chapter 1 we accepted the fact that each business was unique, but looked at the different ways in which we could group businesses together for ease of study. In this chapter we will assume that all business enterprises are identical – whether we are talking about multinational giants like Unilever or the corner shop – and examine the relationship between the business community and the rest of society. To do this we will use the general framework of the systems approach, but in a descriptive rather than an analytical form.

What is a system?

A *system* can be defined as an assembly of parts that are connected together in such a way as to achieve a particular objective. Each part of a system affects and is affected by the other parts, and the removal or change of a part will affect the way in which the system operates. This is a very general definition and can be applied to the physical structure of the universe, to biology, e.g. in the respiratory and circulatory systems of a mammal, to technology, to the functions of a business and to a collection of businesses, each with a different role but with a working relationship. The following definitions will prove useful, not only in understanding the systems approach to problems but also in understanding the relationship between businesses and in bringing order into the complex world of modern business.

1   *Environment* Anything outside a system which has an effect on the way in which it operates. In Chapter 1 we discussed external constraints on business behaviour. These constraints can also be seen as the effect on a business of the environment in which it operates.

2   *Subsystem* A system which is an integral part of another system. A bank is a system; it is also a subsystem of the banking system which, in turn, can be seen as a subsystem of the economic system of the country.

3   *An open system* All systems are open in their operation, that is they are affected by the behaviour of other systems and the environment. An economist discussing international trade will refer to an *open economy*, that is one which is affected by the behaviour of other economic systems. The area over which this interaction takes place is known as the *interface*. Figure 2.1 shows the main components of any system or subsystem.

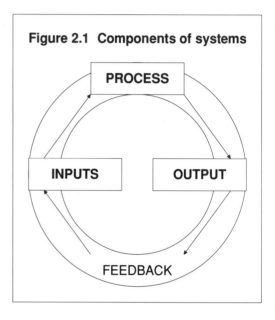

Figure 2.1 Components of systems

Inputs are the resources the system buys in or which are made available to it from outside the system. The *process* describes all the activities that go towards achieving the objectives of the system. The *output* is the result of the process. The output will influence the way in which the system works

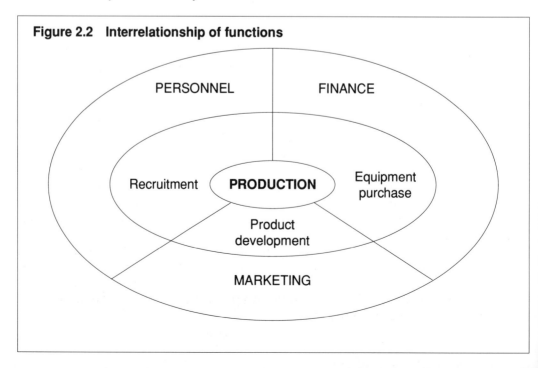

Figure 2.2   Interrelationship of functions

Figure 2.3   People in systems

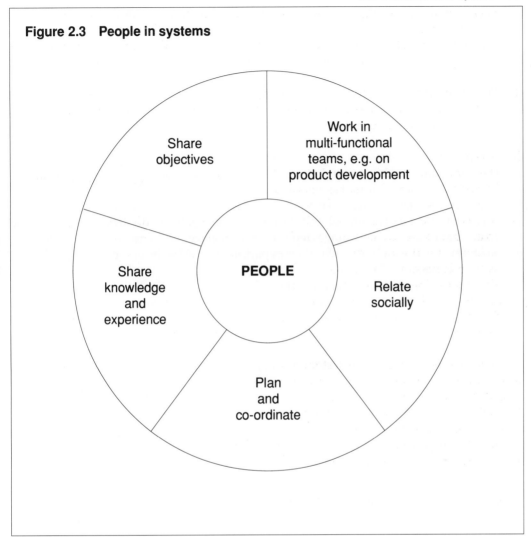

in the future as people respond to the success or failure of their activity. Failure, particularly, is likely to lead to a change in inputs and in the process.

In Chapter 1 we outlined the major functions of a business enterprise. Each of these can be seen as parts of a system. They are interdependent. For example, the way one department operates will affect the operation of other departments in the business. A dynamic and efficient marketing team will place demands upon the production department. It may be necessary for it to change the way in which it is organised to meet the increased demand for its product. A change in senior management (another part of the system) may lead to an increased emphasis on profitability. This implies changes in each of the departments to meet new targets, for example in productivity.

Departments within a business are subsystems, each with its own set of objectives which should support the overall objectives of the business. When trying to achieve its objectives each subsystem must take into account the needs and behaviour of other subsystems.

Figure 2.2 shows some of the ways in which the production department has to interrelate with other departments in the business.

It is possible to analyse a business in terms of the relationships that people establish within the business. Figure 2.2 suggests that the production manager will have to meet other departmental managers on a regular basis in order to co-ordinate the activities of the different departments. These meetings, and similar contacts between people, will have inputs, a process and an output – in other words, a system. Figure 2.3 gives a simple example of this type of analysis.

The individual business is also a part of the overall economic system of the country. It is a subsystem. A healthy economy depends upon the performance of the businesses that comprise it. The state of the economy affects the businesses. The business is therefore an open system.

The systems approach is a useful tool in understanding organisations and ensuring that they work towards a common purpose. With a number of different departments in a business, each with its own management structure and workforce, there is always the danger that an individual department will begin to see its own contribution to the business as the most important. This can encourage departmental managers to chase their own objectives on the grounds that what is good for their department must be the best course of action for the whole business.

When managers are encouraged to take a systems view of the business they are more likely to become aware of the relationship of their work to the work of other departments and the objectives of the business as a whole. It also makes them aware of the dependence of their own department on the efficiency and co-operation of the other parts of the system.

SELF ASSESSMENT

1 What is a system?
2 Distinguish between an open and a closed system.
3 What are the inputs, outputs and processes of your school or college?
4 In what ways can the environment in which a system operates influence the operation of the system?

Business and the economic system

The economic system of a country describes the relationship that exists between customers, producers and the state.

We saw in Chapter 1 that all resources needed to satisfy the wants and needs in a society can be grouped under the headings of land, labour and capital. These resources are insufficient at any one moment in time to satisfy all the desires of people – which are taken to be insatiable. There is therefore the need to choose between the various uses of resources, and this choice implies a *sacrifice*. The true cost of anything is the sacrifice made to obtain it. This sacrifice is known as the *opportunity cost*. The basic economic concepts of *scarcity*, *choice* and *opportunity cost* mean that resources have to be shared out (*allocated*) by society to various uses, a fact that is summarised in the phrase *allocation of resources*.

A simplified model of the economic system has three parts:

☐   *businesses of various types*.   (Businesses use resources to produce goods and services.)

☐   *consumers*.

☐   *the state*.

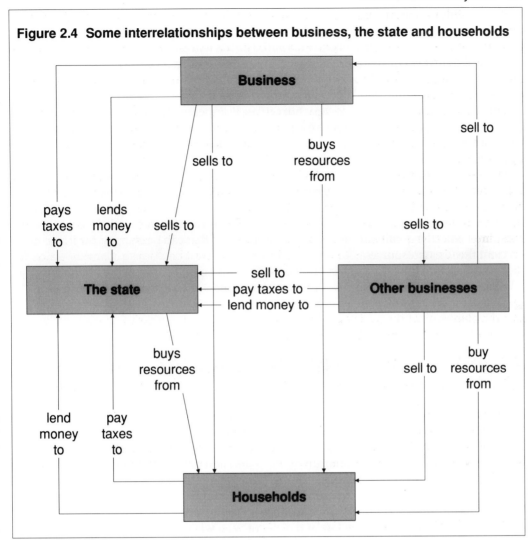

Figure 2.4 Some interrelationships between business, the state and households

The relationship between these parts of the system will, of course, determine the way in which the system works. How much control does the government exercise over the conduct of business? What proportion of the resources of a country are in the control of the government? What standards of behaviour are acceptable in a society? What importance do the people in that society place on certain types of goods and services?

The economic system is a subsystem of the political and social systems of a country, and these will have been determined by historical and cultural factors. Figure 2.4 shows some interrelationships among business, the state and households.

Types of economic system

The two extreme forms of an economic system for the allocation of resources are the *free* or *market* economy and the *planned* economy. Both types of system have ardent supporters whose judgments are often based on political rather than economic criteria. No real economy is totally planned or totally free. Most possess elements of each, which is why they are called *mixed economies*.

Free or market economies

Free economies operate by price. Consumers decide how they will spend the money they have at their disposal. The producers of favoured goods will receive a larger revenue than the producers of less favoured goods. They will therefore be in a better position to buy the resources they need. Some producers will go out of business and the resources freed will be employed in making the goods and services people want to buy.

The idea of a free economy is very attractive. It appears that it is the consumers who decide on the allocation of resources by an accumulation of millions of personal decisions. This idea is known as *consumer sovereignty*. A free market economy also responds well to changes in consumers' wishes, i.e. it is flexible.

Because the decisions happen in response to changes in the market there is no need to use additional resources to make decisions, record them and check on whether or not they are being carried out. The size of the civil service is reduced. It is also argued that competition between producers in a free economy is an incentive to efficiency – the lower the cost compared with the quality of the product and the price that can be charged for it, the more efficient the use of resources.

Free economies do, however, have serious disadvantages – particularly when viewed in relation to the political and social objectives of a society.

Disadvantages of a free economy

1 In many societies it is considered socially and politically desirable that each person should be allocated the minimum amount of resources needed to provide for the basic survival needs of food, warmth and shelter. There is no guarantee that a free economy would achieve this objective. A person with a high level of skill that was in great demand could receive a larger portion of the wealth of that society than a person whose talents, although considerable, were unwanted at that time. There is also no guarantee that individuals would use the resources at their disposal in ways that might be desirable for the collective good of the community, e.g. a decision not to buy educational services.

2 The nature of some goods and services makes it difficult to exclude people who are not willing to pay. Law and order and defence fall into this category. Those who are unwilling to spend more on law and order or who wish to reduce the amount spent on defence are forced to accept the level of service provided by the government.

3 Although the advantages of the price system include the speed with which it reacts to changes in demand, in certain circumstances its response might be unacceptably slow in political and social terms. A rapid change in technology might lead to a high level of unemployment and threaten the political security of the government in power. Cynical observers of the political scene hold that the more unacceptable aspects of a market economy are minimised in the months before a general election.

4 Consumer sovereignty can be seen as the ideal rather than the reality of a modern economy. Many businesses produce in advance of consumer demand and then use advertising to persuade people to buy the goods they have made.

5 Competition between businesses can lead to a duplication of products and a waste of resources. Prior to the nationalisation of the railway system many large towns and cities had several railway stations and tracks each belonging to a different company and, in some cases, duplicate services between towns.

6 The operation of a free market economy depends upon producers having confidence that they will be able to sell what they produce. If they see the risk as being too great they will not employ resources and the general standard of living in a country will fall.

Planned economies

These are sometimes known as *command economies* because the major decisions about the allocation of resources are made by the state. The economic system in planned economies is more responsive to changes in political objectives. The planning system varies from country to country but in general we can say that it will include the following activities:

- [ ] the collection of statistical information relating to the resources available.

- [ ] the setting of overall objectives, e.g. agricultural output will increase by 5 per cent, over a period of time, usually five years.

- [ ] the establishment of objectives at regional level to achieve the overall objectives.

- [ ] the establishment of targets for each production unit – factory or farm – to achieve.

Later in this book you will examine the importance of planning and the planning process in a business enterprise. This will help you understand some of the problems inherent in a planned economy, bearing in mind that economies are larger and more complex than most businesses and that this fact will increase the problems facing a government.

Advantages of a planned economy

1 Resources can be distributed more equitably according to the values of the society. This does not mean that everybody will necessarily receive the same income. Political objectives might regard some parts of the economy as more valuable than others and reward them accordingly.

2 Duplication of resources can be avoided.

3 The state can use its economic power to achieve its own social and political objectives, which may be taken to reflect the collective will of the majority of the people.

Disadvantages of a planned economy

1 The collection of data, the planning process itself and control of planning will all use resources.

2 The lack of scope for individual incentives may lead to a lack of initiative. It is argued that in the market system the desire for profit acts as a stimulus to individuals to undertake risks. The lack of profit motive – it is argued – means that opportunities for improvements which could lead to a more efficient use of resources are missed. In a command economy the incentive offered by the profit motive might be replaced by personal ambition or a political ideal. Some observers of command economies argue that the profit motive does not disappear but is driven underground. Personal profit is sought in gifts, bribery and the black market.

3 A serious problem in command economies – as in market economies – is anticipating the wants of the consumer. Once basic needs have been met people may abstain from

consumption rather than buy goods which they find unattractive or of poor quality. Production usually takes place ahead of demand and, in this situation, command economies can suffer from the same problems of resource waste as market economies. Command economies often try to avoid this problem by making sure that demand exists before production commences. This leads to waiting lists.

The precise proportions of 'free' and 'planned' parts in an economic system and the relationship they have with each other will vary from country to country depending on the interaction of the political, social and economic systems and the cultural history of society.

SELF ASSESSMENT

1 Distinguish between a market economy and a planned economy in terms of ownership and control.
2 Give two arguments in favour of a mixed economy.
3 In what ways is the economy of the UK an open system?
4 Explain why managers in a planned economy might be more aware that they are part of a system than managers in a free economy.
5 Is the profit motive entirely absent in a planned economy? Explain your answer.

Business within an economic system

In general terms the word 'business' is used only in relation to a free market economy or the private sector of a mixed economy. If you read the definition of business given in Chapter 1 you will see that a privately owned business producing shoes in the UK has a great deal in common with a similar, but state owned, business in the USSR:

- ☐ both use the same resources.

- ☐ both aim to generate a surplus, that is they aim to increase wealth as a result of their activities. The surplus of the UK business will be appropriated by the owners of the business who will make individual decisions about the way in which they intend to use it. In the USSR the surplus will be distributed by the central authorities or their agents.

- ☐ both businesses will have constraints on decision making. The constraints will vary in magnitude but will still fall into the same categories as given in Chapter 1.

- ☐ both businesses will undertake the same productive processes.

How can the type of economic system affect a business?

1   The business in a free economy appears to carry a higher degree of risk than that in a planned economy. Sustained losses may cause the failure of the business whereas it is often assumed that in a planned economy uneconomic businesses are subsidised to maintain employment. In practice the business in a planned economy may be dependent on the political objectives of the government rather than market forces. In a planned economy if a business is failing to meet targets it might face closure so that its resources can be redeployed.

2   In a free economy the business has to find its own resources and pay the price asked. In a planned economy resources are allocated to the business. This can mean that the business does not receive resources of the right quality or specification, particularly if the allocation is done by civil servants with little understanding of business requirements.

3   In a free economy businesses are affected by a large number of constantly changing factors. The planning process of the command economy might give an appearance of stability. It should be remembered that the command economy will interact with market systems and is not, therefore, totally protected.

SELF ASSESSMENT

1   Give two important distinctions between a market economy and a planned economy.
2   Give three ways in which a business in a planned economy is (a) similar to and (b) different from a business in a market economy.

Privatisation

The economy of the UK is a mixed economy: some business activities are owned by the state while others are in the private sector. The Conservative Government, elected in 1979, was committed to reducing state involvement in the economy. It did this in a number of ways:

☐   by converting public corporations (nationalised industries for example) into registered public limited companies. The shares of these companies are then sold on the open market.

☐   by ensuring that services such as cleaning, refuse collection and local transport that had been provided by local authorities, health services and similar bodies would be open to tender by private sector businesses. In other words the authority that must, by law, provide the service would have to take the business that offered the service at the best price.

☐   by removing controls and restrictions on the provision of services. This is known as *deregulation*.

Colloquially, all three activities are known as *privatisation*, that is the transfer of

Figure 2.5   Transfer of industry from public to private ownership

The list of nationalised industries which remained in the public sector at the end of 1987–88 is as follows:
British Coal
Electricity (England and Wales)
North of Scotland Hydro-Electric Board
South of Scotland Electricity Board
British Steel Corporation
Post Office
Girobank
British Railways Board
British Waterways Board
Scottish Transport Group
British Shipbuilders (Merchant)
Civil Aviation Authority
Water (England and Wales)
London Regional Transport
The following industries have been privatised since 1979:
British Telecom
British Gas Corporation
British National Oil Corporation
British Airways
British Airports Authority
British Aerospace
British Shipbuilders (warships)
British Transport Docks Board
National Freight Company
Enterprise Oil
National Bus Company

the provision of goods and services from the public to the private sector. Much of the debate surrounding privatisation concentrates on the nationalised industries that have been transferred from the public to the private sector. Figure 2.5 shows the industries that had been transferred by December 1988.

To privatise or not to privatise is a political decision. It is often difficult to reach a decision because many of the industries in question have been part of the public sector for a long time. The provision of a clean, safe water supply and the disposal of sewage were taken out of the private sector in the nineteenth century. In that century railways were subject to statutory limits on the fares they could charge, which considerably reduced their profitability. Coal under private ownership had a poor reputation for health, safety and industrial relations. The British Broadcasting Corporation was established in the 1930s to ensure that neither commercial nor political interests could control an important means of communication.

The length of time these industries have been in public ownership means that nobody, business managers, economists and politicians, who argues about their return to the private sector has recent experience of that type of ownership.

The arguments for and against privatisation follow similar lines to those for a free or planned economy.

For privatisation

1   The profit motive. Without profit to act as an incentive and a measure of success management lacks the drive to increase efficiency by improving services and cutting costs. This results in less customer satisfaction and a waste of resources.

2   State ownership usually means state financing. This is a burden on government spending and increases the public sector borrowing requirement (PSBR).

3   Increased competition will lead to improved standards of customer service and greater efficiency.

4   The transfer of ownership from the public to the private sector will increase the number of people holding shares. More people will have a stake in the productive base of the economy. In 1979 seven per cent of all adults owned shares. By 1987 the proportion had risen to 20 per cent.

5   Nationalised industries are restricted in the amount of funds they can raise on the capital markets. When privatised they have the choice of a wider range of capital which, it is hoped, will lead to a higher level of investment resulting in greater productivity and lower prices.

Against privatisation

1   Competition provides goods and services for people who can afford them. Nationalised industries had a variety of obligations to provide services that might otherwise not have existed because it was uneconomic to do so. People living in remote rural areas were seen to be particularly at risk.

2   It is difficult to decide on the share prices for industries that are sold off because there is no experience of this market. The rapid rise in the prices of some shares immediately

after the companies had been floated suggests that the initial share price undervalued the companies. Critics of privatisation claim that this is selling the assets of the country off cheaply, hence the 'Selling off the family silver' remarks of Sir Harold Macmillan.

3   A privatisation issue is attractive – particularly if the shares are thought to be below their real market value. This attracts funds and makes it difficult for other businesses to raise the capital they need at that time. This money could have been used to finance new investment rather than the transfer of ownership from the public to the private sector.

4   Although privatisation reduces government spending and increases the amount of money it is receiving, it also reduces the revenue the government receives from profitable nationalised industries.

5   During the 1980s nationalised industries achieved significant improvements in output, productivity and cost control. This evidence suggests that a change in ownership is not a necessary prerequisite for improvements in efficiency.

6   There is evidence to suggest that privatisation does not have the revolutionary effect on share ownership that is claimed for it. The rise in the number of shareholders could also be influenced by improved tax concessions for people taking part in employee share schemes.

7   One of the arguments put forward for state ownership of resources claims that certain areas of production are too important to be allowed to be subject to the profit motive. Under this heading we could include water and electricity, especially with concern for safety in the use of nuclear power.

The monetary system

Throughout this book money values will be used frequently to refer to wages, the value of machinery and anything else when we want to allocate a value or compare it with other goods. It will be useful therefore to take a brief look at money and the monetary system in the UK. The monetary system is a subsystem of the economic system.

What is money?
Societies with a low level of specialisation or which generate little or no surplus for trade have little need for money. They may trade their surplus goods by *barter*, that is the direct exchange of one good or service for another. The system works well provided the range of goods and services to be exchanged is limited and the number of transactions undertaken is relatively small. The main problem with barter is finding somebody who has what you want and is willing to accept what you have to offer in exchange for it. This is known as the *double coincidence of wants*. Barter is not unknown in modern western economies. Neighbours exchange services and goods without using money. Someone may take care of the neighbours' garden while they are on holiday and be paid in vegetables. A cabinet maker whose child is tutored in mathematics may pay by renovating the tutor's furniture.

Complex societies use money for most of their commercial transactions. This is because a more flexible and convenient method of exchange is needed to make a large number of exchanges feasible. If you cannot understand this imagine the time and effort needed to find a partner in an exchange using barter. Money, that is any good that fulfils the following functions, is the solution to this problem. Money is:

1   *A medium of exchange*   Money will be accepted in exchange for any good or service, so eliminating the need for a double coincidence of wants.

2   *A store of value*   Under the barter system it is necessary to make purchasing decisions within a short period of time, particularly if the goods concerned are perishable. Someone offering perishable goods for barter will have to take what is on offer before the goods deteriorate.

3   *A unit of account*   When the value of goods and services is expressed in monetary terms it is possible to compare the value of very different goods. How many cows equal one barrel of oil? Using money values it is possible to say. Chapters 4 ('Starting and running your own business') and 6 ('Accounting: an aid to decision making and control') will explore some of the anomalies contained in this oversimplification, but it is still a useful attribute of money.

Money as a *standard of deferred payment* follows from its function as a unit of account. If the value of goods and services can be measured in money then the amount owing can be agreed upon and a future date for payment can be fixed. It is this function of money that makes the purchase of goods and services on *credit* possible.

Types of money

In theory anything can be used as money provided people trust it. In practice it was early discovered that precious metals were an ideal form of money. They were of high value in their own right, they were durable and, because their value was high in relation to their quantity, they were portable. Early traders in Europe used bars of iron from which pieces could be flaked and weighed as payment. The use of the term 'precious' is relative to the society and technology in which the metals are used. Very early in the history of western civilisation it was realised that if the metal was cast into units of standard weight and value (*coins*) many problems in trading would be solved. The guarantee that a coin was of the correct weight was invested in the head of the monarch or emperor. This placed a significant degree of economic power in the ruler. It also carried with it a responsibility to maintain the value of the currency.

Metals are heavy. Over the centuries the amount of goods and services a given quantity of metal would buy became less. To finance their normal business transactions people were having to carry a great weight of coins with them and risking robbery. It began to make sense to leave the gold with a business which had the facilities for safeguarding it and accepting a piece of paper from it promising to pay that amount of coinage when the note was presented to it. These *promissory notes* were a legal contract and the forerunners of our modern *bank notes*. The legal form is still in use.

The history of money is fascinating but to go into too much detail is irrelevant in this book. The detail given so far is intended to take the magic out of the idea of money. We have progressed so far from the societies that used metal as a scale against which they judged value that much of our money has no existence other than figures in a bank account with notes and coins as a convenient way of servicing minor transactions. The notes and coins are worth less intrinsically than the transactions they finance.

This process has occurred because money is a unit of account. Provided records are kept about the value of a person's transactions there is no need for an actual exchange of cash. It has also come about because of abuses to the systems in operation. Criminals like cash because it cannot be traced. Nineteenth-century bank managers were greedy for profit. They realised that they could lend more than they held. The Bank Charter Act of 1844 set in motion a chain of events that concentrated the power of issuing bank notes with the Bank of England and the Bank of Scotland.

In the UK, at the time of writing, the total supply of money can be defined as:

1 *M0* Notes and coins in circulation, plus banks' till money plus banks' balances with the Bank of England.

2 *M1* is known as *narrow money*. This is money which is readily available for use in transactions. The term *broad money* includes narrow money and money which has been saved.

3 *M3* Notes and coins in circulation with the public plus private sector sterling sight bank deposits plus private sector sterling time bank deposits plus private sector holdings of sterling bank certificates of deposit.

4 *M4* M3 plus private sector holdings of building society shares, deposits and certificates of deposit minus building society holdings of bank deposits, notes and coin.

5 *M5* M4 plus holdings by the private sector (other than building societies) of money market instruments (e.g. Treasury bills), certificates of tax and national savings instruments.

This is the *nominal* money supply of the UK, that is the total amount of money expressed in terms of pounds and pence. The *real* money supply is the term used to describe the purchasing power of the nominal money supply.

The neutrality of money
The real economy is about the goods and services which are produced and the efficiency with which this process takes place. Money can therefore be seen as no more than a symbol for these events, a convenient way of representing them and making it easier for transactions to take place. Money is also a good in its own right. People may prefer to hold their wealth in money rather than in real goods or the buying of services.

The value of money can *rise*. *Less* money will then be needed to buy goods and the general price level will *fall*. This situation is called *deflation*. The opposite situation, *inflation*, is characterised by a *fall* in the value of money and a *rise* in the price level. Inflation has been the most prevalent situation in the world in recent economic history.

The monetary sector
The monetary sector in the British economy includes all businesses whose activities are concerned with taking deposits, borrowing and lending money and who are under the control of the Bank of England according to the terms of the Banking Act of 1979. It also includes the banking department of the Bank of England. A brief review of the businesses in the monetary sector and other *financial institutions* will provide you with background information which will prove useful when you study Chapters 7 ('Finance') and 17 ('Business and the economy').

1 The *Bank of England* is the *central bank* and, together with the *Treasury* (a government department), is responsible for the monetary policy of the government, which can influence the supply of money in the economy, the rate of interest and the foreign exchange rate. Later in this chapter we will discuss the relationship which exists

between the business community and the political system. You should note at this level the relationship is very close. The Bank of England translates government policy into practice by its dealings in the monetary system.

2   The Bank of England lends money to the *discount houses*. These institutions are defined as banks under the 1979 Act. Discount houses make their profits by borrowing money from other banks and buying *bills* (evidence of a debt) before the debt is due to be paid. The bills are bought for less than their face value, the price paid being arrived at by discounting from the amount due when they *mature*. The date of maturity is the day on which the debt needs to be paid. Discount houses invest in *Treasury bills* (short-term government debt) and *commercial bills*.

   Discount houses borrow from banks *at call*. The banks can ask for repayment at any time. When discount houses are short of money as a result of this they can borrow money from the Bank of England, or the Bank of England will rediscount bills. The decision lies with the Bank of England not the discount houses. The rate of interest charged or the discount rate for this service is usually 1 or 2 per cent higher than the market rate. In this way the Bank of England can influence interest rates in the economy as a whole. The Bank of England is acting as *lender of last resort*. The extent to which it is prepared to do this will depend on government policy.

3   The *clearing banks* are the banks with which most people are familiar. They have a large number of branches which has earned them the title of the *High Street banks*.

4   *Accepting houses* are banks which specialise in guaranteeing *bills of exchange*. Bills of exchange are used to finance international trade – although the extent to which they are used varies – and were precisely defined by the Bills of Exchange Act of 1882. For the purposes of this chapter it is sufficient to say that they resemble a post-dated cheque where the amount appearing on the cheque is the original amount lent (the *principal*) together with the *interest* payable. A bill of exchange guaranteed by an accepting house is known as a *first class bill of exchange*.

5   There are other financial institutions which are licensed to take deposits from the public.

6   The National Girobank is part of the public sector and provides a range of payment and banking services.

SELF ASSESSMENT

1 Distinguish between inflation and deflation.
2 List the major institutions which form the monetary sector of the economy. Using information from Chapter 1 explain briefly why it is called the monetary sector.

Business and the political system

It is not part of the contents of Business Studies to describe the political system in detail. It is important to remember that politics is about government and whoever governs a country has power over the setting of objectives for the overall management of the country. This implies rules for conduct which will be embodied in law and which will affect business as a part of the society which is being governed.

Politics is also about the relationship between a country and other countries. In the extreme case of war this can mean that a business will be required to produce goods needed by the armed forces rather than the goods and services that people want. It might also mean that businesses are forbidden by government to trade with countries whose political philosophy is considered undesirable, a policy known as imposing *economic sanctions*.

Politics is also about ideas. A government with an ideological commitment to the free market economy rather than a command economy will put into practice policies that will influence business ownership and control. It is also likely to reduce grants to business enterprises and so increase the proportion of costs of production they have to bear for themselves. The reverse is also true. Political commitment to planning might increase grants but put constraints on the decision making activities of the business.

The parts of the political system of a country include obvious organisations such as political parties. Conservative, Labour and the Social and Liberal Democrats (the order is alphabetical!) have a high profile in political activity. Their declared policies are influenced by the behaviour of *pressure groups*, organisations with an interest in having particular policies implemented and who use a variety of methods to persuade the government and individual members of parliament to adopt the policies they advocate. The business community, working through organisations such as the Confederation of British Industry (CBI) can be seen as part of the political system. The CBI, acting as a pressure group, might attempt to persuade the government to follow policies leading to lower interest rates, lower wage increases or reduced taxation if it sees this to be in the interest of its members. Trade unions and the Trades Union Congress (TUC), acting as political pressure groups on behalf of their members, might advocate similar policies but are unlikely to agree about low wages.

The success or failure of pressure groups will depend on the political objectives of a government which in turn will depend on the political ideology of the party. In a democracy it can also depend on the degree of popular support a policy appears to enjoy. Governments are supposed to reflect the will of the people. The more cynical would argue that governments adopt the policies that give them the highest chance of remaining in power.

Business and the ecological system

The ecological system is concerned with the relationship between living organisms and their physical environment. The building of a factory changes the environment of plants and animals. The existence of a pool of hot water, a by-product of a factory cooling system, creates a new environment for plants and animals. The farming methods employed will create or destroy existing environments and can affect the structure of the soil.

Business has always been part of the ecological system. Adverse affects have always received more publicity than beneficial affects. When the activities of business are also seen to have political impact in this area the matter becomes one of public debate and a constraint upon the decisions made by business.

Business and the social system

The social system is the relationship which exists between all parts of society. It is the system of which all other systems we have briefly described are parts. Theoretically it is possible to assume a simple social system. In reality any social system is an extremely complicated amalgam of ideas, attitudes, patterns of behaviour and organisations that have their roots in the economic, religious, ideological, political and social history of the society concerned. Consider the problem of Sunday trading in the UK.

Sunday trading

In the UK a number of services, for example health and transport, are offered legally on a Sunday. Factories which rely on the operation of continuous processes also continue to function. The law relating to the buying and selling of goods and services, however, is complicated and open to abuse. In fact, it is known that the law is flouted by small shops and circumvented by national organisations. In 1985 the government introduced a Bill designed to rationalise the law relating to Sunday trading, the most important effect of which was to extend the ability of shops to open on a Sunday. In support of the Bill was evidence of illegal opening and changing social habits, e.g. the increase in the number of working wives and the growth of shopping as a leisure activity, particularly for items in the do-it-yourself trade, consumer durables and gardening requirements. The government's proposals stated in the Bill met opposition from a wide variety of sources. The Union of Shop, Distributive and Allied Workers (USDAW) opposed the Bill on the grounds that it would lead to more unsocial working conditions for its members. Employees in the retail trade are, for a variety of reasons, difficult to organise into trade unions and tend, as a result, to have less power in negotiations concerning pay and conditions than employees in other industries. The Lord's Day Observance Society resisted on the evidence of the Old Testament of the Christian Bible: 'Six days shalt thou labour and do all thy work: But the Seventh day is the Sabbath of the Lord thy God: In it thou shalt not do any work ...' (Exodus, ch. 20, v. 9/10)

The issue cut across party political lines, the voting decision of individual members of parliament being influenced by the reaction of the voters in their constituencies and their conscience rather than the requirements of their political allegiance in parliament. Although many political commentators agreed that the proposed Act of Parliament was a necessary and belated tidying up process, and despite the lobbying of business interests in support of the Bill, it was defeated. Religion and the social history of shop workers were triumphant.

The above example is an oversimplification and the fact that it has to be so is, in itself, significant. Relatively small groups within the population appeared to have protected their interests to the inconvenience of other people. Perhaps their vocal opposition to the Bill carried silent support from the rest of the voters. The desire to open on a Sunday might have been a desire on the part of big business to increase their profits ... The matter is open to interpretation, and that will depend on each individual's view of the world in which she/he lives!

Conclusion

Business is an integral part of the society in which it operates. Every decision business takes will be influenced by the state and values of the society in which it operates, and will in turn influence the future development of that society. This chapter has outlined business as a part in a limited number of systems. This theme will be developed in Part 3 of this book ('Business in society'). It is important that you appreciate the external constraints on business activity because without such an appreciation you will not understand the internal behaviour of a business organisation described in Part 2 ('The functions of business').

REVIEW

1 Mike Jones looked at the pile of papers that littered his desk and groaned. If this was the price of success it was getting too high. Muttering, he began to sort them into groups.

'Invoices from suppliers ... Ecox are putting their prices up again. Probably that wage agreement they signed last month. That union has got them under its thumb.

'Report from the environmental health people. Now what are they expecting us to do? New guards on all the machines? That will push my costs up. Daren't increase my prices ... too many other businesses doing what I do.

'Only three replies to that job advertisement. There aren't enough young people to go round these days. Wonder if I could get some older people? Shouldn't have put "aged 16–19" in that advertisement.

'Complaint from local residents' organisation about smoke pollution ... sterling falls, interest rates up ...'

a   Classify the systems Mike Jones has mentioned in terms of economic, political, legal and social.

b   Select two of the points made above and list ways in which they could affect the system that is Mike Jones' business.

2   Frampton Ltd manufactures a range of fashion shoes that sell for £50–150 in the shops. The business has four departments: sales, production, personnel and finance. Each department is controlled by a manager who reports to the managing director. The board of directors is dominated by the Smith family, descendants of Fred Smith who founded the business fifty years ago. There is a reluctance on the part of the board to move away from the systems laid down by the founder of the business.

In the 1980s Frampton's sales started to fall. In 1988 the sales manager retired and his place was taken by a much younger person who was determined to make her mark in the company and use it as a stepping stone in her career. In collaboration with the personnel manager, she began a vigorous and innovative training programme for her sales staff. At the same time she expanded the role of the sales department. Advertising was improved and new retail outlets were discovered. Orders began to increase rapidly. The managing director, who had given approval for the experiments, was complimented by the board.

But by 1989 the managing director was becoming concerned by the high level of customer complaints. Orders were arriving late and were frequently incomplete. Quality was falling short of its previously high standard. The buyer for a large retail chain pointed out to him, rather forcibly, that foreign companies managed to produce quality and delivery at a much lower price.

a   Using the diagrams in Figures 2.1 and 2.2 analyse Frampton's Ltd as a system.

b   What are the major subsystems in Frampton's Ltd?

c   From the evidence given list the problems of the company.

d   How might a systems view of the business have avoided these problems?

e   What evidence exists in this case to support the statement 'a business is an open system'?

3   The following extract has been adapted from an article in *The Economist*:

Some (hospitals) might be privatised; others could be bought and run by their own staff; still others could become trusts or charities. They would fix their own pay rates and raise their capital outside the Treasury's iron public sector borrowing rules, bringing into the health service some much needed investment ... If they did not attract enough patients, their management and staff would have to change – or they might close.

Doubters will seize on this last point to argue against floating off Britain's hospitals. Yet hospitals are closed every week, usually on the whim of strategic planners. Much better to use a market test, albeit an imperfect one, to decide ...

The case for relying largely on revenue from general taxes remains strong. That kind of finance is fair, predictable, cheap to collect and avoids the shortcomings of coverage and selectivity that weaken so many insurance systems. Earmarked taxes, from which people could opt out, are a bad idea. Once earmarking was allowed, other taxpayers would plead to opt out of education, or social security, or defence. ('Set the hospitals free', 30 April 1988)

a Explain what is meant by the term 'privatised'.

b Suggest and explain three reasons why allowing hospitals to close as the result of the market test might be better than closure by strategic planners.

c List and outline three arguments that might be put forward by opponents of a privatised hospital system.

d Explain how earmarked taxes (taxes whose revenue will be used for a predetermined type of expenditure) could lead to an improved health service for some people and a worse service for others.

e How would an increase in private financing for the health service affect:

  i insurance companies?

  ii other businesses?

Activities

1 Analyse, as a system, an organisation with which you are familiar . What are the inputs, the major processes and the output? Does the organisation have any subsystems? Is it possible to analyse these in terms of functions and people?

2 Collect as much information as you can about a development project that is causing controversy, preferably in your local area. Analyse the interface of the project with other systems. For example:

  ☐ the local transport network.

  ☐ the surrounding ecology.

  ☐ the political environment.

  ☐ the local economy.

Conduct a survey to find out the reactions of local people.

3 Collect as much information as you can about the 'freeing' of the Eastern bloc economies. Why do the governments of these countries believe it is necessary? What problems are they facing? Does the desire of these countries to free their economies support the arguments for greater freedom of competition in western economies?

4 Conduct a survey to discover people's attitudes to privatisation.

Suggested projects

1 An investigation into the effects of technological change on the subsystems of a business.

2 An investigation into the results of deregulation of a service.

Essays

1 What is a system? How useful is the systems approach in the study of business organisations?

2 Comment on the statement 'All managers must think in terms of the system if the business is to achieve its objectives.'

3 'Privatisation is a matter of great interest to all business enterprise in the private sector.' How far do you agree with this statement?

3 Markets

When you have studied this chapter you should be able to:

□ Define a market.

□ Distinguish between the different ways in which the word is used.

□ Identify the factors that influence the demand for a product.

□ Appreciate the complexity of consumer buying decisions.

□ Define measures of elasticity of demand and supply.

□ Perform simple calculations of elasticity.

□ Identify the factors that affect the overall supply of a product.

□ Appreciate how changes in demand and supply can affect the market price for a product.

□ Describe the classification of markets.

□ Appreciate markets as a constraint upon business decisions.

□ Understand the role of government in regulating market behaviour.

□ Appreciate the need for regulation of market behaviour.

The *market* is part of the environment within which a business operates. In this chapter we shall outline the different types of market, examine the way markets operate and consider some of the implications of market operation both for an individual business enterprise and for society as a whole.

What is a market?

The word 'market' is used in a variety of contexts which, at first sight, seem to have little in common. Read the following passages carefully. You will see that the word 'market' is used in a number of different ways. Can you find anything in common?

A farmer talks of taking produce to market. This market has a physical existence in the local town or city. It is an open space or a building where farmers and their customers meet for the purpose of buying and selling the farm produce. In a town the existence of the market also attracts other traders who erect their stalls on the designated market day. The town is called a *market town* and draws its custom from the surrounding countryside. The sphere of influence (i.e. the area from which the town will draw consumers and producers) will depend on the number of people living in the area and the ease with which goods can be transported. Market towns not only provide a place for the buying and selling of produce and other goods, in the past they were also the places in which labour was hired and the centres for the provision of services such as banking. This is still the case in some rural areas of the UK. In a rural economy, with a relatively sparse population, most business transactions can be fitted into a couple of days in each month and permanent shops may well be a waste of money. Produce is sold from temporary stalls or directly from the cart or baskets it arrives in. Market, in this context, is used to describe a building or open space, in which livestock and goods are bought and sold.

A business can define the market for its product by asking the following questions.

- ☐   Who will buy the product?

- ☐   Why will they buy it?

- ☐   How many will buy it and in what quantity?

- ☐   When will they buy it?

- ☐   Where will they buy it?

- ☐   What price will they pay?

- ☐   Are there any similar products available?

This, of course, only gives an outline of the market for a product. If it is to sell well the business needs to have a lot more information and make a large number of decisions.

At first sight the word 'market' may seem to be used in two entirely different ways. In fact, the uses of the word 'market' have common elements: the product, buyers, sellers, price and place. We can say that the market for any one product is defined by these parameters. The distinction is in the point of view. An economist would bring these elements together in a single succinct definition: a market can be defined as a geographical area over which the price of a good or service is the same.

Determining the market price

The final *market price* for a particular product will depend upon the interaction of the results of individual decisions made by the purchasers of the good or service, the producers and possibly the government.

The purchasers: demand for the product

Individuals decide whether to spend their money or save it. Spending decisions lead to the purchase of consumer goods (food, clothes, etc.), durable consumer goods (washing machines, cars, refrigerators, etc.), and services (hair-dressing, transport, etc.). They may also make investment decisions (house purchase, unit trusts). Savings decisions include building society accounts, savings certificates, deposit accounts, etc.

A business organisation buys labour, raw materials and capital equipment such as the machinery to carry out production. Businesses also buy commercial services, for example banking, advertising and insurance. Governments buy labour and the services of business organisations to build roads, airports and bridges. They buy weapons and consumables (e.g. paper) to help them to carry out their work. Each group has a particular set of constraints which influence its buying behaviour.

Consumer buying behaviour

The consumers who choose to buy one product in preference to other products constitute the *demand* for that product. Total demand for a particular type of product, e.g. the total demand for motorcars in a particular economy, is determined by:

1 *The price of the good or service*   To say that the lower the price of a particular good or service the greater the quantity of that good or service which will be bought is to risk being accused of stating the obvious!

2 *The price of substitute goods and services*   If the price of potatoes rises sharply then rice and pasta products will become relatively cheaper and some consumers will stop buying potatoes and switch to buying rice and/or pasta.

3 *The price of complementary products*   To use a car you need to buy oil and petrol, pay tax and buy insurance. The cost of running a car should be taken into account when deciding to purchase it. When the purchase of one product implies that you must purchase another product then the demand for each will be dependent on the demand for the other. A rise in the price of one such product is likely to lead to a decrease in the demand for both products.

4 *The taste and preference of the consumer*   In Chapter 2 we discussed the working of a free market economy and the idea of consumer sovereignty. In a market economy people make separate and distinct decisions to buy based on their own perception of their life and what is needed to give them satisfaction. Taste and preference is a by-product of an individual's personality. It is for marketing departments to exploit the 'grey areas'; the areas where there is no strong taste and buyers can be influenced to change their choice.

5 *The income of the consumer*   In general the higher the income of consumers the more goods and services they will consume and, therefore, the higher the demand for a particular good or service. This statement must be qualified and a distinction made between *money* income and *real* income.

Money income is income without relation to purchasing power. *Real income* is what you can buy with the money you have. It relates income to the average price level of goods and services; in other words the purchasing power of money. We have mentioned this problem in Chapter 2 ('The business as a system') and we will consider the implications of the value of money in Chapters 6 ('Accounting: an aid to decision making and control') and 15 ('Decision making in business organisations'). In Chapter 18 ('Business and society') we will examine some of the influences on changes in the value of money. To put the situation simply: a high money income and a relatively low price level is likely to lead to an increase in demand. In other words there is a high *real* income. A high money income combined with a relatively high price level (possibly compared with other countries) is likely to lead to a low *real* income.

As a general guide to the way a purchaser's individual choices influence the demand for a good the above analysis is adequate so far as it goes, but it does not answer all the questions a business manager might want to ask.

Consumer motivation

Read the following passage and then try to answer the question.

> Mrs Sherratt is an old age pensioner with an adequate pension from her late husband's firm. She owns her own home, has a comfortable lifestyle and is very fond of drinking tea. For the past five years Mrs Sherratt has been a devoted consumer of brand X. Her only concession to change in that time has been to buy teabags in place of packets of loose tea. It took two years for Mrs Sherratt to make that change. In June 1985 Mrs Sherratt received a legacy of £15 000 on the death of a relative. In the same month she was given, as a gift, a quantity of high quality and extremely expensive loose tea; she appreciated the taste.

Will Mrs Sherratt stop buying brand X tea and buy the more expensive tea?

There is, of course, no way in which we can even attempt to answer that question unless we know Mrs Sherratt very well and could judge how willing to change she might be. Mrs Sherratt might prefer the taste of brand X tea. She might be conditioned by years of careful spending to select the cheaper of two products. She might simply forget to buy the more expensive tea and buy the cheaper brand out of habit. She might be worried in case people realise she has inherited money if her habits change. She might be concerned that her friends would think she was merely trying to impress them. She might ...

In fact, Mrs Sherratt's buying decision would be extremely complex. She may not herself be aware of some of the reasons behind her final decision.

When you remember that Mrs Sherratt is only one of millions of people who buy tea every day, you can appreciate the fact that the analysis of buying behaviour is extremely important. It is, of course, of great interest in marketing and a considerable amount of research has been undertaken in this field of human behaviour. This research tends to confirm the complexity of the buying behaviour of individuals.

Traditional economic theory assumes that all purchasing decisions are made on a rational basis with the objective of maximising the individual's satisfaction. It does not require a great deal of thought to realise that if this were so in all cases, the family shopping would be a mammoth task involving a large number of small decisions. The outcome of each decision would then have to be weighed against the outcome of other decisions to check that the final 'basket' of choices was the combination that would give maximum satisfaction to the family. We can isolate certain groups of factors that influence buying decisions. The particular influence of a given decision, however, will depend on the personality, perceptions, prejudices and education of the individual. It is this that makes research into human buying behaviour so fascinating.

1   *Internal stimuli* The individual has basic physical needs which must be met merely for survival. These are food, warmth and shelter. There are also security needs (protection, safety), social needs (love, group support), status needs from which the individual gets a feeling of self-respect and prestige, and self-actualising needs – the needs which arise for an individual out of her/his own personal goals. It is usual to see the lower order

needs as being those satisfied by straightforward economic buying decisions. Social and status needs may, however, require reinforcing by material possessions, and the satisfaction of self-actualising needs might demand the sacrifice of material possessions.

2 *External stimuli* These can include the impact of marketing on the buying decision – the customer's response to advertising and sales promotion.

3 *Cultural norms* Each person is a member of society and throughout life learns to conform to the demands made by society. Patterns of child-rearing and the formal education system introduce children to the social rules they will be expected to follow and, through reward and punishment, adults enforce adherence to these rules. Although there is a general consensus in society as a whole, sub-groups will have their own rules and children brought up within a group will be expected to conform to the rules of that group. This is a very generalised statement and one which ignores the vast academic research that has gone into the subject. It is adequate for our purposes at the moment. The expectations of a group will affect the buying behaviour of members of that group. If status is measured in terms of a house, a car and a number of consumer durables then this is likely to influence buying behaviour. If success is measured in terms of professional achievement or becoming a successful business owner then this could be the way in which group members measure their success rather than by the possession of certain goods. Cultural norms are not fixed, although they do tend to change slowly. Recent research has indicated that there has been a change in women's attitudes to the point where the standard appeals to their prowess as housewives common to many advertisements for family consumer goods were producing a negative rather than a positive response. A matter of some concern to the producers!

A typical buying decision would include the weighing up of the advantages of one choice compared with others, the rational element, together with the influence of the less obvious factors listed above. The customer might respond through habit or loyalty. There may be an imperceptible shift in cultural norms. We will examine the ways in which a marketing team responds to these constraints in Chapter 8 ('Marketing'). For the moment we are concerned only with defining them.

1 *Primary motives* The customer realises a need for a particular type of good or service. She/He might want entertainment over the weekend, some new clothes or a new stereo.

2 *Selection motives* When there is more than one supplier for a good or service the customer has to make a decision. This decision would be easy if the products of all the suppliers were identical. They are not. What is more, different goods and services can satisfy the same need. The desire for weekend entertainment might be met by a disco, the cinema, sports activities or staying at home and watching the television. Where there are a number of models of the same product, for example the stereo, the buyer has to decide which model has the features that best suit.

3 *Emotional motives* People are not always willing to admit to these motives. Prestige, self-image and comfort are included in this group.

4 *Rational motives* These are the motives that can be given to other people with the confidence that they will be accepted as a good reason for a particular buying decision. Low price, quality, durability and convenience are socially acceptable.

People are not always aware of the motives that rule their buying decisions. This makes it difficult for businesses to discover what markets exist for their product and to design a marketing strategy that will reach potential consumers.

So far we have established that the demand for a product is likely to increase as price falls; that there are a number of general influences on the demand for a product; and that consumer buying behaviour is complex and although we can isolate the influences on an individual's decisions they are so much a product of that person's uniqueness that no outsider could predict the response to a given situation. In Chapter 5 ('Statistics: an aid to decision making and control') we will show how the use of statistical techniques can go some way to helping business with this problem of market analysis.

SELF ASSESSMENT

1 Make a list of all the factors that would influence your personal decision to take a particular continental holiday. Classify the list according to the main influences on the demand for a product.
2 Give two reasons why consumer buying behaviour is complex.
3 Think of three goods you have bought recently. Would you have made a different choice if your income had been higher? What effect, if any, would a general increase in the level of prosperity in this country have on the demand for those goods?
4 Interest rates can be considered as the price of money. List three products whose demand might be affected by the general level of interest rates in the country. Why did you select these products?

Formal analysis of demand

We can summarise the demand for a product graphically in Figure 3.1. Reading from the graph, we can see that when the price is 4p per kilogram, the demand for potatoes in Coxton will be 14 tonnes. A rise in price to 12p per kilogram reduces the demand to 6 tonnes. It is possible to read off the potential demand for potatoes at each price from 1p to 18p per kilogram. A closer inspection of the information reveals that the demand for potatoes in Coxton does not respond in the same way to each change in price.

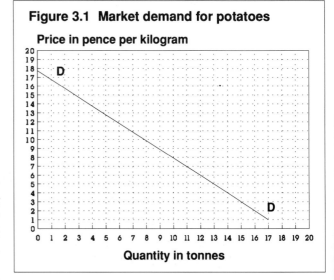

Figure 3.1 Market demand for potatoes

The degree of responsiveness of demand to a change in price is of obvious interest to a business. A measure of this responsiveness is obtained by comparing the percentage change in demand to the percentage change in price. This measurement is called the *price elasticity of demand* or *PED* for short. The calculation of this measure for a change in price from 2p to 4p is as follows:

$$PED = \frac{\text{Percentage change in quantity}}{\text{Percentage change in price}}$$

$$= \frac{\text{Change in quantity}/\text{average quantity}}{\text{Change in price}/\text{average price}}$$

$$= \frac{(15.75 - 13.75)/14.75}{(4 - 2)/3}$$

$$= \frac{2/14.75}{2/3}$$

$$= 0.203$$

When potatoes are sold at 4p per kilogram, the revenue (i.e. price x quantity sold) is £560. A price increase to 6p leads to a revenue of £720. The higher price leads to a higher revenue. A similar calculation for a price change from 14p to 16p results in a fall in revenue from £525 to £280.

In general, if an increase in price leads to an increase in revenue or a decrease in price leads to a decrease in revenue then demand is said to be *price inelastic*. In this case the numerical measurement will be less than 1. If the reverse is true, i.e. an increase in price leads to a fall in revenue or a decrease in price leads to a rise in revenue, then demand is said to be *price elastic*. The numerical measurement is greater than 1. This information is useful to a business in the following circumstances.

☐ If it hopes to capture a larger share of the market by lowering its price. If the market is not responsive to a change in price the business will find itself with a lower revenue and no increase in market share.

☐ Faced with an increase in costs, e.g. a pay rise for labour, the business might be tempted to pass on the extra costs to consumers as a price increase. Inelastic demand would make this possible. If demand is elastic it may leave the business worse off.

☐ Similar to the above case is an increase in tax on a product. The producer has to decide whether to absorb the tax increase, or part of it, or pass it on to the consumer. Again, in an inelastic market it is likely to be the consumer who shoulders most of the tax burden. In Chapter 18 ('Business and society') we shall examine the implications of this for government policy formation in more detail.

☐ A change in the exchange rate can also have implications for a business which exports its goods, imports raw materials or components, or faces competition from foreign firms in the domestic market. If the domestic currency appreciates (becomes more valuable in terms of the amount of foreign currency it can buy) then imports will become cheaper to domestic customers and exports more expensive to foreign customers. If the market is elastic then this could result in a fall in demand for the business's goods abroad but it would minimise the impact of foreign competitors in the home market.

Demand is not only responsive to changes in price. We have seen that the price of complementary and substitute products can also influence demand. *Cross elasticity*, i.e. the responsiveness of demand to the changes in the price of other products, and *income elasticity*, i.e. the responsiveness of demand to changes in income, are also useful concepts. A business would also be interested in how the demand for a product responded to an increase in expenditure on advertising or sales promotion. This is sometimes called *promotional elasticity* or *advertising elasticity*. In each case the variable can be seen as a *force* acting on the demand for a product. The relevant measure of elasticity is calculated by dividing the percentage change in quantity demanded by the percentage change in the variable.

As a general rule, the following will tend to encourage consumer habits that will be translated into elastic demand:

- the availability of good substitute;
- a luxury product, although if it is habit forming people might continue to buy it;
- a market that has shown itself to be responsive to new ideas;
- a feeling of insecurity in the society, leading to an unwillingness to take risks;
- a low level of national income;
- expensive products, which encourage careful consumer buying behaviour;
- products which are bought frequently and in small units.

SELF ASSESSMENT

1 Calculate the price elasticity of demand for a good when a 10 per cent increase in price leads to a 5 per cent fall in the quantity demanded.
2 Give two circumstances in which you would expect the income elasticity of demand for a good to be inelastic.
3 Look at the following list of products. For each product state whether or not you would expect the price elasticity of demand to be greater than or less than 1. Give two reasons to support each of your answers.
   a holidays in the Far East.
   b houses for first time buyers.
   c potatoes.
   d washing machines.
   e musical instruments.
4 Would you expect the price elasticity of demand for a product to stay the same over the whole possible price range? Give reasons for your answer.
5 Jane Harper inserted a series of advertisements in her local newspaper promoting the services of her typing agency. This action increased her promotion costs for that year by 20 per cent. What is the minimum percentage increase in income Jane would need to justify this expenditure? Explain your answer showing any necessary calculations.

The supply of goods to a market

The total supply of goods to a market is determined by the willingness of businesses to supply the product and their ability to do so. Each business will have its own set of priorities when deciding whether or not to supply, and the extent to which a business feels it can satisfy a particular market will be determined by its own unique set of constraints. However it is possible to summarise the general influences on the total supply of a product to a market as follows:

1 *The cost of producing the good compared with the price it is possible to obtain when the good is sold* The higher the price the greater the number of businesses that will be willing and able to produce the product, so the total supply to the market will increase.

2 *The price/cost structure in other markets* A small general store, for example, offering a range of food, tobacco products, newspapers and a video library service finds that, as a result of competition from a nearby supermarket, the profit from the sale of the food lines is declining. By limiting the number of food lines it carries to those which are most profitable and increasing the shelf space devoted to the video library the total profits of the shop are increased. The supply of goods and services to the food market has declined.

Not all businesses would find it so easy to switch from one product to another. Changing the use of agricultural land from one use to another, for instance, could mean a break in production ranging from months to years and a farmer might want reassurance that the high profits that are attractive at the moment will continue for some time before being prepared to risk capital and livelihood in the change.

3 *The technology available to a society* Improvements in technology can increase the number of goods that can be supplied from a given amount of raw material and/or labour. It can, as in the case of home computers, give a product the opportunity to exploit a new market previously denied to it because of high production costs.

4 *The objectives of business* will also influence supply in a market. Profit is important to a business but other factors, not necessarily financial, may sway the final choice of individual decision makers. In the example of the general store given above, the owner of the store might well have decided to accept lower profits if the majority of customers for food were old people who could not easily make the journey to the supermarket. Whether or not the business would survive such a decision and the service continue to be supplied to that market would depend on how much profit the store was making originally. If the switch to the video library was a matter of survival the owner might well have no choice.

The supply of a product to a market is also subject to varying degrees of responsiveness to changes in price (*elasticity of supply*). This can be calculated in a similar manner to price elasticity of demand.

We can summarise the general supply position of markets by a supply curve, as in Figure 3.2. If you compare this diagram of a supply curve with the demand curve illustrated in Figure 3.1, you can see that it is possible to draw them using the same axes. The intersection between the two curves is the point at which the amount that can be supplied coincides with the ability and willingness of the buyers to purchase that good. This is shown in Figure 3.3.

In Figure 3.3 the market price is designated by 0A and the quantity supplied to the market by 0B. The total revenue from sales in that market is market price multiplied by total quantity demanded and supplied. In this example what would that be?

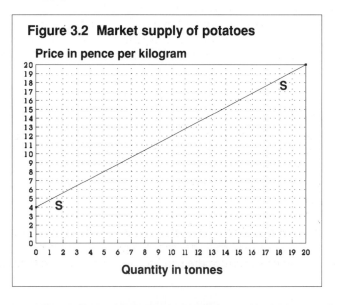

Figure 3.2 Market supply of potatoes

An increase in demand for a product can be caused by a number of things apart from a decrease in price, for example an increase in population, an increase in real national income, a decrease in the price of a complementary product or an increase in the price of a substitute product. This can be illustrated by a shift in the demand curve to the right, as shown in Figure 3.4.

Provided the supply stayed the same the price of the product would rise. A decrease in population or even in part of the population, e.g. a decline in the number of children, a fall in real national income, a rise in the price of a complementary product or a fall in the price of a substitute would shift the demand curve to the left, and the price of the product would fall, as shown in Figure 3.5.

Changes in such variables as technology and the costs of raw materials can have similar effects on the supply curves of a product. Figures 3.6 and 3.7 show the effects of shifts in the supply curve on the price of a product.

You may have noticed that in the analysis given above we have assumed that demand and supply are independent of each other. This makes it relatively easy to study the results of a change in demand or supply. In the real world a business, noting that the demand for one of its products was falling, would be likely to lower production levels and, if possible, switch its resources to a more profitable product. A shift to the left in the demand curve would be followed by a shift to the left in the supply curve. There would be

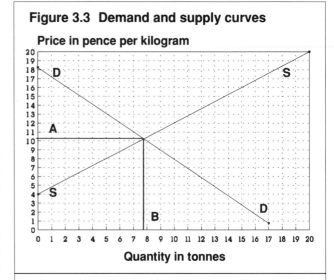

Figure 3.3 Demand and supply curves

Price in pence per kilogram

Figure 3.4 Demand curve shifted to the right

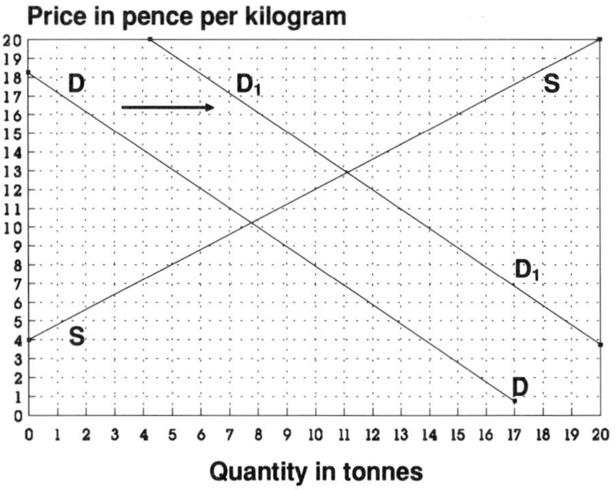

Price in pence per kilogram

Figure 3.5 Demand curve shifted to the left

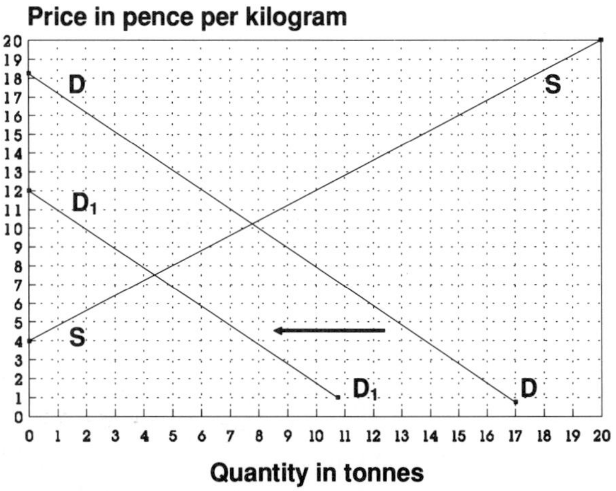

Price in pence per kilogram

a time lag and, depending on how rapidly the producers reacted to the new situation, the price would fall. Figure 3.8 shows the influences on price.

1 Explain how the objectives of firms can influence the supply of a product.
2 Improvements in technology lower the manufacturing costs of a product. Show, with the aid of diagrams, the effect of this on market price:
   a if demand is elastic.
   b if demand is inelastic.
3 By 1995 it is expected that there will be approximately 25 per cent fewer school leavers entering the labour market than in 1989. Explain, with the aid of diagrams:
   a the possible effect on the wages offered to the 16–19 age group if businesses continue to compete for their services.
   b the possible effect on the wages of that age group if businesses attract a greater number of older people into the market.

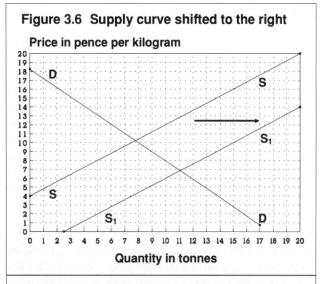

Figure 3.6 Supply curve shifted to the right

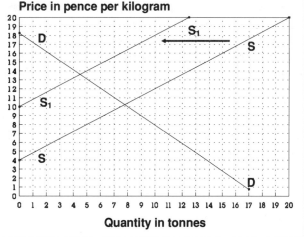

Figure 3.7 Supply curve shifted to the left

4 World coffee prices are affected by agreements between major producer countries to limit their outputs, i.e. quotas are imposed.
   a Show, with the aid of diagrams, the effects of quotas on the world price for coffee.
   b In 1989 producer countries failed to reach an agreement on quotas. What effect would this have had on the world price for coffee?

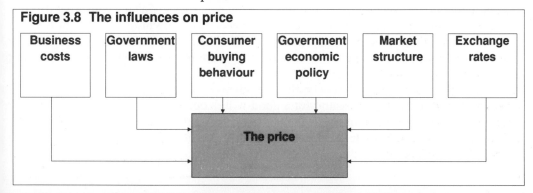

Figure 3.8 The influences on price

Classification of markets

The analysis of market behaviour given so far is general enough to apply to all cases and to provide an outline guide to the way in which you would expect the demand and supply for a product to respond to a number of influences. It is important to remember that this provides a general guide only, and the market for every good and service offered in an economy has its own unique combination of influences.

In Chapter 1 ('What is business studies?') we saw how the wide range of activities in which people were involved could be classified for ease of reference. The same principle can be applied to markets. One way to do this is to divide markets by their geographical size. Other ways include using the type of product or the degree of power a single producer is able to exercise over the market. This is known as *market structure*.

Classification by geographical market

Markets may be described as local, regional, national, continental and world. Companies producing crude oil operate in a world market. This simply means that the users of crude oil, whether in the UK, Malaysia or Japan, will tend to pay the same price for crude oil, and if any difference exists in price the buyers and the sellers will react quickly enough to iron this out. The currency market (the buying and selling of foreign currencies by recognised dealers) is also a world market and dealings in foreign currency in Hong Kong will have an immediate effect on the London Exchange Market. On the other hand the market for a product such as soap powder is likely to be a national market. The marketing team responsible for a brand of soap powder might be able to perceive regional differences in the way in which people respond to their product but whether or not this influences their marketing decisions will depend on the magnitude of these differences and their effects on profits. If the differences were so great that the price had to be markedly different in one region of the country compared with another then they would no longer be operating in a national market.

Classification by product

We have already touched upon this distinction when we talked about consumer goods and consumer durables. The distinction is a useful one in analysing market behaviour because influences upon the buying decisions vary between these categories of goods. Consumer durables, for example, are often bought on credit. As a result of this practice an increase in the cost of borrowing money (the *interest rate*) can be seen as a complementary cost to the buying decision for these goods.

Another major grouping of goods is *industrial goods*. This category includes a wide range of products. The major car manufacturers sell a significant proportion of their output (30 per cent in 1989) to businesses who need cars to carry on their own production role. Cars might, therefore, be called an industrial good. However, they are also a consumer durable because they are bought for the pleasure and convenience of owning them by individuals who do not use them directly as part of their work. The car manufacturer is operating in two markets. This example illustrates the difficulty of making a clear definition of consumer goods.

Possibly the most simple distinction that we can make rests on the idea of *derived demand*. This simply means that the demand for a good will depend on the consumer demand for the final product that particular good will help to make. The following example might clarify the distinction between different categories of goods. A product that can be bought for both personal and industrial use can be defined as belonging to an industrial market when demand for it depends on the demand for the product to whose production it contributes.

> In his budget of April 1985 the chancellor imposed VAT on a number of building operations which had previously been exempt from tax. These included the installation of domestic central heating. By August 1985 the chairman of the heating, ventilation, air-conditioning and refrigeration equipment economic development committee stated, in a submission to the chancellor, that the tax had resulted in a 25 per cent drop in sales immediately after the imposition and demand was still, after recovery, only 90 per cent of the previous year's trading. This was in a market which had been growing at a steady 10 per cent per annum. The situation was causing problems for companies engaged in the manufacture of parts, e.g. central heating boilers and radiators, and businesses which were engaged in the installation of systems. Approximately 4000 jobs had been lost as a result.

The imposition of value added tax had effectively increased the cost of installation of central heating systems. We must assume that this increase in cost had been passed on to the customer in increased prices and, as a result, the demand for these systems had fallen. There would therefore be a fall in the demand of contractors for parts and a fall in the demand for labour by both contractors and manufacturers. The demand for labour and the demand for parts can therefore be seen to derive from the demand for central heating systems. More succinctly, it is a derived demand.

Classification by competitive structure

A Cumbrian sheep farmer takes a dozen lambs to market and returns grumbling about the price taken for them. The only choice had been in whether to sell at that time or wait until a future date, by which time the price might have improved. On the other hand it may have fallen still further. The sheep farmer has no control over the market. She/He lacks power.

A company such as British Telecom has a far greater degree of control over its market. British Telecom is virtually the only supplier of a telephone service in the UK. A decision to increase the price of a telephone call is likely, the management will know, to lead to a reduction in the number of calls made. This reduction in sales for the company will not be as great as it would be if another supplier existed. British Telecom can therefore select the combination of price and projected sales that is most satisfactory to it. The company has some power over its market.

The examples given above are oversimplified but they illustrate the fact that the control a producer has over the market it operates in varies according to the number of buyers, the number of sellers, the type of product, the ease of entry into that industry and the total market share (i.e. the percentage of total sales for a product accounted for by a business) attributable to a stated number of the largest producers. This last concept is called a *concentration ratio*.

Some of the major distinctions in market structure can be classified as follows:

1 *The perfect market* For this to exist there must be a large number of buyers, a large number of sellers, relative ease of entry into the market, and good communications so that people can make informed choices and switch rapidly from one product to another if the price rises. This implies that there is no difference between the different products. Because there are a large number of buyers and sellers no single individual or business

can affect the way the market behaves and a business is a *price taker*, that is it must accept the price offered on the market or not sell the product. It also implies that the demand curve for the firm, although not necessarily for the industry, is highly elastic. Examples of perfect, or near perfect, markets include those for some agricultural products, industrial raw materials and stocks and shares.

2   *Monopoly*   This is a market in which there is only one producer of a given product. If an individual wishes to buy the good or service then they can purchase it only from the monopolist. The power of a monopolist is not absolute. Too high a price may bring government intervention and the threat of increased legal control, and there may be substitute products that are available to the consumer. Before privatisation electrical supply in the UK was a monopoly. If we look at the implications of the domestic heating market we can see that electricity is in fact in competition with piped gas, coal (both of which are monopolies), oil and bottled gas in this market.

3   *Oligopoly*   A market of this type has relatively few producers and a large number of consumers. For practical purposes oligopolistic industries are usually defined by a study of concentration ratios. There may be a large number of businesses producing a particular good but if the five largest firms account for 75 per cent of sales in a particular market then it is reasonable to suppose that the behaviour of that market will be oligopolistic rather than approaching the perfect model. Each business has some control over the market but any change in the behaviour of one business is likely to cause changes in the behaviour of its competitors. An oligopolist, for example, may hesitate to lower the price of the product for fear of instigating a potentially destructive price war in which victory would go not necessarily to the business with the best product, but to the one with the greatest financial resources. An oligopolist is more likely to compete by emphasising the ways in which its product is superior to those of its competitors and to use advertising, branding and packaging to achieve this aim.

SELF ASSESSMENT

1   Explain why the smaller the number of producers in a market is, the greater the market power of individual producers.
2   Give one reason why an oligopolist might avoid lowering the price of a product to gain more custom if it has a number of close substitutes.

Market constraints on business decisions

We began this chapter with the statement that the market is the environment in which a business operates and, so far, we have given a brief description of the way markets operate and a general classification of markets. We shall now look at some of the markets in which a business operates and the ways they can act as a constraint on the decision making process within the organisation.

The labour market

In a time of high unemployment there is a tendency to refer to 'labour' as if each person produces an identical type of labour and therefore belongs to the same labour market. Common sense and experience reveal the fallacy of this approach. Each individual has a unique set of personal abilities and acquired skills which we group together (classification again!) according to our purposes. In general terms we can talk about skilled and unskilled labour but a business is not talking in general terms. A particular business enterprise will have a very specific shopping list for the type of skills it needs in its labour force. If this type of labour is readily available then the business will have no problems. It may even be able to pay lower wages and impose stricter conditions of service than had proved possible previously. If the type of labour it requires is scarce then the business is faced with a variety of questions to be answered: Is it possible to redesign the job so that it can be performed by people with a lower skill level? Can it use machinery instead of labour? If it decides to use machinery, what will be the financial implications of this decision? Can it afford to offer higher wages to attract the sort of labour it wants? The organisation of the market for a particular type of labour can also have implications for a business. A well-organised trade union can make the supply of a particular skill a virtual monopoly. A lack of union organisation can make it easier to pay low wages.

The market for raw materials

In this market the business may not be competing only with firms producing the same goods as itself. Raw materials have a wide variety of uses and the business may find itself competing with other more prosperous producers of different and more popular products who are able to buy at higher prices. Is it possible to use a substitute product? Can research devise a substitute product?

The financial markets

A business both borrows and lends money. Even if it were possible for it to exist in complete financial independence it would still be necessary for the business to be aware of the price of money on the various financial markets, so that it was aware of the opportunity cost of using its own finance for a project. Changes in the cost of borrowing money can cause a business problems in terms of paying debts, investment decisions and, depending on the product, the demand for its own goods. An increase in the interest rate means an increase in the overall cost of living as the cost of mortgages, for example, increases. This can lead to a decline in the demand for certain types of goods, particularly luxury goods.

In Chapter 2 ('The business as a system') we looked at the financial institutions that comprise the market for money – that is those institutions who buy and sell the short-term bills that finance government expenditure and trade. This market affects and is affected by the *capital market* (the market for medium- and long-term debt). A rise in interest rate in one of these markets will attract funds from the other market.

The market for a firm's products

We have dealt with this aspect of marketing at some length in the first part of this chapter. It is necessary to emphasise that the market in which a firm sells its products will affect marketing policy (pricing, advertising, packaging, promotion, distribution and transport), the production policy (quality and quality control, purchasing, research and development, location, production method and organisation), and the financial, organisational and personnel policy of the business. This is true whether or not the business is production or market orientated. The distinction might be that the market orientated firm appreciates the effect the market has on it while the production orientated firm is either blind to that effect or has such a position of market power that it can afford to ignore it.

Each time a business purchases the smallest good or service it is operating in a market. Each time it sells it is operating in a market and a change in any one market creates ripples of cause and effect that spread through interrelated markets.

Government and markets

We have already seen that the workings of a free market economy do not always result in a fair or desirable distribution of resources. A business which has a large share of the market can exert pressure on customers and suppliers to prevent new firms – who may have a better product and be more efficient – from entering that market. Collusion between businesses operating in an oligopolistic market can keep prices high either by agreeing a price between themselves or by limiting the quantity produced or by limiting the level of investment. These agreements are generally illegal but can exist informally. When legal and accompanied by legal agreements they are known as *cartels*. The word is often applied to all such practices, whether legal or not.

Collusion can exist only in an oligopolistic market. The logistics of enforcing the agreement in markets with a large number of producers make it impossible. It therefore seems reasonable to suppose that if more competition could be introduced into a market the businesses involved would become more efficient. Working against this simple solution is the fact that some businesses operate at lower costs if they are large in size. We will discuss the reasons for this in Chapter 10 ('Background to production'). In these circumstances a greater number of firms in the same market would lead to a duplication of effort and a waste of resources. This was recognised when an Act of Parliament established the Industrial Reorganisation Corporation (IRC) in 1966. The purpose of this was to encourage businesses to combine to make better use of resources and so make them more competitive on international markets. The IRC was abolished in 1971.

The opposite trend is represented by the anti-monopoly legislation. In 1948 the Monopolies and Restrictive Practices Act was passed. This established the Monopolies Commission with powers to investigate any accusations of unfair dealing such as price and quota fixing. Collectively these are known as *restrictive practices*. Where there was evidence of such dealings the commission's report was submitted to the minister and the practice could be declared illegal.

By 1956 there was a general feeling that the Monopolies Commission lacked sufficient power. The burden of proof lay with the commission rather than the businesses accused. As a result the Restrictive Trades Practices Act, passed in 1956, established a register for all agreements together with a Restrictive Practices Court. The burden of proof passed to business. A restrictive practice was illegal unless the business could justify it on one of the following criteria:

☐ that the removal of the restriction would lead to a substantial increase in unemployment.

☐ that the removal of the restriction would deny the public certain advantages, for example that abnormally high prices were needed as an incentive to research.

☐ that the agreement was necessary to counteract the existing market power of other businesses, either suppliers or customers.

☐ that the restriction was necessary to protect the consumer from injury.

☐ that the restrictions made the industry more competitive in the export market.

☐ that the restriction was necessary to support another restriction which had been ruled in the interests of the public, e.g. the imposition of production quotas in support of a price fixing agreement.

In 1965 the Monopolies and Mergers Act was passed. *Merger* is a general term to describe the amalgamation of two businesses, whereas *takeover* is the term used to describe the acquisition of one business by another as the result of the purchase of a majority of the shareholding. With collusion forbidden by the 1956 Act the desire to protect their outlets (*forward integration*) or their supplies (*backward integration*), or to control their competitors (*horizontal integration*), persuaded many businesses to undertake mergers. Again this was a cause for concern and the 1965 Act empowered the government to stop and break up a merger or to impose conditions under which it could proceed.

The Fair Trading Act of 1973 established the role of the director general of fair trading with the power to investigate trading activities and refer suspect cases to the expanded Monopolies and Mergers Commission. The Act also reduced the level of market share at which a monopoly situation is said to exist from one third, laid down in 1948, to 25 per cent. Nationalised industries also became liable for trading practices defined as unfair, and restrictive labour practices, for example an attempt by a trade union to take advantage of a monopoly position in a labour market, could also be referred to the commission.

The powers of the Office of Fair Trading were extended by the Competition Act of 1980 to include local authorities, and it was empowered to investigate any trading activity it felt was unfair. The Monopolies and Mergers Commission is still the final judge.

Conclusion

Markets are the environment in which a business operates. It buys in markets and sells to markets. Survival depends on the ability of a business to understand these markets, appreciate the relationship between them and exploit that relationship to achieve its objectives. Chapter 4 ('Starting and running your own business') will offer an overall view of the situation. Part 2 ('The functions of business') will examine the functions of a business in more detail. Because of the widespread effects of market behaviour it was one of the earliest areas of consumer protection and this is an area we will consider in more detail in Part 3 ('Business in society').

A case study: The oil market 1950–1986

The international oil market has received so much attention from governments, economists and the media over the past fifteen years that to introduce it as a case study is to run the risk of becoming boring. The advantages of using it, however, outweigh this.

☐ It is a clear demonstration of the operation of a cartel.

☐ The importance of oil as a raw material and a fuel means that changes in its price have a traceable impact on a wide variety of markets.

☐ The extraction and refining of oil is the work of governments and very large multinational businesses. Many of the issues fall into the realm of diplomacy and politics. A study of the oil market provides material on the interaction between political and economic systems.

□   The price of oil is not a historical issue. For the student this has the advantage of providing continuing material for a case study with the possibility of unforeseen developments.

Background

The most easily accessible oil deposits were found in the USA and in the developing countries of the Middle and Far East and Africa. For many of these countries oil was the only resource they possessed which was easily marketable and which could earn them the foreign currency to invest in development programmes. To buy the technology and expertise of the developed countries a developing country must rely on aid or on what it can earn by its own exports. The importance of oil to the developed countries gave the oil producing countries a valuable resource.

From 1950 to 1970 the price of crude oil (oil before refining has taken place) fell from approximately $1.70 a barrel to $1.30 a barrel. Market power at this time lay with the users of oil rather than the producers, whose income fell.

In 1960 a group of oil exporting countries formed the Organisation of Petroleum Exporting Countries (OPEC). Representatives of each country meet regularly to agree, among other things, the price of crude oil exports. Present members include Algeria, Ecuador, Gabon, Indonesia, Iran, Iraq, Kuwait, Libya, Nigeria, Qatar, Saudi Arabia, the United Arab Emirates and Venezuela. These countries account for approximately 90 per cent of world oil exports and 60 per cent of world oil production. Potentially they have a position of considerable market power if they act together.

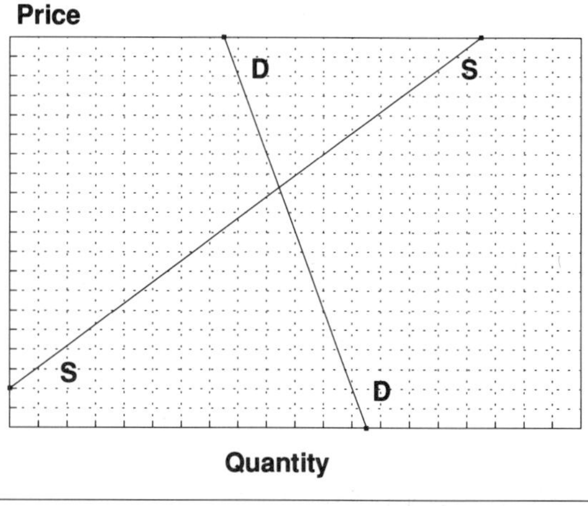

Demand for oil is relatively inelastic. On the simplest level a householder who has invested in oil-fired central heating is faced with capital expenditure if she/he converts to another fuel. The same is true of power stations. Figure 3.9 gives hypothetical demand and supply curves for oil in 1970. Notice that the supply of oil is elastic relative to the demand for it.

In the early 1970s political tensions in the Middle East (notice how many of the OPEC countries are in that geographical area) led to fears of oil shortages. Demand for oil rose as the oil companies and consumers

Figure 3.9 Hypothetical demand and supply curves for oil, 1970

increased their stocks of oil in anticipation of shortages. The world price of crude oil began to rise. Using the terminology we developed in Chapter 2 ('The business as a system') this can be seen as the interaction between political and economic systems – in other words, an example of the way in which the environment it operates in can affect the business community.

The member countries of OPEC took advantage of the movement of the market in their favour. In 1973 they agreed on production quotas which led to a sharp reduction in supply.

The supply of oil, in the short term, was no longer responsive to price changes. It became perfectly inelastic. This is illustrated in Figure 3.10.

By 1980 oil was $28 a barrel. The control of the market by OPEC was by no means perfect and the history of OPEC in the 1970s illustrates some of the problems associated with the management of cartels.

☐ There was a constant tempta-tion for poorer members to break ranks and overpro-duce. In this way they could benefit from the cartel in-duced higher prices and in-crease their own revenue.

☐ Although the demand for oil is relatively inelastic in the short term, the effect of high oil prices was to reduce the level of economic activity throughout the world, and this, in turn, resulted in a fall in the demand for oil. The demand curve shifted to the left, as shown in Figure 3.11.

Internal pressures in the cartel resulted in a split in policy in 1976. A dual pricing system was introduced. Saudi Arabia and the United Arab Emirates decided to keep price rises to the minimum in response to changes in the market demand for oil. In 1980 oil prices rose sharply again as the Iran/Iraq conflict led to a reduction in supplies.

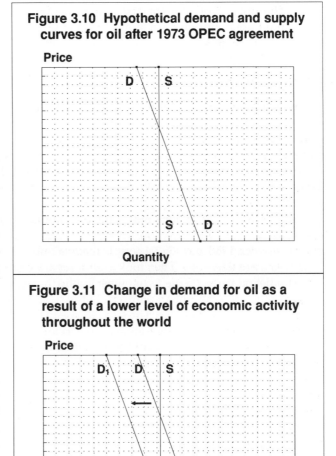

Figure 3.10 Hypothetical demand and supply curves for oil after 1973 OPEC agreement

Figure 3.11 Change in demand for oil as a result of a lower level of economic activity throughout the world

Oil and the world economy

Crude oil is a raw material for a wide variety of products that underpin the economies of the developed countries.

☐ As a fuel it was used to generate electricity, fire boilers, smelt metals and supply commercial transport services.

☐ As a raw material it was used in the manufacture of plastics and synthetic fibres.

☐ It was used by households for heating and domestic transport.

The developed economies had become accustomed to cheap and plentiful supplies of oil. The sudden rise in price had an immediate and telling impact. The explanation given in this chapter is deliberately oversimplified. We will return to this problem at the end of Chapter 17 ('Business and the economy') when you will have a clearer understanding of the working of the economic system. You should remember that the consequences given below were spread over a number of years.

The oil importing countries were immediately faced with an increase in the cost of oil. As a result the total value of the goods they imported exceeded the total value of the goods they exported. The classic response to this situation is to reduce the ability of people to spend money, which would then reduce the demand for imported raw materials (derived demand) and so reduce the overall bill for imported goods. Unfortunately the relative price inelasticity of oil meant that it was other oil importing countries which suffered as a result. Movements in the economy generally are the result of millions of decisions made by individuals and organisations independently. Look at the following example.

> Between 1968 and 1972 a couple made a number of employment and investment decisions. They took jobs in separate towns and bought a house equidistant between the two towns. Public transport was infrequent so they ran two cars. They bought an oil-fired central heating system because it was the cheapest option available. The sudden rise in oil prices in 1973 reduced the income they had to spend on other goods and services. To some extent this was offset by a sharp rise in their salaries (1974 saw settlements which gave wage and salary increases of 25 per cent and 30 per cent) but this was soon eroded by government policies. Wages did not keep pace with the increase in the price of goods.

This pattern, repeated on a less dramatic scale throughout the country, meant that people cut back on their spending. Demand for domestically produced goods and services fell. Employers began to reduce their workforce and the rising level of unemployment contributed to the decrease in demand. Demand for imported goods and services fell and, as the same policies were being followed throughout the developed world, demand for exports fell too.

To some extent these policies have worked for the industrial countries, but this has been at the expense of high levels of unemployment. Unemployment has also been exported to non-industrial oil importing countries. The fall in the demand for industrial goods caused a fall in demand for raw materials other than oil – some of which are imported from developing and relatively poor countries.

By 1985 the changes in the world economy as a result of the initial rise in the price of oil had begun to affect the demand for and the price of oil. Energy conservation had only a marginal effect in industrial countries but in oil importing developing countries rationing was introduced. Households and businesses began to use alternative fuels where this was possible. Oil fields (for example the North Sea) which would have been uneconomic when oil prices were low began to be developed. Not all the new oil producing countries joined OPEC, and this weakened its cartel. In 1986, partly as a consequence of market movements and partly as a result of deliberate decisions on the part of OPEC, oil prices fell to $6 a barrel.

The future development of this case study is now the responsibility of you, the student. You may find it difficult to follow all the arguments used at this stage in your course. A collection of newspaper cuttings will provide you with valuable and up-to-date material for analysis when you are studying Part 3 ('Business in society'). You should not limit your collection to the workings of OPEC and the problems of governments. Remember that changes in the price of oil will have its effects on individuals and businesses.

REVIEW

1 You are the economist of Landun Cars, a medium-sized company producing luxury cars in the £45 000 to £70 000 price range. Your department has isolated the following trends:
- ☐ a sharp fall in the price of petrol;
- ☐ an aggressive marketing campaign by a rival manufacturer;
- ☐ a change in the structure of income tax which favours the higher income groups;
- ☐ sustained growth in the economy generally;
- ☐ a rapid increase in house prices;
- ☐ the stockpiling of raw materials by governments;
- ☐ increased emphasis by businesses on the reduction of costs.

   a Prepare a report explaining how these trends may, or may not, affect the demand for your company's products.

   b Would a manufacturer of a small family car selling at £7500 experience the same impact on its market?

   c To what extent do the manufacturers of luxury cars operate in the same market as the manufacturer of the small family car?

2 Fine Fastenings Ltd produces packaged nails and screws for the do-it-yourself market. The prices of its five most popular lines are given below:
- ☐ Product A £0.25
- ☐ Product B £0.40
- ☐ Product C £1.00
- ☐ Product D £1.50
- ☐ Product E £2.00

The quantities sold are respectively 100 000, 70 000, 20 000, 150 000 and 50 000. The price elasticities of demand are estimated at 0.1, 0.5, 0.4, 1.2 and 0.3 respectively.

   a Calculate the total sales revenue of Fine Fastenings Ltd.

   b What effect would a 10 per cent increase on the price of all the products listed above have on the sales revenue of the company?

   c Fine Fastenings Ltd wishes to increase its sales revenue by £100 000 in order to cover an increase in costs and maintain its existing profit margins. Which products should bear the brunt of the price increases? Explain your answer.

3 Read the case study on oil given at the end of the chapter before attempting to answer the following questions. You should illustrate your arguments with clear sketches of demand and supply curves where these are appropriate.

   a In 1986 OPEC limited production of oil in order to stimulate an increase in the price. Explain the reasoning behind this strategy and comment upon its possible effectiveness.

   b One reason given for the fall in the price of oil has been the world recession. Explain how lower oil prices could lead to a future demand for oil.

   c During the years of high oil prices there was considerable interest in energy efficient technology. Electronic control systems, for example, use less energy than electrical systems. What are the implications of this trend for the arguments you have outlined in answer to **b**?

   d In spite of the fall in the price of oil the search for new oil fields has continued. The table overleaf gives the number of years existing oil fields are expected to last, by geographical area.

Area	Years
Africa	30
Asia	16
Central/South America	19
Middle East	100+
Soviet Union	14
United States	10
Western Europe	18

Given the above information, together with the fact that Japan, the United States and Western Europe are among the world's heaviest users of energy, explain why, in spite of low oil prices, exploration for new fields is continuing.

4 The following article was published in *The Economist*, 22 August 1988.

Fax and fiction: Tokyo

If you thought having a car telephone was fashionable, forget it. In Japan, the latest fad among rising executives is a mobile fax machine (for transmitting documents electronically). Nippon Telegraph & Telephone says that although so far only 12 cars in Japan have fax machines in them, inquiries are running at a 'lively' rate. This is despite a hefty installation charge of ¥248 000 ($1700) plus transmission charges of ¥280 for each sheet of A4 paper. Those who balk at paying that much to equip their own vehicle might in future take a taxi. An Osaka taxi firm has already installed a fax in at least one of its cabs. How long before they make the railways copy them?

The marketing manager of a large manufacturing company reads the above article and decides he needs a fax machine installed in his company car.
  a What rational buying motives might he put forward for this purchase?
  b What emotional reasons might he have?

Activity
The investigation of a local market: the market for private housing.
1 Identify a range of houses prevalent in your area, for example two/three bedroomed terraced, three bedroomed semi-detached, etc.
2 Divide the area into neighbourhoods. If you live in a city this stage may be based on old villages that have been swallowed by the city. In London you may compare Camden Town with Hampstead; in Liverpool, Calderstones with Knotty Ash. In both examples the pairings are random.
3 You will need a sample of house prices covering the range of houses and the areas you have chosen over a period of three weeks. The property guide in the local newspaper will give you a starting point. When you have studied Chapter 5 ('Statistics: an aid to decision making and control') you will realise that this may not be a representative sample.
4 Interview several people who are considering buying a house on the qualities they look for when viewing a house.
5 What are the economic factors involved? Income, the policy of building societies and the role of insurance companies and banks are all important. Visit and invite speakers from these institutions. Your main purpose is to investigate their role in the housing market

but you should remember that they are also part of the capital and monetary systems of the economy.

6 Interview the owners of property. Do they think they have any control over the price they could ask if they wanted to sell? What reasons do they give to support their answers?

7 New houses in the lower and middle price ranges are usually built in anticipation of demand. You need to:

a Compare and contrast these products.

b Discover the percentage of the total market for new houses they command.

c Assemble examples of their advertising, noting any special offers or price reductions that might appear.

d Discover any special problems, for example the availability of sites, the cost of materials, the cost of labour, the attitudes of local government, etc., that may influence their decisions.

8 Investigate the economy of the area, in particular the level of unemployment.

9 Investigate the availability of alternative forms of housing including local authority housing and co-operatives. What is the policy/attitude of the local authority to private housing? What effect does this have on the market for private housing?

You can explore this market for a long time and still make discoveries. The approach is that of the economist – an overall view. However, this investigation will provide you with valuable data that will give an insight into the behaviour of markets and the impact of market structure on the pricing and promotion of products.

Suggested projects

1 A critical appreciation of a local market.

2 The importance of company X's market position on its pricing policy.

3 The impact of demographic changes on the recruitment policy of a business.

Essay questions

1 The market in which it operates determines the strategies of a business. Discuss this statement with reference to the policies of a business concerning:

a pricing.

b production.

c recruitment.

d investment.

2 Outline and discuss the effects of a minimum wage policy on the part of a government on:

a a labour intensive business.

b a capital intensive business.

3 Comment on the factors which might affect the demand for continental holidays:

a in the short term.

b in the long term.

4 A business has a market share of 23 per cent. Its three largest competitors have a combined market share of 40 per cent. Assess the implications of this situation for the first business.

4 Starting and running your own business

The first three chapters of this book have taken a very general look at the world in which a business must operate. After studying these chapters you should realise:

- [ ] that business activity exists to satisfy the needs and wants of people.
- [ ] that although each business is unique, by classifying businesses we can study the characteristics they have in common.
- [ ] that businesses operate in markets.
- [ ] that all businesses carry out the functions of production, marketing, finance, control and personnel.

When you have studied this chapter you should be able to:

- [ ] Identify the reasons for starting a business.
- [ ] Identify the major decisions to be made when starting a business.
- [ ] Define planning.
- [ ] Outline the major stages in the planning process.
- [ ] Appreciate the importance of planning to the business enterprise.
- [ ] Identify external sources of help for a business.
- [ ] Describe the main ways in which a business can be acquired.
- [ ] Outline the main sources of business finance.
- [ ] Describe the internal sources of information available to a business.
- [ ] Appreciate the need for such information.

Why start a business?

There are probably as many reasons and combinations of reasons for starting a business as there are people who make the attempt.

- [ ] An inventor or a person with an original idea for a service might decide to go into business to exploit the idea, rather than try to find somebody else prepared to adopt it.

- [ ] Some people go into business because they hope for a higher standard of living as an owner of a business rather than as an employee.

☐ The desire for independence can also inspire people who are already employed.

☐ Redundancy and the fear of never finding another job may persuade someone to take on the risks of a business. The experience of redundancy can also bring on a feeling of revulsion against being dependent on the decisions of other people and a determination to have more control over life.

Whatever the reason for starting a business there are feelings of conviction, determination and optimism on the part of the *entrepreneur* (that is a person who accepts the risks of business and organises resources to produce a good or a service). The entrepreneur must be careful to find the answers to the following questions if the business is to survive:

1 *Have I the skills, experience and determination to run a business?* The owner of a business is a resource of that business, and will be offering production and management skills to the small business. We can say that the answer to this question lies within the function of *personnel*. The success or failure of all the other functions will depend on the skills of the people engaged in them. Yet even the most skilful workforce cannot succeed if it lacks the support of finance, materials, market and organisation.

2 *What product will I make or what service will I provide?* The answer to this question must go further than a statement of the good or service. Amongst other things it must concern itself with design and quality . The decision will depend upon who will be likely to buy and the ability of the business to produce the good or service. This lies within both the *marketing* and *production* functions.

3 *Will people buy my product?* Who will buy it? Where will it be bought and at what price? Before an answer can be found to these questions the entrepreneur will have to research the market. This activity is part of the *marketing* function.

4 *Can I supply the product at the right time, in the required quantities, at the desired quality and at the right price?* These questions relate to the *production* activities of the firm.

5 *Can I get the product to my customers at the right time, in the right quantities and at the right price?* *Marketing* has the responsibility for answering this question too, together with the problem of informing and persuading people to buy.

6 *Have I the money to buy the necessary premises, materials and machinery? Can I afford to employ labour? Which machines will give me the greatest profit? Which product will give me the greatest profit?* The answers to these questions lie in the function of *finance*.

7 *How am I to combine the different functions listed above so that they will work together and give the maximum reward for the minimum input?* The term used to describe this concept is *efficiency*. The answers lie in the area of *organisation* and *control*.

The first step

Mrs Jones decides to take her three children for a day at the seaside during their summer holidays. She chooses the resort, finds out about train and bus times, discovers the cheapest way of travelling there and books the tickets. The night before she packs a complete change of clothes for the youngest child because experience has told her it is likely to be needed. She makes sandwiches because she cannot afford to buy all the food that will be necessary. In short, Mrs Jones plans her day out carefully.

If you think about your life you will realise that you are planning all the time. A decision to go to a disco will involve other decisions such as who to go with, where the money is coming from, whether your parents will allow you to go, what transport to use and so on. Starting or buying also needs planning. In this section we will look at:

☐   a definition of planning;

☐   the need for business planning;

☐   the contents of a business plan.

What is planning?

A plan is a detailed statement of the way a person or a group of people intend to reach long-term objectives or short-term targets. The difference between the planning of individuals and planning in business lies in the objectives and targets set and in the activities needed to achieve them. The planning process is shown in Figure 4.1.

The principles of planning

1   *Information*   Plans should be based on accurate and factual information. When detailed information is not available the planner will have to rely on experience and judgment. This should not be dismissed as mere guesswork.

2   *Time*   The environment in which a business operates is constantly changing. The plan drawn up for a business will therefore vary according to the period of time for which it is intended. A short time scale demands a detailed business plan. For a longer period the plan will be less detailed.

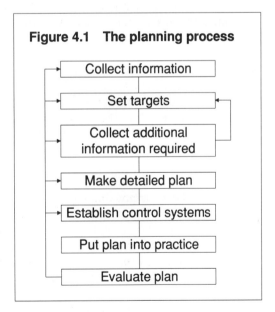

Figure 4.1   The planning process

Collect information → Set targets → Collect additional information required → Make detailed plan → Establish control systems → Put plan into practice → Evaluate plan

3   *Flexibility*   A plan should be constantly changed as circumstances change and more information becomes available.

4   *Control*   The existence of a plan does not ensure success. The progress must be constantly checked if it is to be implemented properly. Control relies on accurate information.

The business plan

It may be months or even years between the birth of an idea and the starting of a business. During this time the would-be entrepreneur should be developing and refining the business plan. There are three reasons for this:

1   A thorough investigation into the costs, markets and available finance, clearly presented will identify the areas of weakness in the original idea and allow them to be eradicated before they cost money or lead to failure.

2   A good business plan will impress people like bank managers, both in its information and the business-like qualities of the person who has drawn it up.

3   The discipline of drawing up a business plan can draw attention to the areas in which the business lacks experience.

Contents of a business plan

1   A brief description of the business will include the goods it intends to offer to its customers, an indication of its market and its sources of supply. How brief this introduction is will depend upon the business. For a small, one person start-up business a hundred words might suffice. A more complex organisation will need a more detailed, and therefore a longer description. This part of the business plan is important if it is to be used to support a request for external investment. Many organisations offering capital to new businesses specialise in certain types of business activity. If they are going to reject a plan it is in the interests of the entrepreneur that they do so quickly. Then she/he can seek more sympathetic organisations without too great a loss of time.

2   Information relating to the personal experience of the entrepreneur will indicate the chances of success to the bank manager or anyone being approached for capital. It can also draw the entrepreneur's attention to her/his own lack of specialised knowledge and suggest the need for a course in, for example, business management before starting to trade.

3   A detailed description of the product would include production costs and the proposed selling price. It should also try to isolate what sets this product apart from all similar products on the market. Is the technology more advanced? The idea innovative? The closer a product is in type to an existing product the harder it will be to attract customers, and the more difficult it will be to persuade people to lend money to the business.

4   The business plan should also include a description of the market at which the product is directed. This will include the geographical area over which it is to be sold, the number of competitors and the special points which will set this business apart from its competitors. It should also indicate the potential for growth in the area.

5   The location chosen for the business should be stated and explained. The explanation might include details of premises and the site chosen in terms of costs and in relation to the market.

6   The methods of production and marketing selected should also be explained and justified. This justification should be related clearly to costs, including labour costs.

7　The business plan should also include the amount of funding that will be required. If the plan is intended to persuade people to invest in the business it should also state the return the investors can expect. For an existing business this statement should be accompanied by the financial statements of the business over several years. A new business might include *projected* financial statements of what is expected to happen.

SELF ASSESSMENT

1　Give three reasons why a business plan is important to the success of an enterprise.
2　List the major headings that should be included in a business plan.

Getting help

The business plan is likely to highlight problem areas in a proposed business. Where can the business get help in solving these problems? If the business is small it will not be able to employ specialists on a full-time basis. It may not be able to afford the services of specialist agencies, for example in areas such as advertising. Where can it get help?

1　*Business courses*　Polytechnics, colleges of further education and other educational institutions offer courses designed to help people judge whether their ideas for a new business have the qualities needed for success, and to help them through the difficulties of establishing a business. Other courses attempt to improve specific skills, e.g. accounting for the small business, computers in business, etc.

2　*The Small Firms Service*　This is provided by the Department of Trade and Industry (DTI) and operates small firm centres in London and other major towns and cities. The centres offer advice on marketing, finance, training, exporting and new technology.

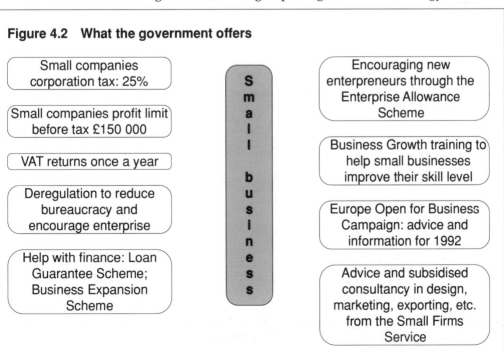

Figure 4.2　What the government offers

Small companies corporation tax: 25%

Small companies profit limit before tax £150 000

VAT returns once a year

Deregulation to reduce bureaucracy and encourage enterprise

Help with finance: Loan Guarantee Scheme; Business Expansion Scheme

Small business

Encouraging new enterpreneurs through the Enterprise Allowance Scheme

Business Growth training to help small businesses improve their skill level

Europe Open for Business Campaign: advice and information for 1992

Advice and subsidised consultancy in design, marketing, exporting, etc. from the Small Firms Service

3   *The Council for Small Industries in Rural Areas (CoSIRA)*   Help from CoSIRA is limited to businesses in rural areas with central populations of less than ten thousand people. CoSIRA offers training courses and a range of consultancy services which give advice on accounting, marketing and finance.

4   *Other organisations*   These can range from government departments to the British Institute of Management, whose Small Firms Information Service provides pamphlets and leaflets of help to the small business.

5   *Solicitors, accountants and bank managers*   These can also provide expert help.

We can summarise what we have learnt so far as follows:

☐   A business must perform a number of functions in order to survive.

☐   Although the individual functions of a business can be studied separately, the profitability and ultimate survival of a business depend upon the way in which they interact. It is useless for a production department to make 5000 items if it is only possible to sell 2000, for example.

☐   Planning is vital if problems are to be foreseen and overcome.

☐   Planning must be based on accurate information if it is to be successful.

☐   It is important for the managers of a business or part of a business to know the extent to which the business plan is 'on course'. In other words they need to be able to *control* the business.

Acquiring a business

A person who wishes to go into business can buy an existing business, invest in a franchise or start a new business.

1   *Buy a business that already exists*   An existing business will have records of sales and profits which will remove some of the uncertainty from the enterprise. A buyer should, of course, insist on seeing these records before she/he buys and have them examined by an accountant. This does not mean that the buyer should not do further research. Accounts are the records of the past performance of the business. They do not say anything about future developments that might affect the success or failure of the business. What effect could the construction of a new retailing development have on other businesses in the town? What are the future plans of the owners of the business? If they decide to set up a similar business in the area will their customers follow them?

The amount of capital needed to buy an existing business can vary enormously. A small shop, bought as a going concern, might be bought for £5000. At the other end of the scale a *management buy-out* can require capital in excess of £10m. Management buy-outs are not new but they received much publicity in the 1980s. They occur, for example, when a large company decides to stop making a particular product and closes a factory. If the management of that factory have faith in the future profitability of the product they may decide to buy the right to make it and the plant and machinery needed to make it.

2   *Invest in a franchise*   Under this system a successful business idea is shared by the person who developed it (the *franchisor*), who sells or 'rents' the use of the idea to other people (the *franchisees*). Under a franchise agreement the franchisees will be required to pay royalties to the franchisor for the use of the idea. They may have to agree to decorate the premises in a particular way or conduct the business according to a certain code of behaviour. These regulations are usually linked to the reasons why the original business was a success. In return the franchisor might provide:

- loans to help in the start-up of the business;
- training in the conduct of the business;
- any special products that are needed;
- the finance for a national advertising campaign;
- a guarantee of a geographical area as the sole market for each franchisee.

Franchising offers the advantages of belonging to a large business organisation combined with the satisfaction and greater control that can be found in a small business. The capital required for buying a franchise can vary from £3000 to £200 000.

There are some disadvantages of franchising, for example:

- *lack of control* The franchise agreement gives the franchisor control over a number of aspects of the business, for example the products that can be sold, the appearance of the business and the source of supply.

- *lack of flexibility* The terms of the franchise agreement may not change fast enough to cope with the changing business environment. This may be particularly true of changes in local circumstances.

- *levy on profits* Most franchise agreements include provision for continuing payments to the franchisor.

Figure 4.3 shows some of the questions a prospective franchisee should check before signing an agreement.

3 *Start a new business* This option carries with it the greatest degree of risk. The business has no history to help you and you will lack the support offered by franchising. On the other hand, it may be possible to begin on a very small scale without risking too much capital. You will also have greater freedom of action. You will not be limited by decisions other people have taken in the past (buying a business) or the limitations placed on you by a franchise.

Figure 4.3 What you need to know about a franchise

?	How long has it been in operation?
?	What is the initial purchase price and fee?
?	Is there a location policy?
?	What services are offered?
?	Do you have access to the records of the franchisor?
?	Is it a member of the trade association?
?	What do existing franchisees think of the service?

SELF ASSESSMENT

1 State two advantages of buying a franchise compared with buying an independent business.

2 Explain one reason why an entrepreneur might prefer to start a new enterprise rather than buy an existing one.

Finding the money

The new business owner has, by now, investigated the idea and decided whether or not it is viable. In this the business plan has helped point out the weaknesses, and professional help has been sought in eliminating them. The decision as to whether or not to purchase an existing business has been taken, and the question now remains as to where to get the money to start this business. There are just three ways in which a business acquires money:

☐ from the money invested in the business by the owner or owners, including any profit which they decide to reinvest.

☐ by borrowing money from private individuals or from another organisation.

☐ by buying goods and services on credit, i.e. having the use of the goods and services before they are paid for.

The basic principles of acquiring capital may be simple but the reality is far more complex. Each business will have its own particular requirements based upon such factors as:

☐ the size of the business.

☐ the stage of development it has reached. Two businesses, for example, with a similar number of employees and making a similar profit, may have totally different capital requirements. One business might be able to fund future investment from profits already made, but its future investment potential might be limited. The other business may need a large injection of capital if it is to take advantage of the market.

☐ the owner of the business, who may wish to retain control; that will mean loans to expand the capital rather than sharing the ownership with other people.

☐ the organisations that make money available to businesses, and which have their own preferences. Some opt for lending to a business with growth potential where there is a large element of risk. Financial organisations such as these will be looking for a business that can give them a return on their capital as high as 45 per cent and will be looking closely at the record of the business in the past, together with the skills of the management team. Another organisation might be prepared to accept lower returns but demand a stake in the business as a condition of making money available.

Basically this is a matter of products and markets. The organisations lending are offering the product 'capital' in the way in which it will give them the profits they want with an acceptable level of risk. The businesses taking the money are buying 'capital'. They will want to buy a product that suits their needs and circumstances.

The end result is a number of markets with what appears to be the same service, namely capital, but with a variety of additional services that make separate products. You should refer back to Chapter 3 ('Markets') if you do not understand this argument.

In this chapter we are not going to concern ourselves with the complications of the markets for money and capital, nor with the factors a business will take into account when deciding on how to finance its particular requirements. This will be dealt with in Chapter 7 ('Finance'). Instead we will look at some basic definitions and the ways in which a very small business just starting up might find its capital in the first years of its life.

1   The owner of the business *invests* money in it. This can come from savings or the sale of possessions. It may be a redundancy payment, a legacy or a win on the football pools. The important thing to remember is that it is the owner's money, to be spent as she/he wishes. If the money is lost, it is the owner's loss.

2   Money can be *borrowed* using possessions as a security. This statement means simply that if someone cannot repay the money then the person or organisation who lent that money can claim or sell that possession in order to recover the money they have lent. An insurance policy which guarantees a payment of £5000 in three years' time may be used as a security for a loan of £2000. The lender of the money will hold all the documents and claim the money due to the borrower if the loan is not repaid. Mortgages are a specialised form of a loan on security. The security in this case is always property. All loans are usually made for a fixed period of time, for a fixed amount and at a fixed rate of interest.

3   *Hire purchase* and *credit sales* for equipment have a great deal in common. The difference lies in the ownership of the item. If a business buys a display refrigeration unit on hire purchase it does not own it until the last payment has been made, although the law does give it some protection against arbitrary repossession by the owner. On the other hand, if it is a credit sale, it will own the refrigeration unit as soon as the initial payment has been made.

4   *Trade credit* is a system whereby a business receives the ownership of goods or services and does not have to pay for them immediately. The time involved can vary. It may be as little as a few days or a week or as long as three months. In some businesses the goods or services bought in can be used and have brought in income before they have to be paid for. This is a death trap for the business which is too optimistic.

5   Businesses can also *lease* equipment. If the equipment is needed for only a relatively short period of time then this can be paralleled to hiring in a domestic situation. A householder wishes to dig over a garden. If the mechanical cultivator is used only once in the year, it is sensible to hire it for two days at a cost of £30, rather than pay £400 to buy it. If the equipment is going to be used continuously then it is better to compare leasing equipment with renting a house. There may be an initial down payment followed by regular payments. This does not increase the capital of a business but by leasing rather than buying equipment it can mean there is more capital for other use.

SELF ASSESSMENT

1   Classify the sources of capital according to the three major ways in which a business acquires finance.
2   List three factors that will affect the capital requirements of a business.

Running a business

A business, like the people who run it and the society in which it exists, is constantly changing. The way in which it develops and its ultimate success or failure depend upon:

1 *People* The person who starts a business might be prepared to work long hours to make it a success. As it becomes more secure she/he might prefer more leisure time to increased profits. The way in which the business develops can be helped or hindered by the available skills in the labour force.

2 *Technology* Changes in technology can make a product or a production method obsolete, that is old-fashioned or out of date. New products will have to be found, new machinery bought and the labour force retrained.

3 *The economy* A high level of unemployment in an economy can mean a reduction in labour costs. It can also mean less demand for the product and a more competitive market. This will have implications for the costing, pricing and marketing of a product. It can also lead to changes in production methods and will certainly affect profitability.

4 *The government* Governments make laws. A change in the laws governing health and safety in the workplace can lead to increased production costs. Other laws might increase the clerical work required of a business. The Data Protection Act of 1984, for example, requires businesses to register if they hold information about an identifiable, living person on a computer. It is the responsibility of the business to make sure the registration is accurate and up to date.

  The government can also affect the general level of demand in an economy by the way in which it raises money and the way in which it spends it. If the government decides to increase the tax on a particular type of good then it is likely that the demand for that good will fall. As we saw in Chapter 3 ('Markets') the extent to which the demand falls will depend on its price elasticity.

5 *Other organisations* The attitudes and activities of trade unions, the activities of pressure groups can also affect the development of a business. A powerful and active trade union can influence working practices and raise the labour costs of a business. A political pressure group might mount a campaign to stop people buying certain types of goods.

6 *The market* The markets in which a business operates will also affect its development. This was dealt with in detail in Chapter 3 ('Markets').

The impact of these forces will vary from business to business and will depend, amongst other things, upon the size of the business, the quality of its management, the finance available to it and the way in which it has developed in the past. Whatever the effect on a business the business plan must be constantly reassessed and modified to take changing circumstances into account. The managers of even the smallest business need information from both internal and external sources.

Internal sources of information

Information from internal sources is found in the records a business keeps. It is tempting in a small business for the owners or managers to believe that they can keep all the necessary information in their head. That way lies disaster. It is easy to be convinced that a project is possible and will be profitable, when five minutes examining records will demonstrate that it is impracticable. Records may be a simple filing system of all documents or a more elaborate system involving a computer. Whichever is chosen the records must be kept.

Chapters 5 and 6 are sub-titled 'an aid to decision making and control'. Both chapters are concerned with the techniques that can be used to help the business pinpoint problem areas, and decide what steps can be taken to make them less of a problem. The techniques are useless unless they are used with accurate and detailed information. A very small business will find the discipline of keeping records sufficient to point up the problems. A larger business must use the techniques outlined in Chapters 5 ('Statistics') and 6 ('Accounting').

Some of these records are for the use of the business alone. Others are required by law.

Legal requirements

1   *Tax*   People employed by a business have their *income tax* deducted from their wages before they receive them. This system is known as Pay As You Earn (PAYE). Once the Inland Revenue has decided on the tax code of an individual the responsibility for ensuring that each person pays the correct amount of tax lies with the employer. Businesses with a large number of employees have found it profitable to computerise their payroll either by contracting out to an agency or by installing their own computer system. Tax on business profits is levied on an annual basis using the accounts of the business. It makes sense for a business to maintain accurate records of payments and receipts to avoid paying excess tax.

2   *Value added tax (VAT)*   VAT was introduced in the UK in 1973. At the moment (1990) it is charged at a rate of 15 per cent on the sale of virtually all goods and services. Necessities such as food for human consumption are zero rated, that is the tax is 0 per cent. A business charges VAT on all sales to customers and pays this money to the Customs and Excise at the end of each quarter. Any VAT the business has paid to its suppliers is deducted from this total. The business therefore pays VAT only on the value it has added to the goods and services it has bought. Hence the name of the tax. A business is liable to prosecution if it pays too little tax. Conversely, it makes no sense to pay too much tax. VAT records are therefore important.

3   *The Department of Social Security (DSS)*   All people in full-time employment have to pay *National Insurance* (NI) contributions towards the provision of the health service and social security payments, including unemployment benefit. Again it is the responsibility of the employer to collect these contributions and forward them to the DSS.

Other records

A business should also keep records of all the activities in which it is engaged. These include:

1   The quantity and money value of raw material, semi-finished and finished goods it is holding as part of its business activity. Collectively these items are referred to as *stock*. Too great a quantity of stock may mean that there is too much money tied up and not enough money to finance other parts of the business. The amount of stock held will depend upon:

□   the costs of holding stock. If the goods held in stock require constant attention to maintain their usefulness then this will add costs in terms of labour. A stock of coal will cost less to maintain than goods that need refrigeration and checking to make sure they are still saleable.

- ☐ the time between reordering and receiving the order is known as the *lead time*. If this is three months for a firm then that firm will obviously carry more stock than a firm which has a lead time of one week.

- ☐ a business that has a *seasonal demand*, that is a demand which is greater in some parts of the year, e.g. Christmas, than at others, will carry a greater stock of finished goods just before the Christmas season than it would at other times of the year. In other words a business must carry sufficient stock to allow it to meet the demands of its market.

- ☐ a business might find that if it orders in large quantities it can buy at a lower price. Of course this must be compared with the costs of storing the goods.

2   The amount of money owed to the business as a result of credit sales, i.e. payment to be made in the future rather than when the sale took place. Customers who receive credit sales are known as the *debtors* of the business. Customers who do not pay their bills are receiving an interest-free loan and the business is deprived of cash. Those two reasons alone should convince a business that careful scrutiny of debtors is sensible.

3   The amount of money the business owes to its suppliers. The businesses to which the money is owed are known as the *creditors* of the business. If a business does not pay its debts it gets a bad reputation. People do not lend money or give credit to businesses with bad reputations.

4   A record of sales according to the season of the year, the customer, geographical area, quantity and value can also provide useful information for future planning. This can mean a lower stock level, planned recruitment of staff and meeting customer demand with ease rather than panic measures that cost money in overtime payments to workers.

5   In a small business employing less than ten people the owner/manager is probably aware of the strengths and weaknesses of the workforce. In larger businesses and businesses with the potential to grow larger it is important that personnel records should be kept. A high absentee rate may alert the business to other problems.

6   Costs change and any business must be constantly aware of the changes. An increase in costs will affect profits. The problem is whether or not the increase in costs is temporary. If it is temporary the business may be able to ignore the increase and endure a lower profit. If it is permanent then production methods may have to change and prices rise. In turn this may mean redundancies and changes in the attitude of people buying the product. A business needs warning of these trends so that it can formulate a plan to deal with them.

7   A cash book should also be kept recording all payments and receipts. At the very least a cash book shows how much money is available.

The larger a business grows the more records it needs to keep to provide the managers with the information they need to control the business and make decisions. This increases the amount of form-filling that has to take place, and therefore increases the workload of the employees. More people may need to be employed and the costs of the business rise.

Computers are useful aids to storing, analysing and reproducing records. Where the burden of filling in forms and providing information becomes too great we describe the situation as a *bureaucracy*. It means, in simple terms, an organisation ruled by the needs of the office.

By now you should have realised that starting and running a business is both more difficult and more complex than simply making a product and trying to sell it.

SELF ASSESSMENT

1 Give three general reasons why it is important that a business keeps accurate records.
2 Select two types of record kept by a business and show the importance of each in the running of the business.

Conclusion

This chapter has given you some insight into the various activities a business must undertake if it is to function and be successful. In Part 2 ('The functions of business') you will study each function in greater depth, but if you are to understand the business world you must remember that a business is a living organism: it is born, and it will, eventually, die. The time of its death will depend on the health of the original idea, the care lavished upon it and the world into which it was born.

Case study A – The Baines nursery

Joseph Baines trained as an engineer. When he was in his late twenties his father, who ran a bookmaking business, wanted to retire, and Joseph took over the business. This was located in a suburb of a large city and close to a small group of shops, including a post office and a pub. There was a large general hospital within five minutes' walk. The betting shop was sited in a side road, twenty yards from a major trunk road. The whole cluster of buildings was the remnant of an eighteenth-century village that had been swallowed up by ribbon development from the town. When Joseph took the business over it consisted of one shop in a semi-detached cottage. The other cottage was his home.

Within five years Joseph was becoming bored. He was uninterested in racing and regarded the management of the shop as an exercise in decision making and administration. On two separate occasions Joseph acquired additional shops but for a variety of reasons did not regard the ventures as successful and sold both. Opening the second shop had involved him in considerable legal expense as his application for planning permission had been opposed by local residents. This experience had made him wary of legal complications.

In 1986 Joseph Baines was in his mid-forties. His children were independent and were living in other parts of the country. He was unwilling to continue in his present occupation for the rest of his working life. As he saw it there were two alternatives open to him. He could sell his existing business and use the capital to start another business, or he could close the business and look for employment. Both alternatives had problems associated with them.

☐ He could not think of another field of business enterprise to which his knowledge and experience suited him. His training as an engineer was out of date and his capital was too small to equip an engineering workshop.

- ☐ The interdependence of the house and betting shop proved a handicap in selling the property. Nobody wanted to buy a four bedroomed house next door to a betting shop and a separate purchaser for the betting shop would have had to invest money in providing staff facilities.

- ☐ The area was one of high unemployment and there were few opportunities for a man in his mid-forties.

It was Joseph's wife who suggested a partial solution to the problem. Mary Baines had been working as a voluntary helper in the nursery class of the local school for fifteen years. She had a wide range of friends and acquaintances based on family, work and social contacts. With her family grown up Mary was anxious to work and had already started to take temporary jobs in local shops. Her preference was to work with children and she suggested to her husband that they should close the shop and open a nursery for two- to five-year-olds.

At first Joseph did not take the idea seriously. It would not solve his employment problem. His involvement with the business would be on a management/administrative level and he knew that once the business was running satisfactorily he would be underemployed. He did, however, have a great deal of respect for his wife's abilities. He saw her as a shrewd judge of character, a firm but kind manager of children and a hard worker. The nursery had very clear advantages.

- ☐ In the short term it would provide him with employment while he looked for another job.

- ☐ It would provide his wife with long-term employment.

- ☐ It would contribute significantly to the family income, particularly when he was earning.

- ☐ It would use their existing resources productively.

Early in 1986 Mary and Joseph Baines decided to go ahead with their plans to open a nursery.

Market research

The Baines approached the social services department of their local authority. Officials confirmed that there was a shortage of nursery facilities in the area, the authority itself having only two nurseries some five miles from the proposed Baines nursery. Informal canvassing in the district produced an enthusiastic response from parents. Mr Baines also phoned a number of nurseries outside the area, posing as a prospective customer, to find out their charges. These ranged from £30 to £40 per week. The nurseries were open from 8 a.m. to 6 p.m. Further investigation into the legal requirements concerning staffing ratios revealed the fact that there was a high staffing ratio for the under two age range. On the basis of this research the Baines designed their product. They did not feel that the accommodation was suitable for this age group.

The product

Nursery services for two- to five-year-olds from 8 a.m. to 6 p.m. inclusive of meals and at a charge of £40 per week for a six day week. Parents booking their children into the nursery for a limited number of days would be charged a rate of £10 per day. This higher charge was to compensate for potential loss of custom.

The social services department

The social workers and officials of this department were both enthusiastic and helpful. They approved the accommodation for twenty-five children, subject to agreed alterations at an approximate cost of £10 000. The business would need to employ four full-time staff, at least one of whom would be a full-time nursery worker.

Financial projections

The Baines drew up the financial projection for their first year of trading, on the basis of twenty-five children at £40 per week for forty-nine weeks, giving a total annual income of £49 000. This is shown in Table 4.1.

Table 4.1

	£	£
Revenue from sales:		49000
Less: Materials	2000	
Wages	40000	
Ins., heating, etc.	1000	43000
Gross profit:		6000
Less: Interest on loan	600	
Tax	1500	2100
Net profit after tax		3900

Funding

The Baines estimated they would need £15 000 to complete alterations and equip the nursery. They intended to introduce £5000 from their own resources and borrow £10 000 from their bank. Their bank indicated its willingness to make the advance on their financial projections, taking into account their experience and reputation in business.

Marketing

At this stage the Baines were sufficiently confident of the success of their venture to invest in some publicity. They had three dozen black and white posters printed announcing a proposed nursery which they distributed to libraries and clinics in the area. The response from prospective customers was gratifying. There were sixty enquiries, approximately 75 per cent of which were prepared to book for the full week and commit themselves to paying for the forty-nine weeks in the year.

Planning permission

The Baines applied to the local authority for planning permission to change the use of their premises. An inspector from the highways department brought their only major setback in the enterprise. He informed them verbally that he would not support their application. He gave the following reasons:

☐ proximity to a major road;

☐ lack of car parking facilities for staff;

☐ lack of car parking facilities for parents which would mean them parking in a narrow road while delivering or collecting their children.

What the Baines did

1 They contacted the brewery which owned the public house. The entrance to the car park of the pub was directly opposite the proposed nursery and was largely unused during the day. The brewery gave verbal permission for parents and staff to use the car park but refused written permission citing possible legal complications. The tenant of the pub was prepared to give written permission to use the car park.

2   They contacted their local councillor and arranged for the hearing of their application before the planning sub-committee to be deferred on the grounds that they had been given insufficient time to prepare their case.

Some points to note

1   The mix of motives that went into the decision to start the nursery.

2   The level of the market research. The costs, in time and phone calls, were kept to a minimum until the Baines were reasonably sure of the viability of their project.

3   The importance of location. The suburban location provided a nucleus of business and professional families who were prepared and able to pay for the services of the nursery. The proximity of two large hospitals increased this catchment area. The siting of the buildings was a disadvantage when it came to obtaining planning permission.

4   The importance of experience and reputation when it came to floating a loan. In Chapter 6 ('Accounting') we will investigate the significance of their personal investment in the enterprise compared with the size of the loan.

5   The external constraints on the Baines' decisions. These included legal constraints on the number of children they could take, the number of staff to be employed and the minimum facilities which had to be provided. The interpretation the highways inspector placed on his instructions was also important. This might be classified as an external personnel constraint.

6   The interaction between the economic and political systems is also clearly illustrated. It is the political system which has the power to approve or disapprove the use of resources. It was through the political system (the councillor) that the Baines gained time to prepare their case.

7   The comparative flexibility in the use of capital as opposed to labour resources. An estimated £15 000 would convert the premises from a bookmaker's shop to a nursery. The time involved would be approximately one month. For Joseph Baines to retrain he would need a minimum of one year and his fees plus living expenses for his family would require an investment of £10 000.

It would be pleasant to report that the Baines Nursery is now in operation. Unfortunately this is a real situation and the decision of the planning sub-committee is as yet unknown. In Chapter 6 ('Accounting') we will assume that the Baines have been given planning permission and use their experiences in setting up the business as an ongoing case study.

Case study B – How not to start and run a business

I was a laboratory technician with a multinational pharmaceutical company. In 1978 they began a rationalisation programme in response to the world recession and the introduction of advanced technology. They needed to shed 500 of the 2500 employees at the plant where I was employed. The area was one of high unemployment and, mindful of their public image, they offered voluntary redundancy to their employees on very favourable terms. I took it.

It was a spur of the moment decision, not thought out at all. I was twenty nine, hated the discipline of arriving for work at a given time – flexi-time was still a thing of the future – hated taking orders and thought that running my own business would give me freedom to do just what I liked. I knew it was going to be hard work – how hard I did not appreciate.

My redundancy payment was £10 000. I bought a car for cash which left me with just over £5000. I decided I would buy a shop. This would provide me with living accommodation as well as a business. The classified advertisements in the local paper gave me several possibilities in what I thought was my price range. I decided on a very busy shop in a small, well frequented shopping precinct. The price of the business was £19 000. Stock was at valuation (s.a.v.). The business market was not booming at the time, the owners were anxious to sell (they wanted to retire) and I was anxious to buy. It seemed ideal.

I went to my own bank for a loan. The manager was unenthusiastic. He pointed out that the shop was on a comparatively short lease and the bank preferred freehold property as a security for loans. The stock was valued at £10 000, I would need a loan for £25 000 at least. I could not understand this. I had the audited accounts of the existing business. It would bring me enough money to live on. He asked me if existing suppliers were willing to continue to supply on credit. I was new to business, he said, they might be cautious. The interest on the loan would be a massive burden on the business.

Four banks later I found my funding. A friend helped me draw up an impressive business plan. £15 000 was the maximum the bank would offer. I took it and went back to the vendors with a proposition. Would they run down their stock until it was at a level I could afford? They agreed. This was my first big mistake. One of the major attractions of the shop was its wide range of stock and its accessibility. The takings plummeted but the vendors were glad to get rid of the place and I was brimming with confidence that I could build the business up again. I moved in.

I can catalogue my mistakes:

1 I thought being your own boss meant freedom. I was a slave to that business. I was there from six in the morning until ten at night. If I was not serving I was doing the books. My social life disappeared. I was sleeping and working.

2 I found I did not like people. Dealing with customers is a different matter to meeting people socially. Some dither, some complain and some are downright rude. The shopkeeper has to keep smiling. If you are rude to them they won't come back.

3 I did not keep my records. Customers bought on credit and did not pay promptly. I did not chase them up. That involved writing letters and at the end of the day I just could not be bothered. The wholesalers were more efficient. I began to find myself with no cash, a bill from a wholesaler for, say, £200, and outstanding customer debts of £300. People don't mind gentle reminders but a distraught shopkeeper knocking on their door demanding payment can be embarrassing. The customer did not come back.

4 I was not really aware of profit margins. I did not shop around for the cheapest supplier. There were four good cash and carry wholesalers in the neighbourhood but I took the easy way out. I dealt with wholesalers who would deliver. Their delivery margins eroded my profit.

5 It took longer to build up the stock the vendors had run down than I appreciated. For six months I had £10 a week to feed myself and buy other essentials. There were times when I had to choose between food and a visit to the local launderette. Even then I tried new

lines that I was sure would work rather than relying on the old tried and tested items. Some new lines sold, too many did not.

6   I had not had a structural survey done on the shop. The lease said I was responsible for repairs. The building was old, incorporated into a modern precinct to add character. It needed a great deal of money spent on it. In my naivety I employed a solicitor to argue the case. More money!

The problems built up. I tried to ignore them but my creditors were not so generous. They began bankruptcy proceedings. The court officials served the papers in March 1985. I was glad to be rid of the place.

> ## Case study C – How to start and run your own business

My family are farmers and small business owners. When I left school I went to agricultural college, then worked in Canada for a couple of years before settling in England. Marriage, two children and the low pay in agriculture set me looking for another job. I went into retail furnishing and, by the time I was thirty, was managing a large furnishing store for a national company. Then the recession hit. People started to find it difficult to make ends meet and the first luxury they cut back on was new furniture. I was made redundant three times in five years. The third time was the last straw. I was unemployed for six months and I made a conscious decision that I would never again be dependent on anybody. I began to think about my own business. I had very clear objectives:

☐   to be independent;

☐   to have the time and money to pursue my own interests;

☐   to work;

☐   to give my children a good start in life.

I also made a list of my advantages/disadvantages:

☐   no money;

☐   considerable experience and contacts in the furnishing business.

It took me another six months to come up with a viable business idea – carpets. I worked hard on my business plan. At the time I did not realise that that was what I was doing, I was just determined not to fail. I came up with the following:

1   *Product* Buying and fitting carpets to order. I rented a small shop on the high street of the local town. I created a display of carpets by using the central cardboard roll and covering them with the scraps of carpet I could buy cheaply from wholesalers as remnants. This gave the illusion of a well stocked shop. A chair, desk, printed stationery and a number of pattern books were the only additional equipment. I took orders from the pattern books, measured the rooms in the evening and, only then, ordered the carpet. I sold on service.

2 *Market potential* Small private houses and the occasional business contract. Potential for development into a large-scale business was limited. I did envisage opening several similar shops.

3 *Competitors* Competition was high. There were two branches of large furnishing businesses in the town. Their delivery times were longer than mine and their service less efficient. For example, if I found the carpet ordered was not in stock at the wholesalers I would call at the house with my samples, give a delivery time and ask if they wanted to re-order. Most customers chose another pattern and I would have it fitted within a week.

4 *Staff* I was the only employee. After six months I used a self-employed carpet fitter who was excellent at the job.

5 *Funding* It cost £500 to pay six months' lease on the shop and equip it. I had bought my house for £4000 and at that time its market value was £17 500. The bank advanced me £2000 on the security of the house. I was able to pay the loan off in twelve months and negotiate overdraft facilities of £3000 to finance the Christmas trade. My trade tended to be seasonal. Everybody wanted their new carpet for Christmas. After Christmas they were saving up for their holidays! The overdraft was cleared by the end of February.

6 *Future expansion* I tried expanding twice. The first time I opened a shop organised on the same lines in a very similar area about twelve miles away. It lost money. The second time I bought the paint and wallpaper shop next door. That, too, lost money. I decided to stay with the trade I knew.

REVIEW

1 Read the case studies at the end of the chapter before attempting the following questions.
   a Compare and contrast the stated motives of each of the entrepreneurs for starting their own business.
   b Using the information given in the chapter analyse the mistakes made by entrepreneur B.
   c Explain the reasons for the comparative success of entrepreneur C.
2 When the Albert Dock was built in the nineteenth century it was the world's largest enclosed dock basin and a symbol of Liverpool's dominance as a port. Changes in shipping technology and the decline of Liverpool as a port left it a derelict monument to past glories. In the early 1980s the Merseyside Development Corporation began an ambitious scheme which converted the existing buildings to provide private apartments, shops, offices and restaurants. The complex also houses television studios and the Tate Gallery. The area now attracts over 1.5 million people each year.

   In the summer of 1986 the visitors included a Chester businessman and his family. For some time he had been considering opening a specialist shop but without any clear idea of the type of goods he would sell. His experience lay in small scale manufacturing. Until his visit to the Albert Dock he had intended to open the shop in Chester when suitable premises became available. He made some preliminary enquiries and discovered the following information:

- ☐ the trading pattern was seasonal. Easter to October was the most profitable period with a further rise in sales just before Christmas. January to March was relatively quiet.
- ☐ takings varied in one shop from £50 per day in the off season to £1200 per day in the peak season.
- ☐ a twelve month lease for the size of retail unit in which he was interested was £10 000.
- ☐ there were a number of specialist shops already trading, apparently with success.

The businessman estimated that he had approximately £30 000 to invest in this enterprise and, with his successful record of trading, envisaged no difficulty in obtaining additional capital from his bank.

a What additional information would he need before deciding on the type of shop to open?

b From the information given in the passage outline the advantages of opening a shop in the development rather than in the nearby city centre.

c What risks are associated with this enterprise?

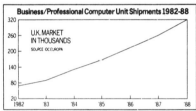
3 Study the extract from the advertisement by Computerland and answer the questions.

a Explain the term 'franchise' in this context. (2)

b Give three reasons for buying a franchise. (3)

c What reasons might there be for the company selling franchises instead of opening the shops themselves? (6)

d Examine the graph and identify three ways in which it may be misleading. (9) 1986 (AEB)

Activities

1 Draw up a plan for a small business. The type of business you choose will depend upon your local area. A small shop, a craft workshop or a mini-company based in your school/college are only examples of a wide range of possibilities. To make the exercise worthwhile you will need to discover the full range of costs you are likely to incur: the cost of premises, length of lease, heating, lighting and insurance, and of equipment and its fitting, material supplies and stocks. Research should be undertaken into the market and the suitability of the location together with possible sources of finance.
2 Invite a bank manager to examine your completed business plan and discuss it with you.

Suggested projects

1 A comparative study of the effect of location on the success of a business.
2 A critical evaluation of a mini-company over a period of twelve months.

Essays

1 The personality of the owner is the most important single factor contributing to the success of a new business. Discuss.
2 Outline the control systems required by a small business and comment on their importance.

Part 2 The functions of business

5 Statistics: an aid to decision making and control

When you have studied this chapter you should be able to:

- [ ] Define the meaning of the word 'distribution'.
- [ ] Define the terms 'variate' and 'frequency'.
- [ ] Apply techniques to a distribution to obtain concise statistics that describe a distribution.
- [ ] Define various measures of central tendency.
- [ ] Define various measures of dispersion.
- [ ] Define the terms 'cumulative frequency' and 'relative frequency'.
- [ ] Use bar charts, pie charts, ogives, histograms and frequency polygons to illustrate distributions.
- [ ] Distinguish between a bar chart and a histogram.
- [ ] Show that the histogram and frequency polygon of a distribution have equal areas.
- [ ] Standardise the variate so as to 'smooth' a frequency polygon.
- [ ] Use the normal distribution to obtain measures to help in decision making.
- [ ] Use the Poisson distribution to analyse a queuing problem.

The problem

Mr Kidani, a small manufacturer, felt the need to diversify. He identified a local market for a new product and confirmed the existence of the market by research. The new product was attractive to him because, except for one component, he already had the machinery and expertise available for its manufacture. This component was, however, something of a problem. No local firm manufactured it, and firms that did make it used most, if not all, of their production themselves. They seemed reluctant to increase their production for him.

This doubt about continuity of supply, together with transport costs should he find a willing producer, led Mr Kidani to consider manufacturing it himself. He calculated as best he could the additional costs involved – extra labour and/or overtime, training and retraining, energy, the price of the machine, depreciation on the machine, plus the opportunity cost of all the above, minus a possible resale value. He concluded that the project was viable.

The largest immediate outlay concerned the machine necessary to produce the component. There were two machines available, one made by Arundel & Co. (which we shall call Machine A) and the other by Butterworth & Sons (Machine B).

There was little difference in the price, Machine A being slightly more expensive. Mr Kidani considered leasing but dismissed the idea as being potentially less profitable than buying.

Raw data

Despite their reluctance to produce for him, Mr Kidani found that other manufacturers were willing to help him to the extent of providing production figures. He obtained figures for five machines of each type, all over a period of twelve working weeks, that is sixty weeks' production figures for each type of machine. These figures are shown in Tables 5.1A and 5.1B.

Table 5.1A				
49	50	51	53	54
56	58	63	40	45
47	48	49	50	52
53	55	56	59	64
41	45	47	49	49
51	52	53	55	57
59	67	42	46	47
50	50	51	52	54
55	57	60	42	44
46	48	33	50	51
52	54	56	58	61
38	45	46	48	43

Table 5.1B				
28	55	47	39	61
52	70	48	42	60
54	47	38	58	51
44	35	56	72	52
46	37	57	50	43
30	55	48	41	60
32	56	49	42	62
54	47	39	59	41
44	66	40	57	52
46	37	58	51	44
33	55	48	65	45
32	56	50	43	64

Mr Kidani estimated that he would need to produce at least 45 components per week. Do these figures help him to decide which machine to purchase?

At first sight the answer must be, 'Not much!' They ought to contain relevant information, but it is far from being immediately obvious. We are in the all too common position of not being able to see the wood for the trees!

The figures as presented are what is known as *raw data*. The objective is to compare the performances of two machines, A and B, but there is little hope of any direct help from the raw data.

Determining the range

A start can be made on establishing some discipline out of the chaos by rearranging both sets of figures in numerical order. This is done in Tables 5.2A and 5.2B. We can now see at a glance the highest and lowest production figures for each machine. The difference between these two extreme values is called the *range*.

Table 5.2A				
33	38	40	41	42
42	43	44	45	45
45	46	46	46	47
47	47	48	48	48
49	49	49	49	50
50	50	50	50	51
51	51	51	52	52
52	52	53	53	53
54	54	54	55	55
55	56	56	56	57
57	58	58	59	59
60	61	63	64	67

Table 5.2B				
28	30	32	32	33
35	37	37	38	39
39	40	41	41	42
42	43	43	44	44
44	45	46	46	47
47	47	48	48	48
49	50	50	51	51
52	52	52	54	54
55	55	55	56	56
56	57	57	58	58
59	60	60	61	62
64	65	66	70	72

Range for A = $\quad 67 - 33 = 34$
Range for B = $\quad 72 - 28 = 44$

This points up a difference between the recorded performances of the two machines.

A distribution

Each set of figures is called a *distribution*. What is wanted is a concise set of measures that will describe a distribution without discarding anything essential. We do not want to throw the baby away with the bath water!

Statistic(s)

Before we go any further we will take a closer look at the differing ways in which we use the word *statistic(s)*. Each item of raw data is referred to as a statistic (singular). Each measure we develop to describe a distribution is also referred to as a *statistic*. This use conforms with the original use of the word which was information collected on behalf of, and for the use of, the state (mainly for tax purposes!).

The mathematical processes that are employed to develop the 'measures' from the raw data are known, collectively, as *statistics* (plural and often written with a capital initial). We shall be using statistics to determine two types of 'measure' (each a statistic). The first type, a measure of the middle, or *measure of central tendency*, will be dealt with immediately. The second type, a measure of how the raw data are scattered, or *measure of dispersion*, will be dealt with later in the chapter.

Measures of central tendency

The mid-range
The *mid-range* of a distribution is, as the name implies, a value that lies mid-way between the extreme values of the distribution.

The constituent of a distribution, in our case a weekly production figure, is called the *variate*, and the figures themselves are called *values* of the variate. Hence the mid-range is the number that lies mid-way between the greatest and least values of the variate. It is the *arithmetic mean* of the extreme values of the variate. From Table 5.2 we can see that:

the mid-range for A = $\quad (67 + 33)/2 = 50$
the mid-range for B = $\quad (72 + 28)/2 = 50$

The mode

The individual items of data are the values of the variate, usually designated x. The number of times each value occurs is called the *frequency* of that value, usually designated f. For example, from Table 5.2A, for Machine A, when $x = 50, f = 5$ (count them!). The sum of all the frequencies is called the *total frequency*, and is, of course, the total number of individual items, in our case(s) 60.

The value of variate that has the highest frequency is called the *modal value*, or just simply the *mode*. It is quite possible for more than one value of variate to have the same frequency, and for this frequency to be more than all the others. Such a distribution is said to be *multi-modal*.

In order to determine the mode or modes of a distribution, it is necessary to count the number of times each individual value of variate occurs. This is easily done from Table 5.2. The results are shown in Tables 5.3A and 5.3B.

We can now see immediately that the modal value for Machine A's distribution is 50. The distribution for Machine B is multi-modal. What are the modal values for Machine B's distribution?

The median

The *cumulative frequency*, designated *c.f.*, of the value of a variate is the frequency of that value plus the frequencies of all values less than it. For example, for Machine A, the *c.f.* for $x = 42$ is 6 and when $x = 46, c.f. = 14$. It is convenient to express the *c.f.* as a percentage of the total frequency, i.e.:

$$\frac{c.f.}{\text{total frequency}} \times 100\%$$

Table 5.3A	
x	f
33	1
38	1
40	1
41	1
42	2
43	1
44	1
45	3
46	3
47	3
48	3
49	4
50	5
51	4
52	4
53	3
54	3
55	3
56	3
57	2
58	2
59	2
60	1
61	1
63	1
64	1
67	1

Table 5.3B	
x	f
28	1
30	1
32	2
33	1
35	1
37	2
38	1
39	2
40	1
41	2
42	2
43	2
44	3
45	1
46	2
47	3
48	3
49	1
50	2
51	2
52	3
54	2
55	3
56	3
57	2
58	2
59	1
60	2
61	1
62	1
64	1
65	1
66	1
70	1
72	1

Thus when $x = 46, c.f. = 14$ or $1400/60 = 23.33\%$.

A full table of cumulative frequencies for Machine A's distribution is given in Table 5.4.

The *median* of a distribution is that value which has as many values of variate less than it as it has greater than it. It is the value corresponding to a *c.f.* of 50 per cent. Looking down the column of percentages in Table 5.4 we can see that because 50 per cent lies between 48.33 per cent and 55 per cent the median lies between 50 and 51.

A more precise value is obtained by straight (linear) proportion, or interpolation.

$$\frac{\text{median} - 50}{51 - 50} = \frac{50\% - 48.33\%}{55\% - 48.33\%}$$

$$= \frac{1.67}{6.67}$$

$$= 0.25$$

so median $- 50 = 0.25$

median $= 50.25$.

SELF ASSESSMENT

1 Determine the median of Machine B's distribution.

(Answers to the self assessment questions for this chapter are on page 115.)

The mean

We defined mid-range as the arithmetic mean of the extreme values of variate. The *mean* of a distribution is the arithmetic mean of the whole distribution. It is the *average* value of the variate.

The mean, usually m, is probably the most important of the measures of central tendency. It certainly crops up very frequently in statistics (plural!).

It can be calculated by adding up all the individual values of x and dividing the sum by the total frequency. However, suppose we had a distribution containing 1000 items and 73 of them were 22, it would surely be rather naive to add 22 to itself 73 times! Far better to multiply 22 by 73 and so obtain a part total with much less effort.

The mean is calculated by multiplying each value of the variate (x) by its corresponding frequency (f), adding up these part totals (fx), and dividing this sum by the total frequency. This is just an extension of Table 5.3, and is shown in full for Machine A in Table 5.5.

Table 5.4

x	f	c.f.	%
33	1	1	1.67
38	1	2	3.33
40	1	3	5.00
41	1	4	6.67
42	2	6	10.00
43	1	7	11.67
44	1	8	13.33
45	3	11	18.33
46	3	14	23.33
47	3	17	28.33
48	3	20	33.33
49	4	24	40.00
50	5	29	48.33
51	4	33	55.00
52	4	37	61.67
53	3	40	66.67
54	3	43	71.67
55	3	46	76.67
56	3	49	81.67
57	2	51	85.00
58	2	53	88.33
59	2	55	91.67
60	1	56	93.33
61	1	57	95.00
63	1	58	96.67
64	1	59	98.33
67	1	60	100.00

SELF ASSESSMENT

2 Construct a similar table for Machine B's distribution and determine its mean.

Grouped data

The mean can be calculated, more concisely, and ultimately more usefully, with a negligible loss of accuracy, by dealing with the values of variate in groups rather than as individuals.

The raw data is split into *classes* of a predetermined size. The chosen size dictates the upper and lower bounds of the classes, that is the *class limits*. All values of the variate that fall between the same class limits are grouped together in the same class.

Table 5.5

x	f	fx
33	1	33
38	1	38
40	1	40
41	1	41
42	2	84
43	1	43
44	1	44
45	3	135
46	3	138
47	3	141
48	3	144
49	4	196
50	5	250
51	4	204
52	4	208
53	3	159
54	3	162
55	3	165
56	3	168
57	2	114
58	2	116
59	2	118
60	1	60
61	1	61
63	1	63
64	1	64
67	1	67
Totals	60	3056

Mean = 50.93

In what follows a class width of 5 has been chosen. This means that, for Machine A, variate values 33, 34, 35, 36 and 37 are grouped in the same class, variate values 38, 39, 40, 41 and 42 in the next class and so on, until all the data is exhausted.

The class limits are 32.5, 37.5, 42.5, etc. These limits reflect the class width, as the difference between successive limits is 5. Note that no value of variate can fall into more than one class.

The grouping is achieved by means of a *tally sheet*. A tally sheet for Machine A's distribution is shown in Table 5.6. It is *a* tally sheet rather than *the* tally sheet because a different selection of class width would need a different tally sheet. Note the conventional way of ticking off the count in groups of five with every fifth tick used to cross out the previous four.

Table 5.6

Range	Tally	Total
33 to 37	|	1
38 to 42	ЦН	5
43 to 47	ЦН ЦН |	11
48 to 52	ЦН ЦН ЦН ЦН	20
53 to 57	ЦН ЦН ||||	14
58 to 62	ЦН |	6
63 to 67	|||	3

SELF ASSESSMENT

Table 5.7

x	f	fx
35	1	35
40	5	200
45	11	495
50	20	1000
55	14	770
60	6	360
65	3	195
Totals	60	3055

Mean = 50.92

Class width 5

3 Draw up a similar tally sheet, class width 5, for Machine B's distribution.

The mid-point of each class is taken to represent all the values in that class, and this is used as the value of x. The total number of individuals in each class is called the class frequency, and is again designated f. These values of x and f are now used to find the mean of the distribution. The method, which is shown in Table 5.7 for Machine A, is similar to our previous calculation (Table 5.5) but is much more concise.

Compare the value obtained in Table 5.7 with that of Table 5.5. Remembering that in this problem we are dealing with components, and therefore whole numbers, is the difference significant? A different choice of class width will produce a different value for the mean. The larger the class width the more values of variate the mid-point is being called upon to represent. The smaller the class width the nearer the calculated mean will come to the value found by Table 5.5. In fact Table 5.5 can be thought of as a calculation of grouped data, with a class width of one!

SELF ASSESSMENT

4 Use your tally sheet from self assessment question 3 to find the mean of Machine B's distribution using grouped data.

Illustrating the data

Consider two plane triangles.

Triangle 1 has sides 22cm by 34cm by 51cm.

Triangle 2 has sides 18cm by 40cm by 49cm.

Compare the two triangles. What can be said about them? They both have three sides! Their perimeters are identical. But they are not the same triangle, are they? In what way are they different?

A very simple way of showing up their differences, or at least some of them, is to *draw them to scale*. It has been said that one good political cartoon is worth a thousand words of polemic. The same is true about the presentation of statistics.

We have two distributions. They each contain 60 values of variate. Their means are quite close. But they are from different makes of machine, so in what way or ways are they different? We can adopt the same stratagem, and draw them to scale.

The bar chart

In the *bar chart* each class is represented by a thick horizontal line. (Some bar charts are shown by means of vertical lines, but this is to be avoided, at least at first, as it can lead to confusion. We will return to this point later.)

The *length* of the line for each class is proportional to the frequency of that class. It is conventional, though by no means universal, to leave a blank space between adjacent lines. A tally sheet is used as before to determine class frequencies. This has been done to help construct a bar chart for Machine A's distribution, shown in Figure 5.1.

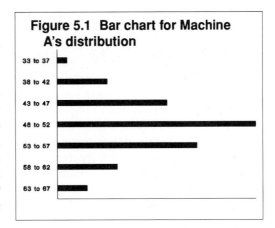

Figure 5.1 Bar chart for Machine A's distribution

33 to 37
38 to 42
43 to 47
48 to 52
53 to 57
58 to 62
63 to 67

5 Use your tally sheet to construct a bar chart for Machine B's distribution.

By looking at the two bar charts we can see that the two distributions are indeed different. A word of caution. It would be foolish at this stage to start thinking about which machine is the 'better'. It is very easy indeed to misinterpret a diagram, unless you keep firmly in mind what the various parts of the diagram represent.

The pie chart

In the bar chart the frequencies were represented by lengths of lines. In the *pie chart*, or *pie diagram*, the frequencies are represented by areas of slices of a circular pie, that is by sectors of a circle. The areas of different sectors of the same circle are proportional to the angles of the sectors, so the angles of the different slices are proportional to the class frequencies. The complete angle at the centre of a circle is 360° so a frequency of say 30 in a distribution of total frequency 200 would be represented by a sector of angle:

$$\frac{30 \times 360°}{200} = 54°$$

The pie chart for Machine A's distribution is shown in Figure 5.2.

The ogive

The *ogive* is the name given to the graph of cumulative frequency against value of the variate. The graph (shown in Figure 5.3 for Machine A's distribution) is a series of straight line segments. It is common practice to 'smooth' out the graph by drawing a continuous curve through the points.

The histogram

The distribution is illustrated in a *histogram* by a series of vertical rectangles. The widths of the rectangles are proportional to the class widths, and the *areas* of the rectangles are proportional to the class frequencies.

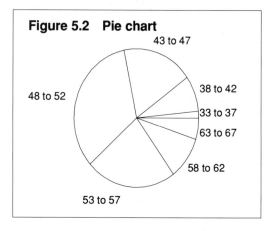

Figure 5.2   Pie chart

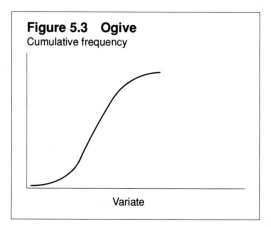

Figure 5.3   Ogive

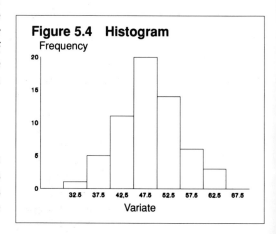

Figure 5.4   Histogram

If the class widths are all the same, the areas are proportional to the heights of the rectangles and hence the heights are proportional to the class frequencies.

It must be stressed that this only occurs if the class widths are all equal. If the class widths differ then the heights have to be adjusted so that the areas represent the class frequencies.

Figure 5.4 is the histogram for Machine A's distribution with equal class widths of 5. Since the left-hand rectangle represents a frequency of only 1, it would in some circumstances be reasonable to combine the first two rectangles. The frequency represented by the first rectangle would then be 6, and the class width 10 (twice the class width of all the others) and so the height of the rectangle would be 3.

A histogram is *not* a bar chart. If all the class widths are equal they look very similar. It is essential to remember that in the histogram it is the areas that represent the frequencies. To avoid possible confusion, it is advisable to construct horizontal bar charts, with a space between the bars.

The frequency polygon

The *frequency polygon* is formed by joining the mid-points of the tops of the rectangles by straight lines. It is conventional to imagine an extra class with frequency zero, at either end, thus completing the polygon. The frequency polygon for Machine A is shown in Figure 5.5.

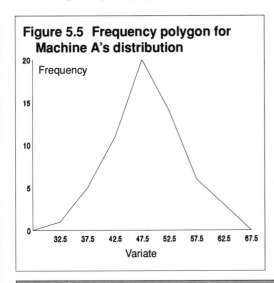

Figure 5.5 Frequency polygon for Machine A's distribution

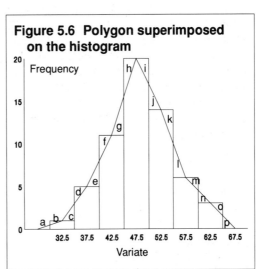

Figure 5.6 Polygon superimposed on the histogram

SELF ASSESSMENT

6 Construct a histogram and a polygon for Machine B.

Figure 5.6 shows the polygon superimposed on the histogram. Elementary geometry can be used to show that :

$$
\begin{array}{ll}
\text{area of triangle } a & = \text{area of triangle } b \\
\text{area of triangle } c & = \text{area of triangle } d \\
\text{area of triangle } e & = \text{area of triangle } f \\
\text{area of triangle } g & = \text{area of triangle } h \\
\text{area of triangle } i & = \text{area of triangle } j \\
\text{area of triangle } k & = \text{area of triangle } l \\
\text{area of triangle } m & = \text{area of triangle } n \\
\text{area of triangle } o & = \text{area of triangle } p
\end{array}
$$

Subtracting from the histogram triangles b, d, f, h, i, k, m and o and adding on triangles a, c, e, g, j, l, n and p turns the histogram into the polygon. It follows that the area of the polygon is equal to the area of the histogram and represents the total frequency of the distribution. This is an important point which we will return to later.

Measures of dispersion

We have dealt with finding the middle of the distribution, the measures of central tendency, but these do not tell us how the values are distributed about the middle. Look at the following two distributions of numbers:

   X   5, 5, 6, 6, 7, 8, 8, 9, 9
   Y   1, 1, 2, 3, 4, 4, 5, 6, 7, 8, 9, 10, 10, 11, 12, 13, 13

Both have a mean of 7 but the numbers in Y are much more scattered or dispersed than those in X. Such scattering is referred to as *variation* or *dispersion*. We have already met one measure of dispersion, the range, from which it is easy to determine the more usual statistic, the *half-range*. It is rather crude, and does not tell us very much.

Quartiles, deciles, percentiles

The median, you will recall, is that value that has as many values less than it as it has greater than it. More succinctly it is the 50 per cent value. The *quartiles* are the 25 per cent (*lower quartile*) and the 75 per cent (*upper quartile*) values. The median is the *middle quartile*. The upper quartile minus lower quartile is called the *inter-quartile range*. As their name implies, the deciles are the 10, 20, 30 per cent, etc., values, while the percentiles are the 1, 2, 3, 4 per cent, etc., values.

Deviation

The *deviation* of a variate is defined as the value of the variate minus the mean. It is, strictly, the *deviation from the mean*, but is rarely given the longer title. Each value of variate will have its associated deviation, so there are as many deviations as there are values of variate. Just as we wanted a single measure of central tendency, we would also like a single measure of dispersion.

The mean deviation

The average or arithmetical mean of the deviations seems the obvious measure to go for. However, a word of caution. If we simply multiply each deviation by its frequency, add up the products and divide by the total frequency, we must of necessity get an arithmetic mean of zero!

A little thought will reveal why this must be so. If we reduce every value of the variate by, say, 5, then the value of the mean must reduce by 5. If we increase every value by 10 we will increase the mean value by 10. It follows then that if we decrease every value of the variate (x) by the value of the mean (m), which is what is done to find the deviation, we reduce the mean value by m, and hence get zero as a result.

To avoid this, obviously useless, measure of dispersion, the *absolute* values of the deviations are taken. The absolute value of $x - m$ is $x - m$ if x is greater than m, and $m - x$ if x is less than m. Either can be taken when $x = m$. Another way of expressing this is to say we take the difference between x and m. The word 'difference' implies 'take the smaller from the larger'.

The standard deviation

It turns out that the mean deviation is not a very useful measure of dispersion. It does not lend itself very happily to manipulation. There is however another method of avoiding the negative values of deviation thrown up by $x - m$, that is to square them, since the square of any number cannot be negative.

The mean of these squares is called the *variance* and the positive square root of the variance is called the *standard deviation*.

We take each deviation, $x - m$, and square it. Then we multiply the result by its frequency, and total up these products. Dividing the sum of the products by the total frequency gives the variance, and taking the positive square root of this gives the standard deviation.

Students of mechanics, or applied mathematics, may recognise that, just as finding the mean of a distribution is like finding the position of the centre of gravity of a system of weights, the standard deviation of a distribution is analogous to the radius of gyration of a system.

On the other hand students of electricity, who have studied AC theory, may realise that we have taken the mean of the squares of the deviations, and then taken the square root of this mean of squares, i.e. we have the root mean square or RMS value of the deviations.

The standard deviation is designated s, and its calculation for Machine A's distribution is shown in Table 5.8. The table repeats the evaluation of the mean from Table 5.7, of which it is an extension, so as to bring the whole calculation together.

Table 5.8 Standard deviation of Machine A's distribution

f	f	fx	$(x - m)$	$(x - m)^2$	$f(x - m)^2$
35	1	35	−15.92	253.34	253.34
40	5	200	−10.92	119.17	595.34
45	11	495	−5.92	35.00	385.07
50	20	1000	−0.92	0.84	16.80
55	14	770	4.08	16.67	233.43
60	6	360	9.08	82.50	495.04
65	3	195	14.08	198.34	595.02
Totals	60	3055			2574.58

Mean = 50.92
Variance = 42.9
St. deviation = 6.55
Class width 5

Populations and samples

We started out with a set of production figures for each of two machines. These machines have, presumably, been producing in the past, and are continuing to produce now, and will do so into the future. The raw data we started with is a *sample* of the production figures. The complete production figures constitute what is called the *population*. You may be familiar with these terms from such things as opinion polls. A sample of those people eligible to vote is taken and this sample represents the population of those eligible to vote. It is very rare indeed to be able to deal with a complete population. It is often far too big, and may even be endless, i.e. an *infinite population*. All that can be realistically done is to take a sample of manageable size, find some things out about the sample, and assume that these things hold good for the whole population. There are various techniques to assist in getting a representative sample, and of assessing the likelihood that it is representative, but they are beyond the scope of our present task. All that will be said is that they work pretty well when dealing with things (production figures for example).

Mr Kidani has obtained a sample for each of two machines. He has no way of knowing whether the samples are truly representative or, in the jargon of statistics, whether they are proper *random* samples. They are, however, all he has, and he must make do with them in deciding which of the two machines to purchase.

The normal distribution

It was said earlier, when dealing with the ogive, that it is usual to draw a smooth curve through the points. This is usually a reasonably easy operation. Doing the same thing with a frequency polygon is by no means as simple. The best way of solving an awkward problem is not to have the problem in the first place. There is no real need to draw an accurate smooth curve through the points (*vertices*) of the polygon.

It is not necessary to draw the curve to realise that it will have a 'bell-like' shape. The larger the sample, that is the more data that is obtained, the more the shape will tend to be bell-like. Experience has shown the validity of this last statement. A distribution of measurements becomes more and more bell-like as the amount of data increases, i.e. as more measurements are taken.

The mathematician Karl Friedrich Gauss discovered a curve that has this distinctive bell-like shape, its formula developed from a consideration of probabilities and their attendant histograms. Figure 5.7 shows the curve we are talking about.

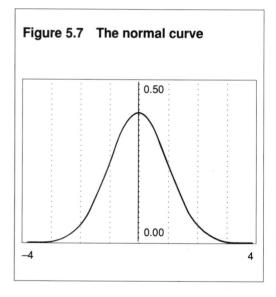

Figure 5.7   The normal curve

This curve is the 'smoothed' polygon of a distribution that has a mean of zero and a standard deviation of one, i.e. unity. Incidentally its mode and median are also zero. The total area under the curve is one, unity. It dies away very rapidly at its extremes, so that despite the fact that it goes on forever in either direction, the whole area can be considered to be confined between $x = -4$ and $x = 4$. For $x = 4$, $y = 0.000\ 053\ 39$, so you can see that there cannot be much area lying to the right of $x = 4$!

The curve is symmetrical about $x = 0$, so we can say that for $x > 0$ the area is 0.5, and for $x < 0$ the area is 0.5.

Also we can say that the area contained between say $x = -2$ and $x = 0$ is the same as the area contained between $x = 0$ and $x = 2$. We will find the last two statements very useful in what follows.

Because experience has shown that a distribution involving measurement tends towards this shape for its 'smoothed' polygon as the amount of data increases, it has become known as the *normal* shape of the population distribution, and is referred to as the curve of the *normal distribution*.

However, the distributions we have do not have: a total area of one; a mean of zero; and a standard deviation of one.

These are minor hiccups, easily dealt with by some simple algebraic manipulations which do not alter the shape of the frequency polygon, and hence of the curve.

1   The area under the polygon equals the area under the histogram. This area represents the total frequency, hence to reduce the area to unity all that is needed is to divide each frequency, and consequently the total frequency, by the total frequency. A variate's frequency divided by the total frequency is called the *relative frequency* of the variate. It measures how likely the variate is to occur in the distribution. It amounts to the *probability* that the value of variate occurs. So far as the curve is concerned, all it does is to change the scale of the vertical (f) axis.

2   In considering the mean deviation it was pointed out that reducing every value of variate by the same amount resulted in reducing the mean by exactly the same amount. It is easy, therefore, to obtain a zero mean for any distribution. All that is necessary is to reduce every value of the variate by the value of the mean. In symbols x is replaced by $x - m$. So far as the curve is concerned all this does is to shift the origin from the value of the mean of the distribution to zero, the new mean. Usually, and for distributions involving measurements certainly, the curve shifts to the left.

3 $x - m$ is, of course, the deviation of x from the mean. Dividing each deviation by the same amount will divide the standard deviation by the same amount (Think about it!). It follows then that dividing each deviation by the standard deviation will automatically create a standard deviation of unity. So far as the curve is concerned all this does is to change the scale of the horizontal (x) axis.

The variate has been changed from x to $(x - m)/s$. This is usually designated as z, i.e.:

$$z = \frac{x - m}{s}$$

Any smoothed polygon will conform approximately to the normal curve provided the value of each variate (x) is replaced by its corresponding z value. The z values are called the *normalised* or *standardised values*. In some contexts they are called *standardised scores*.

In **1** above, it was remarked that areas under the curve now represent probabilities. The area between two z values represents the probability that z lies between the two values. It also consequently represents the probability that x lies between the corresponding two x values. Table 5.9 is a table of areas under the normal curve. The shaded area in the diagram above it indicates the area that is obtained from the table. z is entered to two decimal places, the integral part and first decimal from the left-hand column, and the second decimal from the top row. For example, to find the area corresponding to $z = 1.45$ look down the left-hand column to 1.4, and then along the row under 5. The number .4265 is the area under the curve between $z = 0$ and $z = 1.45$. It is the probability that z lies between 0 and 1.45.

The area between any two z values can be found by exploiting the symmetry of the curve about zero, and the fact that the total area is unity.

Examples

1   Given that a certain distribution has a mean of 57 and a standard deviation of 4, find the probability that a value of the variate is less than or equal to 62.

We have $x = 62$, $m = 57$, and $s = 4$ so the corresponding z value is given by:

$$z = \frac{62 - 57}{4} = \frac{5}{4} = 1.25$$

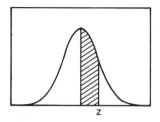

Table 5.9   The normal distribution

z	0	1	2	3	4	5	6	7	8	9
0.0	.0000	.0040	.0080	.0120	.0160	.0199	.0239	.0279	.0319	.0359
0.1	.0398	.0438	.0478	.0517	.0557	.0596	.0636	.0675	.0714	.0754
0.2	.0793	.0832	.0871	.0910	.0948	.0987	.1026	.1064	.1103	.1141
0.3	.1179	.1217	.1255	.1293	.1331	.1368	.1406	.1443	.1480	.1517
0.4	.1554	.1591	.1628	.1664	.1700	.1736	.1772	.1808	.1844	.1879
0.5	.1915	.1950	.1985	.2019	.2054	.2088	.2123	.2157	.2190	.2224
0.6	.2258	.2291	.2324	.2357	.2389	.2422	.2454	.2486	.2518	.2549
0.7	.2580	.2612	.2642	.2673	.2704	.2734	.2764	.2794	.2823	.2852
0.8	.2881	.2910	.2939	.2967	.2996	.3023	.3051	.3078	.3106	.3133
0.9	.3159	.3186	.3212	.3238	.3264	.3289	.3315	.3340	.3365	.3389
1.0	.3413	.3438	.3461	.3485	.3508	.3531	.3554	.3477	.3599	.3621
1.1	.3643	.3665	.3686	.3708	.3729	.3749	.3770	.3790	.3810	.3830
1.2	.3849	.3869	.3888	.3907	.3925	.3944	.3962	.3980	.3997	.4025
1.3	.4032	.4049	.4066	.4082	.4099	.4115	.4131	.4147	.4162	.4177
1.4	.4192	.4207	.4222	.4236	.4251	.4265	.4279	.4292	.4306	.4319
1.5	.4332	.4345	.4357	.4370	.4382	.4394	.4406	.4418	.4429	.4441
1.6	.4452	.4463	.4474	.4484	.4495	.4505	.4515	.4525	.4535	.4545
1.7	.4554	.4564	.4573	.4582	.4591	.4599	.4608	.4616	.4625	.4633
1.8	.4641	.4649	.4656	.4664	.4671	.4678	.4686	.4693	.4699	.4706
1.9	.4713	.4719	.4726	.4732	.4738	.4744	.4750	.4756	.4761	.4767
2.0	.4772	.4778	.4793	.4788	.4793	.4798	.4803	.4808	.4812	.4817
2.1	.4821	.4826	.4830	.4834	.4838	.4842	.4846	.4850	.4854	.4857
2.2	.4861	.4864	.4868	.4871	.4875	.4878	.4881	.4884	.4887	.4890
2.3	.4893	.4896	.4898	.4901	.4904	.4906	.4909	.4911	.4913	.4916
2.4	.4918	.4920	.4922	.4925	.4927	.4929	.4931	.4932	.4934	.4936
2.5	.4938	.4940	.4941	.4943	.4945	.4946	.4948	.4949	.4951	.4952
2.6	.4953	.4955	.4956	.4957	.4959	.4960	.4961	.4962	.4963	.4964
2.7	.4965	.4966	.4967	.4968	.4969	.4970	.4971	.4972	.4973	.4974
2.8	.4974	.4975	.4976	.4977	.4977	.4978	.4979	.4979	.4980	.4981
2.9	.4981	.4982	.4982	.4983	.4984	.1984	.4985	.4985	.4986	.4986
3.0	.4987	.4987	.4987	.4988	.4988	.4989	.4989	.4989	.4990	.4990
3.1	.4990	.4991	.4991	.4991	.4992	.4992	.4992	.4992	.4993	.4993
3.2	.4993	.4993	.4994	.4994	.4994	.4994	.4994	.4995	.4995	.4995
3.3	.4995	.4995	.4995	.4996	.4996	.4996	.4996	.4996	.4996	.4997
3.4	.4997	.4997	.4997	.4997	.4997	.4997	.4997	.4997	.4997	.4998
3.5	.4998	.4998	.4998	.4998	.4998	.4998	.4998	.4998	.4998	.4998
3.6	.4998	.4998	.4999	.4999	.4999	.4999	.4999	.4999	.4999	.4999
3.7	.4999	.4999	.4999	.4999	.4999	.4999	.4999	.4999	.4999	.4999
3.8	.4999	.4999	.4999	.4999	.4999	.4999	.4999	.4999	.4999	.4999
3.9	.5000	.5000	.5000	.5000	.5000	.5000	.5000	.5000	.5000	.5000

From Table 5.9 we obtain the number .3944. A rough sketch is useful in answering a question like this.

The value .3944 is the area marked a in the sketch, whereas we want $a + b$, i.e. z less than or equal to 1.25. Area b is half the area under the curve, i.e. 0.5, so the required area and hence the probability that x is less than or equal to 62 is $0.3944 + 0.5 = 0.8944$.

This means that between 89 per cent and 90 per cent (89.44 per cent) of the values of the variate are less than or equal to 62.

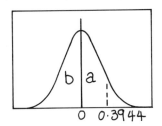

2   For the same distribution what is the probability that x is less than or equal to 49?

$$z = \frac{49 - 57}{4} = \frac{-8}{4} = -2$$

Again a rough sketch will help.

Again the required area is the left-hand tail, this time from $z = -2$ downwards, area a in the sketch. Negative values do not appear in the table, but we can again exploit the curve's symmetry about zero. The area from $z = -2$ to $z = 0$ (area b) is the same as the area between $z = 0$ and $z = 2$ (area c).

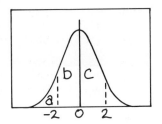

From the table:

$$\text{area } c = 0.4772$$
$$\text{therefore area } b = 0.4772$$
$$\text{but area } a + b = 0.5$$
$$\text{therefore area } a = 0.5 - 0.4772 = 0.0228$$

Let us now return to Mr Kidani's problem, recalling that he had estimated that he would require at least 45 components a week.

For Machine A we have $x = 45$, $m = 50.91$, and $s = 6.55$, so:

$$z = \frac{45 - 50.91}{6.55} = \frac{-5.91}{6.55} = -0.902$$

From the table:

with $z = 0.90$ we get 0.3159
with $z = 0.91$ we get 0.3186

so with $z = 0.902$ we get 0.3164 by interpolation. The area for z greater than or equal to -0.902 (x greater than or equal to 45) is $0.3164 + 0.5 = 0.8164$.

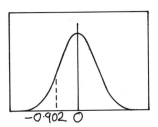

For Machine B we have $x = 45$, $m = 48.83$, and $s = 9.93$, so:

$$z = \frac{45 - 48.83}{9.93} = \frac{-3.83}{9.93} = -0.386$$

From the table:

with $z = 0.38$ we get 0.1480
with $z = 0.39$ we get 0.1517

so with $z = 0.386$ we get 0.1502 by interpolation. The area for z greater than or equal to -0.386 (x greater than or equal to 45) is $0.1502 + 0.5 = 0.6502$.

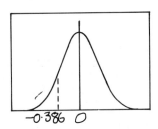

This means that on this evidence, and it is all Mr Kidani has got, Machine A would be expected to attain or exceed the required production of components 81.64 per cent of the time, while Machine B would be expected to do it 65.02 per cent of the time.

Now it is up to Mr Kidani. There are further tests he could do if he is still undecided. There is a test of whether or not there is any difference between the machines. This could be done by hypothesising that both distributions are from the same population. The test, which is beyond the scope of this chapter, would give the probability that they are from the same population. There is then a technique for assessing how likely it is that an error has occurred.

The mathematics cannot make his decision for him. Both machines average above his projected requirements. Machine B is slightly cheaper than Machine A. Are they equally reliable? Would exceeding 45 per week, so as to build up a stock to cover underproductive weeks, involve him in overtime payments? What about storage costs? Items in stock are an asset, but are in effect dead money. It is his money and it is his decision.

REVIEW

1 Calculate the mean and standard deviation of Machine B's distribution using a class width of 5, and hence confirm the figure of 65.02 per cent given in the text.
2 A company produces cylindrical iron bars by a continuous extrusion and cropping process. One machine is set to produce bars ten metres in length with a tolerance of twenty-five millimetres, i.e. the length required is within the range 10 ± 0.025 metres).

The output is monitored by taking a random sample of 100 bars every week and measuring them individually. The results from one week's sample are shown in the table below (measurements in millimetres).

9955	9962	9966	9967	9971	9975	9978	9980	9983	9983
9985	9985	9987	9987	9988	9988	9988	9991	9991	9992
9993	9994	9995	9995	9995	9996	9996	9996	9997	9997
9997	9997	9998	9998	9998	9998	9998	9998	9999	9999
10001	10002	10003	10003	10003	10003	10004	10004	10004	10004
10005	10005	10005	10005	10005	10006	10006	10006	10006	10006
10007	10007	10007	10008	10008	10009	10009	10009	10009	10011
10011	10011	10012	10012	10013	10014	10015	10015	10016	10016
10017	10017	10017	10019	10019	10022	10023	10023	10026	10027
10029	10030	10030	10032	10034	10036	10040	10043	10047	10054

Use these figures to determine:
a What percentage of output can be expected to be immediately acceptable.
b What percentage can be made acceptable by grinding because they are too big.
(*Hint:* Use a class width of 10.)
3 Undersized bars are recycled. It is considered that not more than 10 per cent recycling is acceptable. In the next four weeks the results opposite were obtained. Assuming that this trend continues, determine graphically how long it will be before the machine requires resetting.

	mean	*st.dev.*
Week 2	10004.73	17.80
Week 3	10004.85	18.48
Week 4	10004.68	18.96
Week 5	10004.54	19.49

4 The local librarian wishes to discover what the local population thinks of the services the library provides, and so decides to set a questionnaire.

  a What factors need to be kept in mind when compiling any questionnaire? (6)

  b The replies to the question 'Which of the following do you consider should be given top priority?' are given below.

Alternative answers	Men	Women	Children
Increase the number of library staff	2	6	4
Extend the hours of opening	22	10	6
Buy more fiction books	20	32	25
Buy more non-fiction books	16	27	10

  i Draw a bar chart to illustrate the above data. (5)

  ii Comment on how well you think your bar chart presents this information. (2)

  iii How does a histogram differ from a bar chart? (2)

  c Sixty per cent of those surveyed said that they were satisfied with the service provided by the library. Can the librarian be confident that the majority of the local population would agree with this view if the sample size was:

  i 100? (2)

  ii 200? (2)

  iii What assumptions have you made in your answers to the above? (1)

  d Discuss the advantages and disadvantages of the various ways the librarian could distribute the questionnaire. How could the method of distribution affect the results obtained? (5) 1986 (CLES)

5 a Explain the differences between the following types of sample:

  i random.

  ii stratified.

  iii quota. (6)

  b A firm wishes to fix a piecework rate for its employees and to do this it needs to know the average number of operations per person per day. Rather than make this calculation for all its staff, the firm decides to take a sample.

  i Describe how the firm might decide on the kind and size of sample it would need. (4)

  ii Discuss which of the measures of central tendency would be the most appropriate to use, and explain why you think this is the case. (4)

  c Suppose that workers had previously been paid a flat rate of £25 per day, on the basis of an arithmetic average of 100 operations per day. Suggest why, and at what levels of operation, you might introduce bonus payments, if the results of the sample showed that the arithmetic mean was 100 operations, with a standard deviation of 30. (You may use the table below if you think this is appropriate.) (5)

Proportionate parts of the area under the normal curve Distance from the mean in terms of				
standard deviation in one direction	0–1	1–2	2–3	over 3
Proportion of area in above range	34%	14%	2%	negligible

   d Suppose a worker performed the following set of operations over a 10-day period:
   180 180 150 130 190 200 150 160 170 180
   What would you conclude about the worker and/or the sample results? Explain your
   reasons. (You may assume that the standard deviation remains at 30.) (6) 1985 (CLES)
6 The data given below refer to a manufacturing company, XYZ Ltd. In 1970 the company
   employed a workforce of 2000, but by 1983 this number had dropped to 1000.

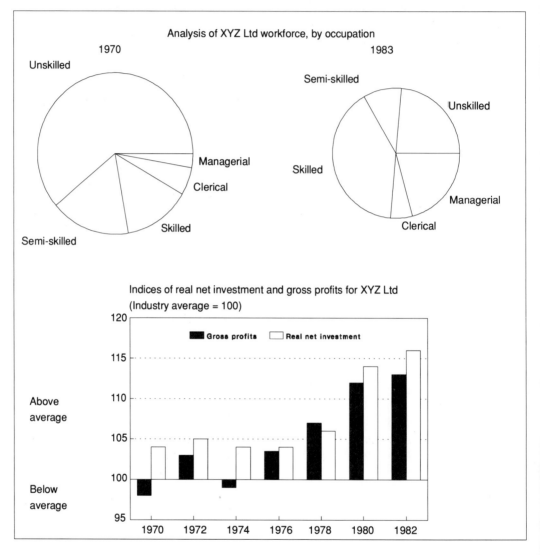

   a State one advantage and one disadvantage of presenting data in the form of a pie chart.
      (4)
   b Give one reason why the pie charts above are of different sizes. (3)
   c Describe briefly the changes that took place in company XYZ Ltd between 1970 and
      1983. (5)
   d Using the data given above, state and explain one possible reason for the decline in
      the number of people employed by XYZ Ltd. (4)
   e Outline three problems the company might have faced as a result of the changing
      occupational structure of the workforce. (9) 1985 (AEB)

Activities

Visit a local supermarket and, with the manager's permission, record:

a The number of customers who approach the checkout in at least twelve five-minute periods.

b How long the cashier takes to deal with each customer.

c The length of the queue.

From **a** calculate the mean (m) number of customers in a five-minute period.

The *Poisson distribution*, named after a French mathematician, can be used to calculate the probability that a chosen number of customers will arrive at the checkout in a five-minute period. The formula is:

Probability that r customers arrive, $p(r) = \text{Exp}(-m) \times m^r/r!$

where m is the mean and $r!$ is r factorial, i.e. r multiplied by every positive whole number less than r. For example:

$5! = 5 \times 4 \times 3 \times 2 \times 1$

You do not need statistical tables to calculate these probabilities. The exponential function (Exp) is given in most sets of four-figure tables and on many handheld calculators, though it usually appears in the form e^x or Inverse Ln(x). Remember that e^{-x} is the reciprocal of e^x.

Calculate $p(0)$, $p(1)$, $p(2)$, $p(3)$ and so on until the number obtained is less than 0.001. This task is not as horrendous as it first appears. We have:

$$p(r) = e^{-m} \times m^r/r!$$

and:

$$p(r + 1) = e^{-m} \times m^{(r + 1)}/(r + 1)!$$

Now:

$$m^{(r + 1)} = m^r \times m \ \text{(law of indices)}$$

and:

$$(r + 1)! = (r + 1) \times r!$$

so:

$$p(r + 1) = p(r) \times m/(r + 1)$$

For example:

$$p(5) = p(4) \times m/5$$

This is an example of what a mathematician calls a *recurrence relation*.

Factorial zero is defined as unity, i.e. $0! = 1$, and $m^0 = 1$ so $p(0)$ is very simple:

$$p(0) = e^{-m}$$

then:

$$p(1) = p(0) \times m$$
$$p(2) = p(1) \times m/2$$
$$p(3) = p(2) \times m/3$$

etc.

Carry on until $p(r) < +0.001$ and then reduce the probabilities to two decimal places.

Next calculate the probabilities of the times the cashier takes to deal with a customer. This is simply:

$$p(\text{a customer takes } x \text{ minutes}) = \frac{\text{Number of customers taking } x \text{ minutes}}{\text{Total number of customers}}$$

We now have two sets of probabilities. The situation can be simulated by means of a table of random numbers. Many books on statistics contain such a table, as do books of statistical tables, and again many hand-held calculators have a random number facility. Assign the

100 pairs of numbers from 00 to 99 first to the probabilities of customer arrival and then to the probabilities of times, in proportion to the size of the probabilities. For example, if $p(0) = 0.04$, $p(0)$ is assigned the numbers 00, 01, 02 and 03, and if $p(1) = 0.07$, $p(1)$ is assigned the numbers 04, 05, 06, 07, 08, 09, 10 and so on. You should find that you use up all 100 pairs.

Start anywhere in the table of random numbers and, going in any direction, pick a pair of digits. This pair will give the number of customers in a five-minute period. The subsequent pairs of numbers give the length of time each customer in turn takes at the checkout. From these numbers see how a queue builds up and compare its length with the lengths recorded in **c** above.

The five-minute period is by no means sacrosanct. If a sufficient number of recorders are available, and the supermarket is busy enough, a one-minute period may be more appropriate.

It does not have to be a supermarket. The same exercise could be used on the cars calling at a petrol station, especially if it is a self-service station.

A worked example should help clarify the technique.

Fifty-five customers were attended to in a period of one hour in a large branch of a clearing bank. The bank has a system whereby all customers join the same queue when entering and move to a teller as one becomes available.

The periods of teller's time occupied by the customers was distributed as follows:

No. of minutes	Tally	No. of customers
1							6
2										9
3									8
4										10
5												12
6							6
7						4
		Total 55

We set about modelling the situation by calculating the probabilities of certain numbers of customers arriving in the next minute. For this we will use the Poisson distribution, and so need the mean number of customers per minute.

Mean $= 55/60 = 0.9167$

Then, writing the probability of r customers arriving in the next minute as $P(r)$, rounding to two decimal places and assigning random numbers in the range 00 to 99 we get:

			Random nos.
$P(0) = e^{-0.9167}$	$= 0.3998$	i.e. 0.40	00 to 39
$P(1) = P(0) \times 0.9167$	$= 0.3665$	i.e. 0.37	40 to 76
$P(2) = P(1) \times 0.9167/2$	$= 0.1680$	i.e. 0.17	77 to 93
$P(3) = P(2) \times 0.9167/3$	$= 0.0513$	i.e. 0.05	94 to 98
$P(4) = P(3) \times 0.9167/4$	$= 0.0118$	i.e. 0.01	99
$P(5) = P(4) \times 0.9167/5$	$= 0.0022$	i.e. 0.00	
$P(6) = P(5) \times 0.9167/6$	$= 0.0004$	i.e. 0.00	
Check sums	1.0000	1.00	

Next we require the probabilities of the number of minutes a customer will occupy a teller's time. This is calculated by:

Probability of using t minutes $= P(t)$

and

$P(t)$ = No. taking t minutes/Total no. of customers

so:

			Random nos.
P(1) = 6/55	= 0.1091	i.e. 0.11	00 to 10
P(2) = 9/55	= 0.1636	i.e. 0.16	11 to 26
P(3) = 8/55	= 0.1455	i.e. 0.15	27 to 41
P(4) = 10/55	= 0.1818	i.e. 0.18	42 to 59
P(5) = 12/55	= 0.2182	i.e. 0.22	60 to 81
P(6) = 6/55	= 0.1091	i.e. 0.11	82 to 92
P(7) = 4/55	= 0.0727	i.e. 0.07	93 to 99
Check sums	1.0000	1.00	

The results from the previous two tables are repeated here for convenience:

Customer arrivals		Teller times	
Random numbers	No. of customers	Random numbers	Time in minutes
00 to 39	0	00 to 10	1
40 to 76	1	11 to 26	2
77 to 93	2	27 to 41	3
94 to 98	3	42 to 59	4
99	4	60 to 81	5
		82 to 92	6
		93 to 99	7

For the simulation we need a table of random numbers such as the one below.

```
03  37  00  74  08  22  41  80  26  04  65  73  73  96  08
05  67  11  42  94  09  42  54  46  71  41  57  92  60  13
06  56  52  08  58  21  65  37  82  31  63  08  07  84  93
01  47  62  40  74  59  38  84  44  69  69  01  62  23  95
06  83  74  40  84  60  10  67  18  01  89  69  37  07  43
53  46  38  18  82  78  48  81  30  44  72  39  59  67  03
37  31  41  31  23  04  27  08  38  69  25  40  62  28  06
15  66  57  82  93  35  84  35  26  64  39  15  21  59  18
47  28  53  42  67  67  89  72  06  33  48  77  32  70  74
37  04  82  85  09  88  07  16  12  83  38  97  83  47  72
59  74  30  52  33  55  83  82  73  98  89  20  82  65  88
96  09  08  00  87  39  11  80  96  73  23  03  49  64  52
40  40  96  65  73  87  66  42  34  90  70  87  47  60  51
67  72  97  43  15  32  55  72  74  08  69  23  57  93  55
87  06  02  82  40  89  97  23  90  26  29  33  57  88  03
66  00  71  77  46  27  56  07  40  28  31  46  06  39  19
28  08  64  17  75  83  42  97  36  34  91  47  98  21  03
01  41  42  40  04  15  18  21  08  80  75  11  18  31  06
78  95  44  64  83  01  49  37  25  55  05  60  45  82  65
58  54  31  54  94  94  70  73  41  15  13  98  14  14  81
```

Figure 5.8A   Simulation with 3 tellers

Minutes	1	2	3	4	5	6	7	8	9	10	11	12	13	14	15	16	17	18	19	20
Random numbers	(18)	(31)	(82)	(52)	(65)	(82)	(77)	(40)	(64)	(04)	(75)	(46)	(40)	(73)	(87)	(93)	(23)	(84)	(58)	(94)
Number of customers	0	0	2	1	1	2	2	1	1	0	1	1	1	1	2	2	0	2	1	3
Teller 1				(42)			(17)			(54)			(15)		(33)				(74)	
Teller 2					(85)						(94)					(09)		(82)		
Teller 3				(00)		(43)					(83)					(67)				(08)
Queue	0	0	0	0	0	2	3	4	2	2	3	4	4	5	5	7	6	7	8	10

Figure 5.8B   Simulation with 4 tellers

Minutes	1	2	3	4	5	6	7	8	9	10	11	12	13	14	15	16	17	18	19	20
Random numbers	(18)	(31)	(82)	(52)	(65)	(82)	(17)	(64)	(54)	(04)	(75)	(40)	(73)	(87)	(09)	(23)	(52)	(58)	(94)	(08)
Number of customers	0	0	2	1	1	2	0	1	1	0	1	1	1	2	0	0	2	1	3	0
Teller 1				(42)				(40)				(46)					(67)			(22)
Teller 2				(85)								(94)						(48)		
Teller 3				(00)		(43)		(77)			(83)		(15)		(33)		(93)		(74)	
Teller 4																				
Queue	0	0	0	0	0	1	0	1	0	0	0	0	1	2	0	0	0	1	4	3

We also need a blank chart similar to the one shown filled in in Figure 5.8A.

The numbers in brackets in Figure 5.8A are the random numbers encountered from the table on page 111. Let us start working our way through Figure 5.8A, starting with the random number 18 from the table, and following the path indicated. We will assume that three tellers are available, all of whom are unoccupied at the beginning of the simulation.

□ Min. 1, Ran. no. 18, this is within the range 00 to 39 in our customer arrival table on page 111, so the number of customers is 0, and of course the queue is also 0.

□ Min. 2, Ran. no. 31, customers 0, queue 0.

□ Min. 3, Ran. no. 82, customers 2, queue still 0.

□ Customer to teller No. 1, Ran. no. 42, so time is 4 minutes.

□ Customer to teller No. 2, Ran. no. 85, so time is 6 minutes.

□ Min. 4, Ran. no. 52, customers 1, so queue still 0.

□ Customer to teller No. 3, Ran. no. 00, so time is 1 minute.

□ Min. 5, Ran. no. 65, customers 1, queue 0.

□ Customer to teller No. 3, Ran. no. 43, so time is 4 minutes.

□ Min. 6, Ran. no. 82, customers 2, all tellers occupied, so queue is 2.

□ Min. 7, Ran. no. 77, customers 2, teller No. 1 is free, so queue is 3.

Figure 5.8A continues in this way to cover a period of twenty minutes.

Notice how, after a slow start, the queue builds up. In fact if you continue beyond the 20 minutes you will find it gets a lot larger!

For comparison the exercise is repeated using the same random numbers, starting at the same point, but using four tellers. This is shown in Figure 5.8B.

The effect on the queue is pretty startling. However, there are 17 'teller-minutes' unused. The numbers seem to be indicating that we need about 3.5 tellers, so perhaps we should repeat, starting with 3 tellers but introducing a fourth after 10 minutes or so, before the customers' tempers start to get frayed! Why not try it?

Essays

1 State and discuss the criteria on which a statistical report should be based. Comment on the extent to which the presentation of data is as important as accuracy. 1984 (AEB)

2 'The collection of statistics is expensive in time and consequently in money. It is not really cost effective.' Discuss.

3 It is very easy to deceive people with the illustration of statistics by means of graphs, bar charts, pie charts and histograms. Detail the methods of deception and how they may be detected and guarded against.

4 a Outline two distinct types of problem where the use of probability techniques might be of help in business, and illustrate, using numerical information, how the analysis might proceed. (15)

  b What non-numerical factors or criteria would be relevant to the problems? (10) (CLES)

Appendix

The random number table on page 111 was created using a BBC Micro and Epson printer. The listing appears below. The program asks for the number of random numbers required, but will produce only the next lowest number divisible exactly by 15 to the number requested. This is because 15 number pairs fit neatly across both the screen of a VDU and A4 paper.

The program next gives the option of printing a hard (paper) copy or just a VDU display. The VDU only display is in paged mode, so it requires the SHIFT key to be pressed to move on. At the end of the table the option is given to repeat the same table or create a new one.

It is, of course, virtually impossible to recreate the table on page 111. That would be roughly equivalent to 'If a million chimpanzees randomly struck a million typewriters continuously for a million years, one of them may just write *Hamlet*'.

Depending upon the dip switch setting on the printer, line 30 may be unnecessary and cause printing to be double spaced.

```
 10 *key0G. 200|M
 20 *key9RUN|M
 30 *fx6,0
 40 CLS:PRINT TAB(5,10);"How many random numbers do you want";
 50 INPUT No%
 60 A% = No%MOD(15)
 70 No% = No% - A%
 80 CLS:PRINT TAB(10,10);"Do you want a printed (Hard) copy
(Y/N)?"
 90 Hard$ - GET$
100 CLS:PRINT TAB(5,10);"Creating numbers"
110 IF INSTR("YyNn",Hard$) = 0 THEN GOTO 80
120 DIMA$(No% + 10)
130 FOR N% = 1 TO No%
140 A = 10E6*RND(1)
150 A = A - INT(A)
160 A = INT(100*A)
170 A$(N%) = STR$(A)
180 IF VAL(A$(N%)) <10 THEN A$(N%) = "0"+A$(N%)
190 NEXT N%
200 IF INSTR("Yy",Hard$) >0 THEN VDU 2,1,27,1,77
210 MODE 0
220 IF INSTR("Nn",Hard$) >0 THEN VDU 14
230 PRINT
240 T% = 10
250 FOR K% = 1 TO N%
260 PRINT TAB(T%);A$(K%);
270 T% = T% + 4
280 IF T% >68 THEN T% = 10:PRINT'
290 NEXT K%
300 PRINT
310 IF INSTR("Yy",Hard$) >0 THEN VDU2,1,27,1,64:VDU2,1,27,1,15
320 VDU 15
330 PRINT TAB(40);"A table of Random Numbers"
340 VDU2,1,27,1,64:VDU 3
350 PRINT "Space bar to continue":A = GET
360 MODE 7:PRINT TAB(5,10);"For another copy press [f0]"
370 PRINT TAB(5,15);"For a different set press [f9]"
```

Solutions to self assessment questions

Self assessment question 1: 48
Self assessment question 2:

x	f	fx
28	1	28
30	1	30
32	2	64
33	1	33
35	1	35
37	2	74
38	1	38
39	2	78
40	1	40
41	2	82
42	2	84
43	2	86
44	3	132
45	1	45
46	2	92
47	3	141
48	3	144
49	1	49
50	2	100
51	2	102
52	3	156
54	2	108
55	3	165
56	3	168
57	2	114
58	2	116
59	1	59
60	2	120
61	1	61
62	1	62
64	1	64
65	1	65
66	1	66
70	1	70
72	1	72
	60	2943

Mean = 49.05

Self assessment question 3:

Range	Tally	Total
28 to 32	IIII	4
33 to 37	IIII	4
38 to 42	HHT III	8
43 to 47	HHT HHT I	11
48 to 52	HHT HHT I	11
53 to 57	HHT HHT	10
58 to 62	HHT II	7
63 to 67	III	3
68 to 72	II	2

Self assessment question 4:

f	f	fx
30	4	120
35	4	140
40	8	320
45	11	495
50	11	550
55	10	550
60	7	420
65	3	195
70	2	140
Totals	60	2930

Mean = 48.83
Class width 5

Self assessment question 5:

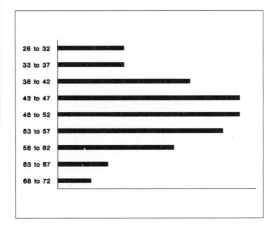

Self assessment question 6:

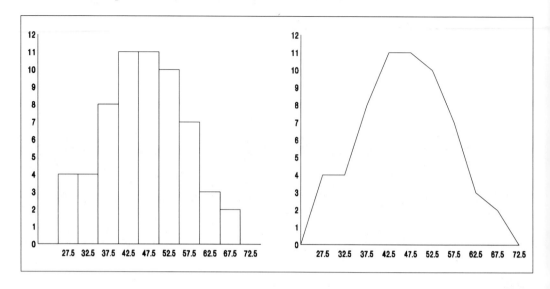

6 Accounting: an aid to decision making and control

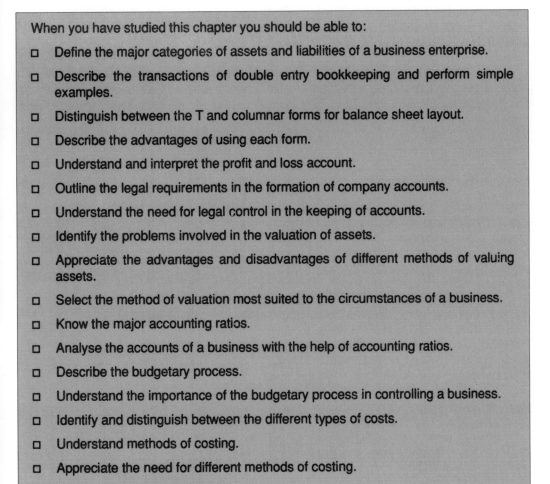

When you have studied this chapter you should be able to:

- [ ] Define the major categories of assets and liabilities of a business enterprise.
- [ ] Describe the transactions of double entry bookkeeping and perform simple examples.
- [ ] Distinguish between the T and columnar forms for balance sheet layout.
- [ ] Describe the advantages of using each form.
- [ ] Understand and interpret the profit and loss account.
- [ ] Outline the legal requirements in the formation of company accounts.
- [ ] Understand the need for legal control in the keeping of accounts.
- [ ] Identify the problems involved in the valuation of assets.
- [ ] Appreciate the advantages and disadvantages of different methods of valuing assets.
- [ ] Select the method of valuation most suited to the circumstances of a business.
- [ ] Know the major accounting ratios.
- [ ] Analyse the accounts of a business with the help of accounting ratios.
- [ ] Describe the budgetary process.
- [ ] Understand the importance of the budgetary process in controlling a business.
- [ ] Identify and distinguish between the different types of costs.
- [ ] Understand methods of costing.
- [ ] Appreciate the need for different methods of costing.

Since people have owned property they have devised methods of keeping a record of what they possessed and its value. They wished to keep an account of what they had and, when responsible for other people's property, they needed to render an account of how they had used it. This chapter is concerned with some of the techniques that have developed, sometimes over centuries, to satisfy this need. In general we will be concerned with the use of accounting information in the following areas:

- [ ] to determine, as accurately as possible, the profit or loss a business has made over a period of time and to provide a statement of the assets and liabilities of a business at a given moment in time. For the moment we will define *assets* as the properties, machinery, investments and cash owned by a business and which are used to achieve its objectives. *Liabilities* are the monies owed by a business.

☐   to provide information to assist owners/managers in achieving their objectives by improving decision making and control.

☐   to provide information to assist people who wish to invest or lend money to a business to make judgments concerning the potential profitability and safety of their investment.

Traditionally the accounting profession has been divided into *financial accountants*, whose professional association is the Institute of Chartered Accountants, and *management accountants*, who are members of the Institute of Cost and Management Accountants.

Financial accountants are primarily concerned with making sure that the accounts of a business are a *true and fair* record of the financial transactions of the business. They may do this by drawing up the accounts of a business from the records kept by the various departments or, acting on behalf of another business, they may examine existing accounts and declare them to be a true and fair record. This process is known as *auditing*.

Management accountants are more interested in the information they can derive from financial accounts. It is this aspect of accounting which is most important in this chapter, although to begin with we will examine some concepts and techniques which are the province of the financial accountant.

Definitions

We have already given brief definitions of assets and liabilities. Now we need to be more precise.

Assets

These are the resources owned by a business. They are classified as *fixed assets* and *current assets*.

Fixed assets

Fixed assets are normally those which the business intends to hold for more than one year and which are not intended for resale. They are the resources the business needs to function, but they may also include investments in other firms.

The conventional order for listing fixed assets begins with the most *illiquid*, that is the asset which is most difficult to turn into cash without loss of value, and ends with the most *liquid* asset, i.e. the one most easily turned into cash without loss of value. This order also tends to reflect the life of an asset within a business. In normal circumstances land and buildings would be the last assets to be sold if the business went bankrupt or into liquidation. It is therefore classified as the most fixed, i.e. the least liquid, asset. Cash is changing all the time, and is therefore the least fixed, i.e. the most liquid, asset.

An outline listing of fixed assets can be given as:

1   *Freehold land and buildings*   The word 'freehold' means that the owner has absolute rights over the land and does not have to pay rent for it.

2 *Leasehold land and buildings* A lease is a legal agreement between the owner of a property, the lessor, and another person, the lessee, that the lessee shall have the use of that property for a specified period of time. The time clause means that a leasehold is both less fixed in terms of ownership than freehold property and also more difficult to sell without loss of value. You should note that in Case Study B in Chapter 4 ('Starting and running your own business') the fact that the business property was leasehold made it more difficult for the prospective business owner to obtain a loan.

3 *Plant, machinery and equipment* After buildings a business needs the physical equipment to produce the good or service. Without them the business could not function, so they are only marginally less fixed than the buildings. This category also tends to be specialised. For example, Austria possesses a nuclear power station which has never functioned because a national referendum went against its opening. Estimates based on media reports suggest that it cost £400m to build and that the sale of parts for re-use or scrap might bring in £30m. That is a fixed asset.

4 *Vehicles* A van or car is both more flexible in use and has a shorter working life than a piece of machinery or a factory. It therefore ranks as less fixed than both.

5 *Goodwill, patents and trademarks* These are easy to define but more difficult to value.

- ☐ *Goodwill* is the favour and prestige a business enjoys which adds value to it beyond the value of its physical assets. It is sometimes defined as the difference between the audited value of a business and the market price it could command on the expectation of existing customers repeating their orders. Unfortunately there is no way of knowing the value of goodwill until the business is sold. To ignore it totally would be to deny an asset of the business. Estimates of goodwill should be conservative.

- ☐ *Patents* are legal documents securing to an inventor the exclusive right to make or sell an invention. Once an inventor (an individual or a company which has the right to claim an invention) has secured the *letters patent* to an invention they may license other people to use the invention. Again this is a legal agreement and the inventor will receive *royalties* in payment for the licence. Patents usually refer to the invention of machinery. In the media – books, films, records, videos – and the world of computer software the equivalent protection is *copyright*. Both patents and copyright attempt to protect the originators of an idea from exploitation by other people and, by allowing a period of years in which they have a monopoly over their idea, encourage further invention.

- ☐ *Trademarks* identify a product and help build up consumer loyalty. If you bought a factory manufacturing the well-known Megamints you would want to be able to continue using that name. A successful trademark is the end result of good marketing and quality control. It ensures continuing sales.

6 *Investments* These are not expected to be held beyond the present accounting period. An accounting period usually lasts for one year. A business that starts trading on 1 August 1991 would end its first accounting period on 31 July 1992.

Current assets

Current assets are those which are 'used up' in the day-to-day operations of a business and which can be converted into cash faster and without potential loss of value. Their listing follows the same convention as fixed assets: the most permanent and illiquid are placed first, whilst cash is last. Current assets include *stock, debtors and prepayments, cash at bank* and *cash in hand*. Debtors are those businesses which have taken delivery of goods but which have not yet paid for them, in other words, firms to whom the business has granted trade credit.

Liabilities

Strictly speaking a liability is a contribution of resources to a business for which a business has to render an account of its use. As we have already seen, the formation of a company gives the business a separate legal identity and the people who run the business must, by law, account for the way in which they have used the money entrusted to them. This will include money lent to the business and also money invested in the business by the owners, that is *shareholders' funds*. Sole traders and partnerships are not subject to the same legal constraints as companies, in that their accounts do not have to be made public, but the accounts of these businesses are treated as if the business is a separate identity from the owner. This has the practical advantage of allowing the owners of the business to keep a clear record of how much money they have invested and therefore of being able to judge the profit/loss position of the business more accurately. In the case of the sole trader the owner's capital would be presented as *proprietor's funds*. The usual practice is to start with owner's funds, follow this with loans which will not have to be repaid in the current accounting year, then current liabilities.

Current liabilities

Payments which will have to be made in the current financial year include provision for repayments of debts expected to mature and other expenses such as tax, bank overdrafts and creditors. There is no conventional order for the presentation of current liabilities.

SELF ASSESSMENT

1 Define the word 'liquid' and explain why cash is the most liquid of assets.
2 Distinguish between current and fixed assets.
3 Define a patent. Explain why patents, goodwill and trademarks are considered assets of a business.
4 Distinguish between shareholders' funds and proprietor's funds. Justify including them in the liabilities of a business.
5 Explain briefly why it is useful for a sole trader to keep the accounts of the business separate from personal accounts.

Accounting principles

Financial accounts are intended to give a true and fair record of the way in which a business has used the money entrusted to it. In order to ensure consistency in the way accounts were prepared, and therefore their comparability, accountants worked to a number of conventions.

☐   The business was regarded as a separate entity from the owners.

□ The accounts included only those parts of business activity which could be expressed in terms of money.

□ A transaction was considered complete when the goods or services were delivered to the customer. This is known as the *realisation principle* or the *accruals concept*.

□ Costs and revenue are recorded in the appropriate time period, that is costs are matched to revenue.

□ The business is assumed to have an indefinitely long existence (the *going-concern assumption*). This means, for example, that assets are valued on the assumption that they will continue in their present use rather than on the value they would have if offered for sale (*net realisable value*).

□ Conservatism implies that accountants are, by profession, pessimistic. They should accept the measurement that gives the most unfavourable interpretation of events.

□ Judgments should be based on verifiable evidence.

□ Both effects of any transaction should be recorded. For example the purchase of stock for cash by a business would lead to a reduction in its cash levels and a rise in its stock levels.

□ Assets are valued according to their cost at the time of purchase (*historic cost*).

These basic conventions of accounting have been added to over the years by changes in the law and internal agreements within the accountancy profession. In 1969 the professional bodies set up the Accounting Standards Committee (ASC) which issues Statements of Standard Accounting Practice (SSAPs). The practices described in the SSAPs must be followed by accountants. In 1973 the International Accounting Standards Committee (IASC) was established to standardise accounting practices between countries, and the Companies Acts have regulated the amount and type of information that companies are required to make available to shareholders and the general public.

Double entry bookkeeping

Double entry bookkeeping is based on common sense. If you go into a shop and buy a sweater for £15 your cash assets have declined by that amount but your physical assets have increased by £15. Newton's Third Law of Motion, which attempted to explain the behaviour of objects in the physical world, states that for every action there is an equal and opposite reaction. Double entry bookkeeping applies the same principle to the activity of recording financial transactions.

□ Action: Stock purchased for £4000 in cash.
Reaction: Cash balances reduced by £4000.

□ Action: Stock purchased for £4000 on credit.
Reaction: Creditors increased by £4000.

□ Action: Business borrows £4000 from bank to pay off £4000 of credit.
Reaction: Medium-term debt increases by £4000.

□ Action: Business pays off £4000 of debt using cash.
Reaction: Cash balance reduced by £4000.

We can summarise the above statements in terms of changes in the assets and liabilities of a business.

❑   Assets+ indicates that as a result of a transaction the total value of assets has increased.

❑   Assets– indicates that as a result of a transaction the total value of assets has decreased.

The same notation can also be applied to liabilities.

❑   Action: Assets+
      Reaction: Assets–

❑   Action: Assets+
      Reaction: Liabilities+

❑   Action: Liabilities+
      Reaction: Liabilities–

❑   Action: Assets–
      Reaction: Liabilities–

We can use double entry bookkeeping to record the transactions of Joseph Baines in setting up his nursery. Let us assume that the present value of the building he intends to use for the nursery is £30 000. He 'gives' the property to the business. Remember that Joseph is a sole trader. The property remains his, but to make his accounting accurate it must be counted as an asset being used by the business. The assets of the business have increased by £30 000 plus the £5000 he intends to introduce from his own resources (savings).

If Joseph Baines decides to close the business he will want this money back. As far as the business is concerned the property and cash invested in it by the Baines family are liabilities. The business has now received assets of £35 000 and, at the same time, incurred liabilities of £35 000. In the terminology of double entry bookkeeping we can say:

❑   Assets: +£35 000

❑   Liabilities: +£35 000

Assets and liabilities are balanced. If you think about the idea of accounting, giving a true and fair record of the way in which resources (*liabilities*) have been employed (*assets*), you can see that this must always be the case.

SELF ASSESSMENT

1 Explain briefly why a business is treated as a separate entity under accounting conventions.
2 Why were accounting conventions established?
3 Give the name of one national and one international body that regulates the accounting profession.
4 What is the realisation principle?
5 A person buys a house for £80 000, pays a deposit of £20 000 and borrows £60 000 from a building society. Explain this transaction in terms of double entry bookkeeping.

Balance sheets

A *balance sheet* provides a summary of the way in which a business has used the resources available to it over a period of time. In Table 6.1 you can see the balance sheet of the Baines Nursery at the start of trading.

Table 6.1 Balance sheet, Baines Nursery at start of trading

Balance sheet: Baines Nursery as at 30 September 1986

Freehold land/buildings	£30000	Proprietor's capital	£35000
Cash at bank	£ 5000		

Between 1 October and 14 November the Baines employ a builder to undertake the necessary alterations. For the purposes of this case study we will assume that the cost of the alterations was exactly the same as his estimate, £10 000. He funded the alterations by borrowing £10 000 from the bank. This gives the following action:

☐   Assets (freehold property) +£10 000

combined with a reaction:

☐   Assets (bank loan) –£10 000

Table 6.2 Balance sheet, Baines Nursery, after alterations to premises

Balance sheet: Baines Nursery as at 30 November 1986

Freehold land/buildings	£40000	Proprietor's capital	£35000
Cash at bank	£ 5000	Bank loan	£10000

The Baines buy fixtures and fittings together with equipment to the value of £5000. Again this is an assets+/assets– transaction.

Table 6.3 Balance sheet, Baines Nursery, after purchase of fixtures, fittings and equipment and grant of bank loan

Balance sheet: Baines Nursery as at 31 December 1986

Freehold land/buildings	£40000	Proprietor's capital	£35000
Fixtures & fittings	£ 5000	Bank loan	£10000
Cash at bank	£—		

The last transaction was not sensible, but it does give us the opportunity to examine two other actions/reactions involved in double entry bookkeeping. The Baines are now short of money. They negotiate an overdraft for £1000. This increases both their liabilities and their assets.

Table 6.4 Balance sheet, Baines Nursery, after negotiation of overdraft

Balance sheet: Baines Nursery as at 31 January 1987

Freehold land/buildings	£40000	Proprietor's capital	£35000
Fixtures & fittings	£ 5000	Bank loan	£10000
Cash at bank	£ 1000	Overdraft	£ 1000

Table 6.5 Balance sheet, Baines Nursery, after first six months' profit

Balance sheet: Baines Nursery as at 31 July 1987

Freehold land/buildings	£40000	Proprietor's capital	£35500
Fixtures & fittings	£ 5000	Bank loan	£10000
Cash at bank	£ 500		

After six months in operation the Baines have accumulated enough cash to pay off their overdraft with £500 to spare. Their cash figure will fall (assets–) but so will the overdraft disappear (liabilities–) and the proprietors' capital will be increased by the amount of their own money now in the bank. This is, of course, a very simple form of balance sheet but it does illustrate the principles contained in all balance sheets. On the right are the liabilities or the *sources* of funds used by a business. On the left the listed assets show *how* these funds have been used.

Table 6.6 Columnar form of balance sheet

Balance sheet as at.....................

	£000	£000	£000
ASSETS EMPLOYED			
FIXED ASSETS	Cost	Deprec.	Net
Freehold premises	4000	1000	3000
Leasehold premises	1000	370	630
Plant and machinery	5000	2355	2645
Motor vehicles	970	200	770
	10970	3925	7045
Investments			795
CURRENT ASSETS			
Stock (inventories)		5500	
Debtors and prepayments		1500	
Marketable (liquid) securities		500	
Bank balance and cash		100	
		7600	
Deduct			
CURRENT LIABILITIES			
Creditors	1754		
Tax and prepayments in coming year	500		
Bank overdraft	451		
Proposed dividends	335		
		3040	
NET CURRENT ASSETS			4560
NET ASSETS EMPLOYED			12400
FINANCED BY:			
SHARE CAPITAL			
Ordinary shares			5300
Preference shares			2100
			7400
RESERVES			2500
			9900
LOAN CAPITAL			
Debentures			2500
			12400

The way in which the balance sheet in Table 6.5 is presented is called the *T form*. It is still in use but most large businesses now use the *columnar form*, as shown in Table 6.6. This has the major advantage of distinguishing clearly between the sources and use of funds and it is generally accepted as an easier form to interpret.

The balance sheet shows the position of a business at a given moment but it does not tell us how the business reached that position, the level of its sales and how the profit made had been divided between the various parties with a claim to it. For this information we need two other financial statements: the *profit and loss account* and the *funds flow statement*.

The profit and loss account

The profit and loss account is a statement of the amount of profit or loss a business has made in a period of time. For convenience and ease of interpretation the information is contained in three sections.

1   *The trading account* This includes the revenue from sales and the costs associated with producing those sales.

   ☐   Revenue – Cost of sales = Gross profit

2   *The profit and loss account* Payments such as interest and directors' fees are deducted from the gross profit to give *net profit before tax*. Tax is then deducted to give *net profit after tax*.

Table 6.7 A profit and loss account
Profit and loss account for year ending 30 June 1987

	£000	£000	£000
SALES			10795
Cost of sales			8650
GROSS PROFIT			2145
Less OVERHEADS			
Administration			
Wages and salaries	235		
Stationery	95		
Heat and light	50		
Rates, rent, insurance	75		
Depreciation	10	375	
Finance:			
Interest	100		
Bad debts	95	195	
Selling:			
Salaries	100		
Distribution	50		
Advertising	150	300	870
Net profit			1275
Corporation tax			383
Net profit after tax			892
Ordinary share dividend			400
Reserves			492

3   *The appropriation account*   To appropriate means to set aside for a purpose or to make something the private property of an individual or an organisation. The appropriation account tells interested parties how the business has used the net profit after tax. A company's appropriation account would include the amount distributed to shareholders, the amount transferred to general reserve and the retained profit.

The presentation of a profit and loss account is shown in Table 6.7.

Funds flow statement

A *funds flow statement* shows the sources and uses of funds employed by a business over a period of time.

If you look at the information given in a funds flow statement and compare it with the information given in the balance sheet you will see many apparent similarities in the information. The difference lies in the period of *time* summarised by each statement. The balance sheet gives the sources and use of funds from the *beginning* of the life of a business. The funds flow statement usually relates to a shorter period of time.

Funds flows are useful to analyse the effects of changes in working capital. Transactions that result in an increase in working capital are sources of funds. Those which lead to a decrease in working capital are funds flowing out of the firm, that is the use of funds. The funds flow analysis shows changes in working capital for a given period.

Value added statement

The *value added statement* indicates the difference between the cost of bought in goods and services and the sales revenue of the business. It is the value added to these things by the effort of the business.

SELF ASSESSMENT

1   Compare the net profit of Baines' Nursery after tax with the amount of money they invested in the business. Assuming banks are paying 10 per cent interest on deposit accounts should the Baines be pleased with the results of their first year's trading? Explain your answer.
2   Distinguish between the columnar and the T form of balance sheets.
3   Distinguish between the balance sheet and the profit and loss account.
4   Distinguish between the balance sheet and the funds flow statement.

The law and accounts

All businesses, no matter what their legal form, are ruled by law in the way they keep their accounts. The main responsibility of the sole trader is to satisfy the inland revenue and customs and excise (VAT) that the correct amount of tax is being paid. Company accounts are regulated by the Companies Acts. Over the years the amount of information they have been required to disclose has increased as the possibilities for malpractice have been discovered, and the idea that businesses are accountable to their workforce and the public as well as their shareholders has taken hold.

Accounting records

Companies are required to make sure that adequate records are kept to show and explain the transactions they have undertaken. They must also be able to:

❑   state, with reasonable accuracy, the financial position of the company.

❑   prepare a balance sheet and profit and loss account that will give a true and fair record of the company's financial position.

❑   keep a daily record of transactions.

❑   keep a record of the assets and liabilities of the company.

The Companies Act of 1985 also contains clauses that state who has a right to inspect these records and when. The penalty of failure to comply with these disclosure terms is imprisonment and/or a fine.

Timing of accounts

The timing of accounts is chosen by the business. If a business starts trading on 1 September 1990 it would make up the accounts of the first year of trading to 31 August 1991. Companies operate in the same way. To prevent companies choosing a date that is convenient to them – just before a big debt is due for repayment when there are plenty of funds available for example – any changes in the accounting period must be notified to the registrar of companies.

Publishing accounts

The accounts of sole traders and partnerships are private. Only the owners of the business and interested parties, such as tax inspectors, have a right to see them. Companies are required to lay before the annual general meeting of shareholders various documents, all of which must be filed with the registrar of companies within a given time:

❑   a balance sheet;

❑   a profit and loss account;

❑   notes (explanations) of the financial accounts;

❑   an auditor's report;

❑   the directors' report.

Disclosures

Companies must also disclose:

❑   the amount of money paid to directors (emoluments);

❑   shareholdings in companies other than subsidiaries;

❑   salaries and other payments to the highest paid employees, for example the managing director;

❑   financial information about subsidiaries.

The costs of complying with the law are high and likely to rise as measures are taken to standardise practice within the EC.

SELF ASSESSMENT

---

1 State one reason why each of the following groups would oppose a reduction in the level of disclosures required of a company:

a Shareholders.

b Trade unions.

2 Give two reasons why a company is subject to more legal constraints than a sole trader.

3 Why is the timing of accounts important?

4 The accounts of a company should give a true and fair view of the way in which it has conducted its business. How does the law try to ensure that this happens?

Interpreting company accounts

Valuation of assets

Strictly speaking the valuation of assets is part of the role of the accountant rather than a matter for interpretation. As we shall see, the way assets are valued can be of interest to potential investors and for that reason has been included in this section rather than in the description of accounts. The only sure way of knowing what an asset is worth to a business is by offering it for sale – hardly practical when it is still needed. We will limit ourselves to a brief outline of the ways assets can be valued, concentrating on the valuation of fixed assets, stock and the effect that changing money values can have on the valuation of assets.

Valuation of fixed assets

Fixed assets such as machinery and vehicles have a limited life span, although at times it can run into decades. Throughout its life an asset's value is falling. If this change in value is ignored the profit declared by a business can appear low compared with the amount of capital employed. It is usual, therefore, to write off some of the value of the machine each year. This appears as a charge on the profit and loss account *before* tax is paid. This charge is called *depreciation*.

By depreciating its fixed assets a business saves on tax and increases profit. However, depreciation itself is not a method of saving up for replacement machinery. That is a decision taken separately by the business when deciding how to use its profit. Depreciation reduces the book value of an asset, i.e. its value after depreciation has been charged. The book value does not reflect the market value of the asset and in itself depends on the method of depreciation used.

The two most common methods of depreciation are *straight line depreciation* and *declining balance depreciation*.

1 The *straight line method* of depreciating assets reduces the book value of the asset by the same amount for each year of its life. An asset which cost £12 000 with an expected life of ten years and a *residual value* (that is the amount the business expects to sell the machine for at the end of its working life) of £2000 would be depreciated by £1000 per year:

$$\frac{\text{Cost of asset } - \text{ Residual value}}{\text{Life of asset}}$$

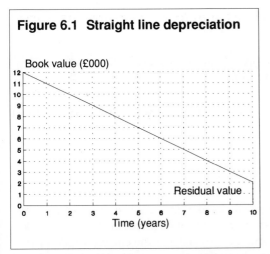

Figure 6.1 Straight line depreciation

Book value (£000)

Time (years)

Residual value

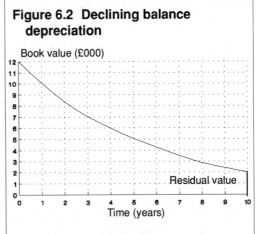

Figure 6.2 Declining balance depreciation

Book value (£000)

Time (years)

Residual value

Straight line depreciation is a simple and straightforward calculation. It gives a higher level of profit to the business in the first years of the life of the machine and is particularly useful when the business is expecting constant returns over the life of the asset. This is shown in Figure 6.1.

2   The *declining balance method* of depreciation reduces the book value of the asset by a fixed percentage calculated to apportion the value of the machine after residual value has been subtracted from initial cost over the expected life of the machine. This means that depreciation is highest in the early years of the life of the machine. The use of the declining balance method takes into account that as the machine grows older its running and maintenance costs are likely to increase and its earning power will decrease. As a machine gets older it is more susceptible to obsolescence and may be more difficult to sell. Figure 6.2 shows declining balance depreciation using the data from Figure 6.1.

Valuation of stock

All businesses hold supplies of raw materials, components and goods which they need to carry out their production processes. Some types of business will also hold stocks of semi-finished and finished goods. The quantity of the stock held by a business will depend on the type of business, its size, the amount of capital it has available and the supply of stock. We will look at the importance of stock levels in more detail in Chapter 11 ('Production control'). In this chapter we are concerned only with the way in which a business allocates value to existing stock for accounting purposes.

In January 1986 a building contractor was offered a quantity of timber sufficient to supply his normal requirements for twelve months. He decided to take advantage of this bargain. In June 1986 he was preparing an estimate for the renovation of a house, his building insurance was due to be renewed and he was hoping to float a bank loan to extend the business. He was faced with the problem of placing a value on the remaining stock of timber for each of these reasons. Should he value the timber at the price paid for it, that is its historic cost, or the cost of replacing it, which was 20 per cent greater?

There are three basic methods the builder might use to solve this problem.

1   *Valuation using a weighted average*   This is the simplest method and can be used successfully when the cost of buying stock does not vary greatly over time. Look at the following example:

Value of stock bought on 1 January £2000 (200 × £10)

Value of stock bought on 1 February £3000 (200 × £15)

Value of stock bought on 1 March £1800 (150 × £12)

The total quantity of stock held on 1 March is 550 at a historic cost of £6800. The value of each unit of stock held can therefore be calculated as:

$$\frac{£6800}{550}$$

$$= £12.36$$

2   *Last in first out (LIFO)*   Using this method all stocks of a similar nature are valued at the last price paid for those stocks. This is a useful method when prices are rising as it takes into account the fact that the stocks used must be replaced at the current market price. Failure to do this might give an artificially high profit in the accounts of the business and result in the payment of too much tax.

3   *First in first out (FIFO)*   FIFO values all stock at the purchase price of the oldest unit used. In the example given above all stock would be valued at £10 per unit until the supplies bought on 1 January were used up, then at £15 per unit until the stocks bought on 1 February were exhausted, and so on.

SELF ASSESSMENT

1   Give two factors which will help fix the level of stock held by a business.

2   Distinguish between LIFO and FIFO as methods of stock valuation.

3   An asset cost £20 000. Its residual value is expected to be £2000 and its life span six years. The business concerned uses the straight line method of depreciation. By how much will it reduce the book value of the machine each year?

4   A business buys stock to the value of £4000 on 1 August, £6000 on 12 August and £10 000 on 15 August. It buys no more stock for the rest of the month. The stock is valued as follows:

    500 items at £20
    300 items at £10
    200 items at £35

What is the average value of the stock held?

5   The price of raw materials is rising rapidly. Under these circumstances which method of stock valuation would you advise a business to use?

The life of an asset

So far we have referred to the 'life' of a machine as if this was a fixed period of time. The life span of a machine can vary according to the situation in which the business finds itself. Museums contain many examples of working machines that are obviously still in existence but whose usefulness is over.

□   *The market life*   A machine is useful only as long as the product it makes sells. As soon as that product becomes obsolete, either through technical advance or because tastes have changed, the machine loses its usefulness, even if it is still in perfect condition.

□   *The technical life* This will depend upon speed of innovation; in other words, how quickly a new model will appear that will make the machine obsolete. The importance of this life will depend upon the degree of innovation. A new model which cuts costs by half will have a greater impact on the business than one which cuts costs by 5 per cent. In the first case it may mean replacing the machine at once to maintain competitiveness in the market. In the second case it may be possible to keep the machine in operation until one of its other 'lives' comes to an end.

The two lives given above are beyond the control of the business. To be safe a business will calculate the *economic* life of the machine on the basis of the shortest of these lives.

The span of time chosen to depreciate a machine can be seen as another life. It should be remembered that as depreciation has an effect on profits, the period of time over which an asset is depreciated is often chosen to minimise tax liability.

Ratio analysis

Managers, shareholders, investors and potential investors want information on the performance of a business so that they can make decisions in their own interest and to further the objectives of the business. The information a group is most interested in varies slightly but, in general, we can say that they are all concerned with liquidity, return on investment and the ratio of equity capital to borrowed funds. *Ratio analysis* is used to isolate the required information.

Ratio analysis compares one piece of accounting information with another. Ratios, once calcuated, must be *compared* with other ratios if they are to be of value in the process of decision making and control. It is usual to compare a given ratio with:

□   the same ratio of the business, measuring performance in previous years.

□   the same ratio of other businesses for both the current time period and over a period of time.

□   an accepted standard based on the cumulative experience of business. We shall see that the accepted standard for the liquidity ratio is 2:1. Too great a degree of variation from that standard might give cause for concern.

Ratios can be presented in the conventional form, e.g. 3:1, as a percentage or as a fraction. The form chosen will depend on convenience and clarity of interpretation.

Liquidity ratios
A business must be able to pay its debts if it is to survive. It therefore needs to hold cash. On the other hand, if it holds too great a proportion of its assets in cash it may be sacrificing opportunities for greater profit. There are two ways of measuring the liquidity position of a business.

1   The current ratio
     Current assets : Current liabilities

2   The acid test ratio
     Liquid assets : Current liabilities

The current ratio includes all current assets and all liabilities which will have to be paid in the current accounting period. It is often suggested that an ideal current ratio is 2:1; the higher proportion of assets being necessary because some assets, e.g. stock, are less liquid than others. In an emergency, therefore, the business cannot be certain that they would be able to dispose of these assets at their book value. A business which carries little stock might be satisfied with a current ratio of 1.5:1 or even lower.

The acid test ratio is an attempt to judge whether a business will be able to meet all its short-term liabilities without the sale or run-down of its stocks. It takes only the liquid assets (debtors and cash) and compares them with current liabilities. An acceptable ratio is 1:1. In this case the business has sufficient liquid assets to cover its immediate liabilities but is not sacrificing additional income.

The analysis of the liquidity position of a business is useful to managers in the management of cash and working capital. We will look at this more closely in Chapter 7 ('Finance').

Investment ratios

Ratios which measure the profitability of a business are of interest to investors and managers. In general investment ratios can be described as providing information on the profitability and growth of a company. The different ratios give different insights into the performance of a business.

1   *Return on equity ratio*   Equity is a term used to describe the capital contributed by ordinary shareholders. Each ordinary share carries the same investment and the same rights and responsibilities. Each share is equal to all others. The return on equity ratio is usually expressed as a percentage. This gives a single figure which is more easily compared with other information; e.g. if you had a sum of money which you intended to invest in ordinary shares you might compare the return on equity ratio of several companies before you made your investment decision.

$$\frac{\text{Net profit after tax}}{\text{Shareholders' funds}}$$

2   *Dividend yield ratio*   If you refer back to the profit and loss account you will see that net profit after tax is not necessarily distributed to the shareholders. The directors of a company may decide to retain profits to finance further growth. This policy will appeal to investors who want their investment to grow in value over time, but will be less attractive to those whose primary objective is a high income.

$$\frac{\text{Dividend per share}}{\text{Share price}}$$

3   *Price earnings ratio (p/e ratio)*   A practical method of estimating the degree of risk involved in a particular investment is to calculate the length of time over which earnings from the investment accumulate sufficiently to cover the initial cost of the investment. You should compare this with the payback method of assessing physical investment decisions in Chapter 7 ('Finance').

$$\frac{\text{Market price of share}}{\text{Earnings per share}}$$

Place yourself in the position of a person considering buying shares in a company when the current market price is £8 and the expected annual earnings per share are £2. It will take you four years to recover your initial investment. Before making the final decision you should ask yourself a number of questions.

[handwritten: OTHER THINGS YOU WOULD EVALUATE.]

a Will the company survive that long? An examination of its liquidity ratios may make you more confident. *[handwritten: eg refer to Ansoff growth strategy - have they a strategy for growth. Level of competition - is the market becoming saturated, the banks, are so entry *refer to Porter]*

b You should also look at the product. Will people tire of it in the next four years or is this only the first stage of its life? After all, the product might sweep the market before it and establish itself in a dominant position.

c You should look at the economy in general. If the product is a luxury and a rise in unemployment is expected you may be less than happy about its prospects in future. *[handwritten: Is it a luxury product or are we coming into a recession.]*

d How else could you use your money? There may be other investments that will pay you back in a shorter period of time. The risk may appear greater but the payback time is less.

e How important is the existing management team to the company's success? Are they likely to stay with the company for the next four years?

Potentially the list of questions is endless. It can include querying future labour relations, the likelihood of new technology emerging, a change in existing laws and so on. The ultimate question for the investor is: How long will this state of affairs continue and will I get my money back before it changes?

4 *Gearing ratio* When you look at the balance sheet of a business you can see that the assets purchased are financed partly by the money the owners have put into the business and partly by borrowed funds in a variety of forms. The relationship between equity capital and borrowed funds is expressed by the gearing ratio:

$$\frac{\text{Long-term borrowing}}{\text{Net assets employed}}$$

Borrowed money has to be paid for in terms of a fixed rate of interest. When the profits of the business are rising this can be seen in terms of a fixed cost that becomes relatively smaller compared with the volume of business generated. In these circumstances borrowed funds are an advantage to the business. When revenue falls the fixed cost of interest payments can be a problem. It can, for example, affect the liquidity position of a business.

There are many more ratios that can be applied to both the accounts and the statistics of a business to help in decision making and control. They will be introduced where they are appropriate in other chapters. Ratios should not be seen as the solution to all problems. Like any form of analysis their value is affected by the quality of the data used and the expertise of the people using it. Some of the problems associated with ratio analysis have already been mentioned in this chapter. We shall now summarise them.

Criticisms of ratio analysis

1   Ratio analysis is an attempt to use information relating to an existing situation to predict the future. The accuracy with which this can be done will depend upon the accuracy of the figures used.

2   Ratio analysis is just one of a number of techniques designed to help in the control of a business and in decision making. The results of ratio analysis must be judged in the context of other information. A business might have an excellent financial history but if the product it makes is about to be made obsolete it would be inadvisable to invest.

3   Ratios used by interested parties external to the business, for example trade unions and potential shareholders, are based on published accounts. These reflect the state of the business at the time they are drawn up and are not necessarily a good guide to that business. In the period before the accounts were published a business might have had an unusually high proportion of liquid assets. This may have been because it was expecting a need for them. It might also have been a deliberate move on the part of management to make the accounts more acceptable to shareholders!

4   When ratios are used to compare the performance of one business with another it must be remembered that they are seldom completely comparable. Businesses have different ways of recording information and differing ways of valuing their assets. This diversity of approach is not always obvious in the accounts but it may invalidate the conclusions drawn from an inter-firm comparison. On the other hand ratios can provide a general comparison between businesses of a similar size, operating in the same market and using similar production processes.

SELF ASSESSMENT

1   A business has issued £1m worth of £1 shares whose market value is now £3. It has also borrowed £400 000. The last dividend declared was 49p per share. Calculate the relevant ratios.

2   Distinguish between the current ratio and the acid test ratio. State one disadvantage to a business of holding too high a level of liquid assets.

3   What value is the dividend yield ratio to a potential investor?

4   Give two criticisms of ratio analysis.

Budgetary control

A budget can be defined as a statement of the financial position of a person, business or other organisation for a future period of time based on estimates of expenditure and proposals for financing them. Budgeting is a process most people are familiar with, if only at the simplest level. A household will plan its expenditure in advance on the basis of expected income. The time period over which a family prepares budgets will often depend on the frequency with which the major wage-earner in the family is paid, usually weekly or monthly. In addition, households will include some longer term planning in these short-term budgets. Provision will be made for bills that have to be paid on a quarterly or yearly basis. Unforeseen circumstances may mean that the budget has to be revised if the family is to achieve its objectives. Budgeting in business has the same characteristics as domestic budgeting:

1 *Planning* The objectives must be set. This is the responsibility of the owner of the business (the board of directors in a company) who will state expected profit levels and proposed expansion to be financed by profit.

2 *Information* In order to forecast expenditure and estimate the amount of money required to fund it a business will need detailed information on production capacity, cost of materials, labour available, degree of any retraining required, the availability and cost of capital and expected sales. In a large business the provision of this information will be the responsibility of the marketing, production, finance and personnel departments in the form of departmental budgets. In a small business it may be the responsibility of the owner.

3 *Co-ordination* In a small business the process of co-ordination is inseparable from the activity of collecting information. The fewer the people involved in the budgetary process the more likely it is that the people concerned have an understanding of the interaction between the different variables. In larger businesses the co-ordination of departmental needs may be the responsibility of the finance department or possibly a committee of departmental heads, depending on the way the business is organised.

4 *Review* Once the co-ordination process is finished the summary is presented to the policy makers. This summary of departmental budgets is known as the *master budget*. The policy makers can then judge the extent to which their original objectives are feasible. They may need to adjust their objectives as a result of the budgeting exercise.

5 *Control* As the budget is put into operation the managers are able to measure their actual performance against projected performance. The techniques used to analyse the difference between the two are contained in *variance analysis*. The information they obtain as a result of this exercise will help in the preparation of future budgets.

In most businesses managers drawing up a budget work on the basis of past information, allocating resources to projects according to their apparent need. This can lead to a waste of resources if the managers are not objective about projects. Some businesses have introduced *zero-base budgeting* in an attempt to overcome this problem. Under this system departmental managers have to justify spending any money, rather than only having to justify an increase in expenditure which is more usual with traditional budgeting. Managers are encouraged to collect detailed information which reinforces the control function of the budgetary process. The business is also in a better position to decide which projects will make the greatest contribution to achieving its aims. The disadvantage, of course, is the additional resources that have to be employed in gathering the information.

A budget period

A budget is drawn up in a period of time before it is to be put into practice. Most businesses use the financial year as a budgetary period. The annual budget is then broken down into quarterly or monthly budgets depending on the needs of the business. In a fast-changing market budgets will be reviewed more frequently. Rather than draw up budgets, with all the work involved, too frequently, a business might draw up several budgets at once, each one based on a different set of expectations about the behaviour of the market and/or output. Once it becomes apparent which budget approximates most closely to reality, that budget can be adopted. This is known as *flexible budgeting*.

Variance analysis

Look at the following example:

> A business has a production budget for 50 000 items over a given period of time. Its actual production is 40 000 items, a variance of 10 000 items or 20 per cent. Should the production manager be concerned about this variance?

The probable answer is 'yes'. A variance of 20 per cent is something to be concerned about. A larger business with the same absolute variance of 10 000 might only have a relative variance of 1 per cent.

Although analysing the variances appears simple the reality will be more complex. It is even more difficult to isolate the factors that caused the variance. In effect the production manager will have to analyse a number of subordinate variances within the production department relating to stocks, personnel, finance, organisation and available machinery. Table 6.8 is an example of a firm's budget, showing actual results and the variation from expected results.

Table 6.8: Budget of Hilife Homemakers Ltd

	Product A		Product B		Product C		Total	Total
	Budget	Actual	Budget	Actual	Budget	Actual	Budget	Actual
Sales (units 00s)	200	175	230	250	150	145	580	570
Sales income (£000s)	1000	875	690	750	1200	1160	2890	2785
Cost of sales (£000s):								
Direct labour	20	15	12	14	22	22	54	51
Direct materials	600	500	450	500	650	650	1700	1650
Overheads	2	1.5	2	2	1	1	5	4.5
Gross profit (£000s)	378	358.5	226	234	527	487	1131	1079.5
Gross profit %	37.8	41	32.8	31.2	44	42		
Selling expenses							50	52
Administrative expenses							10	11
Net income (£000s)							1071	1016.5

Cash flow budgets

The cash flow budget is used here as an example of a departmental budget which contributes to the master budget. It is important for a business to identify the timing of inflows and outflows of cash if it is to meet its payments. Table 6.9 shows a typical cash flow budget.

Table 6.9 Example of a cash flow budget (£000s)

	June	July	Aug.	Sept.	Oct.	Nov.
Cash at the beginning of the month	50	60	75	95	130	145
Add: Receipts from sales	150	160	170	150	100	50
A Total cash	200	220	245	245	230	195
Subtract:						
Wages	70	70	70	50	30	20
Materials	40	45	50	35	20	15
Expenses	30	30	30	30	35	35
B Total outflow	140	145	150	115	85	70
Cash at end of month	60	75	95	130	145	130

The role of the budgetary system

Some of the advantages of the budgetary system are shown below:

- a budget based on full and accurate information can act as a check on senior management and prevent the setting of unrealistic objectives.

- managers who have been actively involved in the budgetary process are more likely to be motivated towards the success of the business.

- by comparing expected results with achieved results managers can discover the weak areas in the business, including their own budgeting procedures, and take steps to strengthen them.

- when all departments are involved in the budgetary process they are more likely to become aware of the problems and constraints faced by other departments. Activity is more likely to be co-ordinated in this situation than if managers had budgets imposed upon them from above.

SELF ASSESSMENT

1 In what way is the budgetary procedure for a small business likely to differ from that of a large business?
2 Give two market situations in which flexible budgeting might be necessary.
3 Under what circumstances would zero-base budgeting be a worthwhile operation?
4 State one reason why a business should always prepare a cash flow budget.
5 Give two ways in which a budget helps a business achieve its objectives.

Costs and costing

Costs are incurred by all the activities a business undertakes. Every decision, no matter how small, involves a corresponding cost. The importance which should be attached to cost in any business enterprise cannot be surprising when it is remembered that:

Profit = Revenue – Costs

Some basic cost definitions are given in this section.

Fixed costs

Fixed costs are those costs which, over a given period of time, tend to be unaffected by changes in output. For example, a factory capable of producing 100 000 engineering parts in a certain period of time might have fixed costs in terms of rent, heating, lighting and the cost of machinery of £100 000 in that time. If the factory only produces 80 000 units it will still have to meet the costs associated with 100 000 units.

The total number of goods and services a business is capable of producing is known as its *capacity*. You should realise that businesses offering services will also have a limit to the total amount they can provide for their customers. A hairdressing salon has a given number of seats, sinks, dryers and stylists. A restaurant is limited in the number of meals it can supply by its kitchen capacity, by seating accommodation, the number of staff, and on the number of meals they can serve. The TV engineer is limited by level of skill and the time spent on the number of repairs possible in one day.

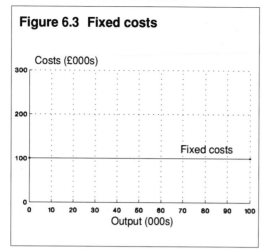

Figure 6.3 Fixed costs

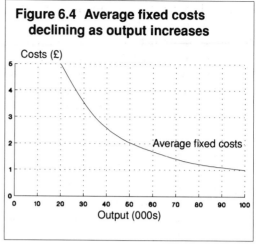

Figure 6.4 Average fixed costs declining as output increases

When a business produces less than the amount of which it is capable we say it is *operating at less than full capacity*. This is usually expressed as a percentage of full capacity:

$$\frac{\text{Number of units produced} \times 100}{\text{Capacity of business}}$$

In the example given above this would be:

$$\frac{80\,000 \times 100}{100\,000}$$

= 80 per cent

Figure 6.3 shows the position of a business with a capacity of 100 000 at a fixed cost of £100 000 in a given period of time.

Average fixed cost is the proportion of total fixed costs carried by each item produced and is calculated by dividing total fixed cost by output. When the business described above is producing at full capacity then the average fixed cost will be £1. When it is operating at 80 per cent capacity the average fixed cost will be £1.20.

Try the same calculation for different levels of output for the above business. You should find that the lower the level of output the higher the average fixed cost. This fact has a significance for businesses when setting prices and deciding whether or not to accept a particular order. Figure 6.4 shows average fixed costs decreasing as output increases.

Variable costs

An increase in output will tend to lead to an increase in the amount of raw materials being used, an increase in the power consumed and an increase in certain types of labour. These costs are known as *variable costs* because they vary with output.

The simplest example of variable costs assumes that the cost of raw materials, labour and power will be the same for each unit produced regardless of the level of output. This simplifying assumption is made to illustrate the concept of variable costs. A business might find that raw material costs decline as output increases because suppliers are willing to reduce the price of orders above a certain size (a *bulk discount*).

Variable costs of £2 per unit produced (the *average variable cost*) would result in *total variable costs* of £20 000 at an output of 10 000 units, £40 000 at an output of 20 000 units and so on until the maxium capacity of the plant was reached. This would give a straight line graph as illustrated in Figure 6.5.

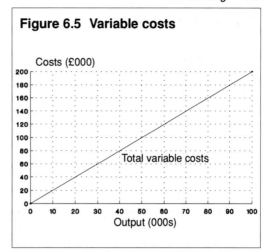

Figure 6.5 Variable costs

Semi-variable costs

The rent of a hired car is a fixed cost, the petrol to keep it running is a variable cost. This marriage of fixed and variable costs is common in business.

Direct cost

Direct cost is a cost that can be clearly allocated to a particular product. The labour and materials will be referred to individually as *direct labour* and *direct materials*.

Indirect costs

Indirect materials will cover stores that are used for all departments, for example lubricants for machines. *Indirect labour* will include the cost of supervision and maintenance among other things.

Overheads

A business performs a number of other functions in addition to production, for example marketing, personnel, research and development and finance. Costs which are clearly attributable to one of these functions are termed *overheads*. They include labour, materials and expenses.

Marginal costs

In economic theory *marginal cost* is defined as the cost of producing one extra unit of output. It is calculated by subtracting the total cost (total fixed costs + total variable costs) of the first level of output from the total costs of the second level of output.

Accountants use the same basic definition of marginal cost but use only direct costs in its calculation. They may be interested in variations in output as low as one, for example in the production of a piece of equipment to order, but will also apply the definition to larger variations in output. We shall explore this idea further when we examine marginal costing later in this chapter.

Imputed costs

This is the cost of using something the business already owns. It can be seen as a method of giving a monetary value to the opportunity cost of using a resource.

Classification of costs

The classification of a cost varies according to the use of the resource and the purposes of the classification. Labour, for example, can be classified in a variety of ways.

- ☐ Labour employed in the production of a good or service is a *direct cost*.

- ☐ Labour employed in selling a product is an *overhead*, unless of course that labour is employed in retailing, when it may be classified as a direct cost.

- ☐ Labour which can be laid off when output falls can be classified as a *variable cost*. A production line worker might be classified as both direct labour and as part of variable costs.

- ☐ When agreements between management and unions make it impossible to lay off labour then labour costs must be regarded as fixed for the period of time covered by the agreement. This situation might also arise if management has a policy of continuous employment.

SELF ASSESSMENT

1 Distinguish between fixed costs and variable costs.
2 Given that a business can produce 150 000 items in a month, its fixed costs per month are £10 000, the average variable cost is £5 per unit and it is operating at full capacity, what is the cost per unit? Calculate the total production costs.
3 The owner of a business described in **2** wishes to make a profit equivalent to 25 per cent of production costs. At what price should the output be sold?
4 Sketch a variable cost curve to show what happens when unit variable costs decline as output increases.
5 State one problem a business might experience in deciding on imputed cost.

The break-even point

What is the lowest possible output at which a business can operate without losing money? The answer is called the *break-even point*. At this level the costs of production are exactly the same as the revenue received from sales, assuming the whole output is sold. The break-even point is illustrated graphically in Figure 6.6.

1 Fixed costs stay the same irrespective of output.

2 Total costs = total fixed costs + total variable costs. As we saw in Figure 6.5, the total variable cost curve passes through the origin. By introducing fixed costs we have added a constant to the equation which defines the curve. The total cost curve always cuts the vertical axis at the level of fixed costs.

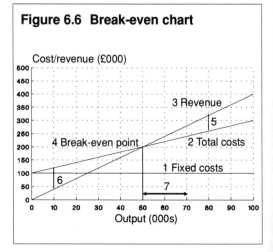

Figure 6.6   Break-even chart

3 The revenue line is found by multiplying the selling price of each unit by the level of output. In this instance the selling price is £4.

4 The point at which the revenue curve and the cost curve intersect is the break-even point.

5 To the right of the break-even point revenue is greater than total cost. The vertical difference between the two curves at any given point will give the total profit.

6 To the left of the break-even point a similar calculation to that described in **5** will give the total losses of the business at any given level of output.

7 If the business is operating at 70 per cent capacity it will still make a profit. The difference between the output at which a business is operating and the break-even output is known as the *margin of error*.

Criticisms of break-even analysis

Break-even analysis is a relatively simple and cheap technique which shows the relationship between fixed costs, variable costs and revenue. It can highlight problem areas that management can then examine in more detail. However the advantages of break-even analysis will be lost if its limitations are not recognised.

1 A break-even analysis is only as good as the information on which it is based. You should remember that the gathering and storing of information generates costs. The greater the degree of accuracy required the more it will cost to gather the information. Too much money spent on accumulating information will reduce the advantages of speed and cheapness associated with the technique.

2 The information on which the break-even analysis is based may have been accumulated for other purposes. Assumptions may have been made when classifying costs that were valid for that purpose but which invalidate the break-even analysis. Direct labour may, for example, be classified as a fixed cost for periods of up to a month. This information may have been used in the drawing up of projected profit and loss accounts to aid in management decision making. Used uncritically for a break-even analysis covering three months it will present a distorted picture. This is a very simple example but it is important to remember that information should not be accepted at face value. Unrecognised assumptions may be built in to its collection and processing.

3 Both simple and complex models are *forecasting* models. A sudden increase in the market price of a commodity, a management–union agreement on pay or the unilateral decision of an international producers' cartel will make the analysis out of date.

4 Break-even analysis assumes all production will be sold. In some ways this is a reasonable assumption if the business is confident in the results of its market research. Break-even analysis translates production into immediate profits. A business might be producing in expectation of future demand, perhaps building up stock in anticipation of the Christmas buying boom. Some of the profits shown by break-even analysis may not be realised in the period covered by it because part of the output will be stored as finished goods.

SELF ASSESSMENT

1 Reading from the information given in Figure 6.6, state whether or not the business will be making a profit or loss at each of the following levels of capacity: 20 000, 35 000, 55 000, 70 000, 90 000.
2 What is the margin of error when output is 80 000 units?
3 State two disadvantages of break-even analysis.

Costing

A business produces 15 000 units per year. The total costs of running the factory, advertising and selling the goods are calculated at £90 000. The cost per unit is therefore £6.

This is the simplest form of costing. Unfortunately it does not help with many of the problems which confront a business and in which cost information is essential if the final decision is to help in achieving the objectives of the business.

Costing and decision making

The following are some examples of decisions in which an analysis of costs is essential.

1 *Make or buy?*   A business uses a large quantity of a certain component in assembling its product. The component is not difficult to make and it is suggested that it would be both more convenient and cheaper if the business was to make it itself. Can it be produced more cheaply than the market price?

2 *Entering a market*   All businesses have a level of profit which they consider acceptable. On entering a new market with a given market price a business will need an accurate assessment of costs to estimate whether or not it will be able to achieve this profit level. We saw a practical example of this in the case of the Baines Nursery in Chapter 4.

3 *Cease or continue production?*   Although a business may be losing money on a product it may be profitable for it to continue to manufacture while the costs of production are fixed. In economic terms this would be known as the *short run,* defined more precisely as the period of time in which at least one factor of production was fixed in supply. A business can continue to produce in the short run provided it can sell enough to cover its variable costs.

4 *Accept or reject an order*   A business may be offered a contract at a price that does not cover the full cost of producing the goods. If the business is operating at less than full capacity it may still be advantageous for it to accept the order.

Each of the situations outlined above will require a different cost analysis and a different method of costing. We will examine costing methods in the next section.

Methods of costing

Costing would be a relatively simple operation if:

☐   all costs could be clearly allocated to one product or area of production. This is known as a cost centre. If you look again at the definitions of costs you will see that overheads and indirect costs may be used by several cost centres. The marketing department may be responsible for several products. How much time does any one person in that department spend on any one product? It may vary with the time of year, or if a product is having unusual problems, and it may also vary according to the role of the person. A product may be of minimal importance to the departmental manager but require a great deal of time from a clerical assistant.

☐ all decisions were of the same type. All make and buy decisions require the same type of costing definitions and the records to be kept could be standardised.

☐ the situation did not change. Unless a business has a very dominant position in the market it will have to take note of its competitors' pricing and promotion policies. Government decisions will also change the environment in which the business operates by increasing taxation or reducing its spending. We can also mention trade unions, changes in consumer buying behaviour, changes in social attitudes and decisions by foreign governments as some of the variables that might cause a business to analyse its costs.

In practice the complexity of the situations faced by a business enterprise and the wide variety of decisions management is called upon to make have led to the development of a number of costing techniques each of which isolates the relevant information required by a decision and/or control problem. In this chapter we will examine just three of these costing methods.

Absorption costing

Absorption costing absorbs the fixed costs and overheads into the production of a good. In a single product business, absorption costing would produce the same result as the total cost approach. In many businesses the same machine can be used for a number of jobs.

> A tea packaging plant makes teabags and boxes them for a number of different brands all produced by the same company. There is no difference in the size of the teabag or box used and the same machinery copes with all brands. (It would be useful if you remembered this when we outline the advantages of standardisation – making every one of a type identical – in Chapter 10, 'Background to production'.) The blends of tea used differ, the number of perforations in the teabag differ between blends and the design of the packaging is distinctive according to the market at which it is aimed. How should the costs of acquiring and running the machines be allocated to each brand?

The costs can be allocated according to the length of time the machinery is used for a particular tea. Thus if the total cost for the running of the machinery over a period of time is £20 000, Brand A might have used the machines for 40 per cent of the time and will be allocated costs of £8000; Brand B is allocated £5000; and Brand C £7000.

Absorption costing is useful in giving a general cost of production, in the valuation of stocks of finished and semi-finished goods and in the allocation of fixed costs between goods when there are reliable production statistics for guidance. It is less useful in the allocation of overheads. When overheads involve services to a product they are difficult to cost subjectively and expensive to cost objectively. The exercise on time management at the end of this chapter should bring this fact home to you, if you have the patience to complete it before the cost in time becomes too great!

Marginal costing

This method is useful if a business has to make decisions on whether or not to accept an order, or whether or not to continue in business. Marginal costing accepts that, in the short run, certain costs are fixed and must be paid by the business whether or not it continues in operation or is operating at full or less than full capacity.

In the definition of marginal cost a distinction was made between an economist's and an accountant's definition. We will use the accountant's definition in the discussion of marginal costing, i.e. *direct costs of production subtracted from revenue*. This ignores fixed costs. They have to be paid so any *contribution* towards them minimises the losses of the business in the short run.

> A loss-making shop has six months to run on its lease, the cost of which is £5000 per year. The owner of the shop regrets renewing the lease, business had already begun to decline at that point, and wishes to discontinue trading. The accountant is less positive, and suggests a closer look at the trading figures. The owner of the shop is legally liable for £2500. To continue trading would incur the cost of bought in stock, heating, lighting, staff and other expenses to a total of £31 000, but would also generate revenue of £33 000.

So the owner of the shop would be *worse* off by stopping trading than by continuing. Stopping trading with six months to run on the lease will produce a debt of £2500. Continuing trading would reduce that debt to £500 – assuming, of course, that living expenses have been taken into account!

> Arkwrights mass produces pressed steel gates. The cost of a single gate to fit a three foot opening is £30, of which £10 can be classified as indirect cost. A leading mail order company approaches Arkwrights and asks them to supply 500 gates at £28 per gate. Arkwrights' first inclination is to refuse. They then look at the order more closely. Their busiest time is in the summer when they operate at 100 per cent capacity. This order is for the period September to December when they operate, on average, at 200 under capacity. The mail order company will be including the product in their spring/summer catalogue which is sent out to agents in February. Arkwrights do some rapid calculations.
>
> □   Indirect costs are £10 per gate.
>
> □   Direct costs are £20.
>
> □   It would receive £28 in revenue.
>
> □   £20 would cover the direct costs of production and it would have £8 to *contribute* to a lowering of their indirect costs.

Arkwrights accepted the order.

Standard costing

Standard costs are decided in advance of production. In this it is similar to budgeting but, unlike budgeting, it is limited to the detailed costs of the production process and takes no account of the overall objectives of the business.

Records of historic costs are, of course, an important element in deciding standard costs. It is also possible to introduce a target into the system. Given the machinery available and its capabilities, and given the type and quantity of the workforce, then senior management may decide what is possible and judge performance against this standard. If the targets set are realistic then they can act as motivators to better performance, as well as giving managers a clear indication of the inefficient areas of their operation. The following example will help clarify the method:

> A department has been given a standard cost for labour of £3.00 per hour. At the end of the accounting period it is discovered that the actual cost of labour was £4.25, an increase of over 40 per cent. Part of this increase could be the result of a negotiated pay rise. On the other hand it could be the result of inefficiencies in other parts of the organisation that resulted in an unacceptable level of overtime being worked.

The difference between the standard cost and the actual cost is known as the variance. The variance for labour, from the example given above, can be calculated as follows:

> (standard quantity x actual cost) / (quantity x standard cost).

SELF ASSESSMENT

1 The sales of a business are falling but it can still cover direct costs. At what point should it cease trading?
2 Define a cost centre as the term is used in this chapter.
3 Give two problems associated with allocating costs to a product.
4 Distinguish between absorption costing and standard costing.
5 State one advantage and one disadvantage of each of the costing methods described in the text.

Conclusion

In this chapter it has been possible to give only an outline of the accounting techniques used in business. It is important to remember that these techniques *summarise* the activities of a business. Giving a monetary value to the opportunity cost inherent in decision making provides information which is open to analysis, the results of which can be used in decision making and control.

Unfortunately the use of money or numerical values can lead to a false sense of security. Figures are often based on human judgment, a fact we shall explore in more detail in Chapter 15 ('Decision making in business organisations'). As a conclusion to both Chapters 5 and 6 you are advised to bear in mind that numerical information is only as good as the care that has gone into compiling it; that compiling information will depend on decisions about what is and is not important; and that compiling information *costs* money!

REVIEW

1 Read each of the following statements and decide whether they are true or false. Give a brief explanation of your answer.

   a A change in the assets of a business must be accompanied by a corresponding change in its liabilities.

   b The acid test ratio of a business must be 1:1.

   c If a company has made a profit over an accounting period its reserves will be increased by that amount.

   d The business accounts of a sole trader are treated as separate from the private accounts in order to facilitate an accurate assessment of the profitability of the business.

   e The purpose of depreciation is to allow businesses to accumulate funds for replacement investment.

   f Fixed costs never change.

   g A business should accept an order only if the price offered will cover all the production costs.

   h If the time period is short enough, all costs may be regarded as fixed.

2 A machine costs £30 000 and has a useful life of five years. At the end of that time it will have a residual value of £5000. The business decides to use the declining balance method of depreciation. The figures are as follows:

   a What is meant by the terms:

      i residual value?

      ii depreciation?

      iii net book value?

Year	Depreciation provision(£s)	Net book value(£s)
1	9035	20965
2	6314	14651
3	4412	10239
4	3084	7155
5	2155	5000

   b From the data given and using the same axes draw graphs to show the effect on the book value of using:

      i the straight line method of depreciation.

      ii the declining balance method.

   c Give one reason why the business might have decided to use the declining balance method of depreciation.

   d State and explain three factors which influence the life of an asset.

3 A company is considering purchasing an existing retail outlet valued at £300 000. The table below gives the estimated increase in income generated by this investment after allowances for expenses.

   a Calculate the average earnings per share, assuming the shares cost £1:

      i if 80 per cent of the funding is raised by 10 per cent debenture stock and the rest as equity.

      ii if 30 per cent is raised by 10 per cent debentures and the rest as equity.

Year	Income (£000s)
1	25
2	50
3	85
4	100
5	150
6	165
7	200
8	225

   b On a graph show the results of your calculations to **a**.

   c Give one reason why this information would be useful to a prospective investor.

   d As a prospective investor give three additional items of information you would require before making a decision.

   e What is the gearing ratio?

   f Give two advantages and two disadvantages of a high gearing ratio to a business.

4 The information given below is a summary of the transactions of a small business during its first year of trading.

	£		£
Cash received		Cash paid	
Proprietor's funds	15000	For stock	25000
Loan from bank	5000	For rent of premises	3000
Sales revenue	40000	For fixtures & fittings	15000
		For rates	1500
		For administration	500
		Owner's drawings	5000
		Heating & lighting	1000

The following information is also available at the end of the accounting period:
☐ the business is owed £2000 by its customers.
☐ there is a stock of goods worth £5000.
☐ cash and bank balances total £1000.
☐ the business owes suppliers £4000.
☐ cost of lease £10 000.

a Draw up the profit and loss account for the firm at the end of the first year of trading.
b Draw up the balance sheet of the business at the end of the first year of trading.
c Comment on the comparative success and failure of the business with the help of the appropriate ratios.
d What other information would you need in order to estimate the business's chances of survival?

5 A business buys a machine at the beginning of an accounting period for £50 000. It is expected to have a useful life of ten years and a scrap value at the end of the period of £5000.

a Compare the book value of the machine at the end of five years using both the straight line and declining balance methods of depreciation at 21 per cent (actual percentage 20.567 to three decimal places).
b In what circumstances might the declining balance method of depreciation be preferable to the straight line method?
c The machine was sold for scrap after eight years. Assuming that the business is still operating profitably, give three reasons why it might have taken this course of action.

6 Reston's Ltd is a small, single product company selling to the industrial market. In 1984 it owned a single factory capable of producing 250 000 units per year with a selling price of £25 per unit. All output was sold at this price. The managing director of Reston's was eager to expand production. The board of directors was less convinced of the advisability of the strategy. As a result the company accountant was asked to draw up projections evaluating the different courses of action open to the business. These were:
☐ **Projection A** Production and selling price to remain unchanged at 250 000 units at £25 per unit.
☐ **Projection B** Use existing plant capacity more intensively. The production manager estimated that output could be increased by 10 per cent, but this would mean overtime payments. The selling price would remain the same.
☐ **Projection C** Expand production capacity to 400 000. If this option was selected the marketing manager recommended a reduction in price of £3 to ensure the sale of all units produced.

The following information was also available:

☐ At the present production levels fixed costs were £2m per year. The increase in overheads arising from the adoption of Projection B would increase these by £275 000, while Projection C would mean fixed costs rising to £4.5m.

☐ Current variable costs per unit are £12. These would rise to £14 for Projection B, but the improved factory layout, discounts for bulk purchase of materials and a reduction in the amount of direct labour required as a result of improved machinery were expected to reduce variable costs to £8 per unit if Projection C was adopted.

a Draw up a report, using diagrams where appropriate, to evaluate each of the three possible courses of action outlined above.

b Assuming the reduction in price was necessary to sell the additional output, comment on the price elasticity of demand for the product, and the implications of this for the business.

c Projection C is adopted. In the first twelve months of operation sales are 350 000 instead of the expected 400 000. Reston's are approached by a large company which offers to buy 40 000 units at £21 per unit. Should the firm accept the order? Explain your answer.

7 Brady Boating is wholly owned by Andrew Brady. The business specialises in the repair of dinghies and day boats for the leisure sailor. Brady inherited the workshop from his father, together with a pride in the fact that it was a family business. By 1985 it was becoming obvious that essential equipment was reaching the end of its useful life. Replacement of equipment, together with an extension to the boat workshop, was estimated to cost £50 000. The bank was prepared to make a loan of £20 000. Andrew Brady had £20 000 for investment in the business but was unsure how he could raise the additional money required by 31 March 1986. At this time a local businessman, Peter Doyle, approached Brady with the following suggestions:

☐ Brady Boating should be registered as a limited company.

☐ an injection of £250 000 capital would be made by Peter Doyle and other interested persons.

☐ the additional capital would be used to update the workshop equipment, open a retail shop selling sailing accessories and clothes and start a catering establishment.

☐ Andrew Brady would be the managing director of the new company.

After careful consideration Andrew Brady decided that he did not want to accept this offer. He preferred to expand more slowly and, as a first step towards this objective, he collected the following budget information:

	Sales (£s)	Cost of sales (£s)	Monthly expenses include: wages and salaries – £1500; rates – £60; heating/lighting/power – £200; transport – £100; miscellaneous – £250. Telephone charges average £150 per quarter payable in November. The business insurance is due for renewal in March. Andrew Brady expects the premium to be £1000.
Sept.	15000	10000	
Oct.	12000	8000	
Nov.	10000	6700	
Dec.	9000	6000	
Jan.	9500	6300	
Feb.	11000	7400	
Mar.	16000	10700	

☐ on 1 November Andrew Brady expects to have a cash balance of £5000.

☐ he allows his customers two months in which to pay their debts, but pays his suppliers in cash.

a Assuming that the business proposition put forward by Peter Doyle satisfies financial criteria, give two reasons why Andrew Brady might have decided against it.

b Prepare a cash flow budget for Brady Boating. Will Andrew Brady be able to finance his own expansion?

8 The cost accounts for the Suntrap Hotel for the period 1 January 1985 to 31 December 1985 are shown below.

	Total number of room/nights let	Revenue per room per night (£)	Variable cost per room per night (£)
April	160	8	6
May	180	10	6
June	220	12	7
July	280	15	8
August	340	15	8
September	170	10	6

Total annual semi-variable and fixed costs are: £1440.

In the past the hotel has had a season of six months per annum from 1 April to 30 September. In an effort to increase profits, the proprietor is considering extending the 1987 season to cover the period 1 March to 31 October. Market research suggests that in each of March and October 100 room nights at £7 per night would be sold. Variable costs are estimated to be £6 per night, and annual semi-variable costs and fixed costs are expected to rise by £100.

a What is the difference between a fixed cost and a variable cost? (4)

b Calculate the profits for 1985. (10)

c What effect would the plan have on overall profits? (2)

d If the hotel were to have opened during March and October in 1985, what is the minimum that would have had to be charged during March and October per room per night, if it were to break even during those months? (6)

e Give four examples of alternative ways for the proprietor to increase profits. (8)
1986 (AEB)

9 a What is the significance of fixed costs and variable costs in determining the break-even point for a product? Illustrate your answer by calculating the break-even point for the figures opposite. (3)

> Sales volume 120 000
> Fixed costs £6000
> Variable costs per unit £5
> Selling price per unit £8

b A certain product sells at £5 per unit. The company plans to manufacture 100 000 units at a variable cost of £2.50 per unit and a fixed cost of £200 000.
 i Draw a break-even chart to represent these figures.
 ii Define the terms 'planned profit' and 'margin of safety'.
 iii Show these on your graph. (7)

c PT Ltd produces three products (X, Y and Z). The relevant data is shown below.

£ per unit	X	Y	Z
Sales price	2.00	2.50	3.25
Direct materials used (at 10p per kg)	0.30	0.40	0.50
Direct labour used	0.90	1.00	1.00
Variable overheads	0.40	0.60	0.85

The company's fixed costs amount to £10 000. The raw material used in these three products is in short supply and may limit the output of PT Ltd.

i State which product the company should concentrate on, assuming that there are no marketing constraints on the products. Support your answer with appropriate figures. (7)

ii It is anticipated that 200 000kg of raw material will be obtained in each month. Showing your calculations, calculate the most profitable product mix and expected profit if the projected monthly demand for X, Y and Z is 5000, 16 000 and 30 000 respectively. (8) 1985 (CLES)

10 OP Ltd produces one product for which a standard costing system was introduced at the beginning of this year. The following standards were calculated for one unit of the company's products:

- □   standard price of direct material £0.45 per kilo.
- □   standard quantity of direct material 12 kilos per unit.
- □   standard direct labour £2 per hour.
- □   standard number of direct labour hours 10 per unit.

a Explain the meaning of each of the above terms. (4)

b Discuss the ways in which the standards may have been set. (4)

c The company budgeted to 10 000 units during May 1985 but, in fact, produced 8000, with the following results:

- □   direct material bought and used (94 000 kilos) £48 880
- □   direct labour used (84 000 hours) £189 000

From the given figures calculate:

i   the standard cost per unit of output.

ii the actual cost for May 1985.

iii the total cost variances. (6)

d Define the following terms, and calculate from the given figures:

i   the material usage variance.

ii the material price variance. (6)

e Explain why the use of 'standard costs' is considered to have advantages over the comparison of actual costs with past costs. (5) 1985 (CLES)

11 a David Woodman is a sole trader manufacturing furniture who is considering forming a company to avoid the problems of personal liability. He is concerned about how to draw up accounts and has asked for your help. Explain the following accounting conventions as they would apply to David Woodman:

Separate entity   Realisation   Historic cost   Double entry (4)

b David Woodman's records show that from 1 June 1985 to 31 May 1986, the following transactions have been made:

Wages to self	£ 7500
Wages to apprentice	£ 3100
New work bench and electric saw	£ 1200
(bought on 30 November 1985 with an expected life of 10 years)	
Lease of premises for a year	£ 2100
Cost of electricity, telephone and other sundries	£ 420
Value of goods sold	£19500
Interest paid on bank loan	£ 400
Repayment of part of loan	£ 500
Sale of old work bench	£ 100
(book value £0)	
Cost of materials	£ 4800

Draw up a profit and loss account for David Woodman for the year ending 31 May 1986, giving as much detail as possible. You may find the following information useful:

☐ stock in hand (materials and finished goods) on 1 June 1985 £2200; on 30 May 1986 £3000.

☐ David Woodman estimates that he spends one-tenth of his time in administration and marketing work, which should be included as an overhead cost.

☐ value of capital equipment on 1 June 1985 was £2500, and it had an average expected life value of five years.

☐ tax is payable at the rate of 40 per cent on profits.

☐ amount owing to suppliers is £500. (13)

c On further examination of David Woodman's records you discover the following:

☐ a table was sold in June 1985 for £250 but the cheque was not honoured and no progress has been made in recovering the money.

☐ a kitchen dresser which cost £800 had been in stock for three years. An offer of £600 has just been received for it.

Discuss in each case what amendments, if any, you would make to the profit and loss account to allow for these factors, and why. (6)

d Briefly explain how the profit and loss account would need to be altered to make it suitable for publication, if David Woodman decides to form a company. (2) 1986 (CLES)

Activities

1 Analyse the published accounts of a company, noting any explanations the accountant considered necessary.

2 Using the information you collected as the result of Activity 1 in Chapter 4, prepare a cash flow forecast for the business.

3 From the financial pages of a newspaper select ten companies whose shares can be bought and sold on the Stock Exchange (that is 'quoted companies'). You should choose well-known companies whose activities are likely to be reported in the press. Keep a record over a period of time of changes in the price of shares, the yield and the price earnings ratio. Over the same period of time find out as much as you can about the activities of these companies and note any changes in the economy or society as a whole that might affect them. Are these changes reflected by changes in the data you are collecting? Attempt to explain any correlations you may observe.

Essays

1 Comment on the usefulness of ratio analysis as a tool for decision making and control.

2 Accounting techniques are designed to present a true and fair picture of the activities of a business. Why is this essential:

a for a sole trader?

b for a public limited company?

3 Discuss the view that budgetary control is an essential part of the co-ordination processes of a business.

4 Outline and comment on the circumstances in which a contribution approach to costing would be more useful than absorption costing.

5 Comment on the value of break-even analysis in the decision making process. What additional constraints should a manager bear in mind when using information provided by break-even analysis?

6 To what extent would ratio analysis enable you to draw meaningful conclusions about the performance of different public companies?

7 a How might inflation distort the annual accounts of a company? (10)

   b Briefly propose a way of overcoming these problems. (5)

   c How might your suggestion affect the convention that 'consistency of treatment' and a 'true and fair view' should always characterise the published accounts of a company? (10) 1985 (CLS)

8 a In what ways would accounting information, when prepared for internal management, differ from that compiled for the use of other interested parties? (15)

   b What kind of information would a supplier require of a new customer ordering £1m worth of raw material on a regular basis? (10) 1986 (CLES)

7 Finance

When you have studied this chapter you should be able to:

□ Describe the use of funds within a business.

□ Appreciate the factors that influence the asset structure of a business.

□ Outline and describe the sources of finance available to a business.

□ Appreciate the circumstances in which a given method of financing would be appropriate.

□ Understand the importance of money management.

□ Define working capital and identify methods by which it can be increased.

□ Outline quantitative methods of assessing investment decisions.

□ Apply quantitative methods of assessing investment decisions to business problems.

A study of the finance of a business is concerned with three areas:

□ the monetary resources of a business;

□ the acquisition of monetary resources by a business;

□ the effective management of monetary resources.

Money and its markets

The common denominator of each of the three areas is the word 'monetary'. In Chapter 2 ('The business as a system') we examined the nature of money and the role it plays in our society. To summarise that argument, we can say that money, in whatever form a society uses it, represents the claim of an individual, a business, an organisation or the state on the collective wealth of the society. In other words how much money you hold is your slice of the cake of national wealth. Whether or not the cake is shared fairly is a problem for politicians and will be decided by the culture of a society. We are concerned with how accumulated wealth, that is wealth that has been *saved* rather than *consumed*, is shared amongst the people who want it.

In simple terms money is a resource and it obeys market forces. Unlike other goods money is not bought or sold; it is *borrowed* and *lent*. The documents which record the transaction of borrowing and lending (referred to as *bills* and *stocks*) are bought and sold. The price of using money is the *interest rate*. If there is a comparatively large amount of money available compared with the demand for it then the interest rate will tend to be low. Should demand rise or the supply of money be restricted then the interest rate will rise.

However, the situation is not quite so simple. Market power operates in the money market just as it does in other markets. The government, for example, is a major borrower and, as a result, is in a position to influence the interest rate. When the banks change their interest rate there is pressure on the building societies to follow suit. Both are hoping to attract funds from a similar group of savers.

The use of funds

In Chapter 6 ('Accounting') we looked at the balance sheet of a business and emphasised the fact that the balance sheet showed the sources of funds used in a business and how these funds had been used. In this chapter we will look at the sources of funds in more detail and examine some of the techniques a business will use in making decisions about the use and management of the funds available.

In the simplest terms a business spends money on acquiring factories and equipment, on buying in the stock to carry on the business and in paying labour and other necessary expenses. Reality is, of course, more complex. Look at the following example:

A couple own and jointly run a small general store in an inner city area. They live in a flat over the shop. Property prices in the area are not high and they were able to buy the leasehold of the shop and flat for £20 000. Stocking the shop needed another £20 000, with a further £5000 each year to meet expenses. In common with many other small businesses the owners did not pay themselves a set wage. Instead they drew enough money from the business each week to meet their immediate expenses and reserved large items of personal expenditure for times when the cash balance of the business was sufficiently high, in their judgment, to cover foreseeable business outgoings and still leave a surplus. At 31 December 1985 the cash balance of the business stood at £15 000.

At 31 December 1985 this business employed a total capital of £55 000. Of this approximately 36 per cent was invested in *fixed assets* (buildings, fixtures and fittings), a further 36 per cent in stock and approximately 27 per cent in liquid assets (cash). The flat in which the couple lived has been regarded as part of the business because it would be impracticable for it to be let or sold separately from the business.

Now look at the next example:

A multinational company decided to sell one of its subsidiaries. Three members of the existing management team decided to buy the business. (This is known as a *management buy-out.*) The price was £10m. For this the new owners got the factory, machinery, existing stock and orders and the right to use the trade name under which the products were already being sold. They also raised an additional £1m.

A breakdown of the asset structure of this business gave fixed assets at 60 per cent of the total, stock at 23 per cent and liquid assets at 17 per cent. Which of the two businesses had made the right decisions in deciding how they would use the money they had available to them? The answer is, from the evidence given here, we don't know! Both may have been right. Equally one or both could be very wrong. The decision about how a business should use its funds and what proportion it should devote to any particular use depends on a number of factors. Some are quantifiable, others depend upon skill and judgment. The following list must be seen only as an indication of the way in which a business might be influenced in the final decision.

1   *The technology used*   A business which uses advanced technology is likely to employ a larger proportion of its total assets as fixed assets. Advanced technology is usually expensive but it can offer savings on labour and materials. If it is easier to use, it can reduce training costs and the need to employ expensive skilled labour.

2   *The nature of the business*   An engineering firm will need the premises and machinery to carry out its work. Stock levels may be kept quite low. A retailer, on the other hand, could have relatively low fixed costs but need to hold a higher level of stock.

3   *The size of the business*   Even within the same industry a small business might show a different asset structure from a large business. It could be that although classified as being in the same industry they are making different products, or that the smaller business cannot afford the technology available to the larger firm. It could be a matter of scale. Small firms might have to buy stocks in larger quantities than they need, but a larger business with greater market power can regulate its stocks according to its needs.

4   *The stage of development*   A new or expanding business is likely to have a distorted asset structure compared with a business in the same industry in a more settled phase of its life.

5   *The size of the market*   A business with a large, constant market for its product will be more likely to use production methods that require the use of a lot of capital equipment.

6   *Management skill*   The asset structure of a business may also be affected by the skill of management. Bad management can produce a bad asset structure.

7   *The government*   Tax concessions can affect the asset structure of a business, as can grants. The effect may be marginal but it still exists.

8   *The state of the economy and business confidence*   A flourishing economy will result in an increase in business confidence and is likely to encourage a business to seek available funds for expansion. An economy in recession could result in investment in labour saving machinery.

Influences on the asset structure of a business are shown in Figure 7.1.

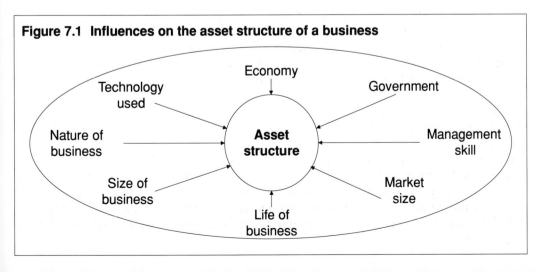

Figure 7.1 Influences on the asset structure of a business

SELF ASSESSMENT

1 What is the asset structure of a business?
2 Explain briefly why the asset structures of two businesses in the same industry can differ.
3 Is there a 'correct' asset structure for an engineering business?

Sources of finance

In Chapter 6 ('Accounting') we pointed out that there are three main sources of finance for any business:

- owners' capital;

- borrowing from other people or organisations;

- obtaining goods on credit.

Owners' capital

In a small business or partnership this is limited to the personal wealth the owners put into the business at the beginning and any profits subsequently re-invested.
Methods of increasing owners' capital are listed below:

- sole traders and partners may use some of their private wealth to give an injection of capital to a business.

- sole traders may take a partner; partnerships can increase the number of partners.

- sole traders or partners could decide to float their business as a company.

- existing companies may be able to issue more shares.

- profits can be left in the business and used to finance further investment. These profits are sometimes referred to as *ploughed back* profits.

Advantages of owners' capital

1   Interest has to be paid on borrowed funds. When the interest is not paid the debtors can start legal proceedings that can result in bankruptcy or involuntary liquidation. Shareholders have no right to demand a dividend. Sole traders and partners are not required to make a profit from their business. A high proportion of owner capital can give stability to a business during its initial development and in periods of economic recession when demand might be falling.

2   The interest on debt is a fixed cost during the life of the debt. This reduces the amount of money available for the owners as profit.

3   Shareholders who do not receive the level of dividend they had hoped for can challenge the directors at the annual general meeting of the company. Theoretically shareholders can vote the directors out of office. This seldom happens in practice. A high proportion of share capital, therefore, can give the directors greater power in deciding to finance growth from retained profits.

Disadvantages of owners' capital

1   The capital is tied up in the business throughout its life. A sole trader can overcome this problem by taking a partner; partnerships may expand in size by taking additional partners. Both sole traders and partnerships can decide to convert to companies. The owners of shares in a company can convert their holding in the company into cash only by selling their shares to somebody prepared to buy them. This is relatively easy if the company is *listed* on the Stock Exchange. The body that runs the Stock Exchange (the *Stock Exchange Council*) will accept a company for listing – and therefore for its shares to be bought and sold by members – only if it meets stringent financial requirements. People holding shares in unlisted companies find it more difficult to sell them. Aware of this problem, the Stock Exchange opened another market for shares in 1980. This is known as the Unlisted Securities Market (USM). The financial requirements needed to enter this market are less stringent than those required for listed securities but they still provide safeguards for people buying and selling shares on the Stock Exchange.

2   A high proportion of owners' capital increases the owners' risk. They may be shareholders in a listed company but if they wish to dispose of their shares at any time they may have to sell for a lower price than they paid, particularly if the dividends of the company have been low compared with the prevailing rate of interest or the dividends paid by other companies.

3   Raising money by issuing more shares is expensive in administrative costs. A *rights issue*, where shares are offered to existing shareholders, is the cheapest method. It is also difficult for a company to estimate the market price of its shares and, if underpriced, there is an additional cost to the company. Issuing shares by *tender* attempts to overcome this problem by stating the minimum price the company will accept for its shares and inviting the public to state how much they are prepared to pay for them.

   Apart from the administrative costs of floating a share issue, owner capital appears the cheapest method of acquiring funds. The opportunity cost of using owner capital, that is the earning potential of alternative investment, should not be forgotten.

Preference shares

Between owners' capital and loans there is a less well-defined area of *preference shares*. The holder of a preference share:

   □   is not an owner of the company.

   □   receives a fixed rate of return but has no legal right to it.

   □   has priority over ordinary shareholders when a dividend is declared.

   □   has priority over ordinary shareholders when the company goes into liquidation.

   Apart from these four points the rights of preference shareholders will vary from company to company. Companies design their preference shares to attract investors who do not want to take the risk of holding ordinary shares and who either do not have sufficient capital to lend to the company or wish to spread the risks of lending money. *Cumulative preference shares* have the right to claim arrears of dividends if the company does not pay a dividend in one year. *Redeemable preference shares* can be bought back by the company after a stated number of years. Some preference shares carry voting rights, others do not. The rights of the preference shareholders are laid down in the company's articles of association.

Borrowing

Borrowing money places an obligation on a business to repay specified amounts of the money borrowed when they are due and to meet regular interest payments of an agreed amount. This obligation remains irrespective of the size of the company. Apart from these basic principles, the terms of loan negotiated between businesses and people or organisations prepared to lend money vary according to the needs of the business and the conditions the lenders feel are required to safeguard their money. The following list of definitions will give some indication of the variety of agreements that can be made between those who borrow and those who lend.

1   *Secured loans*   In return for granting the loan the lender insists on some asset of the business being tied to the repayment of the loan. In the event of bankruptcy or liquidation that lender will then have priority on the money from the sale of that asset for the repayment of that loan. A specialised form of secured loan is a *mortgage*. In this case the asset is always land or property. Unsecured loans are repaid from the fund generated by the sale of all other assets if the firm goes bankrupt or into liquidation. Lenders are less certain they will be repaid. These securities are known as *collateral* for the loan, i.e. properties pledged by the borrower to provide security for the lender.

2   *Syndicated loans*   A syndicate is a group of people who join together to carry out a certain transaction. Where a great deal of money is borrowed no one person or organisation may be able or willing to provide the total sum. In these circumstances a syndicate may be formed to provide the money, with members stating how much they will each lend.

3   *Personal guarantee*   Limited liability protects the owners of a business from the need to repay debts above the amount they have directly invested in a business. A bank lending to a small limited company may demand a personal guarantee that the debt will be repaid. Effectively this removes the advantages of limited liability for the principal shareholders in that they will have to use personal assets to repay the loan if the assets of the business are inadequate.

4   *Debentures*   These are known collectively as *stock*. A debenture is a long term loan which does not have to be repaid until an agreed date (its *maturity*). Debenture holders are entitled to a fixed rate of return each year and have priority over all shareholders. Unlike other forms of debt, debentures can be bought and sold on the Stock Exchange. The company will continue to pay the agreed rate of return to the new owner.

Because the rate of return is fixed when the loan is negotiated the price of a debenture will fluctuate according to the rate of interest. A fixed rate of interest of 10 per cent means that for every £100 the company gains from a particular debenture they will pay £10 each year to whoever owns that debenture. Let us assume that the rate of interest paid by a commercial bank on deposit accounts rises to 12.5 per cent. In practical terms it means that if a 10 per cent debenture stock is purchased at the price at which it was first issued buyers would be sacrificing £2.50 for each £100 of stock bought. The *maximum* price they would be prepared to pay would be one which gave them a return of 12.5 per cent, in this case £80. You should try the same calculation assuming a general interest rate of 8 per cent. The value of stock varies inversely with the rate of interest.

5 *Loans by organisations* It was pointed out in Chapter 4 ('Starting and running your own business') that CoSIRA was prepared to give loans to businesses intending to trade in rural areas. A number of other organisations, for example local authorities wishing to attract industry, offer loans to businesses. Sometimes the organisation offering loans comprises central and/or local government interests as well as private business. A development agency for a region might negotiate a loan for a project that calls on a syndicate of these three interest groups. Finance for Industry (FFI), established by the English and Scottish clearing banks in 1973, provides loans through two subsidiaries: the Industrial and Commercial Finance Corporation (ICFC) and the Finance Corporation for Industry (FCI).

6 *Bank loans* These are possibly the simplest forms of loans available to business. The average bank manager dealing with a small to medium sized firm and responsible to head office for the performance of the branch uses a set of well-defined criteria when making a loan. Like other loans, a bank loan is for a fixed amount at a fixed rate of interest. There is likely to be a demand for regular repayments.

In practical terms a business may simply see its loans as those which will need to be repaid in the next accounting period (*current*) and those which have more than a year to run.

SELF ASSESSMENT

1 What is the minimum opportunity cost to a small business owner who invests £10 000 in the business when the rate of interest paid on bank deposit accounts is 9.5 per cent? What other sacrifices might be involved in this decision?
2 Draw a graph showing the changes in the value of stock with a nominal value of £100 when the interest rate changes as follows: 8 per cent, 10 per cent, 12 per cent, 14 per cent, 11.5 per cent.

Shares or borrowing?

We have already pointed out that the interest on a loan is a fixed charge on the business. That is, it *must* be paid irrespective of the amount of money the business has generated in a year. The higher the level of debt capital in relation to equity capital, therefore, the greater the risk to the holders of equity capital. In addition to the need to service the loans, the dates for repayment may fall at times when the business finds it difficult to meet them. An otherwise healthy business may have a period of poor trading. If it needs to borrow more money it will be at a disadvantage and may have to pay a higher rate of interest and/or accept more stringent terms than it would otherwise have had to do.

The holders of a debt are likely to watch closely the progress of a business they have lent money to. In a small business, for example, a condition of being granted a bank loan might be the careful monitoring of the business by a bank. This can inhibit business decision making.

Financing by borrowing can also have its advantages:

☐ in periods of inflation the *real* rate of return on fixed interest loans falls. This simply means that the interest payments will purchase fewer goods and services as inflation progresses. The same is true of the repayment of the principal. It will be worth less in real terms than it was when the loan was floated.

- the cost of borrowing money is a stated cost which can be useful in assessing the costs of production.

- there are tax advantages in that tax is paid after interest has been paid. This means that a business has to earn more money if it is to give the owners the same rate of return that it pays to subscribers of loan capital.

SELF ASSESSMENT

1 State two disadvantages to a business of borrowing money.
2 A business is expected to grow rapidly over a period of three years. State two possible advantages to the business of funding this growth by borrowing.

Other sources of funds

Medium-term funds
It is usually accepted that medium-term finance is for a period of one to five years.

1 *Hire purchase* Under a hire purchase agreement goods are hired to the user who has the option to purchase them at the end of the hiring period. The ownership of the good remains with the hirer. The funds for hire purchase are provided by specialised financial companies known as *finance houses*. The usual practice is for the finance company to give the full purchase price to the *seller* of the good and negotiate repayment terms with the *buyer*. Both the seller and the buyer benefit: the seller because the purchase price is paid immediately and because the availability of hire purchase can attract buyers; the buyer because the use of the good is immediately available, and not dependent on the accumulation of the necessary capital.

2 *Leasing and hiring* At first sight leasing and hiring appear to be different terms used to describe the same situation, namely that a business does not own an item of capital equipment but pays to use it for a limited period of time. This definition describes *hiring*. A business will *lease* equipment that it needs for a longer period of time. Under a leasing agreement a finance company will purchase a specific item of equipment for use by a business. The equipment remains the property of the finance company but the business has the sole use of it for which it pays an agreed rent. The agreement may be for a given period of time or for the life of the equipment. The terms of each agreement will vary. Specialised equipment might have a maintenance clause. The company leasing it will provide maintenance to avoid problems arising from inexpert handling. Where the technology to maintain a piece of equipment is generally available maintenance is more likely to be the responsibility of the lessee, that is the business leasing the equipment.

Advantages of leasing

- Leasing can help preserve the liquidity of a business. When purchasing equipment will affect current and liquidity ratios, leasing can be an attractive alternative.

- A time lease can give the business the opportunity of keeping abreast with a changing technology. In fields where technology is changing rapidly it may be more sensible to lease a piece of equipment rather than tie up capital in machinery which will be obsolete within a few years.

☐ Like fixed interest loans the leasing payments are constant and are charged against the income of the business before tax is calculated. This reduces the cost of leasing to the business and gives it some protection against fluctuations in interest rates.

☐ A servicing agreement may be both an advantage and a disadvantage to the business. A lease might state that servicing must be done by nominated firms or their own engineers. The cost of such servicing can be high in that the leasing agreement creates a monopoly. To be offset against this are clauses that guarantee substitute equipment during the repair period.

☐ Like all fixed financial obligations, the burden becomes less in real terms during a time of inflation.

Disadvantages of leasing

☐ It is a fixed obligation on the business which may be too great in a recession.

☐ Should the equipment become obsolete before the expiry of the lease it may affect the profitability and competitiveness of the business.

☐ The business has to forgo the advantages of owning the equipment.

In psychological terms, ownership may convey prestige and an impression of stability. In financial terms, assets bought during a profitable time of trading can be a security for loans in less profitable times.

The final decision as to whether or not to lease will depend upon the position a business finds itself in and on the terms of the lease offered. It will take into account such factors as the growth potential of the business, the rate of technological change, the value of the asset to be purchased and management expertise in making investment decisions.

Short-term funds

Funds are generally considered to be short term if they are for less than one year. A *bank overdraft* is an arrangement between the business and its bank to draw more money from the current account, to an agreed limit, than is deposited in it. An overdraft has the advantage of being flexible and, as the amount of money on which interest is paid is reduced with each deposit, can prove a cheap form of finance. Against this is the ease with which the bank can withhold overdraft facilities. This could cause serious cash flow problems for a business which had come to rely on its overdraft.

> The owner of a small shop selling consumer durables holds a limited amount of stock, chiefly for display purposes, and buys only when there is a firm order from a customer. The customer does not pay until the purchase is delivered. The capital available to the owner is adequate to cover these transactions for most of the year. Christmas brings a sharp increase in orders. The owner of the shop finances the Christmas trade with an overdraft. The maximum length of time for which it is needed is two months and during that period there is a steady inflow of payments, thus reducing the overdraft.

Trade credit can also be viewed as a short-term loan. The purchaser does not have to pay for the goods immediately and during that time has the use of the money. No formal interest is paid but the sacrifice of *cash discount* has the same effect.

1 Explain why an overdraft can be a cheap form of finance for a business.
2 Servicing a loan is a fixed charge on the business. In what way can that be an advantage in times of inflation?
3 Distinguish between leasing and hire purchase.
4 A small business intends to increase stock levels in anticipation of a seasonal increase in demand. The owner wants to know the relative advantages and disadvantages of financing the purchases by cash, trade credit or a bank overdraft. Write a paragraph advising the owner on the best course of action.

The internal management of finance

Once a business has assembled its capital, what does it do with it? We have already seen, at the beginning of this chapter, that the asset structure, as it appears on the balance sheet, will depend on the individual circumstances of the business. It is now time to look more closely at some of the problems facing a business when deciding how to use its available capital.

How much cash should the business hold? Economic theory states that *liquidity preference*, that is the desire to hold resources in cash rather than other forms, is governed by three motives:

☐ the *transactions* motive is concerned with the need to have sufficient money to undertake necessary buying.

☐ the *precautionary* motive, which can be summarised as 'just in case'. The money is held to provide security for the business.

☐ the *speculative* motive, which is governed by the desire to have sufficient liquid capital to take advantage of future opportunities for profit.

The definitions of the motives for holding money given here are superficial rather than precise in economic terms. However, they can give some indication of the way in which a business might respond to different situations.

In a period of inflation a business will need to hold a higher cash level than in a period of price stability. When prices are high more money will be needed to finance transactions and more money will need to be held to give security against an unexpected decline in trade. This will not necessarily affect the asset structure of the business. If all assets are valued at current cost the proportion of the total held in cash could remain the same. On the other hand, if fixed assets are valued at historic cost this situation will give a distorted view of the business's position.

When interest rates are high the business is sacrificing more income by holding funds in cash than when they are low. In these circumstances there is a temptation to hold minimum cash balances and invest the rest.

The final decision about how much cash a business will hold will depend upon a mixture of these motives and will be influenced by the circumstances of a business and the judgment of its managers. Even in times of high inflation some businesses are affected less than others.

Working capital

Working capital is defined as the excess of current assets over current liabilities, otherwise known as *net current assets*. In Chapter 6 ('Accounting') we defined the current ratio as

Current assets : Current liabilities

and stated that a frequently quoted ideal ratio was 2:1. It is this excess of current assets over current liabilities that provides the business with the capital it needs to carry on its day-to-day activities. The management of working capital can be crucial to the survival of a business.

Management of working capital

The main objectives in the management of working capital can be summarised as follows:

1   To keep the time lag between the *input* of resources into production and the *payment* for goods and services produced as short as possible. This will reduce the amount of current assets (stocks, debtors and cash) the business needs to invest in at any one time. The same amount of investment is working harder.

2   The financing should be kept as efficient as possible to ensure the greatest possible return on capital employed.

The management of working capital is the application of common sense. They are the principles used by any person managing her/his income.

❑   Do not borrow too much money when the ability to repay debts depends upon uncertain income. If a business is relying on people who owe it money to be able to meet its own liabilities, then the failure of one person to pay will cause problems.

❑   Do not borrow on a short-term basis to finance medium- or long-term purchases: the short-term loans might dry up. The technical term for this is *overtrading*.

❑   Do take into account the opportunity cost. This service/course of action might appear expensive, but what are the hidden advantages (i.e. cost reductions) for the business?

❑   Ultimately, for a business as for an individual, the question is: Will it be able to meet its debts?

The effective management of working capital depends upon the co-operation of all the departments in a business. We can use the control of stock level as an example of this.

The valuation of stocks is usually based on the cost of stocks or their *net realisable value* (that is what the business would receive if it sold them on the open market), whichever is lower. However, the *level* of stocks held will also depend on a number of other factors, for example:

❑   the ability of the purchasing department to maintain a flow of necessary supplies at a rate linked to their usage. If purchasing is erratic the business may have to hold higher stocks than is strictly necessary.

☐   the expertise of the marketing department in estimating future demand and the ability of the production department to maintain a steady flow of production to meet that demand. Overestimating demand can lead to a build-up in stocks of finished goods and, if production is reduced, the build-up of raw materials and components.

Methods of increasing working capital

Working capital can be increased in a number of ways but it is important to remember that each method will carry with it its own disadvantages.

1   By minimising the *cash operating cycle*, that is by reducing the time between the buying of resources and the income generated by the use of resources. This is the best way of improving efficiency in the use of working capital provided it does not lead to such things as poor quality control because the emphasis on throughput is too great.

2   Businesses can also increase their working capital by selling assets and leasing them back. This liberates funds but also commits the business to regular payments of leasing fees which could become a burden on the business if its income falls for any reason. It also reduces the fixed assets of the business and may limit its opportunities of raising loans.

3   A business may use the services of a *debt factoring* company. This is a service in management accounting. The book debts of the business are sold to a specialist firm who will then keep a check on the sales ledger of the company concerned and collect bad debts. In the services it offers debt factoring differs from *invoice discounting*. The latter can be simplistically described as the sale of debts for below their book value to a business which will collect. The difference between book value and the sale value of the debt provides the income of the invoice discounting company. Debt factoring is expensive; it does, however, provide accounting services which can be of great value, particularly to a small business. Both debt factoring and invoice discounting release finance, allow more accurate cash flow projections and save administrative costs.

Increasing the amount of working capital in the business must not be confused with increasing the cash available to a business. Look at the following example.

A small business buys stock to the value of £5000 using trade credit. The owners of the business decided on this course of action because they did not wish to reduce the cash balance of the business.

Working capital before the transaction:
   Current assets (£10 000) – current liabilities (£8000)
   = £2000
Working capital after the transaction:
   Current assets (£15 000) – current liabilities (£13 000)
   = £2000

The assets of the business have increased by £5000, as have the liabilities. Creditors have increased by £5000.

A business which is short of working capital can increase the cash available to it.

1 A bank overdraft is cheap, easy and quick to negotiate and renew and offers flexibility. The value of using an overdraft depends on the use to which it is put. A business that uses an overdraft to provide finance because its debtors are late in paying is paying twice for the same money. If the overdraft is used to increase sales then there is the potential for greater profit. Whether or not an overdraft should be used in these circumstances depends on the judgment of the business manager. Potential profit must be greater than the cost of the overdraft.

2 Trade credit can be tempting but creditors increase the risk of bankruptcy or liquidation. Too many small businesses have failed, particularly in the retail sector, because they have ignored the basic principles of control of creditors. Discounts for prompt payment should not be ignored. They will improve the ability of a business to meet unexpected debts. In other words, they are part of the cash management of a business.

3 Tax and rate payments can often be delayed, but local authorities and government departments are frequently the most aggressive of creditors if the payment cannot be met on time.

4 It can keep careful records of debtors and following up late payers carefully.

If you do not understand the distinction between increasing working capital and increasing the cash available for a business to use, re-read the definition of working capital and refer back to the T form balance sheet in Chapter 6 ('Accounting'). If a business is granted an overdraft of £1000 this will increase cash at the bank by the same amount, but will it change the relationship between current assets and current liabilities?

SELF ASSESSMENT

1 Define the term 'working capital'.
2 How can an analysis of the accounts of a business help a potential investor judge the efficiency with which working capital is managed by a business?
3 Distinguish between increasing working capital and improving the liquidity position of the business.
4 State one disadvantage of attempting to overcome problems related to working capital by increasing the current liabilities of the business.
5 Explain briefly the role of a production department in improving working capital.

Investment decisions

The word 'investment' is one of the many words in the English language that appear to have a number of different usages. An investment can be a siege or blockade in military terms, it can be the purchase of stocks and shares, the decision as to whether or not to buy another business (which is in the area of mergers and takeover bids) or it can be the decision whether or not the business will buy a particular piece of machinery.

All the possible definitions of investment have one thing in common: resources are risked in a venture that might, but not necessarily will, bring future advantage.

☐ A town is besieged. The troops, guns, food, ammunition and the rest of the army are committed to reducing that town. The advantages of a siege are difficult to express in monetary terms. It can only be judged by cost/benefit analysis. If we besiege this town it will cost us £x. If we do not besiege this town its garrison may attack us from the rear.

☐ Buying this business will cost a certain amount of money. On the other hand it will allow us to operate more effectively in the market. What is the cost? What are the potential gains?

☐ Buying this machine will increase our productive capacity/reduce costs/improve our image. What are the costs? What are the potential gains?

The techniques of decision making are all concerned with attempts to measure cost and potential gain. The method chosen will depend on the circumstances of the business.

The payback method

The *payback method* calculates the period of time it takes for an investment to pay for itself out of the profit it generates.

A machine is bought for £10 000. The purchaser makes an estimate of the additional revenue per year that will be generated by using the machine and the annual direct and maintenance costs required to support this revenue.

The machine will give the business an extra income of £8000 per year and will pay for itself in 1.25 years.

	£
Sales	20000
Direct labour	5000
Direct materials	6000
Indirect labour	700
Maintenance	300
Total cost	12000

A short payback period can be useful:

1   When technology is changing rapidly. A business does not want to purchase an expensive piece of equipment and find that it is obsolete before it has been paid for. Of course, this may not be very important. A machine does not have to employ the latest technology to do the job it was designed for effectively. In certain circumstances, however, innovations can carry with them cost and efficiency advantages that put the users of older machines at a disadvantage in the market. The payback method allows a business to estimate whether or not it will 'break even' on the purchase of the machine before it needs to be replaced.

2   It is not only machines that become obsolete. Products, too, can go out of favour with customers before they have brought in sufficient revenue to repay the costs of investment. This is particularly true of high fashion products whose life may be only a few months before another product takes their place. It can also be true of technical products when innovation is moving rapidly.

3   The payback method, like all methods of investment appraisal, can be used to compare the advantages of machines with similar performance but with different costs.

1 Explain why the payback method is a useful technique in a high fashion market.
2 If the original cost of a machine was £20 000 and it is expected to increase profits by £4000 per year, what is the payback period?

Return on investment

The income generated by a machine, over and above the costs attributable to that machine, can be regarded as the 'profit' made by possessing that machine. Of course this figure will still be subject to overheads, tax and other charges before it makes its contribution to net profit. This 'profit' can be expressed as a return on investment in precisely the same way as a potential investor might express the expected dividend on a share as a percentage of the purchase price in order to compare its income yield with alternative investment opportunities.

To compare the income generated by the use of a machine with its total purchase cost would not give a true picture of the return on investment. It is more usual to spread the cost of the machine, minus its value at the end of that time (its *residual value*), evenly over the life of the machine.

> A machine costs £12 000 and is expected to have a life of ten years. At the end of that time the business expects to sell it for £2000. The cost of the machine to the business is therefore £12 000 – £2000 = £10 000. Spread over the ten years of the life of the machine we can say that it is costing the firm £1000 per year.

If we assume that the machine generates a profit of £100 each year then the rate of return on this investment can be given as 10 per cent.

This method of judging an investment provides a useful comparison with the return on other uses to which the available capital could be put. It contains elements of the payback method in that the expected life of the machine and its residual value will be based on the rate of technical innovation and the length of time the market for the products is expected to last.

Neither the payback method nor the rate of return makes allowances for the fact that future money is worth less than present money. Both methods become more precise if the concept of present value is incorporated into the calculations.

Net present value

The idea of *present value* is founded in the concept of opportunity cost. If you have £500 to invest at this moment, and place it in a bank account where it will earn 10 per cent interest, at the end of twelve months you will have £550. It can therefore be said that the present value of £550 in twelve months' time is £500. Re-invested for another twelve months at 10 per cent interest the original £500 would be worth £605, and so on.

How can this information help a business make investment decisions? Let us assume that a business has £5000 and two courses of possible action: it can either leave the money in the bank, in which case it will earn 10 per cent interest; or it can buy a piece of equipment for the business. The managers make some calculations and estimate that the annual income generated by owning the piece of equipment will be as in the table overleaf.

Before they can judge whether this investment is worthwhile they need to know the present value of the income flows. They can calculate this by *discounting*. The simplest way of viewing discounting is to see it as the reverse process of calculating compound interest. Instead of starting with

Year 1	£2000
Year 2	£2500
Year 3	£4000
Year 4	£4500
Year 5	£4000

a sum of money and calculating how much it will earn if it is invested for a period of years and all interest earned is re-invested, we begin with the future sum of money and reduce it by an agreed percentage for each year it has been invested. At the end of this process we have the *principal*, that is the sum of money which, when invested, would have resulted in the future sum of money.

In the example given above the business expected the equipment to earn £2000 by the end of the first year of its use. £1 discounted at 10 per cent would have a present value of £0.909. The £2000 would therefore have a present value of £2000 x £0.909 = £1818. The money earned in year two would be discounted at 10 per cent, but over two years instead of one. The present value of each £1 would therefore be lower at £0.826, giving a total present value for the £2500 of £2065.

To save people the trouble of making individual calculations present value tables have been drawn up which give the present value of £1 over a range of time and at different discount rates. An example of such a table is given in Table 7.1. Many calculators have a discounting function and computers can, of course, be programmed to perform the operation.

Table 7.1 Net present value of £1.00

Years

%	1	2	3	4	5	6	7	8	9	10
1	0.9901	0.9803	0.9706	0.9610	0.9515	0.9420	0.9327	0.9235	0.9143	0.9053
2	0.9804	0.9612	0.9423	0.9238	0.9057	0.8880	0.8706	0.8535	0.8368	0.8203
3	0.9709	0.9426	0.9151	0.8885	0.8626	0.8375	0.8131	0.7894	0.7664	0.7441
4	0.9615	0.9246	0.8890	0.8548	0.8219	0.7903	0.7599	0.7307	0.7026	0.6756
5	0.9524	0.9070	0.8638	0.8227	0.7835	0.7462	0.7107	0.6768	0.6446	0.6139
6	0.9434	0.8900	0.8396	0.7921	0.7473	0.7050	0.6651	0.6274	0.5919	0.5584
7	0.9346	0.8734	0.8163	0.7629	0.7130	0.6663	0.6227	0.5820	0.5439	0.5083
8	0.9259	0.8573	0.7938	0.7350	0.6806	0.6302	0.5835	0.5403	0.5002	0.4632
9	0.9174	0.8417	0.7722	0.7084	0.6499	0.5963	0.5470	0.5019	0.4604	0.4224
10	0.9091	0.8264	0.7513	0.6830	0.6209	0.5645	0.5132	0.4665	0.4241	0.3855

So far we have talked about the income generated by the investment as if there were no expenses involved. In fact the business would need to deduct operating expenses and the production costs associated with the machine before it could judge the 'profit' it would bring. In other words it would draw up a projected cash flow as generated by the machine. This appraisal technique is usually known as *discounted cash flow*.

For an investment to show the possibility of profit the total of all discounted cash flows for the life of the machine should be *greater* than the proposed investment. If the discounted cash flows for a proposed investment of £5000 total £7000 it means that the business would have had to invest £7000 at 10 per cent in order to earn that money. The investment is earning a higher rate of return than 10 per cent.

1 Explain what is meant by return on investment. State one advantage of this method of assessing an investment opportunity.
2 State and explain one advantage of using the discounted cash flow technique rather than other methods of judging the potential profitability of an investment decision.
3 Calculate the net present value of £100 000 generated in five years' time at a discount rate of 8 per cent.

Conclusion

The decisions that face businesses in the raising of capital, the management of cash and working capital and investment decisions have been reduced in this chapter to a few simple principles explained in terms of relatively uncomplicated examples. In reality decision makers are faced with a number of options, each of which will offer advantages and disadvantages which will vary according to the situation of the firm. Changes in technology, the law, the availability and cost of finance may be experiences shared by a number of businesses, but the response of individual firms to these external influences will depend upon the leadership and skill (or the lack of these qualities) of the management, the power of trade unions to influence the decisions of the business, the past profitability of the business and the confidence the management has in its future. In short, financial decisions translate the needs of the various functions of a business into monetary terms, just as management accounting provides summaries of the working of the business in monetary terms.

1 The owners of a small business want to replace an item of powered equipment. They can use accumulated profits or borrow the money to make the purchase. Leasing the equipment is another possibility. The equipment has an expected life of four years. After investigating the different methods of financing this investment, the owners drew up the table shown below. Study the figures carefully before answering the questions that follow.

Method of funding	Initial outlay	Cash outflow per annum (£000s)			
		Year 1	Year 2	Year 3	Year 4
Profits	5	0	0	0	0
Borrowing	2	1	1	1	1
Leasing	0.5	1.5	1.5	1.5	1.5

a What is the price of the equipment?
b On the evidence of the figures given above, which is the most expensive method of financing the investment?
c Give two reasons why the owners of the business might decide on leasing rather than other methods of funding.
d The owners of the business are offered an investment opportunity with an expected rate of return of 15 per cent. How might this affect their final decision?

2 The marketing manager of a business is contemplating a promotion for an existing product. The proposed budget is £50 000 spread over twelve months. Experience suggests that the promotion will boost revenue from the product as shown in the table.

	£
January	5000
February	9000
March	11000
April	12000
May	13000
June	15000
July	14000
August	11000
September	10000
October	8000
November	5000
December	2000

a What is the payback period for this investment?

b Assuming the initial outlay was made in the previous December, what is the net present value of the income flow for the year?

c Would you advise the marketing manager to implement the promotion campaign? Give reasons for your advice.

d Sales of this product are seasonal. In which season would you expect sales to be highest? Justify your answer with reference to the figures given.

3 Banks Ltd produces glass reinforced plastic products for the industrial market. The production manager wants to invest in a machine for one of the processes. The machine design is based on advanced technology of which the employees of Banks Ltd have little personal experience. The production manager has seen the machine at a trade exhibition and is impressed with its specifications and the claims made concerning its importance. He argues strongly for its purchase.

Other members of the management team are less convinced. They point out that the new machine will cost £150 000, whereas the existing machine still has a useful life of five years and replacement with conventional technology would cost just £50 000. The existing machine generates an income of £10 000 per annum after running costs and depreciation (calculated on the straight line method) of £5000 per annum have been deducted. They also point out that alterations to the factory to accommodate the new machine would cost an additional £20 000 and that this sum would have to be paid out again if, in future, they decided to revert to the more traditional technology.

The production manager counteracted with the information that the new machine would generate income of £60 000 per annum after the deduction of running expenses and depreciation (also calculated on a straight line basis) of £30 000.

Banks Ltd normally require a minimum of 15 per cent return on any of their investment projects.

a Assuming that the income figures have remained the same throughout the life of the original machine and that depreciation is based on the working life of the machines with minimal residual value, evaluate the options open to Banks Ltd using the investment appraisal techniques outlined in this chapter.

b Which method of investment appraisal might be most appropriate for the new machine? Give reasons for your answer.

c What other information would you require before making the final decision?

4 Doyle's Electronics Ltd intends to invest £500 000 in an extension to the factory. It is estimated that the increase in income generated by this investment and available to service the capital requirements will be:

Year	Income (£000s)
1	50
2	62.5
3	75
4	87.5
5	100

a Assuming that 80 per cent of the capital required is provided by the company from its own resources and the rest of the money is raised by secured loans at 15 per cent, calculate the annual earnings of the company as a percentage of capital invested.

b Assuming that 80 per cent of the capital required is raised by secured loans at 15 per cent interest, calculate the annual return to the company as a percentage of capital invested.

c What is the significance of the information you have derived from **a** and **b** in assisting the company in making the investment decision? What other factors should it take into account?

5 Freshfields DIY Emporium is a large shop situated in the suburb of a city. It carries a wide range of materials and tools designed to appeal to the home owner and gardener. The emphasis of the range is on decorative and luxury items rather than the purely utilitarian.

Table 7.2   Freshfields DIY Emporium, annual accounts, 1985 and 1986

Balance sheet as at 31 December 1986

	1985		1986	
	£	£	£	£
Fixed assets		60000		65000
Current assets				
Stock	10500		21250	
Debtors	25150		37630	
Cash	5000		1000	
	40650		59880	
Deduct				
Current liabilities				
Bank overdraft	1000		12000	
Creditors	—		—	
	1000		12000	
Net current assets		39650		47880
Total assets		99650		112880
Financed by				
Proprietor's funds		50000		55000
Retained profit		49650		57880
		99650		112880

Profit and loss account

	1985		1986	
	£	£	£	£
Revenue from sales		240000		265000
Cost of sales		160000		176000
Gross profit		80000		89000
Expenses				
Sales	25000		36250	
Admin.	10000		10000	
Heating, lighting	5000	40000	6000	52250
		40000		36750
Interest		100		1200
Net profit before tax		39900		35550
Tax due on profit		11970		10650
Net profit after tax		27930		24900

As many of the customers are commuters, the owner of the shop, a sole trader, offers credit to his customers, many of whom have developed the habit of phoning their orders into the shop during the week. The goods are then delivered on the Friday evening and payment is made at the customers' convenience in the following weeks. All supplies are paid for in cash. There are very few bad debts.

Overall the business made a satisfactory profit but several times in 1986 the owner found it necessary to use overdraft facilities to finance purchases. This trend caused him some concern and he examined his annual accounts for 1985 and 1986 with more than usual care. They are shown in Table 7.2.

a Assuming that all sales are on credit, comment on the average number of days any particular debt is outstanding in both years using the following ratio:

$$\frac{\text{Debtors}}{\text{Sales}} \times 365$$

b The cost of an overdraft at that time was 15 per cent per annum. Calculate the cost to Freshfields DIY Emporium of allowing this credit, comparing 1985 with 1986.

c From the figures available to you explain why the position of the business was worse in 1986 than in 1985.

d The average length of time goods remain in stock can be calculated by:

$$\frac{\text{Finished goods stock}}{\text{Cost of sales}} \times 365$$

What is the average length of time of stock holding by the Freshfields DIY Emporium?

e Outline the ways in which the owner of the Freshfields DIY Emporium might improve his management of working capital. What other factors might he need to take into account before making his final decisions?

f Comment on the liquidity position of the business using appropriate ratios.

6 Micro Ltd is a small private electronics company run by Anne Little, who owns 60 per cent of the equity. It is a fast-growing profitable business with sales of £800 000 over the year ending 30 April 1986, giving a post-tax profit of £600 000. The company is anxious to expand, as the market demand for its product is growing fast. It needs finance, however, to do this.

a i What are the main external sources of finance available to Micro Ltd?

ii What factors should Anne Little consider in choosing which to use? (8)

b Over the next two years, Micro Ltd is planning rapid expansion and it expects sales and profits to increase each year by 25 per cent of the present level. It also aims for:

    stocks = 3 months' sales
    debtors = 2 months' sales
    creditors = 1 month's sales

As no new capital equipment has been bought during the last year, Micro plans to spend £100 000 on replacing existing machines during the next two years, and the same again on new machinery. The present situation of the company is shown on the balance sheet below.

Balance sheet for Micro Ltd year ending 30 April 1986				
1985 (£000s)		1986 (£000s)	1985 (£000s)		1986 (£000s)
410	Shareholder funds	430	150	Land and buildings	150
120	Long-term loans	120	220	Machinery	200
110	Creditors	120	245	Stock	250
170	Bank overdraft	130	195	Debtors	200
810		800	810		800

Stating clearly any assumptions made, calculate the following:

 i the cash required to support this expansion; (4)

 ii the extent to which internal funds will contribute. (5)

 c Using the information given in the balance sheet above, calculate the following ratios:

 i current.

 ii acid test.

 iii gearing.

On the basis of these ratios, make recommendations as to how the company should raise any external finance necessary for its expansion. (5)

 d If it cannot raise the necessary cash, what alternatives are open to the company? (3) 1986 (CLES)

7 a Describe the main options open to British companies if they wish to raise long-term capital. (5)

 b A small engineering firm (Migdal Ltd) consists of four departments, three of which are production departments (P_1, P_2 and P_3), whilst the fourth (D) deals with the administration of the whole business. Data for the four departments is given below:

	P_1	P_2	P_3	D
Number of employees	10	8	8	5
Average wages per employee per week	£225	£200	£150	£100
Fixed costs per week	£2500	£1000	£1500	£1000
Other variable costs: average per employee per hour	£40	£20	£40	None
Capital used, at cost (000)	£150	£100	£50	£10
Working hours per week	30	30	30	30

 i Which of the methods described in answer to **a** above would you recommend if Migdal wished to raise a modest amount of capital and obtain a quotation on the Stock Exchange for the first time? Explain the reasons for your recommendation. (5)

 ii From the data above, prepare a weekly budget of costs for the total business and for each of the four departments. You should assume that each department is to be charged with interest at 10 per cent per annum (assume a 50-week year), and that since D does not earn revenue its costs are to be aggregated and then allocated to P_1, P_2 and P_3 in the proportions of 40:40:20 respectively. (10)

 c What other sources of finance are available to Migdal Ltd, if they finally decide not to get a quotation from the Stock Exchange, and what might be their advantages and disadvantages from Migdal's point of view? (5) June 1985 (CLES)

Activities

1 Investigate the working of the Stock Exchange. Collect as much information as you can about the deregulation of the financial markets in October 1986, and comment on any insights this information may give you into the working of a market.

2 Interview a retailer and a small manufacturer or artisan about the management of their working capital. Pay particular attention to any practices that may seem less than ideal, and the reasons given for following them.

3 Compare the capital structure of a number of companies from their published accounts. Attempt to explain any differences you might observe.

Essays

1 Under what circumstances might a business decide to lease rather than buy a piece of capital equipment?

2 The directors of a company are considering floating it on the Unlisted Securities Market. Comment on the factors which might influence their decision.

3 Discuss the factors which will determine the capital structure of a business.

4 Outline and discuss the methods of investment appraisal a business might use.

5 'The management of cash and working capital is essential to the survival of a business enterprise.' Discuss.

6 'A business that relies too heavily on borrowing to finance capital expenditure is too vulnerable.' Discuss.

7 The following is an extract from the balance sheet of a public limited company:

Ordinary shares	£
Authorised 800 000 at £1 each	800 000
Issued and fully paid 700 000 at £1 each	700 000
General reserve	50 000
Long-term borrowing	
Debentures 10% (2010)	250 000
Capital employed	1 000 000

The company now wishes to raise an additional £500 000 to finance the development of a new product. Assess the implications of the relevant alternative sources of finance. 1986 (AEB)

8 a What is the role of the average rate of return when evaluating investment projects? (5)
  b When might the payback period be a better technique? (5)
  c What advantages and disadvantages would the discounted cash flow technique have over other methods when evaluating investment decisions? (15) 1986 (CLES)

9 Your firm has decided to make a takeover bid for a firm supplying you with raw materials. The question arises as to whether you should offer equity capital or cash.
  a What factors should be taken into account when making the decision whether to offer equity capital or cash? (15)
  b What might be the financial consequences for shareholders of the company being taken over? (10) 1986 (CLES)

8 Marketing

When you have studied this chapter you should:

☐ Understand what is meant by the term 'marketing'.

☐ Know the responsibilities of the function of marketing.

☐ Appreciate the interdependence between the marketing objectives and the overall objectives of a business.

☐ Appreciate the internal and external constraints on business decisions.

☐ Know how a business finds out about its markets.

☐ Be able to select an appropriate method of market research.

☐ Understand what is meant by a target market.

☐ Appreciate the problems a business has in deciding on a target market.

What is marketing?

The function of marketing includes all the activities a business undertakes in order to satisfy the needs of the customer. At its simplest this can be seen as the components of the marketing mix:

☐ getting the *product* right.

☐ suiting the *price* to the market.

☐ telling the customers about the product and persuading them to buy through *promotion* activities.

☐ making sure the product is in the right *place* at the right time.

A definition of marketing that concentrates on decisions concerning the product, price, promotion and place does not give sufficient emphasis to the dynamic nature of marketing activity. Figure 8.1 illustrates the continuous nature of marketing activities.

Figure 8.1 The dynamics of marketing

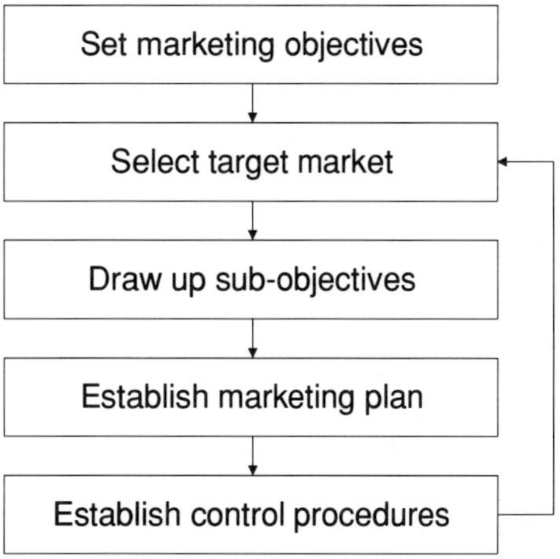

Figure 8.2 Marketing as the interface

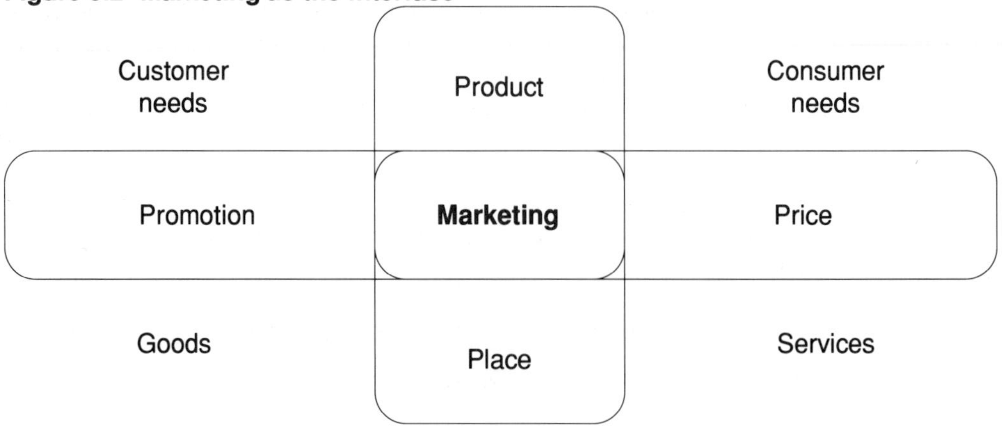

Customer needs	Product	Consumer needs
Promotion	**Marketing**	Price
Goods	Place	Services

Marketing activities include:

- [ ] the need for the business to find out what the market wants.

- [ ] the co-operation between the departments of the business to discover the extent to which it is able to satisfy those needs. This is sometimes called an *internal audit*.

- [ ] the co-ordination of the production and distribution of the product so that it is available to the customer in the right quantities, at the right time and in the right place.

- [ ] communication with the customer and the final consumer.

- [ ] checking the effectiveness of the marketing effort so that improvements can be made for the future.

Marketing can also be seen as the interface between the business system and the market in which it operates. Ideally it receives information from both and, as a result of analysing and interpreting the data, enables the business to function more effectively in the market place. The idea of the marketing interface is shown in Figure 8.2.

A confusion sometimes arises between a marketing and a selling oriented business. The essential differences between the two philosophies are shown in Figure 8.3.

Figure 8.3 Marketing and selling

Selling	Marketing
↓	?
How many have we sold?	What strategy will give us the most profit?
Concentrate on the customers.	What are our strengths, weaknesses, opportunities and threats? (the SWOT analysis)
Concentrate on existing products.	Who are our customers? Who could be our customers?
	Stay aware of the whole business.

Even businesses that have all the outward signs of a marketing approach can sometimes make this mistake. They may have the people with the right job titles, the correct departments can be in existence, but unless the attitudes of the management and people concerned are right the business will still be mainly concerned with selling rather than marketing. The essential difference lies in the attitude of the business towards its customers. The *market oriented* business works hard to make sure that it is producing what the consumer wants now and tries to identify future trends.

So if a market oriented business is one which centres all its activities on the perceived needs of the customer and consumer, the function of the marketing department must include the following activities:

☐ the setting of marketing objectives to support the overall objectives of the business.

☐ the selection of the market the business is aiming to satisfy.

☐ the organisation of the marketing effort.

☐ the drawing up of a plan for marketing.

☐ the organisation of a system of control so that the effectiveness of the marketing can be judged and the plan modified if necessary.

SELF ASSESSMENT

'My job is to sell machines. The machines themselves are technically advanced and customers are not always aware of the advantages they can receive by installing them so I have to persuade – and back up my persuasion with solid facts and figures. I have also got to know what the machines can do and how they can be best adapted to suit the needs of different customers. That means getting back to the manufacturers and telling them what the customer wants. Some of them seem to think that because a machine is technically perfect the customers will be queuing up to buy it. It just does not work that way.'

1 What evidence is there in the above passage to suggest that the speaker is aware of the philosophy of marketing rather than simply selling?

Business objectives and marketing objectives

The overall objectives of a business are the goals, set by senior management, that a business is aiming to achieve in a given time period. These objectives will be expressed in measurable terms and can include a combination of turnover, profit before tax, return on investment and growth. They will be set for varying lengths of time with short-term objectives set for the coming financial year and longer-term objectives reflecting the long-term plans of the business. The short-term objectives will, of course, be set to support the long-term objectives.

The measurable objectives of a business will be set in financial terms. The business has to sell its products to survive and make a profit. The customer also wants to make a profit from the transaction. Goods and services are bought for the benefits they give to the purchaser. The marketing objectives of a business must take this into account if they are to support the overall objectives of the business. Figure 8.4 highlights some marketing objectives.

Figure 8.4 Marketing objectives: where the effort goes

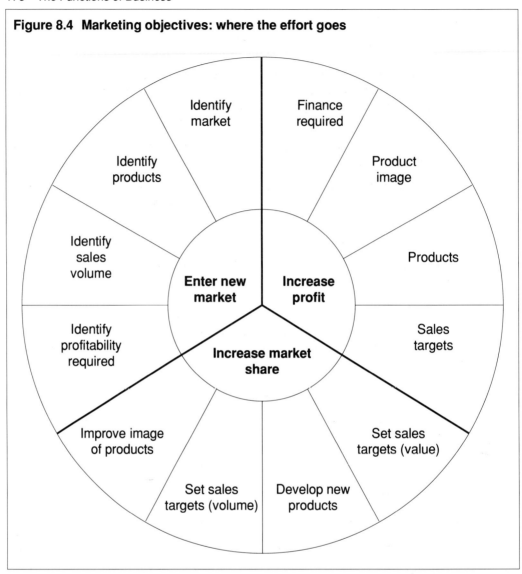

Because the benefits to the consumer of buying a product can be intangible, marketing objectives will include elements that are not expressed in measurable terms.

1   *Image*   This is one of the intangible factors on which customers make their buying decisions. Are they looking for quality, cheapness, expertise or sheer snob value? Do they want to impress their friends with the wisdom of their decisions and evidence of their earning power – or do they want to buy the best possible quality at the lowest possible price? The image a business projects will influence people to buy the product, which in turn will affect the measurable objectives of the business.

2   *Selling*   Sub-objectives set in this area can include:

□   establishing brand loyalty;

□   producing a steady flow of new products;

- finding new markets;

- achieving measurable improvement in sales.

3 *Profit*   A business objective that states that a 10 per cent improvement in profit can be achieved by increasing the profit on sales or by cutting costs. The marketing department will use its knowledge of the customer to decide how big a role it can play in achieving this objective. More specifically its pricing policy will be concerned with:

- setting a price that gives the highest possible return in the shortest period of time – known as *skimming* the market.

- setting a price that is attractive to the largest number of people and so persuading them to buy the product rather than the products of competitors. This is known as *penetrating* the market.

- setting a price that gives a high profit per item – usually applied to luxury products.

- setting a price that gives a high total profit on a large number of products sold – usually applied to cheaper, mass-produced goods and services.

4 *Differentiating the product*   Unless a business is a well-established monopoly or the product is innovative there will be a number of close substitutes for its product on the market. An important objective of marketing can be to emphasise the advantages a product has over those of competitors. This can be done by:

- producing and emphasising a high quality product.

- making the product more widely available than those of competitors.

- establishing a distinctive pricing policy.

- advertising to establish the image of the product.

- featuring distinctive design elements of the product.

If you look carefully at these objectives of the marketing function you will see that they are interdependent.

- The design, quality and distinctiveness of the product will help determine the pricing and the methods used to promote it.

- The selling objectives will contribute to the promotion, pricing and distribution policies.

- The level of profit will be determined by the objectives of the business and the effectiveness of pricing, distribution and promotion policies. This statement assumes that the product is good and is directed to the right market.

- Different markets, particularly with some products, demand a careful mix of product, price, promotion and place.

Marketing objectives, like those of any business function, must support the overall objectives of the business. The achievement of the objectives depends on the right mix of *product, price, promotion* and *place*. The criteria of that mix are dealt with in more detail in Chapter 9 ('The marketing mix').

SELF ASSESSMENT

1 State two objectives a business might be aiming for.
2 Why are the overall objectives of a business expressed in measurable terms?
3 From your own experience give two examples of the intangible benefits a consumer might receive from a product.
4 State one marketing objective and explain:
   a how it can be measured.
   b the difficulties involved in measuring it.
5 Select one common consumer good (e.g. breakfast cereal, washing powder/liquid) and one durable consumer good (e.g. car, washing machine). From your observations of the product, price, promotion and distribution policies, what do you think are their marketing objectives? Give reasons for your answers. You should also make a careful note of any problems you experienced in attempting this question.

The constraints on marketing decisions

In Chapter 1 ('What is business studies?') the constraints experienced by a business were listed as a similarity between all businesses. Now we must look at the specific constraints on marketing decisions, which again can be divided into *internal* and *external* constraints.

The internal constraints

Internal constraints exist as a result of the nature of the business and the situation it is in at a particular time. A manager examining internal constraints should be concerned with the strengths and weaknesses of the business compared with those of its competitors.

1 *People* A business is made up of people, each one of whom will have their own particular combination of skills and personality. Both attributes can become a constraint on the business in achieving its objectives.

   □ In order to achieve the objectives of a business people need to work together. Unfortunately, people tend to have different ways of working and this can lead to conflict. Two people striving for the same objective will decide on the right way to go about it – very different from each other. Each believes their way is right. Both are prepared to fight for their decisions. If they happen to dislike each other as well, nothing gets done while they work out their disagreement.

   □ The need for status can cause a serious problem in achieving objectives. In a large business the production manager and the marketing manager may have equal status. They may be intent upon protecting that status. So when a proposal is put forward that seems to downgrade one department in terms of the other, it may be rejected – not on the merits of the proposal but simply because, in one manager's opinion, it lowers the status of the department. One way to deal with this problem in a market oriented business is to give more authority and responsibility to the marketing staff. The contrasting organisation charts in Figure 8.5 illustrate this.

   □ An important question is 'What skills do the people possess?' Where there is an obvious lack of skills, for example in the advertising department, the business might consider either strengthening its management team by employing people with those skills or buying in the skills by commissioning an agency.

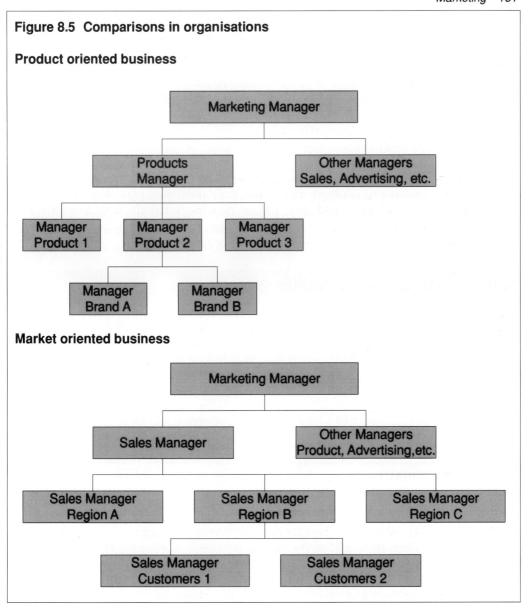

Figure 8.5 Comparisons in organisations

Product oriented business

Marketing Manager

Products Manager

Other Managers Sales, Advertising, etc.

Manager Product 1

Manager Product 2

Manager Product 3

Manager Brand A

Manager Brand B

Market oriented business

Marketing Manager

Sales Manager

Other Managers Product, Advertising, etc.

Sales Manager Region A

Sales Manager Region B

Sales Manager Region C

Sales Manager Customers 1

Sales Manager Customers 2

The importance of people to a business is dealt with in more detail in Chapter 12 ('People and business'). For the moment it is important to remember that the way in which people work together is an important constraint on the ability of a business to achieve its objectives.

2   *Finance* When a business decides to launch a new product, begin an advertising campaign and develop a distribution system, it is investing money. The precise use of the term 'investment' is defined in the Glossary. Usually it is used to describe the purchase of premises, plant and machinery. In fact it refers to any business activity where money is committed to a project involving risk for a period of time. This applies to marketing activities. Before embarking on a project in marketing a business must be aware of the

financial implications. It should, therefore, use the same assessment criteria on the project as it uses when buying a machine.

This is difficult for the marketing department because its objectives include intangibles which can be difficult to quantify. The success of an advertising campaign can be judged by the increase in sales resulting from it. If that advertising campaign is accompanied by a change in distribution policy, then how do you determine which change brought about the increase in sales?

3   *Production*   The production capacity of a business is a major constraint upon marketing. It is pointless to attempt to increase sales if the production department cannot meet the additional orders. Equally it is ridiculous to promote a product on quality if the stated quality level cannot be reached. The production department also has constraints in terms of people (skills and attitudes), finance (existing plant and money available for investment) and marketing (what the market demands from it). These constraints are a combined additional constraint on the marketing department.

SELF ASSESSMENT

1   Explain briefly how each of the following could act as a constraint upon marketing decisions.
   a   A small business realises that it would benefit from advertising. Unfortunately, at the moment, it is experiencing cash flow problems.
   b   Labour relations in a business are poor. As a result production is disrupted and quality control erratic.
   c   The marketing manager of a business is sales oriented, and lacks the imagination to think of the customers.

The external constraints

The market place has been described as a jungle. There are thousands, sometimes millions of potential customers. Unless the business is a monopoly there are competitors, every one of which has their own set of objectives that they are striving to reach.

Businesses are often presented as the ones in control. Yet approximately 80 per cent of new products put on the market fail, and a significant proportion of new businesses also fail. The constraints on a business that come from outside are beyond their control, and they are always changing. Somehow they have to deal with them.

1   *Competitors*   There are very few goods and services that are not produced by more than one business. If the customer is not satisfied by the goods offered by one business it is usually possible to find a close substitute in the products of another business. Dissatisfaction can be in terms of the product, the promotion (which may not offer satisfaction for the customer's needs) and the price at which the goods are offered. A business must take note of its competitors.

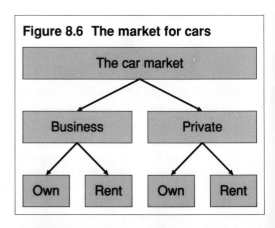

Figure 8.6   The market for cars

Markets are not the homogeneous things they appear to be at first sight. Figure 8.6 shows how the market for cars can be divided into *market segments*.

The business has to find the market segment it is aiming at and direct its policies of product, price, promotion and place to the needs of that group of people. If it is lucky and clever it will find a market segment to which it can adapt its marketing mix closely and in which there are few competitors. When this happens the business is said to have found its *niche* in the market.

2 *Legislation* The customer needs protection. Over the years a body of law has been built up to protect the consumer, in particular from the careless or criminal practices of business.

  ☐ The *Trades Descriptions Act* of 1968 prevents businesses making false claims for the product in advertising. This includes the making of false claims for goods offered at a sale price. The Act stipulates that the goods must have been offered for twenty eight consecutive days at the higher price within the previous six months.

  ☐ The *Finance Act* is passed every year by Parliament to ratify the government's decisions on revenue and expenditure. Central and local government commands a great deal of spending power. A free spending government can provide contracts and, through the people it employs, demand for other goods and services. When a government borrows to finance expenditure it will also push up the rate of interest. This will influence the investment decisions of the business.

  ☐ The *Food and Drugs Act* of 1955 is a constraint upon the production processes of businesses manufacturing food and drugs. As well as laying down minimum conditions relating to the quality of the goods sold it also controls the composition of the products.

  ☐ The *Consumer Credit Act* of 1974 controls the activities of most businesses that offer credit to consumers. The Act came into full operation in 1985. Amongst other things it requires that businesses offering credit should be licensed and that the consumer should have a written statement of the true or annual rate of interest (the APR).

  ☐ The *Consumer Safety Act* of 1978 allows the government to issue regulations banning any products that could cause death or injury.

The responsibility of the supplier of goods and services to the customer is also covered by the law of contract, even when specific laws have not been formulated. In addition the internal laws of the UK are constrained by those of the European Community.

3 *Economic environment* There are times when people feel or are prosperous. There are other times when they have less money at their disposal. How people feel affects their buying decisions. The improvements in communication have made people more responsive to changes in the economy. Media reports of redundancies generate a feeling of insecurity. People tend to save more money, they are less willing to spend and to take on the responsibility of credit agreements. When they feel more prosperous the reverse is true. Again the policy of the business in terms of product, price, promotion and place must take the feelings of the consumer into account.

4 *Technology* Technology has changed very rapidly over the last fifty years. Some of the changes have been government driven. Research and development for defence purposes have provided the knowledge that has created new products. Large

companies with their own research and development departments innovate and create new products that make existing products obsolete. People's needs may stay the same but advances in technology give them a wider choice in the way they satisfy those needs. The customer is not going to pay for a less efficient method of satisfying a need when there are more advanced products on the market. Faced with this situation the business must:

☐ update its products to satisfy customer expectations;

or

☐ find a new product that it is capable of producing with the resources at its disposal.

5 *Other markets* A business buys in labour, finance, goods and services from other businesses. In this situation the business is a buyer in the market and must take account of the conditions of that market. Some of the ways in which this can affect a business are:

☐ a shortage in a particular skill can drive up the price and so make it more expensive for a business to introduce new technology. Conversely, a business employing mainly unskilled labour might find it easier to recruit during a period of economic recession.

☐ an increase in the demand for loans could push up the interest rate, so making it more expensive for a business to invest.

☐ increased demand for a particular raw material on world markets may drive up the price.

Any change in the supplying markets will affect the marketing of a business, particularly in the area of price.

SELF ASSESSMENT

1 For each of the following situations state:
   a the type of business most likely to be affected.
   b the way in which it could affect the marketing policy of the business.
      i An increased awareness of the dangers of food poisoning.
      ii An increase in the price of oil.
      iii A rapid decline in the number of school leavers.
      iv A government decision to invest more funds in science education.
      v A technological advance in communications technology.

Market information

In the previous sections we have discussed the objectives of a business and the internal and external constraints upon them achieving those objectives. It is essential that a business decides upon its objectives with the maximum amount of knowledge about its own situation, the position of other businesses in the market and the way in which the market is moving. This means that the business needs information about:

☐ its own resources and performance which will be collected from its own internal statistical and accounting data.

□   the behaviour and success or failure of the strategies used by its competitors.

□   what the buyers want and how they behave.

All this information will provide constraints on the decisions of the business with relation to product, price, promotion and place policies.

Market research

The activities concerned with collecting information on which to base marketing decisions are known collectively as *market research*. It is customary to divide this into two areas:

1   *Desk research*   which is the collection, analysis and evaluation of information from such sources as government statistics, specialist journals and business accounts.

2   *Field research*   which involves the collection of data directly from a sample of potential consumers.

Although desk and field research are given as two separate activities you should remember that the field research of one business can provide the material for desk research in another business. The person who visits your home with a detailed questionnaire on the type of durable consumer goods you possess, the purchases you have made in the last two years, and the ones you intend to make in the near future, is unlikely to be working for one manufacturer. The data will be used to compile a report on the market for consumer durables in general which will then be sold to interested companies.

The cost of field research is high and requires specialist personnel if it is to be accurate; for those reasons alone it makes sense for many businesses to use the services of agencies rather than to maintain their own departments.

Methods of field research

1   *Questionnaires*   These are the basis of all field research and carry with them a number of problems. It is difficult, for example, to design questions which elicit the information required without ambiguity or influencing the answer of the person being interviewed. If the questions asked are too narrow important information may be lost. If they allow the person being interviewed to make too free a response the information may be difficult to analyse and compare with other responses.

2   *Interviewers*   Using interviewers to ask prepared questions has the twin disadvantages of being expensive and the risk that the interviewer might, consciously or unconsciously, lead the person being interviewed to give a 'desirable' answer. This is known as *interviewer bias*. However, an experienced interviewer can adapt the question to suit the person being interviewed (the *interviewee*). Unfamiliar words can be explained, the purpose of the question made clear. If you look at the disadvantages of the personal interview and compare them with the disadvantages of the questionnaire you will see a close connection. Rephrasing questions takes time and is therefore expensive. It also increases the risk of bias.

3   *Postal questionnaires*   These rely on precise, unambiguous questions and the willingness of people to return them. In a busy life the answering of questionnaires can take a very low priority. Even the provision of a reply-paid envelope will not ensure that the

questionnaire will be answered and posted. Postal questionnaires depend upon an up-to-date mailing list of the type of people who are likely to be interested in the product. There is the risk that the people receiving the questionnaire will see it as part of their 'junk mail'. This can lead to resentment, suspicion of the way in which the name and address has been acquired (a suspicion which can be transferred to the business undertaking the market research) or the questionnaire being thrown away.

4   *Telephone questionnaires*   An interview conducted by telephone appears to combine the advantage of the cheapness of postal questionnaires with the one-to-one contact of an interview. They do, of course, have their own built-in bias that only people with telephones can be contacted. Protection of privacy can cause people to react adversely to this type of market research. Good practice usually begins with a letter to the people about to be interviewed explaining the purpose of the telephone call they will receive and asking them to co-operate.

Both postal and telephone questionnaires reduce the cost of the research but share the risk of bias with personal interviews.

5   *Consumer panels*   These are groups of people who agree to keep a record of all their actions as a consumer. The record might be specific, relating to one type of purchase, or general, relating to a 'basket' of decisions. Again there is the danger of bias arising from the selection of individuals, but the data is objective.

SELF ASSESSMENT

1 Explain why questionnaires administered during a personal interview are likely to be more expensive than postal questionnaires.
2 Give one reason why panels might be preferred to other methods of field research.

Sampling and bias

We saw in Chapter 5 ('Statistics') that the total number of people (or things) from which information could be collected is known as a *population*. With a UK total population of 56m it is unrealistic (and uneconomic) for a survey to include every person. A child of five is unlikely to be either interested in or able to pay for a washing machine. Market research data is based on a *sample* of the total population, that is a part of the whole population whose characteristics are studied to reveal the characteristics of the population as a whole.

At first sight this may appear a simple exercise. You have a product. You think it will appeal to the 18–30 age group. It would be a waste of money to sample people outside that age range. But are you right? If the product is new you may have misjudged your market. Even the manufacturers of established products cannot afford to be complacent about the *market segment* to which they are directing their marketing strategy. They may think their market segment is clearly defined in terms of age, income, sex, occupation and geographical distribution, but changes in society as a whole could change the composition of their markets. An increase in home ownership in the 20–25 age group could increase the interests of this group in domestic appliances and domestic consumer goods such as cleaners. Their priorities in buying decisions may be very different from those of other age groups.

The decision about the sample to be taken can introduce a tendency on the part of the sample to deviate from the true result which would have been obtained if the whole population had been questioned. This is known as *statistical bias*. A decision to aim at a particular market segment when investigating the market will introduce bias.

In Chapter 5 ('Statistics') you were introduced to the idea of the normal distribution. A sample which approximates to this can provide statisticians with information concerning the *probability of error* in the information (the *raw data*) at their disposal. If the sample is small they might use techniques such as the *t distribution* or the *chi-squared distribution*. There is also the *Poisson distribution*. The important thing about each of these techniques is that they rely upon *known* properties of a certain distribution in terms of mean, median, mode and standard deviations. As a result they can be used to make an approximation to the result that would have been achieved if the *whole* population had been questioned. Figure 8.7 gives the major sampling methods used in testing the market.

Figure 8.7 Methods of sampling

Samples using probability

Random sample — Each member of the population has an equal chance of being selected.

Stratified random sample — The population is divided into sub-groups by, e.g. age, income, occupation, geographical area. The selected sub-group is then sampled randomly.

Samples not using probability

Quota sample — The interviewer selects a given number of the population who fulfil certain requirements in, e.g., age and income.

Convenience sample — The interviewer selects a number of the population on the basis of ease of access.

SELF ASSESSMENT

1 For each of the situations listed below state and explain:
   a a sampling method you consider appropriate.
   b the reasons for your choice.
      i The launch of a new breakfast cereal.
      ii The owner/chef of a small restaurant who wants to test customer attitudes to changes in the menu and decor.
      iii A person considering setting up a service business for the people of a certain area.

The reasons for market research

A business needs information on all aspects of the market in which it operates. It also needs to evaluate the effect of its own policies on sales.

1 The population can be classified according to age, sex, occupation and income. The business needs to know if the main demand for its product lies with a particular age/income/geographical grouping in order to adopt effective pricing, promotion and distribution strategies. The grouping, once defined, is known as the *market segment*. If you read marketing magazines you will often see advertisements by other publications, for example newspapers, which give a breakdown of their readership in terms of occupation, income and age. They are using their own market research to target a market

segment and are using that to sell advertising space in their newspapers to businesses which have identified this segment as being their market.

A business may also need to distinguish between its customers and consumers. The customers are the people who buy the products, the consumers are the people who use them. Food, for example, is usually bought by a smaller number of people than the consumers. However, the needs and tastes of the consumer can also influence the buying behaviour of the customer. The interests of the two groups are not identical. The consumer might give priority to taste; the customer's first concern might be price. The business needs to find out which group has the greater power in the buying decision.

2   The product itself is tested. Research in this area may be concerned with monitoring the progress of existing products and people's reaction to them, or it may be concerned with testing reaction to a new market. In the latter case the product may be marketed in a geographical region before being put on the national market. This allows the business to test reaction to the product and to monitor other elements in the marketing mix at a lower cost. This is known as a *test market*.

3   The price at which potential competitors are selling their products is important. For a new product the business has to discover the price which will enable them to achieve the marketing objectives and, through them, the overall objectives of the business.

4   Packaging has the utilitarian function of protecting the goods against damage and deterioration with a view to prolonging its *shelf life* (the period of time for which it can be stored before it must be discarded). For some goods it can also add to the convenience of the retailer. Packaged tea and sugar are easier for the retailer to store and sell. Packaging may also be part of the promotion policy of the business by creating an image which, allied to advertising, can encourage *brand loyalty* on the part of a consumer.

5   Advertising is expensive and a business wants to make sure it is getting value for money. It will be interested in the reaction of the market to its advertising campaign. In Chapter 3 ('Markets') we introduced the idea of demand elasticity. The same concept can be used to analyse the impact of advertising on the market.

$$\frac{\text{percentage change in quantity demanded}}{\text{percentage change in advertising expenditure}}$$

If the market is responsive to advertising, i.e. elastic, the numerical measurement will be greater than 1 and revenue will increase by a larger amount than the additional expenditure on advertising. An inelastic market means that an increase in advertising would add to the costs of the business without a corresponding increase in revenue.

SELF ASSESSMENT

1 A business manufacturing toys is about to launch a toy aimed at the 7–11 age group and retailing at approximately £50.
   a Distinguish between the customers and consumers in this situation.
   b How would it affect the advertising of the business if it was thought that:
      i   the customers had the most market power?
      ii the consumers had the most market power?
   c Give three examples of products in which the distinction between customer and consumer might be important to a business.

Conclusion

1   A market oriented business is one which directs the whole effort of the business to satisfying the needs of the market.

2   The internal organisation of the business reflects the importance of the marketing function. For example, in a marketing oriented business the marketing manager will not report directly to the production manager.

3   The marketing objectives will support the overall objectives of the business.

4   Businesses operate in a dynamic environment. The behaviour of people, other businesses, other organisations, central and local government and international agencies will limit the extent to which it can achieve its objectives and the ways in which it can achieve them.

5   In order to identify a target market, set objectives and devise policies to achieve them in terms of product, price, promotion and place, a business needs information. It also needs information to judge how successful it has been in the policies it decided upon.

6   The collection and interpretation of data needs care.

REVIEW

1 Getfit Ltd produces a range of dried dietary supplements aimed at specialist market sectors, for example athletes, pregnant women and teenagers. Its major customers are health food chains. The company has a high reputation for research and development and for quality.

   Getfit is a subsidiary of a multinational specialising in food production. The parent company has recently taken over a chain of supermarkets. It has been suggested to the board that the Getfit expertise could be used to develop a range of low calorie, own brand food products to be sold throughout the chain. Market research had identified a market niche that these products could fill. The market segment was clearly defined in the product brief.

   a Distinguish between a market niche and a market segment.
   b Outline the market segment for this product, giving reasons for your decisions.
   c Explain how Getfit's reputation for quality and research would be an advantage in this venture.
   d What information would the business need about its potential market?
   e List three ways in which the company could find out this information and comment on the limitations of each method.
   f State three internal constraints Getfit might experience in moving into this market. Give reasons for your answers.

2 Boone's Ltd is a retailing chain specialising in medium-priced furniture. It has stores in most of the major cities and large towns of the UK. Until 1985 it was known chiefly for the quality of its furniture and had a rather staid image. Profits were acceptable but uninspiring.

   In 1984 the board of directors fought off a takeover bid. The fact that they had become a target for such a bid, combined with discontent from the major shareholders, resulted in a radical rethink of company policy. Profit targets were revised upwards, the chief executive was persuaded to resign and someone with a strong marketing background was appointed to the position. The experience of the majority of directors was weighted towards finance.

Six months afterwards the chief executive made a presentation to the board outlining the strengths and weaknesses of the business and recommending some major changes. The following is an adapted extract from the conclusion to this presentation.

'We have an excellent reputation among our customers. They exhibit a high degree of loyalty to our stores. I would remind you that the age profile of our customers is high, and rising all the time. Fifty per cent of our customers are over 45 and their children show no signs of following in their parents' footsteps. If we are to reach our profit target we must widen our appeal and expand our market ...

Customers do not buy a product, they buy a lifestyle. Unless we create an image for our business we can only look forward to declining profits and eventual liquidation.'

a What are the objectives of the business?
b Give two ways in which improved marketing is expected to support these objectives.
c State three marketing objectives the business might establish in order to achieve the overall objectives of the business. What relationship will they have with them?
d Give three examples of what might be included in the new marketing package.
e The business is facing a period of innovation and change. What internal constraints might it experience during the transition?
f Comment on the tactics the business might employ to overcome these constraints.

3 Juskids Ltd produces toys and games for the 5–15 age group. The business is very profitable, with a market share of 20 per cent. Between 1982 and 1988 analysis of sales figures showed some unexpected trends – previously successful products were losing their position in the market and products which it had almost decided to scrap showed improving sales. There were no apparent reasons for these trends so the company commissioned a marketing agency to conduct some market research.

The resulting report confirmed that 80 per cent of their customers were aged between 30 and 45, that 75 per cent had incomes in excess of £15 000 a year, that 70 per cent of them owned cars and that 85 per cent were owner occupiers. The pie chart illustrates their interests.

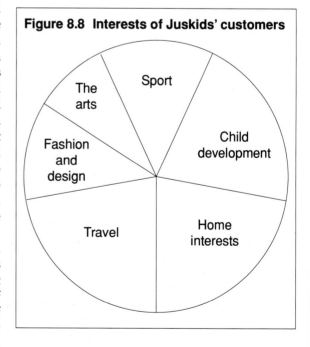

Figure 8.8 Interests of Juskids' customers

The arts

Sport

Fashion and design

Child development

Travel

Home interests

a Distinguish between the customers for a product and the consumers of a product. What significance could this distinction have for Juskids Ltd?

b State and explain one advantage of displaying the information on the interests of customers in the form of a pie chart. To what extent does the pie chart shown fulfil this advantage?

c What additional information would the business need before making changes in its marketing strategy?

d Comment on the relevance of the above information for the marketing strategy of the business.

4 The following extract was taken from the *Liverpool Echo* of 8 August 1989. Read it carefully before answering the questions that follow.

a Explain briefly why perfume sales might be susceptible to higher mortgage rates and inflation.

b Assuming that mortgage rates increased by 4 per cent in this period, calculate the cross elasticity of demand for perfume. To what extent should businesses be concerned about this information?

c Outline one way in which the introduction of expensive new brands could help maintain the sales level of perfume.

> # What a stink!
>
> Higher mortgages stink! And the international perfume market is suffering accordingly.
>
> Last year, British women used £330m worth of perfume. But with inflation and higher mortgages putting the pressure on spending, sales are being hit.
>
> Predictions show that by next year total sales will fall to £320m. Perfume companies are launching expensive new brands to maintain sales, according to a new report from the market research organisation, Euromonitor.
>
> But that just might not work. Women are growing more fickle in their choices, and less loyal to particular brands.

d State and explain three problems a business manufacturing perfume might foresee on reading this report.

5 James Jones was beginning to believe that the people who had shaken their heads at his business idea and prophesied doom just might have been right.

The original idea had been simple. The domestic computer market for micros was saturated and over-sophisticated. Promotions for new models emphasised their outstanding capacity, speed of operation and so on and the prices reflected this. James had argued that there were a lot of people who did not need that degree of sophistication. Education, games playing and word processing on a relatively simple level would satisfy the needs of many customers and perhaps bring more people into the market. He believed that there was a large, unsatisfied demand in third world countries for a cheap, strong micro computer that could use existing software.

First year sales figures had been disappointing. Instead of the 150 000 projected sales the reality was 100 000. It was at this point that James employed a marketing consultant. The resulting report supported his original belief that there was a market for the product – in fact, consumers were very enthusiastic about it. The launch year of Computit, 1989, had unfortunately seen a rise in interest rates. Consumer purchasing power was falling and, although the Jones computer was cheap enough not to need loan financing, people were in fact spending less on luxuries.

The consultant suggested that Jones had misread his market. Computer owners tended to be set in their ways. They replaced existing computers with compatible models so that their own software and text was easily transferable. This consumer loyalty was strengthened by the promotion activities of the established companies who spent a considerable amount of money on informing the market of the technical advances incorporated into their new models. The very cheapness of the Jones computer made people suspicious. Customers tended to think that if the computer was cheap it must in some way be inferior. In the first year of production, this suspicion was supported by poor quality in several batches. Jones put this down to problems in recruiting qualified and experienced staff. Financing of the business had made it difficult to compete in terms of wages and conditions of service with other, established firms.

a What evidence is there in this case that James Jones did not research his market?

b State and explain three possible marketing objectives for James Jones in the first two years of his business.

c What constraints did James Jones experience in achieving these objectives?

d How could James Jones attempt to overcome these constraints?

Activities

1 Select a good or service you might be able to supply to the local community. Undertake a market research exercise on this product and use the statistical techniques outlined in Chapter 5 ('Statistics') to analyse the data. What problems did you encounter? What steps could you take to overcome them?

2 Collect as many cuttings as you can from newspapers and magazines on two external constraints on business activity. Read a little first. It makes sense to choose a constraint which is in the news, for example at the time of writing the interest rate and the environmental lobby would be good choices. Analyse your data. What impact would these constraints have on the marketing functions of the business? What is the response of the business community to these constraints?

3 Select a local business and analyse the constraints on its marketing activities. To what extent do the market in which it operates and the size of the business affect these constraints?

4 Visit the marketing department of a business or invite a speaker from that department. You are interested in the marketing policy for one of their products. To what extent is this policy dictated by internal and external constraints?

Suggested projects

1 A critical appreciation of the marketing objectives of a business.

2 What is the target market for a business?

3 An appreciation of the impact of market structure on the marketing strategy of a business. (This project can be adapted to other external constraints.)

Essays

1 'There is no such thing as a constraint-free environment; the art of marketing is to maximise such possibilities as exist.' To what extent do you agree with this statement?

2 What information will a business need before launching a new product?

3 Comment on the constraints experienced by a marketing director in formulating a marketing strategy.

4 A business is described as being market oriented. What do you understand by this description? Discuss the implications for marketing and production policies.

5 What factors would a manager take into account in deciding on the strategy for marketing a new product?

6 Outline the methods of market research available to a business. What criteria would a business use in selecting methods appropriate to their circumstances?

7 'Marketing is the interface between the business and the rest of the economic system.' Justify this statement.

8 'Sales representatives are there to sell the product they are given.' To what extent do you agree with this statement?

9 The marketing mix

When you have studied this chapter you should:

☐ Understand the general relationship between the marketing objectives of the business and the composition of the marketing mix.

☐ Be able to define products in terms of benefits and type.

☐ Be aware of the product life cycle and the different patterns.

☐ Appreciate the importance of the product in determining the marketing mix.

☐ Understand the role of promotion, pricing and distribution in satisfying customers' needs.

☐ Appreciate the importance of the target market in determining the marketing mix.

☐ Understand the strategies a business might employ to achieve its marketing objectives through the marketing mix.

The elements of the marketing mix

Throughout Chapter 8 ('Marketing') there was constant repetition of the importance of the overall objectives of the business, the marketing objectives and the information available to the business in determining its policies of product, price, promotion and place. This chapter will examine these ingredients of the marketing mix in more detail, demonstrating the different courses of action that are open to businesses – always depending upon the constraints to which they are subject.

The product

What is a product?
The description of a product includes:

☐ technical specifications, for example weight, materials, size;

☐ appearance;

☐ quality;

☐ design;

☐ colour;

☐ use and time of use.

The description is not limited to the physical qualities of a product, sometimes referred to as its *tangible* features. The customers are buying not only the good or service, but also the associated services and the status the product is thought to confer upon them. The description can be extended to include:

- after-sales service;
- status;
- image;
- additional guarantees;
- clarity of instruction manuals/free tuition in use;
- availability of spare parts;
- credit facilities.

The product can also be defined in terms of its final use. These are outlined in Figure 9.1.

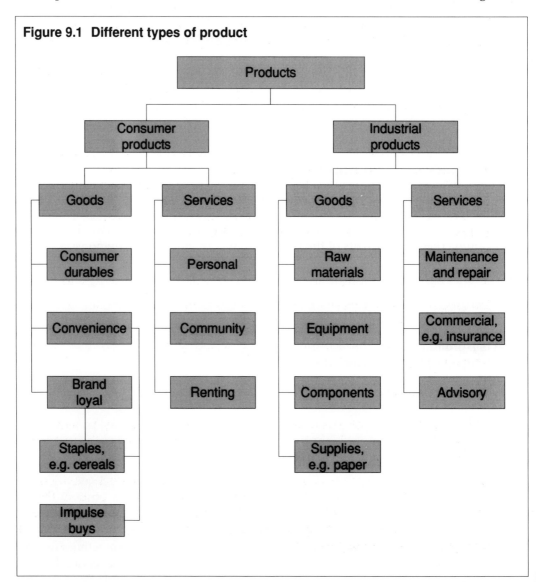

Figure 9.1   Different types of product

1 Industrial goods are those sold to other businesses for use in their production processes or for resale to the final consumer. Industrial goods can vary in price from several million pounds to a few pence. Industrial products can be divided into:

- ☐ machinery and the equipment that goes with it.

- ☐ supplies such as paper, pens, cleaning materials.

- ☐ raw materials and components – wood, metals, car batteries.

- ☐ services to business, for example banking, warehousing, legal, technical and other advisory services.

2 Consumer goods are sold to the consumers to satisfy their immediate and personal needs and wants.

In both markets the elements of the marketing mix are the same, but the emphasis is different. When products are sold in both markets a business may lose sales if it fails to identify and exploit the overlap. There is also a danger that in adapting a product to move from one market to another the features which appealed to the original market might be lost. Products that sell in both markets include cars, office furniture and equipment, and computers. The appeal of industrial products to the consumer might lie in their durability and versatility. A similar range adapted for the consumer market which lacks one of these characteristics but has gained visual impact could very well be a failure.

The product range

The range of products offered by a business is also known as the *product mix*. Businesses which produce more than one good or service are known as *multi-product* firms. The products may be related to each other, for example by using the same raw materials, using the same technology or the same production processes, or they may be totally unrelated. In the latter case the businesses are known as *conglomerates*. The process of increasing the number of products supplied by the business is called *diversification*.

In order to diversify a business might:

- ☐ merge with another business with complementary or different product lines.

- ☐ introduce a new line very similar to those already produced which can be serviced by existing technical and marketing expertise.

- ☐ move into a totally different product area on the basis of its own research and development.

The introduction of a new product always carries with it a certain amount of risk.

- ☐ There may be a lack of expertise in marketing. The product may be technically excellent but a failure to define the target segment of the market on the part of the marketing staff could lead to failure.

- ☐ Patent protection might be inadequate. The success of the product could lead to potential competitors seeking to satisfy the same need with a product that is technically different but has the same use. The battle for market supremacy in video recording systems and the attempts of camera producers to satisfy consumer demand for rapid results are examples of this.

Diversification is a strategy adopted by a business in order to achieve its overall objectives, that is to achieve its desired level of profitability and ensure survival.

The product life cycle

No product has an unlimited life. Consumer tastes will change or the product may become obsolete as the result of changes in technology. In Figure 9.2 you can see a formalised statement of the life cycle of a product. Of course, not all products will have the same product life pattern. Figure 9.3 outlines the different life patterns experienced in different markets.

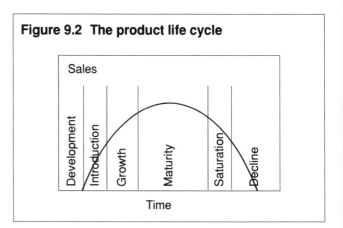

Figure 9.2 The product life cycle

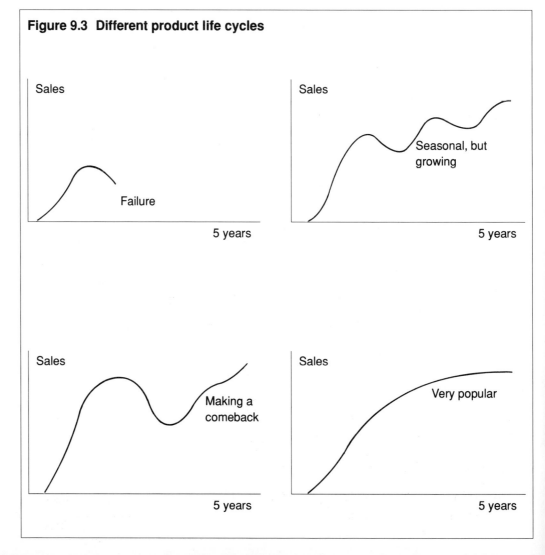

Figure 9.3 Different product life cycles

1   *Introduction/development*   This is the most expensive stage in the history of the product. The costs of research, both technical and marketing, have to be borne, the product is not yet contributing revenue to the business and there is the risk of failure.

2   *Growth*   The product is establishing itself in the market and sales are increasing over time.

3   *Maturity*   The market has been fully exploited (although it may not have reached the sales levels originally hoped for). It is said to be *saturated*. At this stage competition increases as rival firms fight for a bigger share of the market.

4   *Decline*   Total sales are falling.

Businesses may attempt to extend the maturity phase of a product's life by *extension strategies*. These may include: finding new markets and/or new uses for the product; persuading people to use it more frequently; changing the physical appearance or packaging of the product to appeal to new tastes; and developing a new range of associated accessories.

Figure 9.4 shows the relationship between the life cycle of a product and the cash flow generated by it.

If you study this figure you can see that for part of its life a product is taking money from the business and *making no contribution to the profit* of the business. An ideal pattern of product management is given in Figure 9.5.

At any one time the cash flow generated by mature products is helping to nurture the immature products through the early stages of their life cycle. A multi-product business may have a contribution pattern as shown in Figure 9.6.

In markets where sales are seasonal or which are subject to fluctuations the same principle of diversifying the product range in order to provide income is put into practice.

A wider range of products may also increase the selling power of a business and benefit from previous marketing strategies.

Not all the advantages of product diversification are in the

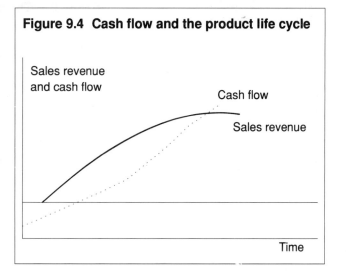

Figure 9.4 Cash flow and the product life cycle

Sales revenue and cash flow

Cash flow

Sales revenue

Time

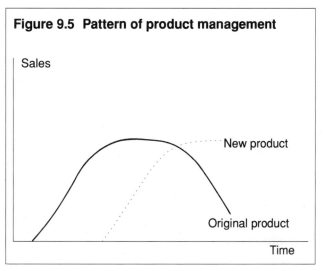

Figure 9.5 Pattern of product management

Sales

New product

Original product

Time

area of marketing. A business may want to use its production capacity more fully and make use of by-products of existing production processes. We shall examine these reasons more closely when we look at economies of scale in Chapter 10 ('Background to production').

The product and the marketing mix

The marketing mix will be affected by:

- ☐ the benefits a product offers the consumer;

- ☐ the type of product;

- ☐ the life cycle of the product;

- ☐ the stage in its life cycle of the product at a given moment.

Figure 9.7 gives the description of a product and shows how each element of the marketing mix might be affected.

As you work through this chapter you will become more aware of this interaction between the elements of the marketing mix – after all, that is how it got its name.

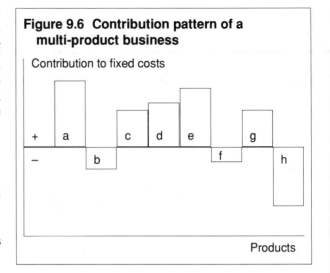

Figure 9.6 Contribution pattern of a multi-product business

Contribution to fixed costs

Products

Figure 9.7 The product & the marketing mix

Is our technology good enough?

How can we communicate with our customers?

What price will the customer pay?

Product: A washing machine

How will we get it to our outlets?

What prices are our competitors charging?

Where will our customers buy?

SELF ASSESSMENT

1 State one problem a business might experience in defining its product.
2 Give one reason why the benefits a business offers as part of its product might be more important than the tangible qualities of the product.
3 A business producing sports shoes places a great deal of emphasis on quality and durability in its advertising. Another business offering a similar range of shoes emphasises the advantages of a healthy active life in its advertising. What does this information tell you about the way in which each business defines its product? Which do you think is right? Give reasons for your answer.
4 State one way in which the position of a product in its life cycle can affect the marketing mix.
5 Give two reasons related to marketing that might persuade a business to diversify its product range.

Pricing

In Chapter 3 ('Markets') we saw how the interaction of demand and supply established the market price for a product. That is an overall view. From the perspective of a business the situation is not so simple. The marketing team have to decide where their product fits into this overall picture. If the product is new they may not be sure which market segment they are targeting.

The price chosen will, of course, be in line with the marketing objectives of the business which in turn will be established to support the overall objectives of the business. A pricing strategy must be decided upon before the method of pricing is established.

Pricing strategies

The constraints on the overall pricing strategy chosen are:

1 *The pricing objectives* These will be designed to support the marketing objectives of the business. Pricing objectives might be set in support of the following areas:

   □   sales;

   □   profit;

   □   growth.

   For example, a price lower than alternative products might be decided on if the business aimed to increase its sales and ultimately its market share.

2 *The type of product and its target market* A high quality product aimed at a high income group might suffer a reduction in demand if its price is low compared with that of its competitors. A great deal will depend upon the consumers' attitude towards the product. Are they buying it for its intrinsic qualities or are they buying it to confer status?

3 *The type of market in which the business is operating* In a perfect market the business is a price taker. It can only react to the existing market price and decide, on the basis of its own costs of production, whether or not it can afford to compete. Some products can be *differentiated* from their rivals. The actual differences may be small but the use of branding and advertising can persuade people that one product is considerably better than another.

4 *Whether the product is innovatory* Innovatory products have a monopoly position in the market. The success of pricing policy in this case will depend on the skill of the marketing team in analysing and evaluating the results of their market research, and also the accuracy with which they describe the product to potential consumers.

5 *The expected life span of the product* As a general rule the shorter the life span the higher the price, to make sure the business covers the costs of development and initial production.

6 *The degree of interdependence within the product range* It might make sense to sell a product at little more than cost if the possession of that product will encourage people to buy accessories to go with it.

Different pricing strategies

1   *Market penetration* has as its main objective the capture of a large share of the market as quickly as possible. In the short term this may lead to lower profits but if the business can establish itself in the market the long-run profits might be high. A great deal will depend on the expected product life and the power of businesses already operating in the market, together with the financial resources of the business adopting this strategy. A short product life cycle will not give the business time to recover development costs if the price is too low. Powerful market leaders with larger financial resources than the producers of the emerging product could follow a policy of price-cutting.

2   *Market skimming* might be likened to skimming the cream off the top of the milk. A high price resulting from high profit margins means a quick recovery of development costs. A business might follow this strategy if its product was technically innovative but it had reason to believe its competitors were likely to launch imitative products in a short time. Fashion products, not only in the garment world but also in games, gimmicks, toys, etc., might also follow this policy. It is a viable option for businesses that expect their product to have a long life span but are in a position to charge a relatively high price in the short term, perhaps with the intention of reducing the price as an extension strategy in the medium to long term.

   A business is likely to select its pricing strategy according to the stage in its life cycle a product has reached, perhaps pricing to penetrate the market in the early stages of the life cycle and switching to a skimming policy when the product is well established.

3   When there are a number of suppliers of a good or service offering it to the same group of people each business will have to match the price of its competitors unless it can persuade consumers that its product is, in some way, more desirable than those of its competitors.

   The more similar (*homogeneous*) the goods and services are, the more the business is dominated by its competitors. Two hairdressing salons may offer identical skills in the cutting and dressing of hair but one might set out to provide a more 'up-market' image. This might justify an increase in the price for its services. It is also likely to mean an increase in the costs of production.

4   *Tendering* is a pricing strategy that is imposed on businesses by market conditions. Governments and local authorities will require businesses to submit a price for a particular job and give a detailed breakdown of costs. Householders engaging builders ask for estimates of the work to be undertaken. The supplier is working without detailed knowledge of his competitors' prices. The customer has the task of ensuring that the prices tendered are for comparable work.

5   The use of *price discrimination* can be seen intuitively as a combination of the strategies of market penetration and skimming. It can be employed when the same product can be offered at different prices to different groups of consumers without the possibility of resale from one group to another.

Methods of pricing

Having established the strategy it intends to follow, the business now needs to work out the price it will charge. This will depend on the costing method it decides to use, which in turn will be dependent on the market in which it is operating and its target profit.

1   *Absorption or full cost pricing*   Total production costs are added together, the required profit added to this, and the result divided by the output. At first sight this method of pricing appears to take little account of the market. A variation of total cost pricing might decide what the market will bear, subtract the desired profit from it and then decide whether or not the good can be made by that business for that price. If the answer is in the negative there may be an investigation into the way in which costs can be reduced; perhaps by changing the quality of the item. This carries with it the danger of accidentally eliminating just those qualities which appeal most to the customer.

2   *Contribution pricing*   When a business has excess capacity or when it produces a number of products it may decide upon the price for a product by contribution pricing. Provided the price covers the direct costs of production and makes a contribution to fixed costs then it will be accepted. In the short term a business with excess capacity might accept orders at below full cost provided the price offered makes a contribution to fixed costs. A business which sees the opportunity of exploiting an additional market through price discrimination may be prepared to price at less than full cost.

3   *Geographic pricing*   The practice of charging a different price in different countries or regions of the same country reflects the cost of transport of the goods. Rather than change prices in one particular country a business might be prepared to take varying levels of profit from different transactions. Another business exporting to Europe could charge different prices according to the region. Of course not all the variations in price between geographical areas will depend on transport costs. The other constraints on pricing must also be taken into account.

4   *Terms*   An important part of pricing is deciding on the terms that will be offered to wholesalers, retailers and the final customer. The two most important are *discounts* and *credit*. Various discounts can be offered:

□   *bulk discounts* for purchases in large quantities.

□   *trade discounts* in this case a manufacturer will set a market price. This is known as the recommended retail price (RRP). Wholesalers and retailers can then purchase from the manufacturer at a price perhaps 30 per cent lower than this price. The RRP has the advantage of allowing the final customer to compare this price with the one being offered by the retailer and so compare the discounts retailers are offering. The RRP replaced resale price maintenance (RPM), which became illegal for most goods in 1964. Under RPM retailers had to charge the manufacturers' prices and so could not compete on price.

□   *seasonal discounts* may be offered to extend the sales of goods which tend to vary seasonally. The discounts will be offered in the season in which demand for goods is low. Figure 9.8 demonstrates how the use of seasonal discounts can change the life cycle of a product.

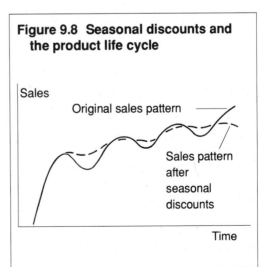

Figure 9.8 Seasonal discounts and the product life cycle

☐   *promotional discounts* or 'money off' offers are part of the general promotional package of the business.

☐   the availability of *credit* and the terms on which it is offered can make an important difference to the price of the good. Strictly speaking credit is not part of the price but in consumer markets when a large proportion of goods are bought on credit terms the customer is likely to see it as part of the price. It should, therefore, be taken into consideration when determining the pricing policy of the business.

SELF ASSESSMENT

1   Explain how each of the following could act as a constraint on the pricing strategy of a business.
   a   As a result of careful monitoring of sales and in-depth market research, a marketing manager decides that one of her products has price elastic demand.
   b   An industry is dominated by four large businesses. A smaller company has an innovatory product and wants to enter the market.
   c   A business selling to a high volume, low price market has a rise in costs.
2   Distinguish briefly between pricing strategies and pricing methods.
3   Figure 9.9 shows two product life cycles. For each one explain how the changes indicated by the dashed line could have been achieved through alterations in pricing strategies.

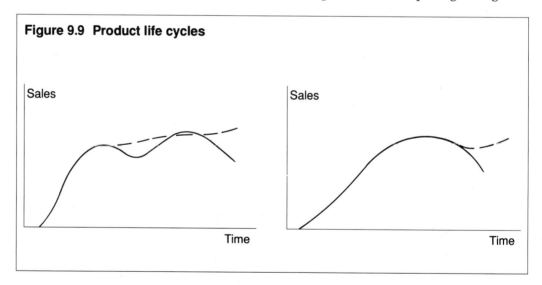

Figure 9.9 Product life cycles

Promotion

Promotion is about communication. It is used to describe any activity of a business that tells potential customers about its products, persuades them to buy, or reminds them that the products are still on the market. Promotional techniques are also used to build an image of the business, for example by emphasising its contribution to research and development or its commitment to the environment. Figure 9.10 shows the large number of promotional techniques that are available to a business.

Figure 9.10 Promotional techniques

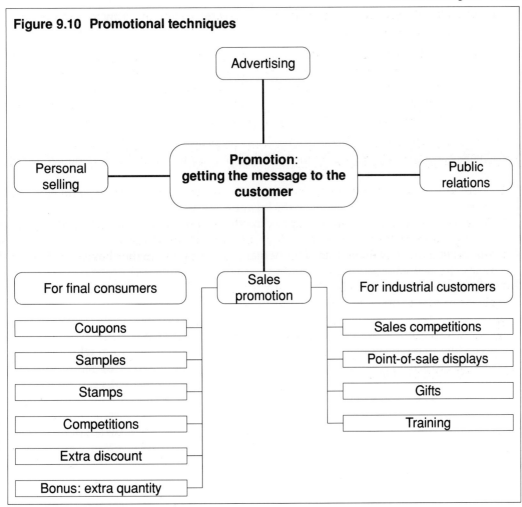

Promotion is important to a business because it can:

☐ persuade people to buy its products and, by generating sales, contribute to the income of the business.

☐ emphasise features of a product that market research has shown to be important to potential customers.

☐ tell people about new products.

☐ build up an image of the business, e.g. for quality, which will make people more likely to buy its products in the future.

☐ extend the life of existing products.

☐ give answers to problems that may have arisen.

☐ justify changes in the policy of the business.

☐ give information about where and how a product can be purchased.

Because promotion can have a big impact on a wide variety of business activities, it is important that it is carefully planned. This planning should involve the setting of objectives for promotional activities that reflect the overall objectives of the business and the marketing objectives and that take into account objectives set for product planning, pricing and distribution policies. There are four main promotional activities:

1   *Advertising*   This is the paid publication of information, ideas and persuasion by a business through a given medium, for example television.

2   *Personal selling*   Oral promotion from one person to a prospective customer or customers with the purpose of making sales.

3   *Public relations*   Placing news about the business with the media in the hope that it will be reported. The business does not pay directly for this 'publicity'.

4   *Sales promotion*   Any marketing activity that is not included in the above.

Advertising

The choice of advertising medium will depend upon:

1   *The market segment*   Magazines and television companies analyse their readers according to interests, age, tastes and income to provide information which they can then use to sell advertising space. A brief glance through marketing magazines will provide examples of the media advertising their advertising potential. Feature articles in magazines can provide a vehicle for advertising.

2   *The amount of money available for advertising*   Media which, in turn, spend money advertising themselves will charge more for advertisements.

3   *The size of the market*   It is pointless for a small business to advertise nationally unless its product is both unique and expensive. Products of this type are often advertised in specialist magazines or, in the case of consumer goods, by word of mouth.

4   *The medium chosen*   This should also relate to the product. Different people read different magazines and watch different programmes. The efficiency of the medium in selling is recognised by attempts to restrict advertising of certain products when it is felt the advertisers have an unfair advantage.

Advertising is not simply a matter of devising an attractive poster and expecting the customers to flock to buy the product. The customer is informed and persuaded to buy in stages.

- The customers have to be made *aware* of the product.
- The *interest* of the customers must be aroused.
- The customers are given *information* to convince them that the product is a good one.
- The customers are persuaded into *action*.

The design of the advertisements used will change according to the stage of the product life cycle. Some people are more reluctant to buy new products than others. Some people can't afford new products; this is true if the business has adopted a skimming price strategy.

Advertising can be either very cheap or very expensive according to the medium chosen. Only goods with large markets will find national television advertising an economic proposition. Unless advertising increases demand it will add to the total cost of the product.

When a business has a 'family' brand name, that is a brand which is common to a number of products, the cost of advertising can be spread over all the products. This may have unfortunate results if one product receives bad publicity.

Personal selling

Personal selling is expensive. Its success depends on a well trained sales force who know their product and the advantages it can offer. It does have a number of advantages:

- the customer can ask questions. The salesperson knows immediately the major problems that concern the customer and can answer them.

- the salesperson can adapt the sales message to the needs of the customer. This could include pointing out the way in which the product can be modified to suit the needs of that customer. Advertising can only point out a few of the possibilities of a good product. It is up to the salesperson to make sure that the customer is aware of all the possibilities.

- the salesperson can negotiate the order, taking the customer's needs in terms of finance and delivery dates into account.

The importance of selling varies from market to market. The selling of complex industrial machinery relies on a good sales force. In established consumer markets selling is less important. However, there is a distinction to be made here. The manufacturers' sales forces persuade wholesalers and retailers to stock the products. It is the salespeople of these businesses that have direct contact with the customer. The producer of the goods may have little say in their training. It is for this reason that the manufacturers of certain types of consumer goods appoint agents (car dealers) or employ their own staff (cosmetics demonstrators in shops) to make sure that their products are sold in the right way. This is an example of the interdependence of the promotion and place elements of the marketing mix.

Public relations

This covers a very wide range of activities. It might be an article in a newspaper about the growth of the business, sponsoring a local sports contest, becoming involved in an educational project with local schools or a report in the editorial section of a magazine on a new product that has potential.

Businesses want publicity. It helps keep their products in the public eye, which will generate more sales, and it is cheap. An additional advantage is that while people may not take too much notice of advertisements unless they are specifically intending to buy, they do read the articles and are less sceptical about information given in them.

No business wants bad publicity. To avoid this the public relations department feeds the media with favourable news stories and devises ways in which the business can be seen to be doing good. The public relations department must also be ready to counteract negative reports in the media about the business. It must give the business's point of view.

Sales promotion

The importance of sales promotion in a market will depend on the type of market in which the business operates. In a market dominated by a small number of powerful producers all manufacturing similar products, price competition carries with it the dangers of a price war and reduced profits. Under these circumstances branding and well-designed packaging supported by advertising is a familiar promotion strategy. To boost sales in the short term, and perhaps gain or retain the brand loyalty of wavering customers, special offers, money off coupons, competitions, and redesigned packaging to direct the product to the changes in the market, might all be employed.

Sales promotion and advertising are aimed at distributors as well as the final consumer. Wholesalers and retailers are more likely to stock a product if they are offered in-store display units or if there is the promise of a national advertising campaign. Unless a producer has control of its own retail outlets it needs to persuade people to stock its goods.

SELF ASSESSMENT

1 Look at Figure 9.10. Classify the different promotional activities listed there in terms of advertising, personal selling, public relations and sales promotion.
2 Explain briefly the one way in which promotion can be affected by other elements of the marketing mix.
3 Give one reason why it is essential that the objectives of advertising, personal selling, public relations and sales promotion are interrelated.
4 A business has recently suffered bad publicity. As part of a rationalisation programme it has closed one of its factories, making 2000 people redundant. The factory was in an area of high unemployment and intense trade union activity ensured coverage by the national media. The same week an accident at another of its factories resulted in the death of three people and the severe injury of another ten.
   a Explain why these events might affect the sales and image of the business.
   b What promotional techniques might the business use to counteract the effects of the bad publicity? Give reasons for your choice.
   c What would affect the success or failure of the business in achieving their promotional objectives in this case?

Distribution

Distribution is concerned with getting the product from the producer to the buyer in the right quantity, in the right place and at the right time. Distribution is expensive. The business has to make decisions about:

☐ the number of *warehouses* it will need, and where they are to be located. These decisions will depend on the market for the goods and the costs involved. Remember that a warehouse will cost money and will add to the overheads of the business.

☐ the *stocks* that the business needs to hold. Do customers want the product on demand, or are they willing to wait? A business making goods to order might keep no more than a few samples of the work so that potential customers can see it. A business that is producing for the mass market will have to keep the goods flowing freely into the shops.

□ the type of *transport* that can be used. Different methods of transport may be more or less cost effective depending on the cost of transport in relation to the price of the good, or the type of good being transported in relation to the speed with which it is required. Drugs can be sent by air, so too can out of season fruit and flowers. Coal, which is cheap in relation to transport costs, is moved by sea, rail and road depending on the distance involved. Transport is also a service. Cost disadvantages may be outweighed by the efficiency of that service.

□ the *communications* that are used. This includes the ways in which orders are processed and the systems that are used to ensure no mistakes are made. A lost order form means a dissatisfied customer. A lost invoice affects the accounting function of the business. Both will lead to additional clerical work that will increase costs.

□ the method of *packaging*. We have already seen that the packaging used by a business can be an integral part of the sales promotion. However the business also has to decide how the goods will be packaged for distribution. How many packets of cereal to a box? What type of boxes to use? How fragile are the goods?

The problems of distribution can be summarised under three headings:

□ the physical means of distribution;

□ the organisation of distribution;

□ the type of service the customer requires.

Physical distribution

Physical distribution is concerned with the movement, storing, handling, packaging and warehousing of all types of products. The physical distribution method used by a business is important for two reasons:

□ it can add significantly to costs. The proportion of total costs caused by physical distribution varies from industry to industry. It may be as low as 10 or as high as 30 per cent.

□ it makes a big contribution to customer satisfaction. Customers like to know when their order is going to arrive, that it will arrive on time and that it will be accurately filled.

Objectives of a good distribution system are likely to cover:

□ sufficient stocks to meet the majority of orders at any given time.

□ the minimum period of time within which the majority of orders will be met.

□ a maximum allowance for damage in transport.

□ the speed with which orders are received, acted upon and dispatched. This might involve stating a time period that will apply to the majority of orders from the time of receipt to the time of dispatch.

If you look at the above objectives you will see that several contain the phrase 'the majority of orders'. The business has to make decisions comparing the costs of holding extra

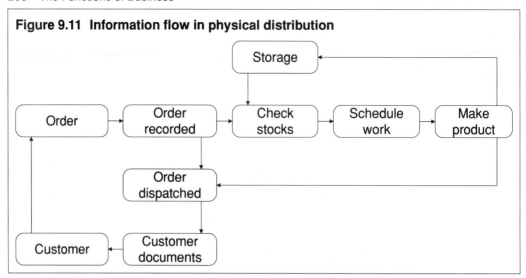

Figure 9.11 Information flow in physical distribution

stocks with the extra custom they would receive from the marginal customers. The managing of stocks is dealt with in more detail in Chapter 11 ('Production control').

Figure 9.11 shows the flow of information through a physical distribution system.

Channels of distribution
The channels of distribution are the organisations that a product passes through in the chain of production. The main ones are shown in Figure 9.12.

1   Direct to a *retailer*. If the product depends for its reputation on the quality of its after-sales support this might be the best route. Large retailers with market power will buy direct from the manufacturer. They might impose their own quality control, designs and branding on the manufacturer.

2   Direct to the *customer*. Specialist manufacturers may follow this route using mail order. Local markets may be inadequate for their needs but they do not wish to lose control over the product by selling to a wholesaler or a retailer. This is a traditional method of distribution for perishable goods. Farm shops and markets give farmers the opportunity of selling their produce fresh to the consumer. Trade exhibitions provide a point of contact between the manufacturers of industrial goods and the businesses which are their consumers.

3   Through an *agent* in an organised commodity market. A world market for commodities like tin, pepper, sugar and wheat results in the growth of specialist businesses trading in these commodities.

4   Household consumer goods such as washing powders may be sold direct to the retailer but will also follow the traditional path of manufacturer to *wholesaler* to retailer to consumer.

Customer service
The whole of distribution policy is aimed at providing a service to the customer. Customer service has been given its own section because it provides the link between distribution and the rest of the marketing mix. Because customers vary in their requirements it is often

Figure 9.12 Channels of distribution

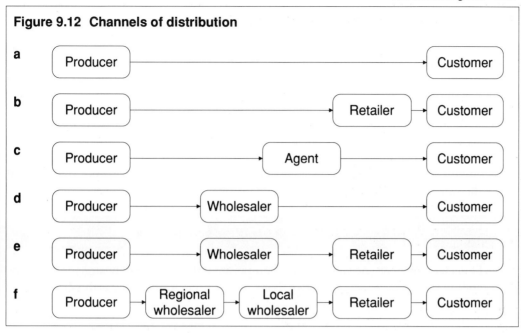

necessary for a business to have several distribution policies according to the market segments at which their products are aimed. The product itself and the company's pricing and promotion policies will influence the distribution channel chosen. A business that has spent a great deal of money promoting a luxury image for its high priced product is unlikely to distribute it through supermarkets. Distribution exists to meet the needs of the customer – not simply to get products to the destination. Remember, it is the right quantity, at the right time and in the right place. It is the needs of the customer that determine the meaning of the word 'right' in this context.

SELF ASSESSMENT

1 List the decisions a business has to make when deciding on a system of distribution. Explain how each of these areas could affect the customer's attitude to the business.
2 Distinguish between physical distribution and the channels of distribution.
3 Explain briefly the role of distribution in the marketing mix.

Conclusion

1 The marketing mix consists of the activities involved in determining the:

□ product,

□ price,

□ promotion,

□ place,

with which the business will attempt to satisfy the needs of its customers.

2   Each area will have its own objectives which support the marketing objectives of the business.

3   The areas are interdependent so that, for example, decisions on the nature of a product, its quality, design and life, will have implications for the pricing, promotion and place policy of the business.

4   The constraints on the elements of the marketing mix will be determined by the overall constraints on the marketing policies of the business.

5   The nature of the mix will vary from business to business, although businesses operating in the same markets will tend to show similarities.

A case study: the problems of football

When Fiona was fourteen she was an ardent supporter of the local first division football club. Her ambition in life was to go to a match. For some time her ambition was thwarted by her mother who felt that football grounds, with their reputation for violence, were no place for her daughter. Fiona's father was not a great deal of help in the matter either. His support for the team was shown by listening to radio commentaries and watching televised matches. He was too old he said, when his daughter pleaded with him, to spend Saturday afternoons standing on freezing cold terraces. Besides, he had far too much to do.

Fiona and her father personalise the major marketing problem facing British football clubs – a poor image and the development since 1945 of rival attractions. A number of football clubs face financial problems and unless they get their marketing right could face closure.

The product and promotion

At first sight the product is no more than a game of football, the winners of which will gain points to determine their place in the league table or will go into the next round of a competition. In fact this product has a number of components, including the state of the ground, the conditions offered to spectators, and the safety of the ground, in terms of both health and safety and the danger of crowd violence. The style of play offered by the team and the star quality of the leading players are also important. Most teams have a hard core of regular supporters, the numbers related to the degree of success a team is enjoying. A run of defeats will reduce the attendance at matches. A successful run in a European competition will result in higher gates. Not all teams can be successful and the cost of players can be high. The most sought-after players operate in a continental market and some European clubs can offer transfer fees of three and four times the maximum paid in the UK.

Most clubs augment their income by diversifying. The club shop will sell a range of items in the club colours and using its name and insignia. These will sell, not only to the match attenders but also to the army of television supporters. Lotteries can bring in useful income. Commercial sponsorship too can help offset the running costs of the club. It is important to remember that the success of all these ventures will depend on the success of the club in playing football. A club that reaches a cup final might double its takings from trading activities and find it easier to secure lucrative sponsorships. A bad playing season can see a slump in revenue.

For many clubs the ground itself is a valuable and underutilised asset. It is open to the elements and too heavy a use is not advisable. Installing artificial pitches enables the ground to be used all the year round, and not only for football matches. Not all clubs approve of such pitches. Inevitably they affect the play and some would argue that the quality of the artificial turf leaves a great deal to be desired.

Part of the general product package are the facilities offered by the clubs. Cold, open terraces might be part of the tradition of football but are not likely to attract a family audience when rival amusements offer more comfort. Refreshment facilities are often minimal. Some clubs are already improving these areas.

The problems associated with crowd violence are a matter for the football industry as a whole to solve, although individual clubs can make their contribution. The distribution of tickets for away matches can help control the type of supporter who represents the club. Ticket-only schemes have the dual advantage of providing some degree of control over supporters and giving the club a secured income. Violence at one match will reflect on the image of the industry and have repercussions for other clubs.

Price

Pricing reflects the desire of supporters to congregate together and contains a control element for 'away' supporters. Basic ticket prices – standing room only – vary little over the country as a whole. A price range between £2.50 and £3.50 appears to be the average (1986). This gives access to the part of the ground usually favoured by supporters of the home team. Supporters of the team playing away may be charged between £3.00 and £5.00.

The place

Inner city football clubs would seem to be ideal candidates for a move to a greenfield site. The existing ground could be sold for development and the new land would be relatively cheap, with ample car parking. Many supporters do not live within walking distance of the ground. Travel to the outskirts of the city could be easier, particularly if there was motorway access. Traffic congestion during home games would disappear. Against this is the fact that the 'place' is often an important part of the product and promotion. Would supporters have the same feeling for the team if matches were played in an anonymous stadium? Would a change in location affect brand loyalty? Most fervent football supporters would predict disaster if it was suggested the place should be changed. For the club the problem is in judging how long it would take its supporters to develop a loyalty to the new place.

Professional marketing in football is a relatively new phenomenon. The captive audiences of the pre-1939 era when the 'match' was the standard Saturday afternoon occupation for whole communities have been falling steadily. There is still a great deal of support for some teams. Can the football clubs capitalise on this? More important, do they want to do so, or is the ruling ethic still that of a club rather than a profit-making business? To what extent do players, ground, success, image and prestige contribute to defining the product?

REVIEW

Exercises

1 Wainwrights is a small engineering business producing a single product. The total capacity of plant is 25 000 units per annum, but sales seldom exceed 80 per cent of this figure. The product is priced on a full cost basis with overheads of £60 000 allocated to sales. Direct costs are £7 per unit produced.

   a Assuming that Wainwrights' objective is a 20 per cent profit expressed as a percentage of turnover, at what price should they sell the product?

   b Wainwrights are offered an additional contract for 4000 units at £10 per unit. Should they accept the order? Justify your answer, explaining the assumptions you have made.

   c As a result of an upswing in the market Wainwrights' sales rise to 95 per cent capacity. Calculate the profit as a percentage of turnover assuming the product was sold at the original price.

   d In view of the change in market conditions outlined in **c**, should Wainwrights change their pricing policy? What other information would be needed to answer this question?

2 A business manufactures a household consumer product. Until recently its marketing drive has been based on the concept of the perfect housewife. Periodic promotional campaigns have been sufficient to maintain its market share but this is now being eroded by its competitors. Market research suggests that women find the advertising approach condescending. The product itself is technically superior to that of its immediate competitors and the advertising elasticity of demand for the market as a whole is greater than 1. Suggest ways in which the business might revitalise its product. What factors, other than those above, might it need to take into account when deciding upon its tactics?

3 The retailing market for a range of products has five large companies with respective market shares of 12.0, 11.9, 11.3, 6.8 and 4.0 per cent. The rest of the market is served by businesses with a more limited product range and serving geographically isolated markets.

   a Describe the possible effects of this product structure on the price, sales and promotion policies of the businesses concerned.

   b What additional information might you require before making a judgment on this?

4 Jason Designs manufactures clothes which it sells directly to quality, up-market retail outlets. The brand name is respected for quality and its imaginative but conservative interpretation of fashion trends. The business is also extremely successful in the export market, particularly to North America. This market accounts for 40 per cent of its sales.

   In 1986 Jason Designs invested in additional capacity with the objective of entering the high fashion market, targeting the 16–25 age group. A range was designed and the production department experienced no difficulty in operating within the cost and quality parameters set for it. These were lower than those of the original range but still high when related to that of the rest of the market. The problem lay in naming the new range. One faction within the business was in favour of keeping the original label with the possible addition of the word 'young'. The opposing group advocated inventing a totally new name, perhaps with a discreet press leak to the glossy magazines concerning its origin.

   Outline the arguments for and against the two approaches to marketing the new range given above, stating any additional information which would be necessary before a decision could be reached.

Activities

1 Analyse three issues of a popular magazine. You should attempt to identify the target readership in terms of age, sex, occupational category, income, interests, why they read that magazine and what subjects they are not interested in. Your analysis should cover both the advertisements and the editorial content. Would you use that magazine as a medium for advertising if you were trying to promote:

   a detergent?

   b high fashion clothes?

   c an expensive range of kitchen equipment?

   d products based on micro-chip technology?

Explain your answers and find magazines that would be ideal vehicles for the advertising of the products listed above.

2 Survey the market for a product, either good or service, that you intend to offer. Analyse the results of your market research using the statistical techniques outlined in Chapter 5 ('Statistics'). Draw up a projected balance sheet and profit and loss account for your business over the first three months of its life.

3 Select a locally produced good which is marketed nationally. Discover, through observation and interview with the marketing manager, the marketing mix used by the business in question. What are the reasons given for the policy? You may repeat this exercise for a variety of products, being careful to compare and explain the results of your investigations.

4 Select a range of advertisements and analyse them according to whether they can be considered informative and/or persuasive to the market segment they are aimed at, the wants they are designed to satisfy, and the stage in the product life cycle. Pay particular attention to any advertisement that uses statistics to support its selling points. Are these in any way misleading? What additional information would you require to make an informed buying judgment?

5 Select a product that has been the subject of a recent *Which?* (the magazine of the Consumers Association) test report. Make a list of the features you, or somebody you know, would find desirable when choosing that product. On the basis of this list select the model you would buy. Compare your selection with the *Which?* test report. Does your choice vary from the 'best buy'? If so, in what way? Would the information given in *Which?* influence your final decision? What insight has this activity given you into consumer buying behaviour?

Suggested projects

1 A critical comparative study of the distribution channels used by two businesses manufacturing the same product.

2 An evaluation of the promotional methods used by a small business operating in a local market.

3 An appreciation of the impact of market structure on the marketing strategy of a business.

4 A critical investigation into the extent to which a non-profit making organisation operating in the public sector needs to promote its activities.

Essays

1 A business manufactures a number of diverse products, some of which it subsidises. Comment on the view that such behaviour constitutes a waste of resources.

2 A business uses a single brand name to promote a range of products. Comment on the possible reasons for it adopting this strategy and discuss the problems associated with it.

3 Identify and discuss the information a business will require before deciding on the pricing strategy for a new product.

4 Discuss the view that costs are the most important determinant of price.

5 A business is aware that the demand for its products is relatively price elastic. How may this information influence its marketing strategy?

6 Comment on the factors a business will take into account when deciding on the distribution channel for its product.

7 To what extent can advertising be considered a waste of resources:
   a for the individual business?
   b for the industry in which that business operates?
   c for the economy as a whole?

8 A business is described as being 'market orientated'. What do you understand by this description? Discuss the implications for marketing and production policies.

9 An enterprise invests a large sum of money in promoting its corporate image with particular emphasis on the contribution it makes to the community. Comment on the reasons for such a strategy.

10 'It is essential that the marketing team distinguish between advertising and promotional activities. They attract a different population.' How far do you think this is true?

10 Background to production

When you have studied this chapter you should:

- Know what is included in the production function of business.
- Understand the reasons for classifying production.
- Appreciate the importance of production planning.
- Know the necessary steps in production planning.
- Know the stages in product design and understand the importance of each stage.
- Appreciate the contribution value analysis makes to achieving the objectives of the business.
- Understand what is meant by economies of scale and how they might be achieved.
- Know the factors affecting location and siting and appreciate how they will vary according to the type of business.
- Understand the factors affecting plant layout.
- Distinguish between the different types of production.
- Identify the circumstances in which type is appropriate.
- Understand the importance of specialisation, standardisation and simplification.
- Define economies of scale.
- Distinguish between the scale and size of a business.
- Distinguish between internal and external economies of scale.
- Appreciate the importance of the production function.

What is production?

The production function is that part of business activity which converts raw materials, components and finished goods into new goods and services. The production process can take a number of forms:

- changing the form of raw materials so that they become more useful, for example the smelting of ores and the refining of petroleum.
- combining components so that they form a new product, as in the car industry.
- using premises, equipment and other products to help provide a service, such as banking.

Production activity can be classified in two ways:

☐ by level;

☐ by process.

Classification by level

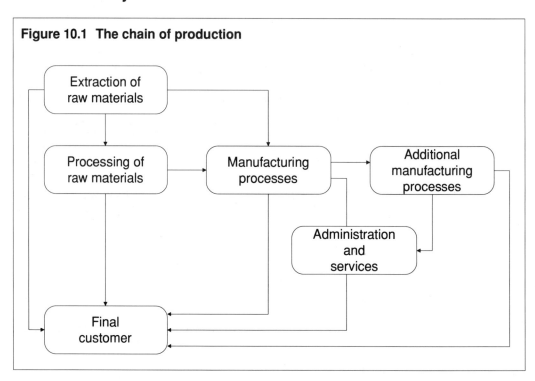

Figure 10.1 The chain of production

Figure 10.1 shows the classification of production according to the point a production process occurs in the route from raw materials to the finished product to the final consumer. This route is sometimes known as the *chain of production*.

Figure 10.2 illustrates some of the activities that appear at each stage in this chain.

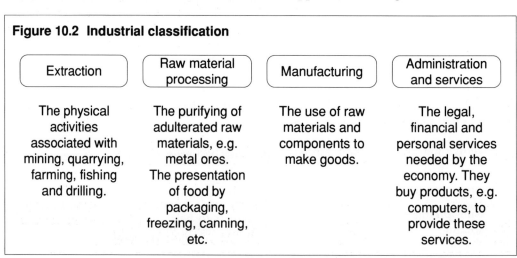

Figure 10.2 Industrial classification

Extraction	Raw material processing	Manufacturing	Administration and services
The physical activities associated with mining, quarrying, farming, fishing and drilling.	The purifying of adulterated raw materials, e.g. metal ores. The presentation of food by packaging, freezing, canning, etc.	The use of raw materials and components to make goods.	The legal, financial and personal services needed by the economy. They buy products, e.g. computers, to provide these services.

Classification by process

This method of classification is limited to manufacturing industries. It groups businesses together according to the method used to make a product.

1 *Analytic methods*   These are methods of production which reduce materials to their parts in order to extract useful products. Oil refining is a good example. The analytic method may be undertaken to obtain one main product. There are usually *by-products* which a business may use if they exist in sufficient quantities. By-products may also be sold to other businesses.

2 *Synthetic methods*   These combine raw materials and components. Synthetic methods cover a wide range of industrial processes from the assembly of goods such as televisions, computers and cars to the cultivation of bacteria for antibiotics and alcohol.

3 *Continuous methods*   The technology used in the creation of some products, for example electricity and oil, requires that production runs are continuous. Usually they are only stopped for maintenance, and this can be after a number of years' continuous production.

SELF ASSESSMENT

1 What do you understand by the term 'production'?
2 Why is it useful to classify the different types of production?
3 Give two ways of classifying production by process.
4 Look at Figure 10.1. Name two types of business you would expect to find at each stage in the chain of production.
5 State two reasons why it is useful to classify businesses according to the process they use.

The production plan

Like the other departments in a business, production has to set objectives that support the overall objectives of the business. These objectives might include:

□ the level of *productivity* required. This is not simply a matter of stating how many items will be produced in a period of time. It also takes into account the finance, equipment and labour that have been used to achieve that output. The difference between *productivity* and *production* levels is shown in Figure 10.3.

□ quality levels.

□ production costs.

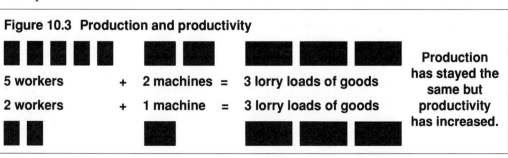

Figure 10.3 Production and productivity

5 workers + 2 machines = 3 lorry loads of goods

2 workers + 1 machine = 3 lorry loads of goods

Production has stayed the same but productivity has increased.

The constraints on the production department reaching its objectives are identical to those affecting other departments in the business.

1   *Finance*   The amount of finance available for investment in plant and machinery will affect such things as the labour productivity of the workforce and the amount of wastage during production processes. It will also affect the ability of the business to compete for people with scarce skills.

2   *The skills of the workforce*   A business with a good training programme is less likely to suffer from this constraint. Changes in technology may put certain skills at a premium. In this situation the ability of a business to achieve its production targets will depend on its ability to recruit people.

3   *The available technology*   This can affect production in three ways: by limiting the amount that can be produced because of the technology already in the business; by making it difficult to compete in quality standards when other businesses have superior technology; and by the need to redesign or find new products when a change in technology makes existing products uncompetitive.

4   *The market*   Production and marketing are interdependent. Production has to produce goods in the right quantity, to the right quality and at the time when they are required. If they do not produce the goods people are willing to buy then the products will not sell. It is the function of the marketing department to keep the production department well informed about what the market wants.

5   *Legislation*   Central and local government legislation can affect production processes by imposing health and safety conditions, or by controlling the level of emissions (e.g. smoke) a factory is allowed to make, which could mean changing the method of production.

6   *The state of the economy*   A booming economy could mean that a business experiences difficulty in buying inputs, either because the price is too high or because they are scarce in relation to the demand for them. It is usually a combination of both.

SELF ASSESSMENT

1   What is the relationship between the overall objectives of a business and its production objectives?
2   Explain how production objectives could contribute to a business achieving maximum possible profits.
3   Which of the constraints on the production function achieving its objectives would you classify as internal constraints and which as external constraints? Why did you make this decision?
4   State and explain three ways in which the market could act as a constraint on the production function.
5   State and explain two ways in which a change in technology could be a severe constraint on a business which had neglected its training programme.

Putting the plan into practice

In order to achieve its objectives the business must discover the constraints on its decisions and then find the answers to the following questions:

- □ which location?
- □ which site?
- □ what plant layout?
- □ what method of production?
- □ what scale of production?
- □ what is the best way of working?
- □ what controls are required?

The ways in which businesses attempt to answer the last question are dealt with in Chapter 11 ('Production control').

Location

The selection of a location for a factory, workshop or retail shop is essentially a problem of cost and the availability of a market. For the owner of a small retail shop the location problem may be confined geographically to one small town. The manufacturers of a consumer durable, on the other hand, may have the choice of a number of countries. The importance of any particular influence on the final location decision will depend on the type of business, the size of the business, the demands of the production processes and the importance of the market. The list of factors influencing the final choice of location is a long one but will not be applicable to all businesses.

1 *Labour* A business is interested in labour with specific skills. It may be attracted to an area because there is a high concentration of labour with those skills available. On the other hand it may prefer an area with unskilled labour rather than compete with other businesses for skilled labour in short supply. Its final decision may depend upon the ease with which its production processes can be simplified and with the quality of further education provision. In some industries the availability of labour is not a major factor. The existence of valuable mineral deposits will encourage a mining company to move the labour to the job. The exploitation of the North Sea oil fields can be seen as an extreme example of this situation.

2 *Services* The major services required by a business are power (gas and electricity), water, drainage and waste disposal. In a modern industrialised economy this is unlikely to be an important element in the location decision, in that they will be readily available in the quantities required. In more remote areas and in less industrialised parts of the world this could be more important. A business requiring a large amount of electricity could overload a limited local electrical supply. This in turn may require the provision of additional capacity in the supply of electricity, perhaps by the business itself.

3 *Transport* A good transport system can allow a business greater freedom in its choice of location. The decision is likely to be influenced by the cost of transporting the raw

Figure 10.4   Influences on location

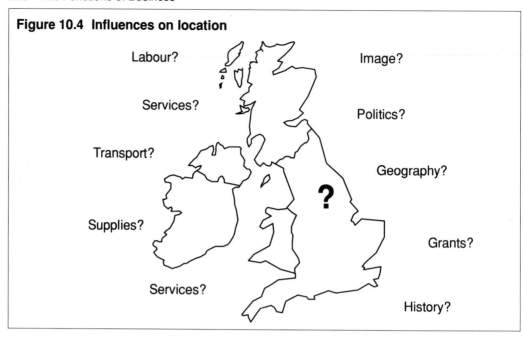

Labour?

Services?

Transport?

Supplies?

Services?

Image?

Politics?

Geography?

?

Grants?

History?

materials compared with the cost of transporting the finished goods to the market. Heavy transport costs for raw materials will predispose a business to move closer to its sources of supply. Where the costs of transporting the finished goods to the market are the greater, the business is more likely to be situated closer to the market. On the other hand a business buying bulky, expensive to transport, raw materials from a wide area may find no advantage in being located close to one source of supply. It might be an advantage in this case to minimise the costs of transporting the finished product, i.e. it would locate close to its market. Figure 10.4 shows some of the influences on location.

4   *Source of supply*   The importance of the source of supply of raw materials and components will depend upon the transport system available. In addition, managers responsible for the purchasing of supplies often prefer to be close to their suppliers.

5   *Local services and amenities*   We have already pointed out that the existence of a good system of technical education can be important if the business is faced with the need to train or retrain its workforce. The existence of a good primary and secondary system of education, a range of housing, shopping facilities and entertainment provision can also be a factor in a location or relocation decision. An entrepreneur whose business has no outstanding location requirements might choose to locate to satisfy a personal lifestyle rather than for strictly economic reasons and so, perhaps, contribute to the drift away from urban to rural areas.

6   *History*   Once an industry is established in an area it requires powerful economic reasons to force it to leave. A group of businesses producing the same type of goods can lead to the establishment of ancillary services which, if it moved to an entirely new location, it would have to provide for itself, and at a higher cost. It is likely that local colleges would provide suitable training courses which would not be economic without a concentration of industry, and there would be a pool of labour with the relevant skills. A business with several locations within a given area might want to locate a new plant

within that area to maintain communications and control. The unwillingness of businesses to move too far away from their existing location is generally referred to as *industrial inertia*.

7   *Central and local government grants*   These can be seen as an attempt on the part of central and local government to provide just the powerful economic incentive required to overcome industrial inertia. The decline of older industries has left a number of areas of the UK with chronic problems of high unemployment. The provision of low interest loans, low rents and special grants for capital investment are designed to attract industries to these areas. The most severely affected areas are known as *development areas*, with those less severely affected called *intermediate areas*. Figure 10.5 shows the pattern of regional assistance in the UK in 1989.

The Enterprise Initiative offered by the Department of Trade and Industry (DTI) offers the opportunity to buy advice in marketing, design, finance and exporting (among other things) from private consultancy firms. In general there is a sliding scale of aid granted to the businesses concerned. For example, the marketing initiative is managed for the DTI by the Institute of Marketing. The DTI pays half the cost of 5 to 15 days of consultancy, but in development areas it will pay two thirds of the cost.

The European Community has its own regional fund which will provide money for governments, local authorities and businesses which are prepared to undertake certain types of initiative. These include training, research and development, job creation and the development of energy supplies.

Unfortunately, if the grants are seen as the major reason for moving a factory, and other location factors are not given due weighting, the end of the subsidy, particularly if accompanied by a general recession, can mean that these are the first factories to close.

8   *Geographical factors*   The climate is obviously the deciding factor in businesses engaged in farming and horticulture. Although there are some marginal crops whose high value and demand can make them economic to grow under artificial conditions, for example the growing of tomatoes in the UK, most crops are grown in areas where the climate suits

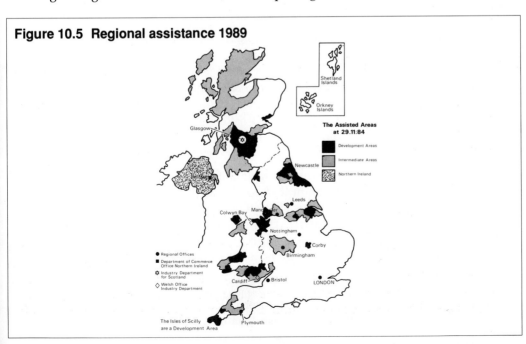

Figure 10.5 Regional assistance 1989

The Assisted Areas at 29.11:84

Development Areas
Intermediate Areas
Northern Ireland

● Regional Offices
■ Department of Commerce Office Northern Ireland
✿ Industry Department for Scotland
◇ Welsh Office Industry Department

The Isles of Scilly are a Development Area

their demands. Various other geographical factors will affect farming. The height of the land above sea level, the physical and chemical structure of the soil and its topography.

Manufacturing industry is less dependent on climate but can be influenced by the geological structure of a particular area both in terms of the topography of the region and whether or not the subsoil will be able to bear the loads placed on it.

9 *Politics* Unstable governments, governments opposed to private enterprise, and the threat of war might deter investment in a country. Equally they may be ignored if the projected returns from that investment are sufficiently high in the short term.

10 *The image of the area* In the UK the north has a poor image – a mix of poor industrial relations, a run down environment, violence and inertia. Many advertisements now concentrate on the positive aspects of living in the industrial north.

In recent years there has been an increasing awareness that location decisions are made by people who have to move with their business or persuade key staff members to move with it. The human factor in location decisions cannot be ignored. Figure 10.6 shows the weightings different types of business will give to location factors.

Figure 10.6 Location factors and business classification

Type of business	Criteria
Production	
Non-manufacturing	Resource availability
	Access
	Cost
Manufacturing	Market
	Access
	Resources
	Services
	Cost
Distribution	
Warehousing	Customer service
Retailing	Access
	Cost
Services	
Banking	Customer location
Insurance	
Legal	
Personal	

Location decisions are part of the long-term planning of the business. The selection of the location means that capital is committed to the acquisition of land and premises, employment of a workforce and the installation of plant. The risk inherent in a change of location contributes to industrial inertia. That is not to say that business location never changes. In the past forty years changes in technology and in society have resulted in significant shifts in industrial location. This is less obvious in the small geographical area of the UK, but it does exist.

1 Production is becoming increasingly international as specialisation increases and technology improves. A business can manufacture components in Korea and assemble

the final product in the UK. Ford organises its production on a continental basis in Europe with Ford UK producing some parts for other Ford plants in Germany and Spain, and importing some other parts for production in the UK.

2 Changes in the demographic structure of the population, including the age and geographical distribution, mean that businesses have to reassess location decisions to maintain delivery standards and the required level of customer service.

3 Advances in technology and communications can give businesses greater freedom in the selection of location. It may allow them to exchange an expensive site for one in a low-cost area, thus releasing funds for expansion.

4 A trend away from large production units to smaller factories gives a business the opportunity to rethink its original location decisions. The business could make this decision because of changes in the production process or as a result of new ideas on plant organisation. Smaller production units may be seen as leading to higher levels of productivity than larger units.

SELF ASSESSMENT

1 Which location factors do you think would carry most weight with:
   a a small retailer?
   b an arable farmer?
2 State and explain how changes in the demography of a region could influence the location policy of a business.
3 What do you understand by the term 'industrial inertia'?
4 Explain briefly why location decisions are part of the long-term planning of a business.
5 A region is hoping to attract more manufacturing business to its area. What advantages of the area do you think it should stress in its promotional literature and advertising? Why?
6 A country develops an extremely efficient transport system over a period of twenty years. Would this have the effect of concentrating or dispersing business activity? Explain your answer.

Siting

The site of the business is the actual area of ground which a business will occupy within a given geographical location. Many of the factors affecting siting are, at first glance, the same as those affecting location. However there are differences. A location decision will be concerned with the transport network available to the business, for example, whilst the siting decision will place greater emphasis on the access a business has to that network.

1 *Availability of transport* A site giving good access to the national motorway network will have advantages over a similar site five miles distant that involves a journey using busy roads. Transport can also affect the availability of labour.

2 *Local bylaws and the reaction of local inhabitants* Local authorities may have regulations about the level of noise, smells and traffic that they are prepared to tolerate in a particular area. Even when these do not exist, or where there is some doubt as to whether or not the

business is infringing them, local people might form pressure groups to prevent the building of a particular type of factory. Widespread publicity following industrial accidents which have affected the local community can have repercussions for other businesses in the same industry regardless of the level of their safety precautions.

3   *National and international pressure groups*   These can also attempt to influence the siting of a particular enterprise. A threat to the wildlife of a region may give rise to opposition, regardless of the attitudes of the local people.

4   *The size, cost and physical qualities of the sites available*   Where the production processes require heavy machinery a large, flat site with a subsoil capable of bearing the weight of the machinery will be a priority. Land will also be required for the storage of raw materials and finished products together with parking space for private cars. This type of land is more likely to be available at a reasonable cost away from city centres, hence the growing popularity of sites on the outskirts of towns known as *greenfield* sites.

5   *Provision of services*   This can often depend on the attitude of the local authority. The willingness to provide industrial estates and to provide, or help to provide, for the disposal of industrial waste and to lay on gas, electricity, water and sewage services to a greenfield site is not a statutory duty of a local authority and will depend upon local attitudes and needs. The existence of a good infrastructure for electronic communication is also essential for some businesses, particularly those in the financial sector.

For some businesses the major factor in the choice of site may be the proximity of similar businesses so that they can take advantage of economies of scale. In this case the design of the building to be used, whether a factory, an office block or a retail shop, will be dictated by the site available. Both single and multiple storey buildings have their advantages and disadvantages and individual businesses will have their own priority in requirements.

1   *Costs*   A multi-storey building will have lower site costs. Single-storey buildings, particularly those using modern building technology, will have lower building costs.

2   *Organisation of departments*   A single-storey building may make the flow of goods from one department to another easier to organise and automate and so lower handling costs. A multi-storey building may have the same effect in a service industry, for example retailing or insurance. Departments will have a well-defined area which will facilitate control.

3   *Ventilation and use of natural light*   Both are easier in a single-storey building and therefore reduce costs. On the other hand heating costs are likely to be lower in a multi-storey building with a lower ratio of external surfaces to working space.

4   *Use of floor space*   The location of heavy machinery within a factory will be limited by the ability of certain parts of the building to bear the load. This is less of a constraint in a single-storey building.

The location and siting decision, like most business decisions, is an exercise in opportunity and comparative cost. In other words, which location will give the lowest cost of production and marketing for the least sacrifice? Transport costs can often be the deciding factor.

1 Distinguish between location and siting problems.
2 Explain briefly how the correct choice of site can help a business achieve its objectives.
3 In what way is a siting problem an exercise in opportunity cost?
4 How might political factors affect the siting policy of a business?
5 From your understanding of location and siting problems explain, briefly, why greenfield sites would have attractions over more established sites.

Layout of plant

In planning the layout of the production area of any business the objective is to position machinery, equipment and people to get the maximum productivity from the available resources. The business will define the objectives of the plant layout in terms of:

- improving or maintaining quality;
- controlling costs;
- improving the utilisation of machinery;
- increasing flexibility in the use of resources;
- controlling the progress of an order.

The final form of a good layout will vary from business to business. Before starting a layout plan the answers to the following questions must be available.

1 *What is the available space?* This should take into account the height of the working area as well as the floor space. The planners will require the exact dimensions of the building including any unusual features. Pillars supporting a roof can be obstacles to the free flow of staff and materials unless they are taken into account in the original plan.

2 *What type of work is going to be done?* It is obviously desirable that dirty and/or dangerous jobs should be separated physically from other activities. Jobs requiring an unusual degree of concentration may also need to be separate.

3 *What volume of work is going to be done?* One stage in the production process may be common to a number of products, and therefore more machinery will be used. Unless this is given proper weighting in the layout design there will be overcrowding. For example, designers of supermarkets have to take into account the number of people who are expected to use the shop when deciding on the width of aisles.

4 *Can people and stocks be clearly seen?* There is an old saying 'out of sight, out of mind'. People tend to forget what they cannot see. It is important that stocks and work in progress should be clearly visible. This is important for dangerous substances that are likely to need regular checks. Again, in a retail outlet, if customers cannot see what they want displayed then some of them will assume that it is not in stock and sales can be lost.

It enables managers and supervisors to be more effective if they are able to see what is happening. It also allows management and union safety representatives to make sure that people are following health and safety procedures.

5   *What storage will be necessary?*   A business will always have storage requirements. It may be the storing of superfluous machinery, the storing of stocks of raw materials and components, the storing of work in progress or finished goods. If these requirements are not taken into account at the planning stage of layout, then the stores are likely to encroach upon working space. Again this can lead to breaches of safety regulations, for example storing goods under staircases where they present a safety hazard in case of fire.

6   *What communications will be necessary?*   It makes sense to position machines that work together close together. This reduces handling and the risk of wastage. Measuring the number of movements between one part of the production process and another can give valuable information for this type of decision. It also makes sense to position management stations close to the area of responsibility. It is very easy to forget to pass on an important message if you do not have regular contact with the person concerned.

7   *Are there any special servicing requirements?*   Machines that need servicing from the rear should not be placed against a wall. Power points and fuse boxes should not be hidden behind machines. These points may seem like common sense, but are easily overlooked.

8   *What equipment is going to be used?*   Heavy equipment will need structural support. Once it is in position it will take effort to move it. It may make sense to decide on the positioning of heavy equipment first and design the rest of the layout to fit this.

Plant layout can be a complicated problem and a number of mathematical/computerised analytical techniques are used to find the best possible solution. These include network analysis and simulation.

SELF ASSESSMENT

1 State and explain two ways in which the vertical and horizontal dimensions of a store should be considered when planning its layout.
2 Give two advantages and two disadvantages of an open plan office.
3 In what ways can the plant layout help in communications and people management?
4 A workshop has two machines which are used in sequence. They are positioned with a third smaller machine between them. The original justification for this was the utilisation of space. State and explain two problems that might be associated with this layout.
5 Assuming a machine has been positioned without thought of its servicing requirements, what costs would this incur in terms of labour, output and health and safety?

Production design

The long-term production decisions a business must make include the methods by which the good or service will be produced. Some constraints on this planning process include:

   ☐   the cost of the product;

   ☐   the size of the market;

   ☐   the size of the business;

   ☐   the technology required;

   ☐   the skills available.

The traditional types of production design are *job*, *batch* and *flow* production.

Job production

The term 'job production' describes a situation in which a single product is completed by one person or a group of people. Servicing a car, the making of a piece of furniture to the specification of an individual customer, and the design of a computer system to meet the requirements of an individual customer can all be seen as examples of job production. The organisation of job production will be a relatively simple matter when the product is simple and demand is relatively small. When demand increases or the product is technically complicated the demands on the organisational abilities of management increase. This can increase the costs of production to such a level that management will seek alternative methods. Whether or not they adopt them will depend upon the needs of the product, the willingness of the market to pay the necessary price to cover costs and the availability of sophisticated technology to help limit the increase in costs. Job production is the most common form of production in very small businesses.

Advantages of job production

1   The product can be tailored to meet the needs of the customer. This is not impossible using other types of production but job production does give more flexibility in this matter.

2   When things go wrong it is easier to isolate the source of the problem, although it is not necessarily easy to analyse the problem! The owner of a garage, for example, faced with an irate customer complaining about the standard of servicing on a car, will know which of his mechanics was responsible for the servicing. It may be more difficult to find out why that particular job went wrong. The fault may lie in the skill of the mechanic, the degree of supervision, a fault in a piece of equipment or a failure on the part of the customer to provide sufficient information or permission.

3   The workforce has a greater involvement with the product. The sight of a completed job gives a person greater satisfaction than contributing to a small part of a project. Either working alone or as part of a small work group individuals prefer to see what they have achieved and to know that their contribution was an important part of the final product.

Disadvantages of job production

1   When job production is used to make a complex technical product tailored to the needs of customers the sales force will be relatively large and a high degree of technical expertise will be required. Smaller firms may overcome this problem by using the services of an agent. The cost of selling will then be spread over all the firms employing the agent as a principal. Effectively the agent is selling knowledge of the market and technical skills. The business employing the agent is reducing the overheads of maintaining a sales force.

2   The business is likely to need to own or lease a wider range of machinery. Machine A may be required to produce parts for jobs X, Y and Z. Depending on the importance of the time factor and the cost of re-setting Machine A, the business may need the use of more than one machine to meet the delivery dates for its orders. Delivery dates are set by the market. A firm is less competitive if it offers a delivery date six months after a firm order

is placed than one who can offer a delivery date two months after the order is placed. The truth of that statement will, of course, depend upon the uniqueness of the product concerned. A business with a virtual monopoly in a market is in a far stronger position than one competing with a number of firms offering close substitutes for its product.

3   Job production requires a flexible workforce. The technically simple product presents few problems. A more sophisticated product demands a highly skilled workforce able to do a wide range of specialised tasks. This can be expensive in labour costs. Add to this the need for highly competent supervisors and a flexible management team able to undertake technical supervision, costing and labour management and it becomes clear why more economic methods of production have been developed.

Job production is different from plant layout using the *job shop* approach. In the latter the workspace is organised in terms of functions. Machines to perform a given operation will be grouped in work centres and different products will take a different route through each work centre. A furniture business could have work centres for cutting, turning, staining, assembling and polishing, among others.

SELF ASSESSMENT

1   State three products that might be made using job production methods. Explain why job production is appropriate in each case.
2   Identify one instance in which job production is used as a positive marketing point.
3   A small company produces hi-tech goods for a world market. Why might it need an agent?
4   Distinguish between job production and job shop production.
5   A flexible workforce suggests a high skill level. State and explain two problems this might cause a business.

Standardisation, specialisation and simplification

Before we examine batch and flow production we should look at the qualities needed for job production. Using job production there is the potential to produce a unique good or service, that is one which is unlike any other on the market. This is not always necessary. A measuring jug used by a cook must be reasonably accurate in its measuring abilities but that is all. A nut is a nut provided it fits the bolt it was intended for. It does not require a great leap in imagination to see that if you can design a simple item that can be used by a large number of people for a variety of purposes, then it will be easier to produce. Simplifying a product reduces the possibility of mistakes in its manufacture. A simple product needs a less skilled labour force because people become highly skilled at a small range of tasks. A simple product needs a smaller range of machinery.

A product might be simple because of its nature, as in the example of a measuring bowl, or it may be made simple by design. In the latter case we talk of *standardisation*.

Standardisation means that the goods produced conform to a standard. We will concentrate on the business which wants to make as many nuts as possible. To do this the business will have to make sure the nuts fit as many bolts as possible. This problem has been made easier for the business because over the last 170 years the users of bolts and nuts have realised that if they all use the same size range (*standardise* their requirements) there will be separate businesses that will provide these parts in large quantities and far more cheaply than they could do so themselves. The standards set are very precise. The internal diameter of a nut that varied more than 0.025mm above or below the standard set would make that nut useless for the bolt on which it was supposed to be used. Of course, the variation which can be tolerated will depend upon the physical size of the nut in question. A nut used in the manufacture of a car will have a more precise tolerance level than the nut used to hold on the propeller of a ship. When a product has been simplified and standardised it becomes easier to make. The labour does not have to be so skilled, and machinery can be devised to take over the more routine tasks. It becomes easier for people and machines to be given a specific job to do. Staff and machines can be *specialised*.

These principles may seem common sense to you. If you live in an industrialised society you are used to the idea of buying spare parts when some household object goes wrong. You are familiar with the fact that people perform highly specialised jobs to help make a product. It will do you no harm to remember that the knowledge of these principles has been part of human knowledge for many thousands of years. The deliberate exploitation of them has a much shorter history. Adam Smith wrote his *An Inquiry into the Nature and Causes of the Wealth of Nations* in 1776. He isolated the division of labour (a sub-set of specialisation) as a major contribution to the wealth of nations. In that work, Smith was simply summarising the experience of the economy of contemporary England and its near continental neighbours. Individual businesses, both in the UK and the USA, began to appreciate the advantages of standardisation in technical goods. In ordinary household products the three principles have a longer history. Abraham Darby produced cast iron cooking pots to a standard design and, for his time, in large quantities. He used superior technology to produce an old design economically. In the early eighteenth century the Lombe brothers had a silk factory that was considered ahead of its time. It was fifty years before the market for cotton goods persuaded manufacturers that they should follow his example. Standardisation, simplification and specialisation can be part of job production. They become more important when a business uses batch or flow production methods.

SELF ASSESSMENT

1 Define standardisation, specialisation and simplification.
2 What relationship exists between these three concepts?
3 State and explain two reasons for a manufacturer of a consumer durable to need to standardise product components.
4 Give three ways in which standardisation, specialisation and simplification can increase the profits of a business.
5 How has the application of these three concepts improved your lifestyle?

Batch production

A batch of goods is simply a group of products which undergo production at the same time. The simplest example is a batch of loaves. These are the loaves that are put into the oven, by the baker, at the same time.

Batch production can be defined as a method of organising the work on any product so that it is divided into a number of operations and each operation is completed for a group of products (the batch) before it is moved on to the next operation. Under batch production all items in a particular batch move from one process to another simultaneously. This can lead to organisational problems. For example if the batch is too large and one operation takes longer than another then staff and machines can stand idle while they wait for the next batch to reach them. One solution to this problem is to have a 'buffer' stock of work in progress that can be drawn on. This ties up capital in stock and has an effect on working capital.

Advantages of batch production

1   Compared with job production it can lead to a saving in the amount of machinery used.

2   It enables a costing system to be employed which can allocate costs to each completed product.

3   The system generates a large quantity of stock between different production processes. Although this ties up capital it can also act as a buffer. The existence of such stocks can give management greater flexibility in organisation.

Disadvantages of batch production

1   A large amount of capital is tied up in work in progress.

2   There is a long production time for making each part. Any one item in a batch will not be completed significantly before any other item.

3   There is a need for a very efficient system of control in planning and production. This can be time consuming for management.

SELF ASSESSMENT

1   Define batch production.
2   Explain briefly why moving from job to batch production might save money for a manufacturer.
3   Why may batch production cause storage problems?
4   Outline the major costs, specific to batch production, that a business will incur.
5   State three types of business that use batch production and explain why.

Flow production

We have already seen that in batch production each item in the batch has to wait until all other items have completed that stage of the production process before it can move, with the rest of the batch, to the next stage of production. Flow production is a method of organising the work processes where each individual item being produced moves on to the next stage of production immediately. This eliminates the waiting time and the existence of large quantities of stock and work in progress. On the other hand it requires the business to be very specific about the design of the product and demands a high degree of standardisation in terms of tools, methods and parts used. Machinery is arranged in lines according to the order of its function in the overall process and the operators tend to have a more limited range of tasks to perform. For flow production to be viable in terms of the investment required there must be a comparatively large and steady market for the goods being produced. The product, therefore, must appeal to a wide range of customers. Flow production utilises the concepts of simplification, standardisation and specialisation to a far greater extent than either job or batch production.

Flow production has been accused of reducing the status of the workforce to that of mere cogs in a machine, taking from them their pride in their jobs and the satisfaction inherent in seeing a completed product. The amount of investment in machinery to keep the line flowing and the disruptive effects of a breakdown or bottleneck in any part of the line can impose constraints on other parts of the business. The purchasing department, faced with the costs of an idle production line, might find reliability the most important priority in its purchasing mix and give price a far lower priority than it might have done under conditions of job or batch production.

On the other hand, the use of flow production has brought the majority of consumer durables within the reach of a greater number of people than before.

The choice of production method is complex for a business. It can be said to depend on:

- the stage of development a business has reached;
- the nature of the product;
- the size of the market;
- the frequency of demand.

A start-up business making a standard good, e.g. furniture or clothes, is likely to work on a job production method. The orders are unlikely to be big and will not justify the large investment in labour and machinery for batch or flow production. As the orders increase they may move towards batch production, and several large orders for a range of garments for a specific line might make batch production viable, but these orders may not be repeated.

Some businesses will never make the transition. The owner may want to produce for only a limited market or be unwilling to undertake the additional risk. The production of luxury goods with high status appeal is likely to be undertaken by job production methods.

An international company producing antibiotics does so under conditions of batch production, as do breweries. Both industries have the same basic task: to provide the ideal environment in terms of food and warmth for micro-organisms to flourish and give off their desired by-product. In the case of beer the by-product is alcohol, for the drug companies, antibiotics. The organisms are different, the temperature, food and end product are different, but the principles are the same. Essentially the process is the loading of a large vessel with the required food, the monitoring of the temperature and the production of a *batch* of the product. It has much in common with our earlier example of a batch of loaves.

In a large brewery the products of this type of batch production are likely to be processed using flow production methods. It will be the responsibility of the production manager to make sure that batches are ready to feed the bottling production line. This combination of production methods is common in industry.

A machine may have a variety of uses but needs to be retooled when moved from one use to another. Retooling is the term used for resetting a machine to do a different job. With some machines using, for example, computer and/or laser technology this can be a relatively simple task. Other machines require the services of a skilled toolmaker to make the change. It therefore makes sense to make a batch of products which need the same tools before changing the machine to make another batch of products.

SELF ASSESSMENT

1 Distinguish between job, flow and batch production.
2 Why might a business use a combination of all three production methods?
3 Give three types of products that could be produced using flow production methods. Justify your choice of products.
4 To what extent does the size of the market influence the method of production used?
5 State and explain one reason why standardisation is important in the adoption of flow production.

Scale of production

Economists use the term *economies of scale* to describe a situation in which production costs fall as the scale of the organisation increases. We have already examined some of the factors that will cause this to happen, for example fixed cost per unit will fall as output rises (average fixed costs). Discounts for bulk purchasing might also reduce material costs. Economies of scale can occur in all aspects of a business's activities. We will examine them in this chapter with the emphasis on production.

1   *Technical economies*   Technical economies of scale are the true production economies. These arise where the costs of expanding capacity increase more slowly than the increase in output. The fixed cost per unit will fall. As a simple example let us assume that it costs £100 000 to buy a machine with the capacity to produce 100 000 items, and £150 000 to buy a machine with a production capacity of 200 000. Assuming all other costs stay the same, the first machine will produce units at a cost of £1 while the second will produce units at a cost of 75p.

   A business may have a machine that is operating at 50 per cent capacity whilst the rest of the factory is operating at full capacity. If the business expands to the point where that machine can be operated at full capacity then production costs will fall.

2   *Buying economies*   Buying economies do not come only from discounts. Purchasing is a specialised skill and someone with a narrow range of goods to purchase for his company is more likely to develop expertise in the products available, the reliability of the suppliers and an understanding of how often and in what quantities the products will be needed. Such a division of labour is possible only in a large business.

3   *Marketing economies*   The costs of advertising, distribution and sales promotion are high and can be a large proportion of the total cost of a good produced by a small or medium-sized business. Large businesses can undertake advertising on a national scale secure in the knowledge that spread over their total output the addition to the cost per unit will be minimal. Should advertising increase demand for a product over and above the cost of the advertising (advertising elasticity of demand greater than one) there may be technical economies possible in addition to the marketing economies. In industries where the production unit is relatively small, either by tradition or because of the nature of the business, or the technology employed dictates relatively small-scale production there may be attempts to gain marketing economies by co-operation. Agricultural marketing boards are an example of such co-operation.

4   *Financial economies*   Large businesses have more assets, more products and greater reserves than smaller businesses. This reduces the risk of lending to them and they can, as a result, often negotiate loans at a lower rate of interest than smaller businesses. The risk associated with launching a new product is less traumatic for a large business with the resources to cushion the shock of failure.

5   *Administrative economies*   These include not only the ability to pay for and use efficiently the services of the best management ability available, but also to employ sophisticated computer systems that would be beyond the financial resources of a small business.

The five economies of scale given above can be considered as *internal* to the business. Large industries and a concentration of an industry in one area can often benefit small firms as well as large. Separate administrative services, such as the computer processing of payrolls, are available to all firms. The provision of suitable educational courses by local colleges, maintenance services offered by independent companies and the existence of businesses specialising in the production of certain components can all reduce the costs of individual businesses. These are known as *external* economies.

SELF ASSESSMENT

1 Distinguish between internal and external economies of scale.
2 In what ways might a medium-sized business benefit from internal economies of scale?
3 Distinguish between the size of a business and the scale of its activity.
4 State and explain one way in which a business might enjoy marketing economies without increasing the scale of its business activity.
5 How might the provision of suitable BTEC courses by a tertiary college lower the costs of a medium-sized manufacturing industry?

Conclusion

It is important to remember that the production processes of a business do not exist in isolation. An inefficient production department which delivers faulty goods or fails to deliver on time can lose sales for the business. On the other hand the production department is subject to constraints.

Production in extractive and manufacturing industries has the most physical presence of all business activity. It is difficult not to be aware of sheer size of plant in some industries. The plant owes its existence to the market for the goods it makes and if that market should decline or the marketing department fail to exploit it then even the largest factory will close.

REVIEW

1 Musaji Pressings Ltd are considering relocating their factory. The managing director consulted the senior management team for their views on the matter. The following is a summary of the reports they submitted.

☐ *Production manager* A greenfield site, preferably in the same area, would allow him to reorganise the shop floor and gain considerable economies. He did not want to move out of the immediate area because a number of his major suppliers were in the vicinity.

☐ *Finance manager* Sell up on the present site, so releasing the large amount of capital tied up in the land and buildings and lease a purpose-built unit fifty miles away.

☐ *Marketing manager* Agreed with the finance manager. The fifty mile move would take them closer to their major markets. It would also put them in the centre of the motorway network.

☐ *Personnel manager* Advocated staying in the same place and modernising the building. He pointed out that local colleges met many of his training needs and courses might be difficult to set up in a new place. He was also concerned about his ability to recruit staff with the necessary skills.

The final decision was to move to a greenfield site in the area favoured by the finance manager.

a Explain why there is a conflict of interests in the reports of the managers.

b State and explain three problems the production manager might experience as a result of this move.

c In view of the final decision, what do you think are the priorities of the business?

2 The text below was taken from an advertisement by the Merseyside Development Corporation. You are the company secretary of a medium-sized business producing consumer goods. The board of directors is interested in moving to Merseyside.

a What information would you request your staff to discover in addition to that given in the advertisement?

b Prepare a formal report for submission to the board outlining the advantages and disadvantages of relocating your plant in terms of:

i finance.

ii the workforce.

iii communications.

iv the market.

v production.

Investment Thrives on Our Banks

Nowhere is the power of economic regeneration more apparent than on the Mersey Waterfront.

Today, it has become the site for a community of flourishing new businesses.

The internationally acclaimed Albert Dock is the vibrant hub of Merseyside's rapidly expanding leisure and tourist industry.

Executive housing has been encouraged by an improved environment and increase in confidence.

These achievements have enhanced the quality of life bringing the promise of employment and prosperity.

It's a programme of change which owes its existence to the dynamism and vision of the Merseyside Development Corporation.

Prime development land has been reclaimed and opened up, essential infrastructures established.

Private sector investors were quick to respond to what will become the major investment opportunity of the 1990s.

They were spurred on by the benefits of a workforce specially trained for their needs and the prospect of financial assistance.

Past successes have substantially extended the MDC's sphere of influence.

Now the MDC's hard work opening up new development land along both banks of the Mersey is creating the foundation on which the next wave of private enterprise will take shape.

So get the facts now. Call Eileen Wall on 051-236 6090.

3 Joan Logan used the Enterprise Allowance Scheme to set herself up in business as a wood carver. At first the business developed slowly but in 1988 a major furnishing chain expressed interest in her work. Initially they placed an order for 500 bases for table lamps. On the strength of this Joan employed another skilled worker, and the two of them were just about able to fulfil the order for the agreed delivery date. The lamps sold well and the furnishing chain was back with additional orders. Joan was unwilling to refuse the business but she knew that the two of them could not keep working fifteen hours a day to fulfil the orders.

  a Outline the major methods of production.

  b State and explain three ways in which Joan could attempt to solve her problem.

  c Select one of your answers to **b** and outline three problems Joan might face if she adopted this solution.

Activities

1 As a group select a simple craft product with which you are unfamiliar. Origami (the art of folding paper) might provide suitable examples. It should be possible to make the product using job, batch and flow techniques.

  a Make a realistic assessment of direct labour and material costs.

  b Divided into three groups, each using a different production method, learn how to make the product. The learning process can be judged complete when products of an acceptable saleable standard are being produced. Calculate the cost of the learning process in terms of direct material and labour for each group.

  c Continue to make the item for at least an hour.

  d Comment on the following aspects of the exercise:

    i Assuming that you want to cover all costs, including development costs, and make a profit of 10 per cent on costs, what is the break-even point?

    ii Analyse the difficulties experienced by each group. This should include problems of materials and equipment, quality control and wastage rates, learning times, group attitudes to the exercise (Did some members of the group think the exercise a waste of time? How did this affect their productivity and performance?), bottlenecks experienced and reasons for them.

There is no guarantee that your experience will reflect the conventional wisdom relating to different types of production. If there is a difference can you explain it? You should remember that each individual has a unique set of skills and aptitudes and the problems you have encountered reflect those of a production manager. Why might these problems be intensified in a period of relatively full employment?

2 Visit several business organisations analysing the production function in each according to the outline given in this chapter. Your selection of businesses should include examples of job, batch and flow production organisation and, if possible, businesses operating in a variety of markets. Interview the production manager. What does she/he see as the main problems? Is it the market, people, finance or equipment that provide the biggest constraints on decision making?

Essays

1 The concept of economies of scale suggests that large businesses are more efficient in their use of resources than small businesses. If this is so why do small businesses survive and what justification can be offered for the investment of government money in the small business sector?

2 Outline and comment on the interrelationships which exist between the marketing and production functions.

3 'The location decisions of a business are relatively independent of considerations of market and supplies.' What are the implications of this position for:
   a the business?
   b attempts by central and local government to control or influence location decisions in the private sector?
4 What factors contribute to making a business 'footloose'?
5 What do you understand by the term 'production function'? Comment on the role of the production plan in the overall planning process of a business.
6 Discuss the factors a business would take into consideration in planning the layout of its production processes.
7 'Job production is limited to the craft specialist.' How far do you agree with this statement?
8 'Flow production can produce goods at lower unit cost than either job or batch methods.' Comment on the conditions necessary to make this a true statement.

11 Production control

When you have studied this chapter you should be able to:

☐ Understand the need for control in the production function.

☐ Outline the main methods of control.

☐ Outline the process of product design.

☐ Understand the importance of product design.

☐ Appreciate the role of value analysis.

☐ Describe the function of purchasing.

☐ Discuss the role of purchasing.

☐ Explain the purpose of stock control.

☐ Comment on the importance of stock control.

☐ Define quality control.

☐ Outline the methods of quality control.

☐ Appreciate the need for quality control.

☐ Explain the meaning of work study.

☐ Discuss the role of work study.

Businesses need to make decisions on:

☐ the product;

☐ the purchasing of materials;

☐ the control of stocks;

☐ the quality of the product;

☐ the management of people making the product.

Compared with the decisions outlined in Chapter 10 ('Background to production'), these decisions are relatively short term. A factory, for example, could be in existence for fifty years and owned by the same business for that time. During its life it might produce twenty different products as it responds to market changes. Suppliers will change and the level of stocks the business is prepared to hold could vary every year.

The fact that the decisions are short term does not mean they are less important. They can be seen as the responses the business makes to the information it collects as part of its control process, i.e. the constant checking required to make sure the production function is on target in making its contribution to the overall objectives of the business.

The product

The product is the good or service the business sells to make a profit. This is a very simple definition. Reality is much more complex. There are very few products which fall neatly into one or other of those two categories. Most products contain both a physical element and a service element. Consider the statement below. The person who made it works in the purchasing department of a large company.

> 'We seldom buy on price alone. For example, it is no use buying something at a saving of £10 per unit if the delivery is likely to be late. We have got to keep that production line going otherwise the extra cost will wipe out any savings in our purchasing.'

He went on to explain the other factors which go into the mix of a purchasing decision. The goods he was buying were engineering components. He was the customer for another business in competition with other producers. Providing the quality was right, the service a business could offer him in terms of delivery dates and security of delivery was an important element in making the final decision.

Let us look at another example, this time in a consumer market.

> A person wanted to buy a two seater settee. He finally found the design he liked in the furnishing department of a large store. The sales assistant quoted a delivery time of three months. The man asked if he could buy the display model, pointing out that there was a three seater settee in the same design which could be used as a display model for both two and three seater settees. His request was refused. The customer was annoyed at the poor service. The business lost a sale and the goodwill of the customer.

The product of a retail store is service, and in the opinion of this customer the service was poor. On the other hand the store policy could have been based on the knowledge that customers liked to see what they were buying and in satisfying one customer they may have lost three more. Perhaps the fault lay with the purchasing department who had not made sure that there were sufficient stocks to meet demand, or with the manufacturer who could not meet the demand. Whatever the truth of the situation the good being sold did not overcome the reluctance of the customer to tolerate the level of service, and a sale was lost.

The buying decisions of individual customers are a complex mix, and not simply rational decisions based only on price and quality. Goods are appreciated not only for what they do but also for the overall contribution they make to the needs and lifestyle of the customer. Service must, therefore, be an important element in the product, whether it is a consumer good or an industrial good.

SELF ASSESSMENT

1 State two ways in which the efficiency, or otherwise, of a marketing department can affect the efficiency of the production department of the same business.

2 Explain how the satisfaction of a customer may be affected by the materials and service in the following:
   a car servicing.
   b hire of a television set.
   c purchase of a washing machine.
   d purchase of a new car.
3 Explain, briefly, the role of each of the following in satisfying the customer:
   a The design of a product.
   b The delivery date.
   c The quality.

Design of the product

The design of any product is not simply a matter of an attractive appearance, although the importance of this should not be underestimated. An unpleasant job becomes less repellent if the tools to be used are attractive to look at. This can increase the productivity and job satisfaction of the workforce as they are made happier in their working environment. A good appearance can also help attract initial sales. However, to ensure a high level of repeat orders the equipment should also be easy, safe and economical in use.

The responsibility of the design team can, therefore, be defined as interpreting the needs of the customer and translating these needs into a form suitable for use, and which the production capacity of the business can produce without incurring excessive costs.

The design 'team' in the business can be the responsibility of the production manager. In a small business it will not exist as a separate entity and it is unlikely that any professional designers will be employed, although the DTI do offer a subsidised design service for small businesses. In a small business producing goods such as fabrics, clothes and jewellery the designer might also be the entrepreneur. Design in these areas tends to have a higher profile than design in the manufacture of industrial machinery. This does not mean that the design of a piece of machinery is unimportant. In fact it can be considered more important because the health and safety of the user may be at stake.

The design process

Every product has a design, whether it is consciously developed as such or not. The process of designing a good may be an integral part of the marketing and production decisions or it may be a defined progression which is consciously evaluated by the business at each stage. Whichever is the case the stages given below will be present.

1 *The idea* This may come from the marketing department. Research has indicated a product is required and there are no competitors in that field. It may be the original idea of a person intending to start a business. Remember, a service has to be designed to meet the need of customers. At this stage an outline of the idea is laid down.

In a business manufacturing consumer durables this will take the form of a draft specification. A *specification* is a detailed description of the product, including the type of materials to be used, size, colour, etc. The draft specification for a washing machine would include the number of wash programmes, the spin speed, the size, colour range and any other qualities that market research has suggested is needed for success. For a fabric it would include the basic design, colours and material to be used. Even at this stage there will be close co-operation with production. The initial design process will use resources, and if it is developed in isolation the opportunity cost of failure will be high.

The original idea should contain specific data to act as a guide for the future stages in design. This information should include:

☐   The standards of reliability, performance and quality required (market research).

☐   The appearance that is most likely to be acceptable (market research).

☐   Any particular quality that may appeal to the buying public. Volvo, for example, recently stated that catalytic converters (a part designed to cut down harmful emissions in exhaust gases) will be fitted to their cars free of charge. This may be an act of disinterested social responsibility on the part of the company; or it may be that they see this as a positive marketing stance.

☐   The maximum price at which it will sell (marketing and production).

☐   The maximum cost of design. You should remember that design costs are production costs.

☐   The maximum quantity that will be needed. In Chapter 6 ('Accounting') we saw that the cost per unit can be influenced by the scale of production.

☐   Any special safety features or operating features that should be incorporated. For example if a machine operator will need to use two controls at the same time or in a particular sequence it makes sense for them to be situated together and for the layout of the controls to reflect the sequence. On the other hand if the use of two controls together is potentially dangerous then the design can incorporate safety measures to inhibit this. Some safety features are required by law, e.g. roll-over bars on tractors and safety belts in cars.

2   *Testing*   At this stage the initial idea is tested for viability. The assessment of the concept takes place on a relatively small scale using mock-ups, scale models and mathematical calculations to test the viability of the idea. The methods used will vary according to the product. The increased availability of computer technology has made this task easier in complicated projects. The speed with which computers can process data has meant that a number of alternative solutions can be tested in a shorter period of time.

3   *Prototype*   The information gained from the second stage is used to make a full scale model. This is to make sure that the increase in scale does not introduce more problems into the production.

4   *Specifications*   are laid down for the production of the good.

5   *Production*   For some products this may be a test production run and the products will be test marketed to see if they are acceptable to the market. If the product is a failure the production will go no further. Large and expensive products cannot have a 'test' run – it would make the product prohibitively expensive. For such goods the second stage is likely to be extended.

The design process is one of problem solving and the minimisation of risk. Look at the stages closely. You will see that they echo the planning pattern that has already been repeated several times in this book.

SELF ASSESSMENT

1 State two ways in which each of these departments in a company could influence the design of a new product:
   a Finance.
   b Marketing.
   c Personnel.
   d Production.
2 Using the flow chart illustrated in Figure 11.1 as a guide, draw up a flow chart for the design process of a simple good.
3 Most households own a plastic bucket. The shape of all buckets is very similar. If a company decided to enter this market could it by-pass the design stage? Explain your answer.
4 State and explain two reasons why a business would build a prototype of a new product.
5 List three products whose design is limited by legal restrictions.

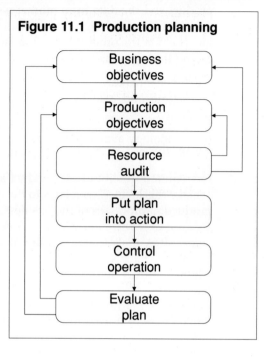

Figure 11.1 Production planning

- Business objectives
- Production objectives
- Resource audit
- Put plan into action
- Control operation
- Evaluate plan

Value analysis

Value analysis is an approach to evaluating the effectiveness of producing a component or product. It is an exercise designed to answer the question: Can we achieve the same result more efficiently and therefore at a lower cost? The stages in value analysis emphasise the role the different business functions play in the development of a product.

Value analysis is not concerned with a particular product. It is interested in the function that product has for both the business and the customer. For a business manufacturing shelving units the function of a screw is to hold a shelf bracket to the wall; the same screw may also have a decorative function that is important to the customer. By defining the function of the component or product rather than the item itself, value analysis encourages the business to seek alternative methods of performing that function and so improving efficiency and reducing production costs.

Stages in value analysis

1 *Defining the function of the product* If the product is a component then this stage should produce a precise statement of what it must do if it is to perform its job correctly. A good definition may immediately suggest more cost effective ways of achieving that function. The definition of a finished good should also take into account the market for which it is designed. A company producing wristwatches for the luxury market might lose the market if they used a cheaper metal casing in an effort to control costs.

2 *Collection of data* At this stage the company may only *think* it knows what the product is. They need detailed information if they are going to evaluate it. This information should include:

☐   detailed technical specifications of the product.

☐   marketing information. The existence of similar products, the life expectancy of the product and the data from market research will all have a role to play in the final decision. A major design exercise will not be worthwhile if the product has a limited lifespan. On the other hand value analysis might be used to identify strategies to extend the lifespan of the product.

☐   a detailed breakdown of costs to indicate the areas it may be advantageous to investigate and also to define the constraints on any changes that might be suggested.

☐   the technology available to make the product. This should include details of new developments and their possible effects on production costs and quality control.

☐   the required quality of the product and details of the control procedures used to achieve this level. This relates to the quality required by the market but also to the production processes of the business.

3   *Evaluation*   It is likely that a number of alternative solutions will be suggested to the same problem. Each solution will then be evaluated against the criteria established by the original product definition.

Value analysis is not limited to the existing products of a business. It can be used by a firm entering a market for the first time to decide the market segment it is aiming for. Its importance lies in its integrated approach to the problem. An effective value analysis team would contain experts in each of the major business functions.

SELF ASSESSMENT

1 List the business functions that would need to be employed in a successful exercise in value analysis.
2 Why is it important to define the function of a component simply and with care if the process of value analysis is to be profitable?
3 How might knowing the function of a product help the business to extend its lifespan?
4 A business is thinking of replacing a solid wood finish to one of its products with a synthetic material. State and explain one constraint on this decision.
5 Outline briefly the way in which value analysis could help determine the market segment for a new product.

Inputs and outputs

A business buys raw materials, components and semi-finished goods and puts them through a variety of processes that make them more useful. The end result of this process may be sold to another business to become a component or semi-finished good at the start of its processes or it may be sold direct to a consumer. Many businesses do both. A car battery is useful to the owner of a car who sees it as part of current expenditure. It is also essential to car manufacturers who regard it as an item of stock. The input of one business is the output of another business. In this section we are concerned with the input to the business, that is the purchasing function and the monitoring of stock levels within a business.

The purchasing function

The importance of purchasing varies according to the type of business. In service industries materials may be a very small part of the final cost of a product. In a manufacturing business the material cost may be a large proportion of the final cost. In the latter case it is essential that the right stocks are bought at the right price, in the right quantity and at the right time. The role of purchasing goes beyond this simple statement. The purchaser is a buyer in a market, who knows what products are available in that market and who can make this information available to the design department. The purchaser should also be able to advise on delivery times, which is essential information for stock control.

In order to fulfil this function in achieving business objectives the purchaser needs detailed information about suppliers. A good supplier requires cultivation. This is part of the overall approach of the purchaser. If the supplier is to meet the needs of a business then information is necessary about what those needs are, and it is a function of the purchasing department to supply this information. Suppliers also tend to be more co-operative if they are paid on time and in accordance with other terms laid down in the initial contract.

Suppliers may, in fact, perform part of the design function of the business. When a specific part is required the customer will provide the supplier with detailed specifications. In this case the supplier has little or no part to play in the design. When the customer states only the general function of the product to be purchased and the size of any interconnecting parts (pipe diameter, etc.), then it is the supplier who designs the product. This means that the purchasing department must have knowledge of the alternatives available and the complete 'package' (quality, price, service) so that a decision can be made as to which one will be in the best interests of the business.

The quality of raw materials and components are as important to the customer as the way in which the product is made. Customers do not differentiate between the two. The quote given below was made by the managing director of a small garment manufacturing company. She had just turned down a lucrative order from a chain store on the grounds that the quality of the material they supplied her with was unsatisfactory.

> 'They can fool about with their own reputation if they like but this business is my bread and butter. The material was far too thin for skirts. A skirt would be coming apart at the seams in the first two weeks. No matter how careful my girls are, no matter how well I check, stitches alone won't hold the garment together.'

It is important that a business can be trusted to supply the agreed quality. The final customer seldom makes distinctions. If a car breaks down it is the manufacturer who is blamed, not the business that supplied a faulty component.

The supplier must also be able to produce the quantity of goods required, when they are required and at the right price. A delay can cause production stoppages and slowdowns, lay-offs in the workforce and a possible loss of future orders for the customer.

The importance of the purchasing function will be recognised if you remember that a business can be defined as an organisation that buys in goods and services which it then uses to produce other goods and services to be sold at a profit. Without purchasing a business cannot exist.

SELF ASSESSMENT

1 State and explain two differences in the role of a purchasing manager for a retail chain and an engineering company producing industrial machinery.

2 From the information given above list the responsibilities of purchaser and supplier to each other.

3 Give a brief explanation of the ways in which a supplier can affect the success of the final product. How does this influence the purchaser?

4 Read the quote given above from the managing director of the garment manufacturing company. Do you think she made the right decision? Give reasons for your answer.

5 State and explain three ways in which poor purchasing could increase the costs of a business.

Stock control

Stock control is concerned with assessing the materials needed according to projected output, storing the materials in a suitable manner (that is to keep them safe and in good condition), and issuing materials when required. The relationship between purchasing and the stock control activities of a business will vary according to the size of the business and the organisational decisions.

The maintenance of the 'right' level of stocks is very important to the health of a business.

1 In many industries the cost of materials used to make the product is a high proportion of final cost. Stocks can represent a considerable investment for a business.

2 Stocks cost money to store. These costs can be seen as the opportunity cost of holding the stock. Stocks do not earn any money. If a business holds a stock valued at £10 000 then it is sacrificing, at least, the interest on £10 000 held in a bank at, say, 10 per cent. It is also sacrificing potential profit. The minimum cost of holding this stock can be seen as £1000 per annum. In addition there are the costs of storage and the risk of stocks deteriorating in value.

3 Stocks are frequently a major part of working capital and this can have implications for the liquidity of the business.

The ideal situation in stock control is to hold stocks for the shortest possible period of time between ordering and the conversion of stocks into goods sold for a profit. In this way the cost of holding any one item of stock is minimised. This ideal cannot be realised by the work of the stock control department. It will rely on production efficiency generally and the organisation of the factory to achieve a rapid throughput of work.

Stock levels

We have already established that it is desirable for a business to keep stocks as low as possible. On the other hand if stocks are too low then there is a danger of production stopping because of a shortfall in materials. A business will have a minimum stock level, sometimes called the buffer, safety or insurance level, below which it will not allow stocks to fall, and a maximum stock level, above which the costs of holding the stock outweigh the advantages of holding it. The minimum and maximum of stock held are relative rather than absolute figures and will depend upon a combination of factors.

1 *Storage space and costs*   Space used to store materials can be seen as space that could be used for manufacturing. In some businesses there may be a physical shortage of space that puts a clear limit on the amount of stock they can hold safely and without risk of excessive spoilage.

2 *The lead time* This is the interval of time between the identification of the need for an order and the availability of that order to the production department. It is *not* the same as delivery time. Lead time includes ordering, delivery and receiving time. The longer the lead time the higher the minimum level at which stocks will have to be held.

3 *The amount of capital available* This will influence the stock level. This does not mean that a successful business will hold a higher level of stocks than a similar but less profitable business. In fact the reverse might be true. Lack of available capital might force a business to hold a lower level of stock than it considers strictly desirable.

4 *The type of stock* Perishable goods will be kept in smaller quantities than non-perishable stock to reduce the risk of loss. The 'life' of stock does not depend only on whether it is likely to deteriorate; it also depends on the lifespan of the final product. If the product goes out of fashion the stocks bought in to make it will be useless.

5 *The economic ordering quantity* This will determine the amount of stock bought at any one time. Discounts available might offset the costs of storage and encourage a business to raise its minimum stock level.

6 *External factors* These can influence the level of stocks held. A business might hold a high level of essential stocks if it can foresee a future shortage brought about by a possible crop failure or pressure on supplies as a result of war.

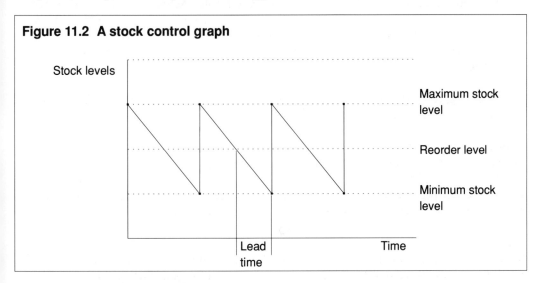

Figure 11.2 A stock control graph

Figure 11.2 is a simplified stock control graph. Its value lies in its illustration of the main elements within stock control. It illustrates a situation in which there is a known quantity which must be ordered at regular intervals. This is characterised by a situation in which:

□ demand is known and reasonably constant;

□ all other costs are known;

□ items arrive on time.

Figure 11.3 Product demand patterns

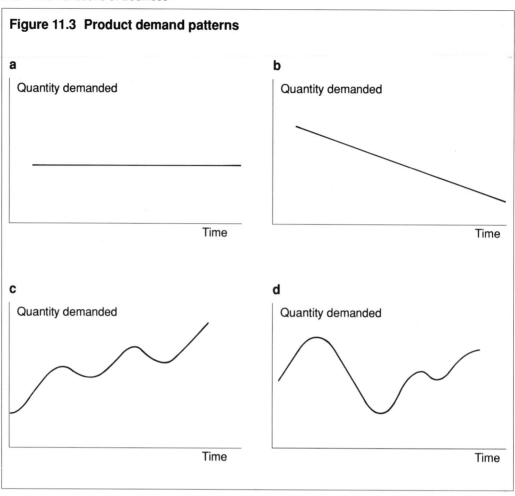

1 Unusual weather conditions lead to reports that availability of an important raw material crop is likely to be below normal. What might be the reaction of a business which uses this raw material? What other factors would it take into account before reaching its final decision?

2 Figure 11.3 shows a series of graphs representing the demand patterns of four products.
   a Using the same axis, sketch four graphs showing the pattern in the fall of stock levels as a result of these demand patterns.
   b Which demand patterns could be illustrated by a graph similar to Figure 11.2? Give clear reasons for your answer.

3 What do you understand by the term 'economic ordering quantity'? Why is it important?

4 State and explain two problems a business might experience as a result of irregular lead times. What role has the purchasing department to play in the solution to these problems?

5 A newspaper ran the headline 'Business stock levels down!' The article that followed suggested that this provided evidence of an impending economic recession. Give a brief explanation of why the conjecture might be accurate.

Quality control

The production department, like all other departments in a business, will have targets set to contribute to the business plan. In addition the production department will also have *quality* targets. The desired level of quality is not necessarily the best quality attainable for that product. The tennis racket made for a professional player will have to stand greater stresses than that used by an amateur. The professional will pay more for that quality. Quality control can be seen as minimising the rate of failure within limits set by costs and the market price. There may also be safety standards to which a product must conform. Quality control is also important when applied to material stocks and work in progress. After all, the further a faulty part progresses in the production process the greater the cost of scrapping or reworking the product of which it is a part. There are additional costs if the product reaches the market. Consumer law states that a product must be of merchantable quality, that is able to perform the function for which it is intended. Although the retailer takes the first responsibility for this situation, a manufacturer whose products do not satisfy the customer is likely to find distribution outlets reluctant to stock its products.

The objectives of quality control

The objectives of quality control are to make sure that the product:

- □ will satisfy the needs of the customer.
- □ will work under the conditions it will experience.
- □ will operate in the way in which the customer wants and the publicity claims.
- □ can be produced by the business within the cost constraints.
- □ can be repaired in the time claimed on the majority of occasions.
- □ satisfies health and safety requirements.

Quality and costs

Once a business has decided on the degree of quality suited to its market, maintaining that level of quality will cost money. Products will be scrapped if they do not meet the required standards, inspectors will have to be employed to ensure the standard is reached and production may be slowed down.

There is the opposing view. Quality control is cheap. Get the quality right and the business is unlikely to be faced with unexpected costs when the product is found to be faulty by its market. The cost of quality can be low if it is built into the objectives and organisation of the business. It can be divided into:

1 *The costs of prevention* The careful monitoring for potential faults will eliminate these before the product has left the design stage. If a business is sure it knows what the market wants then there is less chance of wasting money on a product which is either of too high or too low a quality to appeal to the market segment at which it is directed. A training programme and business ethos that instils quality objectives into employees will save money in the future at relatively little additional cost.

2 *The costs of control* The cost of employing people to check that the product meets the agreed standard at all production stages.

3   *The costs of failure*   Not only in the scrapping and reworking of materials, and the loss of production time, but also in the damage to the company's reputation.

Where the output is high, quality control inspectors will work on a sample of goods and use the statistical techniques from Chapter 5 ('Statistics') to analyse their findings. When results are unacceptable, changes in suppliers, working practices, selection and training techniques might be necessary. Poor quality is not necessarily the result of careless workers.

SELF ASSESSMENT

1   A business decides that it is losing its market share because the price of its product is too high. Give two problems it may encounter in trying to reduce the price, assuming profit margins will stay the same.
2   State and explain three reasons for poor quality control.
3   Give three ways in which value analysis could help reduce the costs of quality control.
4   Select two objectives of quality control and explain why they are important in a business achieving its overall objectives.
5   Explain briefly why the highest quality a product can reach is not always the 'best' quality for a business to aim for.

Work study

Work study is a body of techniques that analyse the tasks to be performed (work measurement and/or motion study), the time that is needed to perform the tasks (time study) and the setting of standards for a given task. Work study can:

- increase productivity by reducing unnecessary effort and saving time.

- reduce the risk of injury to a worker and so improve health and safety.

- reduce costs by reducing time lost through absenteeism caused by injury, and wastage caused by bad working practices.

- increase the degree of satisfaction felt by the worker.

- help the personnel function in devising effective training schemes.

The stages of work study

Work study can be divided into *motion study*, *time study* and establishing standards by which a work can be evaluated.

Motion study
Motion study is a detailed evaluation of the way in which a task is carried out. Its main objectives are to:

- make the job easier.

- make it safer.

- improve quality.

- increase productivity.

Frederick Taylor was the first person to seriously consider improving productivity – and therefore profit – by teaching the workforce to move efficiently. Workers should use the minimum amount of energy in doing a job and so tire less quickly. Since Taylor's early studies at the beginning of the century a body of knowledge has grown up. This includes such things as an emphasis on smooth and continuous motion, using gravity to help the work, placing tools in the order in which they are used and establishing a rhythm of work.

The expert studying a problem can use film or video to observe movements in slow motion. The analyst then labels each action. If a worker spends time searching for a tool then this suggests that reorganisation of the workstation would increase efficiency. Effort in lifting causes tiredness so the use of a machine could increase productivity and reduce the likelihood of accidents.

Time study

Once the additional machinery has been installed, the workstation organised and the workforce trained, a time study can be undertaken. This allows a time to be set for a particular job and so can help in costing. A time study can be conducted using a stopwatch study, that is the timing of each action, a sample of the time taken to perform a given task over a specified period of time and the use of data from the records of the business.

Stopwatch studies

These are supposed to be conducted by watching a normal worker operating at a normal speed. This is the main drawback of the method. It is difficult to decide what is meant by a normal worker and people find it hard to behave naturally when they know they are being observed, particularly if they feel threatened by the observation.

Work sampling

This avoids some of the problems associated with the stopwatch method. For much of the time the worker is alone. The analyst takes observations at intervals and analyses the statistics to determine the pattern of work. Although the results are less accurate than the stopwatch method over a period of time they may be more accurate. The person being observed is more likely to relax and work at the normal pace.

Work study has positive benefits but its introduction is often treated with suspicion. The workforce need to be reassured that any increases in productivity will not lead to a reduction in the number of jobs. Changes in working practice may be resented even when the original practices were both tiring and inefficient.

SELF ASSESSMENT

1 State and explain three ways in which work study can improve the efficiency of a business.
2 Why does the effectiveness of a time study depend upon a careful motion study?
3 Give two reasons why a stopwatch study may not give accurate results.
4 Distinguish between stopwatch studies and sampling.
5 Give three possible consequences of worker antagonism to a time and motion study.

REVIEW

1 Shields Ltd manufactures portable radio-cassette recorders. It entered the market early and enjoyed considerable success. Recently, however, sales have been falling. The popularity of the product has encouraged new entrants into the rapidly growing market, some of which are considerably larger than Shields and have spent large sums of money promoting their products. The board of directors at Shields are not convinced that this is the answer for them. They instigate a thorough investigation into the problem.

a Distinguish between a fall in sales and a fall in market share.

b Explain briefly why the directors are not prepared to accept new entrants into the market as the cause of the problem.

c Which business functions would be involved in the investigation? State one contribution each function would make to the investigation.

d How could value analysis help Shields Ltd in prolonging the life of its product?

2 Tom Parker works in the purchasing department of a large manufacturing company. One of the lines for which he is responsible is a component used in the assembly of a major product. At the end of 1989 the main supplier of this component ceased trading and for the last six months Tom has been buying from five different businesses. He has drawn up the following table to compare the promised lead time of each business with the actual lead time on their last ten deliveries.

Supplier	Promised lead time (days)	Actual lead time of last ten deliveries (days)
A	8	12, 9, 8, 11, 13, 12, 11, 12, 14, 13
B	14	9, 12, 15, 13, 14, 14, 16, 13, 14, 15
C	16	16, 16, 15, 17, 18, 20, 17, 16, 14, 17
D	20	25, 24, 26, 24, 23, 25, 23, 26, 27, 23
E	23	23, 21, 22, 25, 25, 24, 27, 27, 29, 31

a What do you understand by the term 'lead time'?

b Give two reasons why the lead time is important to the business.

c On a graph show the variations in lead time for each supplier.

d State and explain two problems the trends shown by the figures could cause for the business.

3 A business buys in a component used in the assembly of its product. It uses the component at a steady rate of 50 000 per month and prefers to keep a month's supply in stock; lead time is two weeks. The maximum amount of stock the business prefers to hold is 200 000.

a Draw a graph to show the changes in the stock of components over six months.

b At what level of stockholding should the business reorder?

c At the end of the third month the supplier is involved in an industrial dispute which lasts for a fortnight. Assuming no other supplies are available sketch the consequences for the business on your graph.

d How might the business react to each of the following situations?

i An increase in the price of the component.

ii A shortage of working capital.

iii Stockpiling by governments of an essential raw material.

iv An expected rise in the demand for the final product.

v Improvements in stock control techniques.

4 Greenfingers Nursery specialises in propagating shrubs and trees for the mail order market. The owners of the nursery were very concerned when a consumer report identified their business as the one giving the lowest level of customer satisfaction in a group of ten nurseries surveyed. One of the partners was not too concerned, and pointed out that Greenfingers was the largest nursery in the survey and she doubted that the sample used was valid. 'After all,' she said, 'they are asking people to write into them and the ones who write will be the ones with complaints. It stands to reason that we will have more complaints simply because we do more business.' Her partner was not consoled and in a meeting put forward the following areas in which they had to review their quality control:

☐ labelling.
☐ condition of plants.
☐ packaging.
☐ distributors.

a Give three reasons why quality control is important to a business enterprise.
b Do you think the first partner was accurate in her assessment of the situation?
c Give two quality control objectives Greenfingers Nursery might establish for the areas of concern given above.
d What problems in quality control might Greenfingers experience?

5 A business has developed a new product of advanced technological design. It was expected that the demand for the product would be low at first, rising steadily over a period of six months to 20 000 units per month. Production levels were set at 15 000 units for the first twelve months of the product's life. In fact, actual orders rose steadily to 40 000 units over a period of six months.

a Draw a graph showing the relationship between output, projected orders and actual orders.
b Outline the marketing problems the business may experience as a result of this situation.
c Assuming that it is impossible to expand production capacity before the end of the twelve month period, how might the business increase the supply of the product? What difficulties might it encounter given the nature of the product?

6 Examine Figure 11.4.

a What problems might the business face as a result of this pattern of sales and production?
b How might:
i the production department,
ii the marketing department,
attempt to solve these problems?

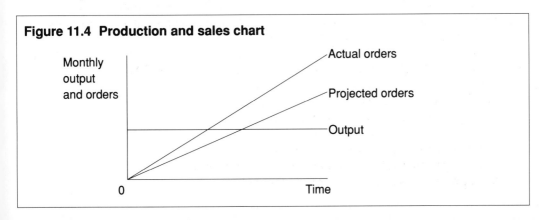

Figure 11.4 Production and sales chart

Activities

1 Select several brands of a product. Hairdryers, washing machines, personal computers are possible examples. Analyse the design features of each example. From your own knowledge outline the constraints on the design. Which, in your opinion, is the best design and why?

2 Select one item of stock you would need to buy in if you were running a small shop. You can choose any type of retailing operation. Using *Yellow Pages* or another local directory, identify possible suppliers of this line. Discover the terms on which they are willing to supply. Which would be the best supplier for you? What assumptions and decisions did you have to make before you could arrive at your conclusion?

3 Quality control applies to the academic work of students as well as the production of goods and services! Keep a diary for a month. In this diary you should note:
   - quality objectives negotiated between yourself and your tutor.
   - methods used to monitor the quality of work produced.
   - the process by which improvements in quality are achieved.

Suggested projects

1 Can business X improve its stock control?
2 A critical evaluation of quality control within a business.
3 Can business Y improve the use of its canteen facilities?

Essays

1 Elms Ltd has identified a market opportunity that could be met by extending its product range. In what way could value analysis help Elms decide:
   a whether it should enter the market?
   b the design of the product?

2 Discuss the contribution the purchasing department makes to the success of a business manufacturing power tools for the DIY market.

3 Comment on the opinion that the maintenance of buffer stocks is a waste of money.

4 What are the main objectives of a stock control system? Discuss the importance of the clear definition of such objectives to the successful running of a business.

5 'Quality control is cheap... it is the least expensive and most important function in the business organisation.' How far do you agree with this statement?

6 Discuss the constraints upon a business enterprise when deciding on a policy of quality control.

7 Carstair Ltd is embarking on a programme of cost reduction and rationalisation. As personnel manager write a report explaining how the related work study programme should be presented to trade union representatives.

8 Comment on the view that a work study programme is to the benefit of employees.

9 Outline and comment on the interrelationships which exist between the marketing and production functions.

12   People and business

When you have studied this chapter you should be able to:

□   Describe the interdependence of people and business.

□   Outline management theories.

□   Appreciate the contribution that theorists have made to the development of management techniques.

□   Criticise the different theories.

□   Distinguish between the different types of groups.

□   Apply the definitions of groups to different situations.

□   Define and distinguish between the different types of leadership.

□   Appreciate the need for different types of leadership in different situations.

□   Define motivation.

□   Outline the ways in which businesses attempt to motivate people.

□   Appreciate the relationship between methods of motivation and the theory.

□   Appreciate the limitations of motivation techniques.

Businesses are the creation of people. They are organisations brought into existence to satisfy the needs and wants of society. They have an effect on the lives of people they employ by the way in which they are organised, the wages they pay, the social opportunities they may or may not offer and the degree of job security they can ensure.

In turn, people influence the growth and development of businesses: as customers with their buying decisions, as owners and employers by investment, purchasing, marketing and production decisions, and as employees by their *efficiency* in their job.

People also influence business by the choices they make as citizens. The way in which individuals decide to vote will affect the political climate in which a business has to operate. Individuals with strong opinions on particular matters may join together in an organisation to publicise their concern and to try to persuade decision makers to take notice of their point of view (pressure groups). An environmental *pressure group*, for example, might influence the siting of a business.

The general relationship which exists between people and business organisations is illustrated in Figure 12.1.

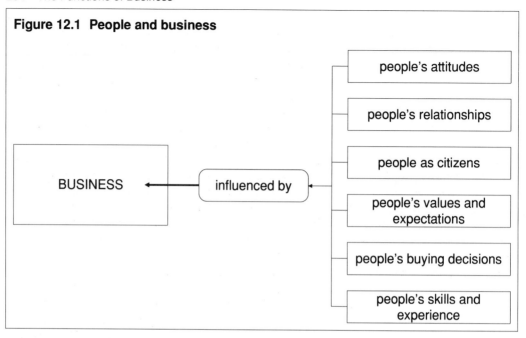

Figure 12.1 People and business

People as individuals

Each member of the human race is the unique product of heredity and environment. People inherit physical characteristics from their parents and their expectations of life are moulded by their unique experience. This is a very simple statement and you should be aware that psychologists are still investigating the relative importance of hereditary and environmental influences on the development of *personality*. In this section we shall look at the way in which the needs, personalities and attitudes of individuals are important influences on the efficient running of a business enterprise.

The needs of the individual

What do people need to make them happy and contented? If you asked this question of any one person they could probably give you a long list of specific needs. It is also likely that at different times in their life some of those needs would have greater importance than at others. In an attempt to provide a simple framework of needs Abraham Maslow in 1970 drew up a *hierarchy of needs*, shown in Figure 12.2.

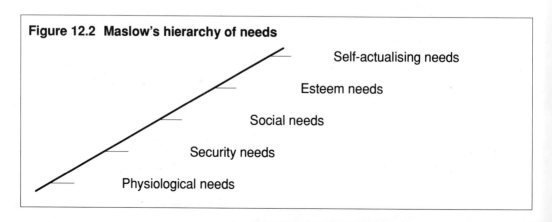

Figure 12.2 Maslow's hierarchy of needs

Maslow argued that a person would seek to satisfy lower level needs before moving on to the next level of needs. If it is not possible to satisfy needs then the person experiences frustration to which the response may be *apathy* ('What is the use of trying? There is no chance of success.') or *aggression*. Aggression may be expressed verbally, for example by blaming other people for lack of success. In extreme cases it may result in physical violence either to people or to things. The nineteenth-century Luddites, faced with new technology that rendered their skills redundant and their livelihoods at risk, resorted to machine wrecking. Twentieth-century workers faced with the same problem might use the organised power of trade unions to express the same frustration.

Maslow argued that in modern industrialised societies the lower level needs were enjoyed by most people. The way to persuade people to work more productively, i.e. to motivate them, was to offer them the opportunity of satisfying higher level needs, for example control over their working arrangements, or their need for independence.

Maslow developed the idea of *self-actualising needs*. These are unique for each individual. They are the needs that a person must satisfy if they are to realise their full potential. The range of these needs is vast – as varied as the people who attempt to achieve them.

The hierarchy of needs is a good explanation of the way in which people behave. People go to work to earn money to satisfy their *physiological needs*, to buy the entertainment that satisfies social needs and the products that contribute to their status. Some people are prepared to sacrifice lower order needs in the short or long term for self fulfilment. The artist starving in his garret may be hoping for future wealth or could be prepared to make the sacrifice for Art.

Persuading people to work

A need is something that people lack. They feel that their life would be enriched if this lack was fulfilled. They therefore take steps to satisfy the need. The reasons they seek this satisfaction are their motives. Figure 12.3 illustrates the process of need satisfaction.

There is no guarantee that the actions of individuals to satisfy their needs will contribute to the objectives (the needs) of a business. For example, social needs might be met in the working environment. An employee who pursues this type of satisfaction may not give satisfaction to the managers and owners of the business.

At the beginning of this century very little thought was given to the role of people in the workplace. Jobs tended to be traditional in design, hours of work were long and discipline strict. Since then a number of people, both managers and academics, have studied this problem and produced a variety of solutions.

Figure 12.3 The process of need satisfaction

Motivation to satisfy need

Identify need

Action to satisfy need

Satisfaction of need

Frederick Taylor (1856–1915)

Frederick Taylor, writing at the beginning of this century, saw people as motivated by money. He saw them as economic in their needs. He argued that if jobs were designed to make maximum output possible, and *personnel* were recruited for their ability, trained thoroughly and paid well according to output, they would work more productively, achieve higher pay and the business would make more profit. Taylor envisaged a system in which the employee received a fair share of the additional profits made by the business. Unfortunately this element of his ideas was often ignored by management. When this happens it can lead to fear for job security. As a result unofficial limits may be put on the amount of work people might do in a day, the controlling force here being the opinion of the people an individual works with rather than the management of the business. In certain types of job money can be an important *incentive*. The place of work does not offer satisfaction for all needs. Some people do not want independence and control over their job. They would prefer a high money wage which they can use to purchase satisfaction of their other needs outside work.

Elton Mayo (1880–1949)

In the 1920s Elton Mayo conducted important research that suggested that the most important influence on the way in which people behaved at work was the people they were in contact with during the day. When people felt they were appreciated for their efforts, when they enjoyed the company of the people they worked with, they would work more productively. These experiments gave weight to the idea of man as a social animal.

The most publicised experiment in this area is known as the *Hawthorne experiment*. The Western Electric Company of Chicago had been experimenting to find the ideal light levels for maximum productivity in their company. They were surprised to find that wide variations in the level of lighting had little effect on output. Mayo led the research team from the Harvard University School of Business Administration that was invited to study this phenomenon. The published research resulted in an increased emphasis on the provision of sports and social facilities, a tendency to organise production so that people worked in small groups rather than on assembly lines and a management style that was consultative and supportive rather than authoritarian.

Henri Fayol (1841–1925)

Fayol was primarily concerned with the principles and practice of management. He analysed the main activities of management as follows:

- planning;
- organising;
- communication;
- co-ordination;
- control.

He believed that the application of these principles to business behaviour would allow managers to run businesses positively, making clear decisions and communicating them to the workers. This would give employees clear objectives to work to and increase motivation.

Although much of Fayol's work appears to support a rigid formula for successful management, in fact he was aware of the importance of adaptability in the skills required by a manager. He also emphasised the need for organisations to show a 'human' side by considering the needs of their employees and attempting to meet them.

Douglas McGregor

McGregor published *The Human Side of Enterprise* in 1960. In it he outlined *Theory X* and *Theory Y*.

Theory X states that people are inherently lazy and uninterested in work. They lack ambition and desire security above anything else. As a result they require constant direction and supervision by management if they are to be effective as workers.

Theory Y, McGregor's own theory, suggests that all people can be motivated to work productively and it is the responsibility of management to provide the ideal circumstances to persuade them to do so.

Frederick Herzberg

Writing at approximately the same time as McGregor, Herzberg analysed characteristics of jobs. He came to the conclusion that these could be divided into two categories.

□ *Maintenance factors* are good heating, lighting, pay and social facilities. People do not work any more productively because these are present but if conditions deteriorate then their work output can decline. Poor maintenance factors can cause job dissatisfaction.

□ *Motivators*, for example a sense of achievement, the giving of responsibility, the prospect of promotion, lead to higher work output and job satisfaction. Herzberg described the building of motivators into a work situation as job enrichment.

Recent research has moved away from the simple approach and has given weight to the idea of the *complex* person. This can be summarised as follows:

1   People change throughout their life. At one point their work may be the primary source of need satisfaction, defining them as people and providing them with a social life. Later the more important satisfactions may come from their personal lives or from voluntary work. The importance of work therefore changes.

2   As people develop they are subject to a wider variety of influences. This includes the way in which the organisation in which they work affects them. Motives which they did not know they possessed or dismissed at the age of twenty might be dominant at the age of forty. Someone who places a high value on money at twenty may be more influenced by promotion prospects and security twenty years later.

The work of the theorists discussed so far can be referred to as content theories of motivation. These are concerned with the particular features of a job that motivate individuals. These might be found in the needs of the individual or in the conditions of the job itself. *Process theories* are concerned with how motivation works. Figure 12.4 outlines the expectancy theory of motivation.

Expectancy theory is apparently less useful to managers in a business than content theories. It offers no guarantee that the satisfaction an individual is seeking in performance will be found within that enterprise. By placing values on the different ways in which needs can be satisfied the individual may well reject work as the method most likely to give satisfaction.

A simpler process theory concentrates on the modification of behaviour. Good practice, that is behaviour which contributes to the achievement of the objectives of the business, is rewarded promptly by an increase in pay, promotion or praise. Behaviour which goes against the organisation achieving its goals is not rewarded. Many people apply this theory of motivation to the way in which they bring up their children.

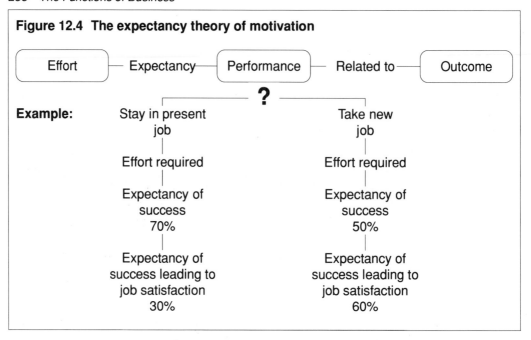

Figure 12.4 The expectancy theory of motivation

SELF ASSESSMENT

1 The Hawthorne experiment suggested that people worked better if they felt valued. What evidence in the text supports this conclusion?

2 Give two reasons why the theory of 'the complex person' might be more realistic than preceding theories.

3 State two ways in which the theories of Frederick Taylor could be seen as a threat by employees.

4 A man decided to start his own business. For the first two years he had sufficient money to buy essentials and no more. Does this argue against Maslow's theory of a hierarchy of needs? Give reasons for your answer.

5 Distinguish between Theory X and Theory Y.

Personality

Personality can be described as the total of an individual's behavioural and emotional tendencies which distinguish her/him from other individuals.

Over the years psychologists and psychoanalysts have attempted to describe and analyse broad patterns of personality in an attempt to classify people and so achieve a broader understanding of the ways in which they behave. A great deal of research has gone into this subject but we shall only look at the classification of personality by type and the implications of this approach for a business.

Classification by type

1 *The extrovert* Extroverts are people who are primarily interested in people or things outside their own self. Eysenck distinguished between *stable extroverts* and *anxious extroverts*. Stable extroverts are very good at making contact with people and are often

Figure 12.5 Classifications of personality

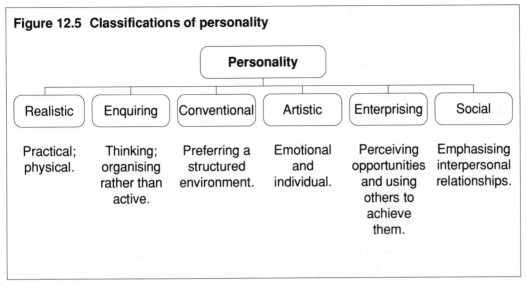

successful in jobs that require constant contact with people in order to persuade them into a course of action. Anxious extroverts, on the other hand, generate more tension. They can be found in high pressure jobs, frequently those with a deadline to meet.

2   *The introvert*   Introverts have a tendency to withdraw into themselves and seek their stimulus to action from their own resources. The stable introvert prefers quiet jobs with little human contact whereas the anxious introvert takes this tendency to the extreme. The anxious introvert can be the truly creative person in the business.

Some businesses use personality tests to assess the suitability of applicants for a particular job. There is some debate about the usefulness of these tests. An individual might have the potential for enterprise – that is the ability to see opportunities and influence other people to achieve them – but may not have had the experience or encouragement that allows such skills to develop.

Figure 12.5 illustrates further classifications of personality.

SELF ASSESSMENT

1 Select five occupations in business and state which personality type might be most suited to each.
2 Give three reasons why the personality of an applicant might be important in the selection of personnel.
3 Select one career with which you are familiar. What type of personality would be most suited to it? Why?

Groups

If each person in the business enterprise is a unique product of heredity and environment with a complex and changing pattern of needs and a distinct personality pattern, what happens when people try to work together? The answer is that most people tend to modify their behaviour, to a greater or lesser extent, to suit the people they come into contact with, and the needs of the job. In doing so the group gradually establishes an acceptable code of behaviour, known as the *group norm*, to which each person adheres.

Group norms can also be imposed upon the group by management and reinforced by education and training. In many cases the standards of behaviour imposed by management are modified by the group when working. This can lead to problems. For example a strict code of practice relating to the wearing of safety helmets may be adjusted to a style the workers concerned consider more attractive. It is also likely that the style would be against the safety regulations of the employing business, for example it might leave hair exposed to moving machinery. People in that group who did not conform to the accepted pattern of behaviour might be subjected to pressure to do so. The pressure might take the form of comments designed to make the non-conforming individuals feel inferior. Whether or not the pressure would be successful would depend on the strength of character or stubbornness of the non-conformists as opposed to the leadership qualities of the people trying to make them conform. Look at the following example:

> A group of college lecturers arrived at work to find an official union picket line from another union. It was the policy of their union to recommend that its members should not cross such picket lines. At first approximately two thirds of the lecturers were prepared to cross the picket line. The one third who refused to do so had a high proportion of the older members of staff whose length of service and seniority carried weight with their colleagues. In the end considerably less than a third of the staff *did* cross the picket line.

This example illustrates the complexity of individual reactions to a situation.

1   The senior staff had no power over their colleagues in making this decision. However the habit of the more junior members of staff of giving weight to the opinions of these people was carried over into a non-work situation.

2   As more people joined the senior staff in their decision so there was more pressure on the rest of the group to conform.

3   The group norms in this situation were partly defined by the recommendations of the trade union.

4   The designated leader of the group, i.e. the head of department played a neutral role. She did not (and could not) use her authority in this situation.

5   The older members of staff had worked together for a number of years and had built up friendships outside the workplace. This gave their stand a cohesion that their opponents lacked.

6   The final result depended on the interpersonal relationships of the people concerned. Had the senior members of staff not been respected in their work roles, or had there been resentment against them for the way in which they dealt with their colleagues, the group decision might well have gone the other way.

Read the example carefully. There are several different types of groups involved.

1 The lecturers were members of the staff of a college with 250 members of staff and 4000 students, many of whom they only met occasionally. They were also members of a union some of whose members they will never meet. Groups to which people belong, but do not have daily contact with all the members, are known as *secondary groups*.

2 Both the college and the union exist for distinct purposes, as does the department to which the lecturers belong. Groups which are formed as a result of the actions of an organisation are *formal groups*. They are part of the structure of the organisation.

3 When people meet each other at frequent and regular intervals we describe the group they belong to as a *primary group*.

4 When people form groups because of common interests and on a casual basis we refer to these groups as *informal groups*. Should they make rules for joining the group and elect people to perform jobs related to the group it would then become a formal group.

Six people meet once a week in a local pub. Their common interest is gardening. For an hour or so they discuss plans for their gardens and then part, to meet again the next week. Sometimes one member of the group will volunteer to order a certain type of seed for the rest, or another will offer the loan of a tool. One day they decide to form a gardening society. They advertise in the local newspaper for people of similar interests to join them, book a hall, hold a meeting, draw up rules, declare an annual subscription and become affiliated to the national body. There is one person responsible for funds (the treasurer), one for the minutes of the meetings and correspondence (the secretary) and one who runs the meetings in an orderly fashion (the president).

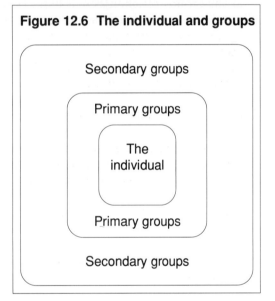

Figure 12.6 The individual and groups

Secondary groups

Primary groups

The individual

Primary groups

Secondary groups

The first group was informal. When it became a society it was formalised, that is it had a structure and had to adhere to agreed procedures. Figure 12.6 shows the relationship between the individual and different types of groups.

SELF ASSESSMENT

1 What is a group?
2 Distinguish between formal, informal, primary and secondary groups.
3 Suggest two ways in which a group can modify the behaviour of an individual.
4 Using Maslow's hierarchy of needs explain how membership of a group can satisfy some of the needs of an individual.
5 Analyse a formal group to which you belong in terms of its relationship to secondary groups and the informal groups within it.

Leadership

In discussing groups it was implied that *leadership* affected the behaviour of groups. It is now time to examine this idea in more detail. We will look at:

- ☐ the way in which leaders arise out of a group.
- ☐ the types of leadership that can be exercised.
- ☐ the way in which the type of leadership is affected by the needs of the group.

The theory of leadership

Leaders are present in both formal and informal groups. A teacher standing in front of a group of students, a supervisor in a factory, and the managing director of a company are all exercising the power of leadership. They have, hopefully, clearly stated objectives and they are organising the group in their control to achieve those objectives.

In any group of friends there is likely to be a leader; the person who says 'Let's do this. I'll get the tickets, you find out the time of the buses.'

Both leaders, the first in a formal group, the second in an informal group, have the power to make people do what they want. The interesting question is: How does a leader emerge from the group? There is no single answer to this question. It is likely that the emergence of a leader depends on the interaction of a number of factors.

1   The character of the leader. People who accept and/or are given leadership tend to have certain characteristics in common. They are sociable and willing to make contributions to discussion. They are likely to be more intelligent than the rest of the group and have problem-solving abilities.

2   Leadership depends on the type of task being undertaken.

3   Leadership depends on the personalities of the rest of the people in the group.

4   Leadership may be imposed on the group or the leader may be elected. The election of a leader does not have to be formal. It could be no more than a consensus among group members that one person has the ability to lead.

Imposed leadership may come into conflict with the informal group leader. In circumstances where the informal leader is dominant then the informal group norms will be followed rather than the norms imposed by the formal group, for example a business. In extreme circumstances this can lead to low productivity, poor quality work and the failure in the business as a whole to achieve its objectives.

The power of a leader can come from a number of sources.

1   The ability of the leader to reward co-operation, for example by recommending them for promotion.

2   A fear on the part of members of the group that if they do not co-operate they will be punished, either actively by disciplinary action or passively by a failure of the leader to reward.

3 A charismatic personality, that is the sort of personality that has a special charm or appeal that is capable of inspiring people.

4 Expert knowledge will be accepted in situations where that knowledge is relevant.

5 Organisational power is given to a person who has been elected or appointed as a leader.

The power enjoyed by the leader over the performance of a group is likely to rest on a combination of the above factors. The ability to direct the group to achieve the objectives set will vary according to the personality and motivation of the leader, the degree of expertise possessed, the personal interaction of the leader with the group and the group norm. Some of these variables are illustrated in Figure 12.7.

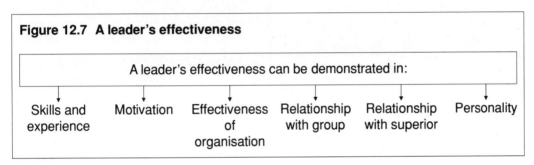

Figure 12.7 A leader's effectiveness

A leader's effectiveness can be demonstrated in:

Skills and experience | Motivation | Effectiveness of organisation | Relationship with group | Relationship with superior | Personality

Leadership styles

1 The *autocratic leader* sets his own objectives, allocates tasks and insists on obedience. As a result the group becomes very dependent upon him. The members of the group do not have the necessary information to make their own decisions. Because they are dependent on the leader there is little cohesion among group members and output, although high under supervision, may not be of good quality. Members of a group with autocratic leadership frequently appear dissatisfied with their leader.

On the other hand autocratic leadership can be necessary in certain circumstances. The discipline imposed by the armed forces was based on the need to move large numbers of troops from one part of a battlefield to another very quickly and to condition them to obey orders instantly.

2 The *democratic leader* encourages participation in the decision making process. She consults with members of the group and 'sells' the final decision to them, working on the assumption that people will work better if they know and believe in their objectives. This style of leadership requires good communication skills on the part of the leader. It results in greater satisfaction on the part of the group, the quality of output tends to be good and the members of the group make a large number of suggestions. True democratic leadership increases the satisfaction within a group.

Figure 12.8 shows a range of leadership styles from the completely autocratic to the extreme of democracy, that is laissez-faire leadership.

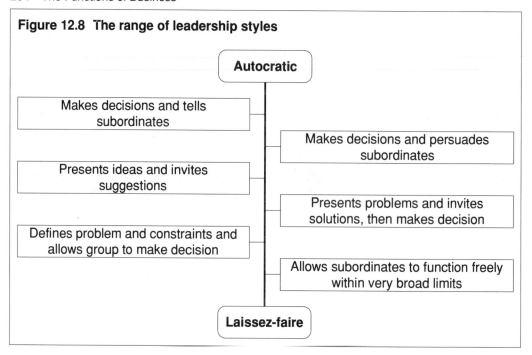

Figure 12.8 The range of leadership styles

The type of leadership employed by any individual will depend on a number of factors:

1 *The task that is being undertaken* We have already seen that military, authoritarian discipline was developed to meet the needs of the battlefield.

2 *The traditions of the organisation* Organisations develop their own patterns of behaviour. An organisation with a tradition of autocratic management would put pressure on individual managers to conform. This is an instance of the development of group norms.

3 *The type of labour force* Highly skilled people will have more to offer in a democratically led group than people lacking experience. In the latter case autocratic leadership may be the only option open to the manager if the job is to be completed.

4 *The size of the group* Autocratic leadership becomes more likely as the number of people a manager controls increases. The greater the number of people the greater the risk of a democratic style degenerating into confusion.

5 *The personality of the leader* Some people are more suited to one leadership style than another. This might be the result of personality, experience (or lack of it) or insecurity.

6 *The personalities of the group members* Some people may prefer to be directed in their work, either from lack of interest, from previous experience of autocratic leadership or because they believe that the manager is paid to take decisions and responsibility.

7 *Time* The time available to complete a task will also influence the leadership style. Persuasion and consultation take time, even if the result is a more efficient workforce.

It might appear that the style of leadership should change according to the situation; the democratic leader becoming autocratic when a rushed order has to be completed, with inexperienced staff or in an emergency. Research suggests that the majority of people prefer their leaders to have a definite leadership style. Leadership style often reflects the personality of the leader. It is therefore realistic for selection procedures to include a clear definition of the personal qualities expected in a successful candidate.

There is evidence to suggest that the behaviour of the group influences the behaviour of a leader. A low achieving, apathetic working group is more likely to encourage the leader to use an autocratic style with a strong emphasis on reward and punishment.

SELF ASSESSMENT

1 Give two circumstances which affect leadership style.
2 From what you know of the needs of individuals explain briefly why people may prefer a definite leadership style.
3 Distinguish between autocratic and democratic leadership styles.
4 Explain why a high achieving work group is likely to encourage a democratic style of leadership.
5 What type of leadership would you expect to be used in the following circumstances?
   a A research laboratory.
   b An army unit on active service.
   c A group of friends planning an outing.

Motivation

In the first part of this chapter we looked at people in terms of their needs and personalities, the way in which they behave in groups and the leadership of those groups. In this section we will examine the way in which this knowledge of people might be used to motivate them, that is to make each person want to work more productively towards the objectives of the business. These techniques have been derived from the theories of the researchers such as Maslow, Mayo and Herzberg outlined at the beginning of the chapter.

Individuals are unique and group norms vary widely from business to business. What might motivate one group of employees might have the opposite effect on another group. Motivators may also vary for the same group of people over time.

Money as a motivator

As profit acts as a measure of success of a business, so many people judge their success or failure and the esteem in which they are held by the employer in terms of the remuneration received for the job done.

Remuneration can be seen as a maintenance factor (page 314). Provided employees are satisfied with their conditions of work then relatively low pay can be tolerated. Dissatisfied employees will often focus on low pay relative to the earnings of other groups of workers when engaged in a dispute with employers.

Money can act as an incentive to work more productively. Pay buys the goods and services that people want to satisfy other needs. The more boring the job, and the less its intrinsic interest the greater the importance of money as a motivator and incentive to effort.

Methods of payment

There are two basic methods of payment, time rate and piece rate.

Time rate

Using this system of payment employees receive wages or salaries according to the amount of time they spend at work. No account is taken of the quantity of work done or the quality of that work, although if an employee is not competent then there is the possibility of training or dismissal. Time rate is easy and cheap to calculate and is often used when it is difficult to measure accurately the amount of work done. It can also be a temptation for an employee to do the minimum possible. Time rate is used in many occupations including most office work. People working on an assembly line are also paid time rate because it is difficult to assess the contribution of the individual to the final product.

Piece rate

This involves payment at an agreed rate per item produced or job completed. Piece rate payment can act as an incentive to work more productively; the more you produce the more money you get. It does mean extra costs in checking quality and, in some occupations, more care has to be taken over health and safety in case the desire for speed overcomes safe working practices. This system also puts pressure on management to provide the work and the necessary materials, otherwise the lack of security inherent in it will lead to job dissatisfaction. Commission paid to salespersons is a form of piece rate.

Many businesses use a combination of time and piece rate payment. Employees will receive a basic time rate which will cover the time spent in setting up tools and compensate for periods when work is slack. After an agreed *quota* has been reached a piece rate system will come into operation. This method provides the security missing in payment by results but retains the incentive element.

Bonus payments

The simplest form of *bonus payment* is an agreed sum of money payable to workers for an agreed outcome. Bonus payments can be paid for good timekeeping or for producing more than an agreed amount in a given period of time. They may be paid to individual workers or to a group of workers. Bonus payments must be simple to work out, easily understood by the people who receive them and cheap to operate. They must also be seen to be fair, otherwise they will cause resentment. A feature of bonus payments is that they can come to be regarded as a standard part of pay, and they therefore lose their incentive effect. Failure to declare a bonus in this situation can also lead to resentment.

Productivity deals are sometimes regarded as a form of bonus payment because they usually lead to higher rates of pay or a bonus for increased output. A true productivity deal will also involve significant changes in working practices in order to reduce both the amount of time wasted and staffing levels and to introduce greater flexibility.

Employee share ownership plans

In recent years these have been advocated as an ideal way of involving employees with the company they work for and therefore motivating them to identify with the objectives of that company. Tax concessions in recent budgets have stimulated interest in these schemes, not least because they can provide the business with a cheap way of raising equity capital. It is important to remember that only a certain proportion of the total shares of the business will be made available to employees and these are usually distributed on the basis of length of service. This can cause problems when people are excluded from the scheme. Where share ownership is accompanied by good communications it can achieve its purpose of motivating, but it can be seen by the workforce as a management device to obtain cheap money.

Some management buy-outs (where the management of a subsidiary company buys it from the parent company) have encouraged the employees to take a share stake in the company as part of their drive to raise capital and to involve the workforce.

Profit related pay

This can vary from a simple bonus scheme in which a proportion of the firm's profits are distributed to employees in accordance with position and length of service, to a system in which a proportion of the pay of the employee is related to the profit of the business. If successful the employees are likely to be given the motivation to work more productively to increase the profits of the business and so increase their own earnings. However the profit of a business does not only depend on factors within the control of the business. Market conditions, in some cases unforeseeable, can lead to excess profits or abnormally low profits. Management too can be criticised under this scheme if other employees blame a shortfall in profits to its inadequacies. In other words, profit related pay could be a demotivator, adding to, rather than subtracting from, resentments.

Other money incentives

Businesses offer a variety of payments according to the job to be done. These include extra pay for working unsocial hours, e.g. a night shift, and pay for a dirty or dangerous job. In general the more complicated the payment system the greater the opportunity for disputes to arise and the fewer the incentive or motivation benefits experienced by the business.

Fringe benefits

Fringe benefits are payments in kind. They do have a money value for employees but this is disguised in the provision of goods and services. Figure 12.9 shows some of the fringe benefits offered to employees in the UK.

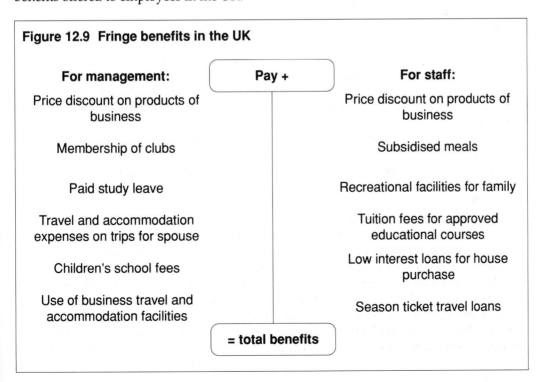

Figure 12.9 Fringe benefits in the UK

For management:	Pay +	For staff:
Price discount on products of business		Price discount on products of business
Membership of clubs		Subsidised meals
Paid study leave		Recreational facilities for family
Travel and accommodation expenses on trips for spouse		Tuition fees for approved educational courses
Children's school fees		Low interest loans for house purchase
Use of business travel and accommodation facilities		Season ticket travel loans
	= total benefits	

Fringe benefits are often of more value to an employee than an increase in pay. Many are difficult to tax and although there has been some effort to make taxation reflect the true value of the benefit this is often difficult to quantify. Fringe benefits also define status within a business, for example the model of car offered is seen to reflect the value the business puts on the work of an employee.

SELF ASSESSMENT

1 Select three methods of payment and suggest circumstances in which each one could act as a motivator. In what circumstances would each cause resentment?
2 Distinguish between time rate and piece rate.
3 State one advantage to employees of a share ownership plan.
4 State three situations in which the level of profits of a business might fall through no fault of its own.
5 Select three examples of fringe benefits. What type of person do you think they would appeal to and why? In what way could they motivate a workforce?

Non-financial motivators

People tend to be motivated if they are interested in the job, feel respected, enjoy the company of the people they are working with, have status and promise for future advancement in terms of the training and promotion prospects that the business offers to them. If these conditions do not exist then it is likely that the workforce will feel alienated. An 'us and them' situation will exist which will make people reluctant to exert themselves in achieving tasks. In other words the *morale* of the business will be low.

Leadership (page 262), communications (page 284) and the *prestige* of the business (page 6) all have a part to play in raising the morale and increasing the level of motivation of a workforce. In this section we will concentrate on the way in which job design and participation in decision making can achieve this aim.

Job enlargement

This is concerned with widening the variety of tasks within a given job. It can also be described as the redesign of jobs. The tendency towards specialisation in the workforce, partly as the result of introducing technology and partly as a result of a drive for greater efficiency, has led to many jobs becoming smaller in scope. This has reduced the control of the worker over her/his day. Seemingly endless repetition of a task can lead to boredom and a lower standard of work. Given a variety of tasks, the worker can assign those which require less concentration to a time of day when their concentration levels are low.

Jobs may be *rotated* to produce the same effect. A worker may spend so much time on one task before being moved to another task or even another department. The following statement was made by a worker on a production line. He was talking about the effect on him of the economic recession which had led to the closing of a number of factories in his town and the closing down of all but one production line at his factory.

'I suppose I should be grateful I've still got a job but it's boring all the same. I never stayed in a job for more than a few years. When I got fed up with a place I would move on. Same sort of work but different people and a different place. It made life more interesting. Can't do that now. We used to swap around in here. Nothing formal but the supervisor turned a blind eye. A week or so on one line and then we would change to another. Now that there is only one line working that has gone too.'

This is not an example of job rotation and job enlargement being deliberately used to motivate. It does, however, illustrate the needs these schemes are designed to satisfy.

The addition of tasks to a job can meet with resentment. Workers might see it as an attempt on the part of management to make them do more work for the same money.

Job enrichment

Job enrichment is the process of increasing the degree of responsibility workers take for their own work and the formal recognition given to it. This can also increase the promotion prospects of employees by adding to their range of experience. Job enrichment might give employees more control over the way in which they organise the work, over the allocation of tasks to members of a group and over quality control. Job enrichment, to be successful, should be supported by a training programme so that workers can acquire the additional skills they will need.

Participation

When people take an active part in reaching a decision they are more likely to feel a sense of commitment to putting the decision into practice. There is a great deal of evidence to support the theory that *worker participation* in decision making is a highly effective motivator. Where participation is imposed on a workforce without adequate training or preparation the sense of commitment lessens. In such cases workers may resent the calls on their time. Shop-floor representatives must be seen to have real influence in the decision making processes and the information needed must be available to them. If not, there is the danger that management might use their superior knowledge to initiate the course of action they wish and worker representatives will be regarded as a rubber stamp.

Quality control circles

Quality control circles are a relatively new development in British industry. They can be viewed as a special development of worker participation. A small group of workers meet regularly to discuss problems they are experiencing in their jobs. They attempt to find the solutions to the problems. Management offers the resources to the workers to put their solutions into practice. A quality control circle works on the assumption that all workers have experience of the jobs they are doing which may be more relevant and immediate than the more theoretical knowledge of management.

The different motivational techniques have in common the idea that the greater the responsibility, recognition, respect and status accorded to individuals within a business, the greater the individuals' sense of involvement in that business and therefore the greater the degree of motivation. The solution to industrial problems is made to sound simple. In practice, of course, the success or failure of a scheme for improving motivation can depend on a number of factors.

1   The state of industrial relations within a business. We have already seen that people judge new events in the light of their experience. In an organisation with a history of poor industrial relations any scheme of management is likely to be viewed with suspicion. Even if there has been a complete change in management personnel the new men may inherit the reputations of the old.

2   The attitude of trade unions could be a deciding factor in success or failure. A trade union might see a management scheme for worker participation as usurping their role in the organisation.

3   The accuracy with which the original problems have been diagnosed will also contribute to success. Job enlargement, job enrichment, participation and quality control circles might seem an additional burden to a workforce whose apparent lack of motivation was due to overwork!

4   The way in which a scheme has been introduced can also be significant. An imposed scheme will meet with more resistance than one in which prior consultation has taken place.

5   Allied to the last point is the impact of management style. A business with a tradition of autocratic management will find the workforce more apathetic and unwilling to co-operate than a business which has encouraged suggestions in the past. An autocratic manager may start out with good intentions but his personality and, perhaps, a feeling of insecurity may cause him to retreat thereby increasing the problems for future attempts.

SELF ASSESSMENT

1   Distinguish between job enrichment and job enlargement.
2   Give two reasons why job enlargement might lead to resentment.
3   Give three possible effects on a business of a poorly motivated workforce.
4   Outline and explain two circumstances in which worker participation could improve the product quality.
5   Read the quotation on page 268. What needs was the person attempting to satisfy? How might his employers have satisfied those needs?

REVIEW

1   The growth of Marionette Enterprises had been a rather haphazard process. It had started in the mid-1970s, in a workshop in a converted nineteenth-century factory, making marionettes. These had proved a success but, realising the need for diversification if the business was to survive, John Stephenson, the owner, had added high quality toys, well-crafted in wood, to his product range. As each new product was introduced a new workshop was acquired. By 1980 Marionette Enterprises had eight separate workshops scattered about the same industrial complex and a small rather pokey office in a different location entirely.

   As far as production was concerned this slightly unorthodox system appeared to work very well. In financial and administrative terms it was less successful. Each workshop had its own complement of machinery, all rather old but still operating smoothly. The senior skilled operator in each workshop accepted responsibility for organising the work, quality control and training. Stephenson believed that if he could rationalise his production processes he could buy additional machinery which could be shared by all sections of his business. Wood off-cuts from the more expensive toys could be used to make a range of cheaper, mass produced toys. In addition his own task of management would be made easier. Accordingly in 1985 he rented a purpose-built unit on a modern industrial estate designed for small and medium-sized businesses. He recruited a production manager with extensive experience and reserved for himself the role of marketing and financial manager. Within a year it was obvious that something had gone badly wrong. The reputation for reliability the business had built up was suffering from delayed orders. There was an increase in customer complaints concerning quality and levels of absenteeism and lateness seemed unusually high. The production manager placed all the blame on the workforce. They did not, he claimed, understand the need for factory discipline.

Stephenson was naturally worried about the situation and when he met Michael Carr, one of his original employees, outside the local supermarket, he took the opportunity to sound him out about the situation in the factory. Carr looked embarrassed but after some persuasion offered the following reasons for the problems of Marionette Enterprises.

'Well, I don't know if you are going to like this but we were doing nicely the way we were. The work had to be done and we knew exactly what we had to do. You would come in, give us an order, tell us the completion date, after that it was up to us. I suppose we did get into bad habits. For instance if an order was going well and there was no other work outstanding we used to cover for each other if we wanted a half day off. The lads got used to that and it helped if there was a child ill. It added a bit of flexibility. At least two of the wives went back to work because they knew we would be able to cover most emergencies. We never bothered with this clocking on and off either. If somebody arrived ten minutes or so late they made up the time during the day. Young Joey thought he was on to a good thing when he first came but we soon sorted him out. We got hold of him one break and pointed out it was not a holiday camp. If the work did not get done and done properly we would all be out of a job. When machines broke down we would phone up one of the other shops and one of us would stick the wood into the van, drive over there, machine it and bring it back. That is how we used to get your rush jobs done. Now all this organisation is getting us down. Every time we try to get a job done we seem to be breaking some rule or other.'

What can John Stephenson do?

13 Business organisation and communication

When you have studied this chapter you should be able to:

□ Identify the factors that determine the organisation of a business.

□ Define the principles of organisation.

□ Distinguish between authority and responsibility.

□ Apply the principles of organisation to business.

□ Construct an organisation chart.

□ Comment on the value of an organisation chart.

□ Distinguish between different types of organisation.

□ Define communication.

□ Appreciate the importance of communication to a business.

□ Distinguish between the different channels of communication.

□ Identify the barriers to communication in business.

□ Define and explain communication nets.

□ Appreciate the role of the grapevine in business.

□ Explain management by objectives.

□ Appreciate the role of management by objectives.

In Chapter 2 ('The business as a system') we defined business in terms of organisations and systems. In Chapter 10 ('Background to production') we looked at specialisation, standardisation and simplification as aspects of organising production. In this chapter we are going to look more closely at the principles of organisation as they apply to the whole business.

A word of warning! There is no such thing as an ideal organisation. What works for one business may be potentially disastrous for another – even though they make the same product, are approximately the same size and use the same technology. The final organisational form of the business will depend on:

1   *The size of the business*   The larger the business the more likely it is to have specialised departments. We saw in Chapter 4 ('Starting and running your own business') that the small business owner has to undertake most of the business functions personally. In the

intervening chapters we have implied that these functions could be carried out by specialists.

2   *The traditions of the business*   A family business might remain faithful to a certain type of organisational structure, for example, long after it should have changed to meet contemporary needs.

3   *The number of products*   A business with a large number of products might organise so that each product had its own marketing, production and so on.

4   *The geographical spread of the business*   A business whose factories are widely separated will have a different organisational structure from one with only one factory or whose factories are within easy reach of each other.

5   *The preferred style of leadership*   Autocratic leaders will want to have control over decision making. This will affect the final structure of the organisation.

6   *The type of technology used*   Joan Woodward, writing in 1958 (*Management and Technology*), came to the conclusion that businesses using similar technology or production processes, even if they were operating in different industries, tended to have very similar organisational structures. The same study came to the conclusion that certain types of organisation were more appropriate for certain types of technology, judging by the relative success of the businesses studied.

7   *The personnel employed*   Individuals have different skills and aptitudes. When the senior personnel of a business changes it is not unknown for the organisational structure of the business to change to make the fullest possible use of the abilities available to it.

8   *The environment in which the business operates*   A rapidly changing environment, for example in technology or the market, requires an organisational structure that is able to respond quickly to a change in circumstances.

9   *The objectives of the business*   A change in objectives will lead to a change in the organisational structure of the business. A decision to grow by entering new markets and developing new product lines could lead to an organisational structure that placed greater importance on marketing and research and development, in a business that had previously given equal weight to marketing and production.

SELF ASSESSMENT

1   From your study of production explain why the type of technology used by a business might influence its organisational structure.
2   Give one reason why there can be no ideal form of business organisation.

Principles of organisation

In this section we are going to look at the decisions any business manager, other than in the very smallest business, has to make about the way in which the organisation will work.

In a small business the owner will undertake all the activities of the business, and will:

- [ ] make decisions relating to the long-term objectives of the business.

- [ ] make sure the work in the business meets these long-term objectives.

- [ ] make the good or service that is the reason for the existence of the business.

- [ ] undertake to raise and manage finance, employ staff and solve, or try to solve, legal, financial and personnel problems that might arise.

- [ ] provide the services that keep the business going, e.g. acting as a receptionist, cleaner, etc.

As the business grows larger, division of labour takes place and these roles are performed by different people. It is the relationship of these roles to each other that is determined by the principles of organisation.

Authority

Authority is the ability of a manager to make decisions that will affect the behaviour and conditions of subordinates. This ability is an integral part of the manager's role in the organisation.

Authority contains within its definition the concept of power, that is the possession of control and/or influence over others. All power in an organisation is not necessarily linked with authority. Groups in the workforce have power. They can establish group norms that actively undermine the output targets set by management. Individuals have power in their response to orders. Even on the simplest level, people have it within their power to decide on the extent to which they will conform to the instructions they have been given.

The extent to which people are prepared to accept authority depends on a number of factors.

1 *The environment in which they live* All societies have individuals who are vested with authority. Large, complex societies tend to have more rules and regulations and people to enforce them than simpler societies. People who have been brought up to be 'law abiding' are more likely to respect authority when they meet it.

   The existence of a high level of unemployment in an economy is likely to make people more careful of observing the rules of the workplace in case they lose their jobs. In the early nineteenth century when industrialisation was in its infancy employers complained that people had no sense of discipline – they did not understand the importance of getting to work on time – because in their previous employment, or lack of it, in agriculture they had had a more relaxed attitude to timekeeping.

2 *The sanctions available* Businesses support the authority of their managers with a variety of sanctions, e.g. dismissal. They also reward employees for acceptance of authority, e.g. by promotion.

3 *The willingness of managers to employ the authority they possess* Some managers are reluctant to enforce decisions. They may not wish to be unpopular. Subordinates may take advantage of this situation.

4 *The personality of the manager* This might be described as the leadership qualities possessed by an individual. A respected manager can gain a greater degree of co-operation than one who is disliked or seen as incompetent. The greater the experience

and technical skill of the manager the more likely it is that subordinates will accept the exercise of authority.

5   *The success of the organisation in motivating its employees*   The greater the identification of the employee with the objectives of the business the greater will be the acceptance of the authority of management.

6   *Unwillingness to accept responsibility*   Some people prefer to be told what to do. Life for them is easier that way.

7   *The type of organisation*   Some organisations have a tradition of autocracy. They are more likely to attract and recruit people who are willing to accept authority.

Opposition to authority is more likely to be subversive than direct. Subordinates are therefore likely to use tactics such as denying they received instructions, working to rule, inventing excuses, and possibly damaging equipment so that a job becomes impossible. Direct opposition can be personal confrontation or a wildcat strike. Workers who feel that the production line on which they work has been set too fast have been known to use this tactic.

Responsibility

The authority to make decisions carries with it the obligation to ensure that they are carried out and the liability for the consequences of that decision.

SELF ASSESSMENT

1 Distinguish between authority and power.
2 Explain why an inexperienced manager may have difficulty in exerting authority.
3 What methods are used to support authority in an organisation with which you are familiar?
4 From your own experience list ways in which people resist authority.
5 Describe the relationship between authority and responsibility.

Delegation

Delegation is the act of entrusting another person to carry out an act for which you retain responsibility. The person delegated must be given the power to perform the task (*authority*) and will have a responsibility to see that it is completed satisfactorily. The person who delegates will still be responsible for the task. An example from education might help to clarify this distinction.

> The headteacher of a school is responsible for the standard of education offered by the school and certain legally defined responsibilities relating to the welfare of the students. In a village school the job may be done by one person who is also the only teacher. In a large secondary school it is impossible for one person to carry out all the work. Apart from other considerations she/he will not have the expertise to teach the range of subjects to the standard required. The heads of department will, therefore, have responsibility for their own subject area. They must *account for* the way they exercise their responsibility to the headteacher.

If you place yourself in the position of the headteacher in this example you will see that before you were prepared to delegate authority you would want to be sure that you could *trust* the people concerned and you would also want some form of *control* over their activities.

Centralisation, that is where the majority of decisions remain the responsibility of relatively few people, can be seen as the opposite of delegation. *Decentralisation* is not the same as delegation but may often be accompanied by it. For example a business which makes several products may decide to divide the organisation so that there is a management, production and service structure for each product. The major decisions concerning that product would be made by the senior management of that division. This can be explained by saying that control has shifted sideways (horizontally). Delegation implies a downward shift in control (vertically).

Even in decentralised organisations some functions might still remain centralised. Significant economies of scale in purchasing might mean that the buying function is controlled from the centre. The importance of investment could have the same effect on the financial function, with divisions working to an agreed budget and requiring consent from head office for expenditure above an agreed maximum. The relationship between authority and responsibility with delegation is illustrated in Figure 13.1.

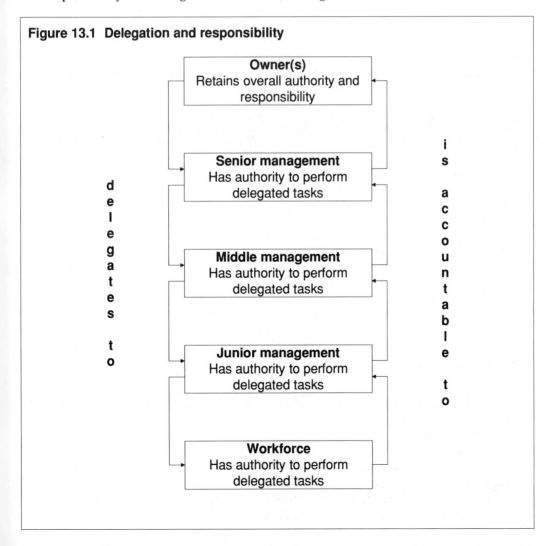

Figure 13.1 Delegation and responsibility

As usual in the study of business there is no one correct answer. Some arguments which support centralisation are:

1   It facilitates rapid decision making. In a situation in which a business has to respond quickly to external pressures, such as changing market situations, centralised control reduces the amount of time spent in co-ordinating the activities of a number of different departments or divisions.

2   A business with a tradition of autocratic leadership might find decentralisation or delegation difficult to achieve. It can be a demotivator for people to have the theoretical power and authority to take certain decisions only to have these decisions over-ruled by more senior management.

3   Senior management have experience of decision making and, presumably, have achieved their present position by showing that they are successful decision makers. It is reasonable to expect that they will make better choices than people with less experience.

4   Centralised control provides senior management with an overall view of the position of the business and allows them to make decisions in terms of allocation of resources that contribute to the overall health of the business and the achievement of long-term objectives. Most people tend to regard the activities in which they are engaged as being of prime importance. This can lead to marketing departments taking decisions without sufficient knowledge of production capability.

To summarise the above arguments, centralisation gives control to a comparatively small number of good decision makers who can use their power to achieve the most effective use of resources to promote the strategic objectives of the business. It can also lead to problems.

1   Centralisation can cause a delay in decision making. If too many decisions have to be relayed through a number of people then there is greater likelihood of error. We shall look at this problem in more detail when we discuss communications.

2   There is a limit to the amount of work people can cope with. If senior management have too many decisions to make then the quality of their work will be affected and one of the chief advantages of centralisation will be lost.

3   Centralisation implies the existence of a comprehensive system of control. The operation of any system in business costs money. Centralisation can be judged as being more expensive than decentralisation or delegation.

4   Centralisation limits the opportunity for middle management to learn decision making skills. If their job is simply to put into practice decisions which have already been made they cannot develop experience in evaluating the evidence before making a choice.

5   Decentralised organisations might be more aware of individual problems than the senior management in centralised organisations. This may take the form of being aware of conditions in their own geographical area or the problems inherent in producing or marketing a particular product.

The final decision about the degree of centralisation in a business enterprise will depend on the skill of top management and their leadership style, including the amount of trust they have in the skill and experience of their subordinates. It will also be influenced by the size and geographical dispersion of the business units, the importance of the decisions to be made in relation to the overall objectives of the business and the degree of independence each part of the business possesses.

SELF ASSESSMENT

1 Define delegation.
2 Distinguish between centralisation and delegation.
3 To what extent can a manager delegate responsibility?
4 A manager has a group of inexperienced subordinates. Give one advantage and one disadvantage of delegating in this situation.
5 Give one reason why the growth of a business is likely to lead to an increase in delegation.

Span of control

The span of control is the number of subordinates a manager directs. The number will vary according to the situation in which control is being exercised, which in turn depends upon:

☐ the experience and personality of the manager concerned.

☐ the nature of the work. The simpler or more standardised the task the less need there is for managers to make decisions and therefore the more people they can control.

☐ the experience of those being controlled and their degree of commitment to the work.

☐ the cost of limiting the span of control. The fewer subordinates a manager controls, the more managers that are needed.

☐ supervision. Too much can limit initiative and enterprise.

☐ the type of management style. A manager who can delegate effectively can control more subordinates than a manager who lacks the confidence to do this.

☐ the structure of the organisation. Figure 13.2 shows the different shapes of a business employing 1000 people when the span of control is altered. The smaller span in Figure 13.2a results in more levels of hierarchy – levels of management between the senior manager and the shop floor – which could cause communications problems.

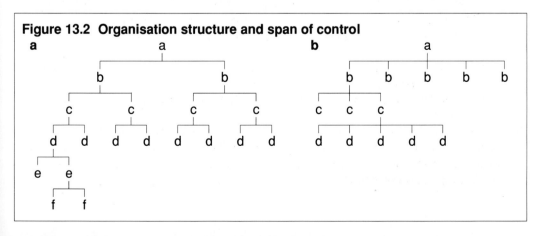

Figure 13.2 Organisation structure and span of control

The chain of command

The chain of command in an organisation is the line of authority and responsibility that transmits instructions and reports from and to senior management and the shop floor.

If the chain of command was observed in all businesses different levels of management would be insulated from all contact with anybody but their immediate subordinates and superiors. This is seldom the case. Managers have informal contact with other people either socially or as a deliberate policy to keep them in touch with the operation of the business. Some senior managers deliberately operate an 'open door' policy, that is they are accessible to people from different levels of the hierarchy. This does have the advantages of improving communications, motivation and ensuring that managers are accountable for their decisions. On the other hand it can make managers feel insecure when their superior challenges the correctness of their decision on the evidence of a subordinate.

The span of control suggests that an individual is accountable to only one person. In practice people are often accountable to several superiors depending on the responsibilities that are defined as part of the job.

The shape of organisations

To summarise, so far we have said that people bring into the business organisation their own personalities with their individual pattern of needs. Within that organisation they will be members of a number of groups both formal and informal, and in each group they will have a role. In order to achieve its objectives the business needs to direct the people working in it, co-ordinate the needs of the individual so that they are harnessed to the objectives of the business and operate control systems to check that the people working there are fulfilling the needs of the business. It is now time to look at the overall shape of the organisation.

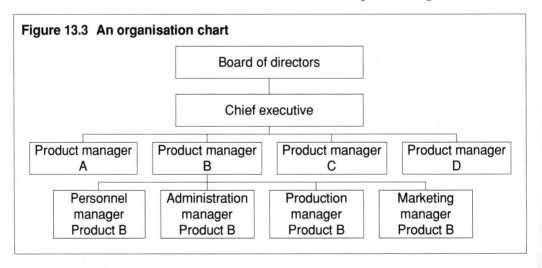

Figure 13.3 An organisation chart

Figure 13.3 is an example of an organisation chart. It is a statement of the major roles in an organisation and their relationship to each other in terms of authority and responsibility. It demonstrates the hierarchy of the business, that is the rank and order of each role. The example given in Figure 13.3 is conventional. Each level in the hierarchy has a defined position and orders flow down the levels and information flows upwards. We will examine the implications of this type of pyramid structure in terms of effective management when we discuss communications later in this chapter.

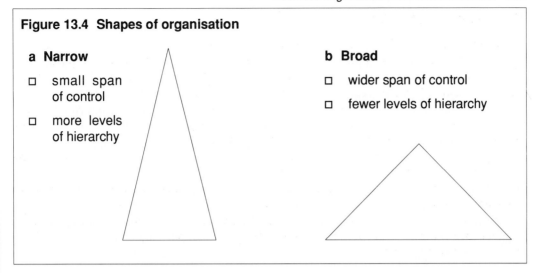

Figure 13.4 Shapes of organisation

a **Narrow**

☐ small span
    of control

☐ more levels
    of hierarchy

b **Broad**

☐ wider span of control

☐ fewer levels of hierarchy

Figure 13.4 shows two of the shapes the pyramid structure can take. Although the pyramid structure is the most common it can be supplemented or replaced by other organisational structures.

The matrix structure

If you re-read the section on design in Chapter 11 ('Production control') you will see that the design team is drawn from a number of departments and, very probably, from different levels in the hierarchical structure of the business. The design problem is one of many business problems that demands a range of skills and knowledge.

Figure 13.5 gives a simplified matrix showing the members of a design team and the roles they are expected to play in the design process.

The matrix approach to organisation may be used in a business organised on hierarchical lines when complex problems need to be solved rapidly. By calling on a variety of expertise it saves time in communication and minimises the chance of impossible ideas being considered for too long.

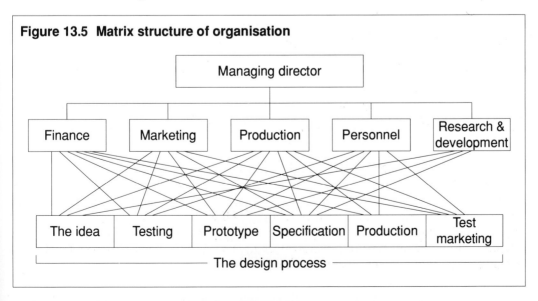

Figure 13.5 Matrix structure of organisation

Matrix organisations may be deliberately designed. Figure 13.6 illustrates the organisation of a college of further education. There is a clear chain of command from lecturers, through senior lecturers, principal lecturers, heads of department and vice principal to the principal. Now look at Figure 13.7 which shows the structure of the same college after re-organisation.

The responsibility for organising subject teaching has been shifted down the hierarchy to principal and senior lecturer level depending on the degree of responsibility involved. Heads of department have functional responsibilities. They will be required to take their expertise in these areas to team meetings to solve problems relating to the college as a whole, e.g. the overall pattern of courses offered by the college, the allocation of staff to subject areas, etc.

The original organisation structure of the college might have team meetings for heads of department but in this case they may have promoted and defended the interests of their own departments rather than bringing specialised knowledge to bear on the problem in hand.

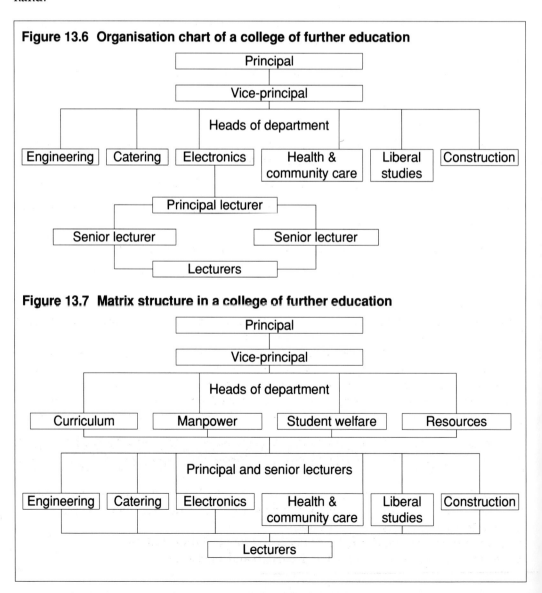

Figure 13.6 Organisation chart of a college of further education

Figure 13.7 Matrix structure in a college of further education

Networks

A network can be defined as a system of criss-crossing lines or channels. We talk about a network of roads, railways and canals. To get from point A to D using these networks a person would select the route that was most suitable at the time. Figure 13.8 shows that to get to D there are two possible routes, one through B the other through C. The route through B is shorter but the road is blocked by snow. Route C is chosen.

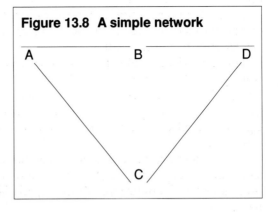

Figure 13.8 A simple network

To stretch this analogy a little further let us suppose that D is a problem to be solved and B and C are people who can help A solve it. B would be preferred but is engaged on another problem. A and C therefore co-operate on the problem. When a similar problem arises in the future it might be A and B who co-operate on it.

Analogies are dangerous when they are taken too far. From this analogy you should take the following points about the network system of organisation.

- There are no levels of hierarchy.
- Membership of problem-solving groups is formed on an ad hoc basis according to the people available and the problem to be solved.
- Composition of the network can change without formality, e.g. hiring and firing.
- It is likely that all members of the network will be considered equal in skill, although the skills may not be identical.
- Each member of the network is responsible for her/his own work.
- The leadership of teams will vary according to the task in hand.

Networks can appear in a variety of businesses. A group of independent dress designers may co-operate in staging a fashion show. Systems analysts and programmers working on a freelance basis may co-operate on individual projects.

At its simplest level the appearance of a network may depend on personal contacts. In the case of the fashion designers they may have attended the same college. The systems analysts may have worked for the same company. Networks can also be sustained with a loose formal structure. A newsletter may be published, or regular meetings held at which people can make new contacts who might be useful to them and reinforce old contacts.

SELF ASSESSMENT

1 Give three circumstances in which a business would decide on a small span of control.
2 Under what circumstances might a manager implement an open door policy?
3 Give one use of an organisation chart.
4 Give three factors which might influence the shape of organisations.
5 Distinguish between functional organisation and a network.

Communications

A discussion of networks as an organisational structure is a useful introduction to communications in business in that a network owes its existence to communications. You will be able to judge the importance of the connection at the end of this section.

Throughout this book we have made the assumption that people communicate with each other all the time. Now we will examine the nature of communication, its problems and the relationship between communications and organisation.

What is communication?

Communication can be defined as 'the use of a common system of symbols, signs and behaviour for the exchange of information, ideas and emotions'. To make the definition more precise we need to look at the phrases contained in it in more detail.

1   *A common system of symbols, signs and behaviour*   The symbols can be words, either written or spoken, numbers, facial expression and the use of the body to convey a message. The use of words and numbers (written or spoken) is termed verbal communication. The use of facial expression and body language is termed non-verbal communication. The tone of voice in which a phrase is uttered can also influence its meaning. The phrase 'He's a worker' could be spoken in a complimentary sense meaning 'He works very hard'. It could have political connotations of 'He does the type of job which is defined as being part of the working class in my philosophy'. Or, from the other end of the political spectrum, it could be used derisively as in 'He is only a worker'. The same expression will be interpreted in different ways according to the tone of voice and the facial expressions of the person who uses it.

2   *Exchange*   This word implies that communication is a two-way process. One person communicates an idea, the second person responds to it. The response is known as *feedback*. Feedback may modify the first person's view of the situation. The extent to which it does so will depend on the strength of the evidence and that person's willingness to accept it.

Barriers to communication

A barrier to communication is any physical or psychological feature that prevents the clear transmission of a message from the sender to the receiver. The main barriers to communication are as follows.

1   *Lack of expertise* on the part of the receiver or sender. The inability of the sender of a message to give clear, concise and precise instructions either in oral or written form can cause distortions in the message and lead to misunderstandings. An extreme example is a situation in which one or both parties have an imperfect knowledge of the other's language. People with expertise in a task often underestimate their own knowledge and assume it is shared by other people. In this instance task instructions may be minimal on the assumption that the other person will know what to do.

2   *The use of specialised terms and jargon* can also act as a barrier to communication because people without the specific educational background and experience will not be able to understand them. These are sometimes known as semantic barriers.

3 *Perceptual differences* can also cause communication problems. People interpret the world about them in different ways. Past experience in life can predispose people to optimism, pessimism, suspicion and trust. A subordinate receiving praise from a superior that past experience has proved untrustworthy would be unlikely to take the praise at face value and look carefully for the hidden message – which might or might not be there.

4 *The length of the lines of communication* can lead to messages being lost or distorted. An organisation with too many levels of hierarchy could suffer from this problem. You might find it useful to note the effect that differing spans of control have on the levels of hierarchies in a business (page 279). Conversely if too many people report to a manager there may be insufficient time for clear communication.

5 *Information overload* is a term used to describe a situation in which the amount of information received is too great for a person or organisation to process. When this happens information is lost and/or ignored. As a result decisions are taken on insufficient information or on information that an individual has decided is important. Think about this carefully. You may have experienced information overload after researching for an essay. You have more information than you need. What do you include in the essay? What do you leave out?

6 *Prejudice* can cause communication problems. This is a subdivision of perception. People of another creed, colour, class or country can trigger unreasoned dislike in some people. Anything they say will be interpreted through the expectations of the receiver.

7 *Physical distance* can also cause problems. Although communications using telephone networks, telex and fax are excellent, people are more prepared to ignore instructions from a distance than those given face to face, or written instructions from somebody they know is close to hand.

8 *Machines break down.* Other systems cease to function. No matter how carefully a message is phrased, even to a willing receiver, if the telephone is out of order or a strike is in progress it will not get through.

SELF ASSESSMENT

1 Define communication.
2 State and explain the type of barrier(s) to communication you might find in the following situations:
  a A person new to computing reading the 'Computer News' in a quality newspaper.
  b The marketing manager of a business confronted by a detailed report on a product's market. The report contains a lot of statistics.
  c A mother explaining to her fifteen-year-old daughter why she does not want her to go to a disco. The daughter's problems in explaining to her mother why she must go.
  d A Kashmiri student who has just arrived in the UK attempting to find his way to the university halls of residence in an English city.
  e The finance director of a company with production units in five widely separated sites in the UK.
  f A supervisor sees a worker operating a dangerous machine without the necessary, but uncomfortable, safety equipment.

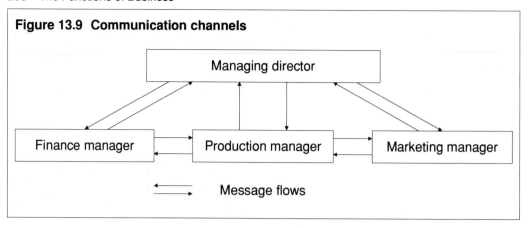

Figure 13.9 Communication channels

Channels of communication

Channels of communication are the lines through which messages pass from sender to receiver in an organisation. These are shown in Figure 13.9.

Channels from superior to subordinate are known as *downward*, those from subordinate to superior as *upward*, and those between people of equal status in the hierarchy as *horizontal*.

Downward communication (vertical)

This is communication between a superior and a subordinate. It is used to:

- □   issue instructions about the way in which a job must be done.

- □   explain the importance of the job in relation to other parts of the organisation.

- □   explain the rules of the workplace and why they exist.

- □   encourage or discipline the subordinate as a result of past work.

- □   motivate the subordinate.

Downward communication should be aimed at increasing a person's understanding of the business and avoiding alienation. Too often it is used to deliver instructions and criticisms!

Upward communication (vertical)

Subordinates can be wary about giving their superiors too much information – particularly about things that have gone wrong. Successful businesses see mistakes as part of the learning process for both senior managers and the people who have made the mistakes. In more traditional businesses a mistake could go against the subordinate when it comes to promotion. Upward communication usually takes the form of a written or oral report on the completion of a task. The person making the report can be tempted to suppress evidence or paint a glowing picture of the progress made. This gives more senior managers a false picture and can lead to bad decisions.

Horizontal communication

Horizontal communication takes place between people on the same level of hierarchy in the business. The main purposes are to:

□ make sure that different parts of the business are working together. An example might be the production and marketing directors of a company meeting the finance director to ensure that their plans for expansion can be financed.

□ resolve any interdepartmental problems or conflicts.

□ provide support by sharing problems and the solutions that have been found for them by other members of the group.

Communication networks

An organisation chart can show the major lines of communication within an organisation. It does not show the pattern of communication within small groups. This can be better understood by an appreciation of communication networks. Communication networks show the pattern of transmission and feedback of information of smaller groups within an organisation both horizontally and vertically.

The diagrams illustrated in Figure 13.10 are based on the work of Alex Bavelas in 1948. He drew a number of conclusions about potential leadership, problem solving abilities and group satisfaction based on these patterns of communication.

The leader of group 1 is likely to be C in that C will have the most power in deciding which messages will be transmitted to the rest of the group. The lack of contact between members of the group and the lack of opportunity to exchange ideas means that originality and problem solving within the group is likely to be low.

Contrast this with the interchange of messages in group 5. The volume of messages means that problem solving is likely to be slow. There will be a large number of ideas to be assimilated before a solution is reached. On the other hand this profusion of ideas is more likely to lead to originality of solution. Any member of this group can be the leader.

Groups 1 and 5 are the extremes. In groups 2 and 3 the leaders are likely to be C.

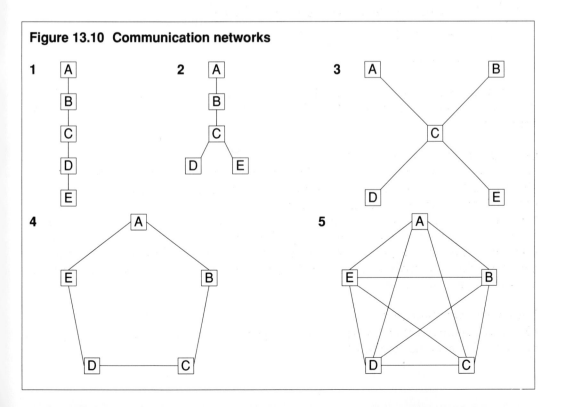

Figure 13.10 Communication networks

The grapevine

The grapevine is the term applied to informal channels of communication within an organisation. Teachers in schools have been known to complain that the sixth form know more about what is happening than they do. How do they find out? The answer is simple. In a day school sixth-formers live near the school. They are in touch with the local community. One knows a builder who has tendered for a contract; another has overheard a parent governor discussing a proposed expansion; ... This and other information is put together with more precision, analysis and effort than they are prepared to put into an essay. The speculations are likely to be close to the truth.

The dangers inherent in a grapevine lie in two major areas:

☐   when the people in the official channels of communication feel that they have been ignored and their status is threatened.

☐   when the information is inaccurate.

The latter case tends to happen when the employees of a business have not been given sufficient, understandable information about a major change in the business that will affect them. Technological change might start wild rumours of redundancy, for example.

The grapevine flourishes when management pays insufficient attention to communication through the formal channels. People like, want and need to know what is happening. The future of the organisation will affect their future too.

SELF ASSESSMENT

1 Distinguish between horizontal and vertical channels of communication.
2 Define the grapevine, illustrating your answer with examples from your own experience.
3 Give two reasons why upward vertical communication could fail.
4 A company decides to establish a sports club. Give one advantage and one disadvantage of this.
5 Distinguish between a communication channel and a communication network.

Communications and information technology

The process of rapid innovation in information technology has led to a claim that communications and organisations are being revolutionised. It can be accepted that the potential for revolution exists. Whether or not it will be as great as some of the claims suggest will depend upon the interaction of a number of factors.

1   Technology can help to increase the speed with which information is transmitted, its clarity and its availability. However, the type of information transmitted, the words used and the willingness and ability of the receiver to make use of the information, are still of vital importance.

2   Improved technology can lead to changes in the organisational structure. It can reduce the need for different levels in middle management and so reduce the number of levels in the hierarchy. This will reduce the chances of error in communication.

3   Improved technology can lead to greater centralisation. When this divorces decision makers, geographically, from the production processes this can mean that important information is lost. The nuances of the situation may be missed.

4   Technology relies on well-trained people to use it. Poorly trained operators and antagonistic users can sabotage the most advanced technology.

5   Improvements in technology can break down barriers between people by providing a 'common set of symbols'.

6   Information technology can only improve verbal communication. It may improve communications by distancing people and minimising the effects of prejudice.

SELF ASSESSMENT

1   List three production and three marketing problems which might arise as the result of poor communication.

2   Give two ways in which improved communication technology can lead to improved communications and two ways in which its effect may be neutral.

Management by objectives (MBO)

Management by objectives is a process of management that emphasises the role of leadership and communications in the organisation and control of a business. It is a method of managing managers rather than the workforce at large.

There are three basic elements in MBO:

- ☐   the identification of agreed goals by a manager and a subordinate.

- ☐   the definition of the subordinate's responsibilities in terms of agreed results.

- ☐   the use of agreed goals and responsibilities to control the progress of the business.

Advantages of MBO

1   People work better when they have a clear understanding of what they are expected to achieve and how their activities will contribute to the overall objectives of the business.

2   The process of deciding on objectives and responsibilities improves communication between manager and subordinate. By improving feedback it helps with future decision making.

3   It improves training by making managers aware of their own needs and the training needs of subordinates.

4   It provides opportunities for growth and development.

5   By setting identifiable, short-term targets it increases an individual's sense of achievement and provides opportunities for recognition.

Disadvantages of MBO

1   The assessment of objectives can appear judgmental and threatening if senior management lack the necessary interpersonal communication skills.

2   When unrealistic objectives are set the resulting failures can be demotivating.

3   Management of all levels must be convinced of the value of the exercise otherwise it will become a meaningless routine.

The general process of MBO is outlined in Figure 13.11.

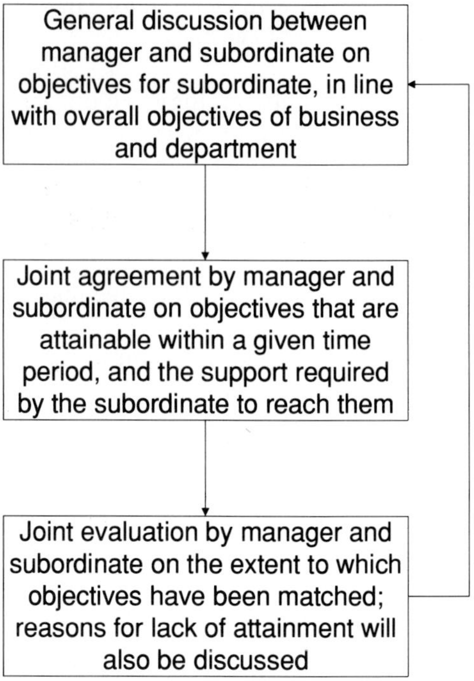

Conclusion

People are the building blocks of organisations. They can be organised into working groups and given structures to operate within, but unless they have the motivation to work within those structures they will, either consciously or unconsciously, adapt them to their own needs. At the beginning of this chapter it was pointed out that business exists for, by and because of people. A person is more complex than the most sophisticated techniques and technology employed in the business world. This chapter can do no more than indicate the complexities of the problems implicit in managing them.

Figure 13.11 The process of management by objectives

General discussion between manager and subordinate on objectives for subordinate, in line with overall objectives of business and department

Joint agreement by manager and subordinate on objectives that are attainable within a given time period, and the support required by the subordinate to reach them

Joint evaluation by manager and subordinate on the extent to which objectives have been matched; reasons for lack of attainment will also be discussed

REVIEW

1   Figure 13.12 shows the organisation chart of a manufacturing company.
  a   Using the information given in Figure 13.12 to illustrate your answer, define:
    i   chain of command.
    ii   span of control.
    iii   levels of hierarchy.
  b   Given this organisational structure, what communications problems might the business experience?
  c   Sketch an alternative organisational structure and explain its advantages over the one illustrated in Figure 13.12.
  d   Give three factors a business would take into account when designing its organisational structure.
2   John Carstair, personnel manager, was looking forward to a quiet pint at his local. It was Friday night and the week had been a disaster.
    Monday   The car broke down on his way to work. He was late. When he arrived he discovered a party from the Amsterdam head office touring the site. His secretary said they had been looking for him.
    Tuesday   A delegation representing the trade unions objected to changes in working practices. They claimed they had not been kept fully informed of the changes. John

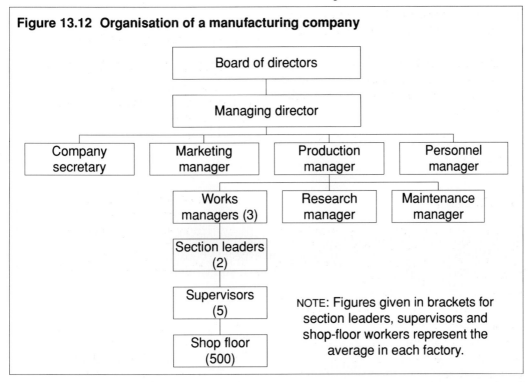

Figure 13.12 Organisation of a manufacturing company

NOTE: Figures given in brackets for section leaders, supervisors and shop-floor workers represent the average in each factory.

had pointed out, with very little success, that he had sent memos to all concerned and arranged for posters to be printed for the shop floor. His secretary informed him later that there had been a delay in the printing.

Wednesday Relatively uneventful.

Thursday Head office was considering the relocation of their UK plant. John's wife was distinctly upset at the thought of moving to another part of the country. What about the children's education?

Friday Garage phones to tell John the car needs a lot doing to it – about £500 worth! The pub was full and noisy. John bought his drink and made for the quietest corner. A voice hailed him. 'John, come and join me'. It was his managing director. John sighed and changed course. His boss was as disgruntled as John.

'I gave careful instructions about those changes in working practice. Joe (the production manager) assured me they would be carried out to the letter. What do I find? Chaos.'

'Not really surprising.' John was still thinking about his own troubles. 'It's reckoned that 30 per cent of all instructions are lost at each level of management. We've got five levels in our place. The shop floor will get ...'

'Excellent John. I knew I could rely on you. Let me have a report on Monday outlining what we can do about it. Now, have another drink – on me of course.'

a What is meant by 'levels of management'?

b If John is right about the loss of information at each stage of management what percentage of the original message might reach the shop floor?

c Outline three possible barriers to communication experienced by this business.

d 'The local pub on a Friday night is an unsuitable place to give instructions to a subordinate.' State and explain three reasons in support of this statement.

Figure 13.13 Communication in groups

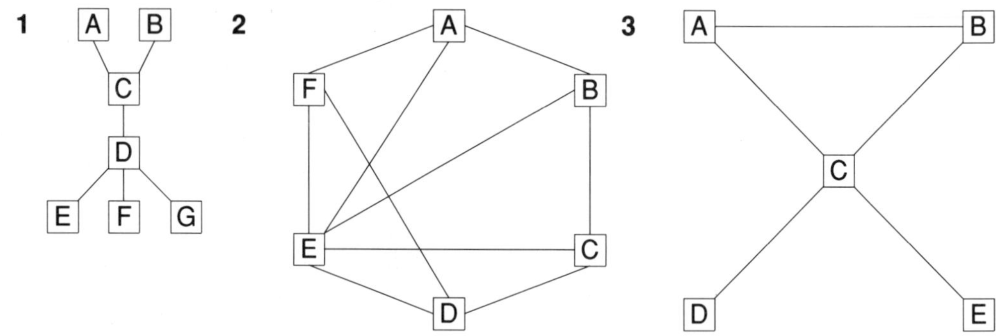

3 The diagrams in Figure 13.13 show communications in groups.
   a Which person in each group would you expect to become the leader?
   b For each group describe a business in which you would expect to find this pattern of communication.
   c State and explain three principles to be observed in the organisation of group communications.

4 Dorcas Training Centre is a management agency for the Training Agency providing off-job training for Youth Training (YT). The centre offers training in upholstery, joinery, cabinet making, catering and the caring services. As the majority of trainees are classed as premium grade, that is they require additional support in basic literacy, numeracy and life-skills, an important part of the role of staff is to provide this education through the medium of their vocational training.

   The staff of the centre consists of a manager and eight supervisors. All are men in their mid-thirties to early fifties and the majority have recent experience of redundancy. Their qualifications are good in their particular field and all have taken or are taking City and Guilds courses to train them as technical teachers.

   In October 1986 a new deputy manager was appointed from within the staff. This caused some grumbling. There was a faction in the rest of the staff who considered the man unsuitable for the job. The atmosphere in the staffroom was not pleasant. Partly for this reason, and partly because of the responsibilities of his job, the new deputy manager ceased to spend his breaks in the staffroom and spent most of his time in his office.

   By Christmas the situation had worsened. The new deputy manager had begun to comment on the way in which the supervisors were conducting their training. The supervisors took the view that they were the experts in their field and they knew what was necessary for the trainees to know and the best ways to convey this knowledge to them. The situation reached a climax when one of the supervisors was appointed to the civil service and celebrated his departure by telling the manager that the reason he was leaving was the unwarranted interference and incompetence of the new deputy manager.

   The manager consulted the deputy, who put forward the following points:
   - the ill-feeling was not quite as widespread as the departing supervisor had suggested.
   - the main instigator of the ill-feeling had been the departing supervisor, who had believed that his administrative experience made him more suited for the deputy manager's job than the man appointed.
   - some of the supervisors were not training in accordance with the philosophy of YT. Rather than devising ways of educating the trainees using their experience,

they were relying on classroom lessons, imparting knowledge through instruction and typewritten handouts.

The deputy manager went on to point out that, although it was the stated policy of the centre that any handouts should be prepared by the trainees to give them experience in the use of office equipment, the supervisors had fallen into the practice of preparing these materials themselves, and doing their own photocopying. Their justification for this being the length of time it took to explain to the trainees what was required and the high error rate. It was his statement that all reprographic equipment in the centre was for the use of trainees that had caused the initial outburst of grumbling.

The manager was extremely concerned about the situation outlined to him. His own direct contact with the supervisors was relatively small. He decided to interview each one individually, in the presence of the deputy manager, and try to discover their points of view. Approximately fifty per cent of the staff interviewed declared themselves to be dissatisfied and cited the deputy manager's interference with their training methods as the principle reason.

a What reasons can you suggest for the existence of this situation? You should present your analysis in terms of communication problems, leadership and group behaviour.

b What steps might the manager take to resolve his problem?

c Outline the possible consequences for the quality of training offered by the centre if the problem is not resolved.

Activities

1 Observe a meeting. You can simulate this by asking another group of students to solve a simple problem, for example placing objects in ranking order. This activity works well as a group activity because the group interaction is complex and it can be difficult for one person to observe and record all the elements of behaviour.

a Does one person dominate the group? If so, how? What mannerisms, gestures, tone of voice, verbal expressions did that person use to gain dominance? For example, one student assisting in this exercise gained effective leadership by sitting in the seat normally used by the tutor and using the gestures and tone employed by the tutor. The other students in the group did not appreciate this – the tutor and the observers did!

b Was any conflict generated during the discussion? Who disagreed with whom and what were their positions?

c Were any members of the group non-participating? Can you give possible reasons for this?

d What was the pattern of communication around the table? Did the participants address the group leader or did they tend to speak to the people beside them or opposite to them?

e Was the general attitude of the group supportive? You can get a rough estimation of this by classifying every remark said. Implied compliments, jokes, and tension-relieving comments will tend to indicate a supportive group. Remarks that can be classified as aggressive and denigrate the opinions of others can be classified as non-supportive. Be careful with this observation. The words used are often the least important part of the evidence. Analysis of an extremely argumentative meeting with a number of departmental heads fighting for their fair share of resources produced evidence of an extremely supportive group.

When you have completed the analysis present your results in the form of diagrams and tables. What insights into group behaviour have you acquired?

2 Produce an organisation chart for an organisation with which you are familiar. What are the limitations of this chart? Does it reflect all the communication patterns in the organisation?
3 Design a questionnaire on delegation and communication to be answered by the senior management team of your school or college.

Suggested projects

1 A critical appraisal of the communications between a business and its customers.
2 A study of the effects of the introduction of information technology into a business.
3 Should a business employ a safety officer?

Essays

1 Distinguish between informal and formal systems of communication. Discuss the symptoms of a breakdown in the system of formal communication within a business enterprise.
2 Outline the major classifications of leadership style and comment on their appropriateness in a business organisation.
3 Outline the organisational problems that may be encountered as the result of a merger between two businesses. Comment briefly on the ways in which these problems might be overcome.
4 Discuss the factors a business should take into account when considering the decentralisation of the buying function.
5 'The bigger the business, the more complex the organisation and the greater the problems of communication.' To what extent do you agree with this statement?
6 Business studies textbooks have been known to state that the ideal span of control is six. Is this necessarily true?
7 Distinguish between authority and responsibility. Comment on the importance of these concepts for a business enterprise.
8 'The boss does nothing. He has a big office, fancy furniture and all he does is give orders.' Discuss this view of the role of a chief executive in a large business.
9 Discuss the impact of information technology on the structure of business enterprises.

14   Managing people

When you have studied this chapter you should be able to:

- [] List the constraints on a business in its use of people.
- [] Distinguish between the internal and external constraints.
- [] List the information contained in a manpower plan.
- [] Explain why this information is necessary.
- [] Define the stages in recruitment.
- [] Understand and explain the importance of each stage.
- [] Distinguish between a job description, a job specification and a job requisition.
- [] List the different methods of recruitment and explain when each might be useful.
- [] Describe the main methods of training.
- [] Understand the importance of training to a business.
- [] Indicate how the effectiveness of training can be measured.
- [] Outline the main legal constraints on employment, resignation, dismissal and redundancy.
- [] Outline the ways in which the effectiveness of a personnel policy can be judged.
- [] Understand the need for protection.
- [] Outline the legal responsibilities of employers and employees in maintaining a safe working environment.

In Chapter 12 ('People and business') we described the uniqueness of each individual in terms of needs and personality. We also looked at the theories concerning the ways in which they could be motivated and, in Chapter 13 ('Business organisation and communication'), at the theoretical structure of an organisation and the way it can contribute to motivation. In this chapter we will examine the practical aspects of managing people, that is the personnel function.

The personnel function is practised by the prospective business owner when personal skills, qualities and shortcomings are examined before starting a business. It is also practised by the owner employing no more than one or two people, the supervisor on an assembly line in a factory employing 7000, the marketing, production and finance managers in organising and managing their departments, and the board of a multinational company when appointing a managing director.

The personnel function can be divided into three main areas:

☐   the *use* of people;

☐   the *motivation* of people;

☐   the *protection* of people.

There is some overlap between these areas. The use and protection of people can contribute towards motivation. Attempts to increase the motivation of individuals will influence the ways in which they are treated as employees and the degree of protection, over and above that required by law, which they are offered. As you work through this chapter you should be aware of this integration, although each element of the personnel function will be treated separately.

The use of people

Any business must be able to answer the following questions before it can use its staff effectively.

1   What are the objectives of the business in the long and the short term? Changes in marketing, production and financial strategies will all influence the number and type of people employed. A business with an objective of growth may need to recruit someone skilled in the management of mergers. Or they may employ another business to provide that skill.

2   What is the size of the existing workforce? What skills do they possess? What is their training potential? It may or may not be cheaper to recruit somebody who already possesses the required skills than to retrain people already employed.

3   What numbers, skills and training will be required by any projects to be undertaken in the next few years?

4   What finance is available to carry out the changes needed?

5   To what extent is the existing staff utilised? For example, a business wishes to expand. If it has a number of staff who are already working short time there may be no need to recruit. If they are working overtime then the only way to expand may be through recruitment unless changes in organisation and/or the introduction of more advanced technology could use the existing workforce more efficiently.

These are all internal constraints that a workforce imposes on a business in attempting to achieve its objectives. A business is hiring labour and is, therefore, operating in a number of labour markets depending on the skills of the people it wishes to employ.

The labour markets and the economy generally impose additional *external* constraints on its decisions.

1   What is the state of the economy? Even in a depressed economy some businesses are more prosperous than others. A business wishing to expand will find it easier to recruit the right type of labour at a lower price when the economy is depressed than when it is expanding. A prosperous economy with a shortage of the required type of labour might

cause a business to retrain rather than recruit, or to simplify certain jobs so that they can be performed by people with less skill.

2 A shortage of labour may be the result of technical change rather than an expanding economy. In depressed economies undergoing technical change, for example, it is likely that the skills associated with the new technology will be in short supply and therefore will command higher prices than other skills.

3 What is the wage rate paid by other firms? A business may want this information so that it does not pay more than is necessary. It may also want it so that it can outbid its competitors in the labour market. A multinational company moving into an area at a time of relatively full employment might use this information to set a wage level for certain skills 25 per cent higher than those of other businesses in the area.

4 Have trade unions negotiated any national agreements with respect to working conditions with which the business will have to comply? Will a change in production technology result in the employment of less skilled, possibly non-unionised, workers?

Internal and external constraints are shown in Figure 14.1.

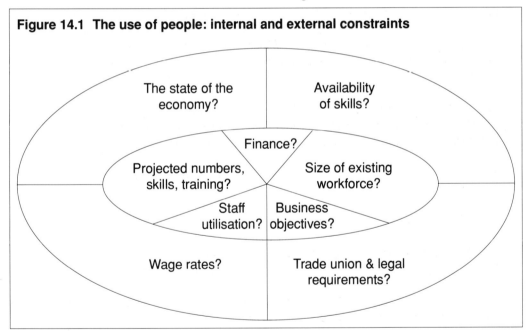

Figure 14.1 The use of people: internal and external constraints

If the type of question asked above seems familiar that is not surprising. The information they provide will form the basis of the *manpower plan* (so-called despite the increasing proportion of women in the workforce!), a part of the overall business plan and subject to the same general constraints as the main business plan and the plans of all other departments within the organisation. A completed manpower plan will contain the following information:

- jobs that will appear or disappear in the time period covered by the plan.
- training needs, including any retraining.

□ the recruitment or retirement or redundancy programmes that will need to be implemented.

□ the implications for industrial relations.

□ the necessary control systems to ensure that the manpower plan continues to serve the objectives of the business.

The manpower plan (see Figure 14.2) will also have implications for the decisions of the production and marketing departments. Its needs will contribute to the master budget.

SELF ASSESSMENT

1 Define the personnel function.
2 Give two internal and two external constraints on the personnel policy of a business.
3 State three ways in which a manpower plan can help a business operate effectively.
4 Explain how:
   a a change in technology
   b an increase in the level of activity in an economy
   will affect the manpower plan of a business.
5 Give two ways in which the needs of the production department can affect the manpower plan of a business.

Figure 14.2 Outline of manpower planning process

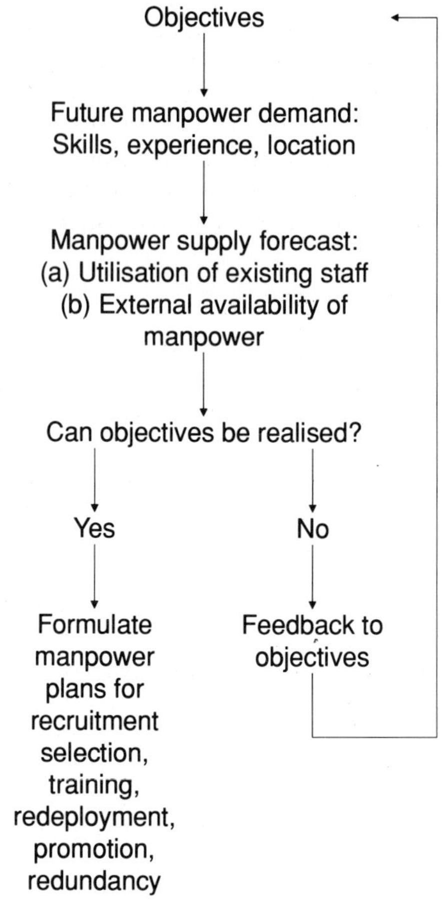

Objectives

↓

Future manpower demand: Skills, experience, location

↓

Manpower supply forecast:
(a) Utilisation of existing staff
(b) External availability of manpower

↓

Can objectives be realised?

Yes → Formulate manpower plans for recruitment selection, training, redeployment, promotion, redundancy

No → Feedback to objectives

Once the manpower plan has been drawn up the business can begin the process of organising its labour force to help achieve the business objectives. This will involve a number of activities:

□ recruitment;

□ selection;

□ training;

□ appraisal;

□ redeployment;

□ promotion;

□ redundancy/retirement/dismissal.

The activities have been listed in this order to reflect the experience of a person employed by a business. They could also reflect the way in which someone running a one person business might assess personal needs and skills in relation to ambition. Figure 14.3 charts the progress of an imaginary clerical worker in the first three years of employment by a business. You will notice that some of the activities listed above recur throughout this person's career.

Figure 14.3 Progress of a clerical worker over a period of three years

Recruitment and training
↓
Induction training
↓
Appraisal
↓
Job training, Department A
↓
First annual appraisal
↓
Redeployment
↓
Second annual appraisal
↓
Supervisory training
↓
Promotion

Recruitment

Before you go out to buy something you usually take the trouble to decide what you need. A business purchases materials needed for its production processes according to the specifications laid down in the design of the goods it is making. It is the same process when it comes to hiring people.

In Chapter 4 ('Starting and running your own business') we said that a prospective business owner should examine the skills and personal qualities she/he possessed, and match those skills against the ones needed to run a particular type of business. In the same way, when employing people the owner should have a clear idea of the job they are expected to do and the skills and personal qualities which will be needed to do that job successfully. This is also important in *motivating* people. People engaged in work which is beyond their ability, or which they consider boring, are unlikely to work with enthusiasm.

The stages in defining a job and the skills needed to perform it efficiently are:

- □ job analysis;
- □ job description;
- □ job specification;
- □ recruitment profile.

Job analysis
Job analysis is a detailed examination of a job, the tasks performed, the skills and personal qualities needed to perform them successfully and the circumstances in which they are performed. Job analysis is used to:

- □ select personnel, either by employing people from outside the business or by redeploying or promoting existing staff. Redeployment is the term used when staff are moved from one part of the business organisation to another to perform a different task of the same status as their previous job.

- □ establish the training needs for a particular job. This will also help to minimise training costs by a more careful matching of existing skills and aptitudes in the people employed with those required by the job.

- help in the selection of suitable equipment and prevent waste on the purchase of unnecessary equipment.

- identify the experience of people who have performed a job and assist in the process of staff development and promotion.

- help in establishing rates of pay and account for differences in payments made to different members of staff.

- isolate the possible risks of accident and assist in the design of equipment and procedures to reduce the risks.

Job analysis, therefore, is not simply to help in recruitment. The activity can be seen as a fundamental part of the personnel function. It may be expanded into *job evaluation*, which attempts to put jobs in the order of their importance to the business. Job analysis is not an easy operation to carry out successfully.

1   It is a very slow process. Observing a job might give an outline of the tasks that need to be performed but it can be misleading in terms of the skill needed to perform that task. A skilled operator will make a job look easy. If you observe a plasterer at work it does not appear to take a great deal of effort to provide a smooth finish to a wall. An attempt to do the same job yourself will demonstrate the level of skill required. Watching the plasterer tells you nothing about the mental decisions being made, for example about the consistency of the plaster for the type of surface being worked on.

2   Observation will produce very little useful information when much of the work is carried out mentally. A manager attempting to solve an organisational problem may be simply sitting at a desk and staring into space.

3   When questionnaires or interviews are used to analyse a job the attitudes of people can influence the way in which they answer questions. A person seeking promotion might be tempted to exaggerate the complexity of her/his present job.

4   People do not always remember all the tasks that comprise their job. Some tasks may be performed infrequently, perhaps only once a year, and are easily overlooked.

Good job analysis will use a variety of methods and also use information already existing about the job, e.g. from work study reports. Observation and interviews with the person doing the job and with the manager responsible can be supplemented by analysis of the equipment and materials used. Together this information will give a more accurate picture of the job.

Job description
A job description is a broad statement of the purpose, scope, duties and responsibilities of a particular job. It will normally contain:

- the title of the job;

- a broad statement of the duties;

- who the person doing the job is responsible to;

- who will report to the person doing the job.

A job description places a job in the context of the organisation. It contains elements relating to *role, authority, responsibility, communications* and *span of control*. It also defines the degree of *specialisation* relating to a job.

Job specification

A job specification is a more detailed development of a job description. It states the physical and mental abilities required. This is usually expressed in terms of activities, requisite knowledge, and the type of judgment required, together with the factors affecting such judgments, and the factors affected by such judgments.

Job analysis, job descriptions and job specifications are described here as part of the recruitment procedure of a business. They also provide invaluable information for the following personnel functions:

☐ they can help in the selection of staff for promotion. A knowledge of acquired and practised skills can enable managers to identify people who have the necessary aptitudes for a higher graded job.

☐ they can be used to identify training needs for the business as a whole and for individuals as part of staff development. In the latter case training needs can influence promotion decisions and act as a motivator.

☐ they can provide an objective statement of the job to establish targets which should be achieved by people performing the job. These are called *performance standards*.

☐ they can provide an objective standard against which the efficiency of the staff engaged in a particular job can be judged. This is known as *staff appraisal*.

If you read the uses of job analysis, job descriptions and job specifications carefully you should become aware of the fact that they are likely to become a subject of dispute between the owners of a business and their employees.

A very precise job specification places a weapon in the hands of people who are dissatisfied with the way in which they are being treated. They can refuse to perform a task on the grounds that 'It's not my job'. When that particular task has been widely performed on a 'goodwill' basis prior to the dispute there could be delays and organisational problems as a result of this response.

A job specification which is imprecise can contribute to *demarcation disputes* between trade unions. In this case a union will claim a task should be performed only by its members. This is usually a matter of concern when a union feels its members' jobs are threatened.

The use of detailed job specifications in the appraisal of staff can lead to disagreements between the person being appraised and the appraiser. When this involves people who have to work together this can have a detrimental effect on working relationships and the efficiency with which a job is performed. In open appraisal schemes where the person being appraised has access to the report a tick by the statement 'Not yet ready for promotion' can act as a demotivator and a potential source of conflict between the two people concerned.

Job requisition/recruitment profile

This will exist formally in large organisations where the job of recruiting staff is given to a person who may have no direct knowledge of the job itself. It is designed to allow the person responsible for selecting staff to understand the requirements of the job and know enough about it to be able to answer any questions the applicant might ask. A recruitment profile for a skilled operative would be drawn up in consultation with the production manager but the interviewer might be a specialist in the personnel department. A job requisition will include details of the work involved, conditions of employment, necessary qualifications, and the amount of experience and personal qualities required.

The job requisition is the final link between the job and the person who will be employed to perform it. The person responsible for filling the post must now decide where to find that person.

SELF ASSESSMENT

1 Distinguish between a job description and a job specification.
2 Give two ways in which a job analysis can help a business.
3 Distinguish between job analysis and job evaluation.
4 Give two reasons why all businesses should have a recruitment profile.
5 Explain why it is important for managers to be careful in the construction of job specifications.

Selection of personnel

When a vacancy exists a business may fill it either from its existing labour force (*internal recruitment*), or by employing another person (*external recruitment*).

Internal recruitment

When using internal sources the business may promote or redeploy individuals. Redeployment means that the business transfers staff from one area of activity to another. The use of internal sources can have the following advantages:

1 It is cheaper than other methods of recruitment. There is no need for extensive and expensive advertising and, because the people are already known in the organisation, there is less chance of having to re-advertise. It is also faster, and this in itself will save costs.

2 Labour is redeployed when it is no longer needed in its present activity. The alternative might be short-time working or even redundancy. Internal recruitment can be seen as a way of avoiding expensive redundancies and of giving workers a greater feeling of security. In some circumstances businesses may agree with the trade unions concerned that all vacancies will be filled from internal sources. This is likely to happen where unemployment in an area or a skill is high.

3 Promotion prospects can act as motivators to staff. They are more likely to take on additional responsibilities that show they are suited to promotion.

4 Internal candidates know the way in which the organisation works. They do not have to learn the systems or the unspoken codes of practice that operate in any organisation. They will become more effective more quickly than external candidates.

5 Internal recruitment can be said to be more certain than appointing people from outside the organisation. Application forms, interviews and references can be no substitute for the in-depth knowledge of an individual's personality, strengths and weaknesses that day-to-day contact provides.

Internal recruitment does have its disadvantages. When it is the result of agreements with trade unions it can mean that available candidates are not suited to the job and will be less efficient in performing it than somebody recruited from outside the organisation. Jealousy is not unknown and a newly promoted person can find former colleagues unco-operative.

External recruitment

When it is necessary and/or desirable to recruit from outside the organisation a business has a number of methods to choose from.

1   *Recommendations from existing employees*   This can be seen as an extension of internal recruitment. The people recommended are likely to have some knowledge of the workings of the business if only by hearsay. They are more likely to know people already working for the business and will be less likely to leave. The people making the recommendation will also have an interest in making sure that the person concerned is suitable for the job. The extent to which a business will consider personal recommendations will depend on known qualities of the person making the recommendation.

Personal recommendation can operate on a variety of levels in a business. It may be a manager who has met and worked with somebody outside the organisation and sees in the skills offered a valuable contribution to the business. It may be a production worker recommending a child, or the child of a friend, to the personnel department. In the latter case many of the advantages of internal recruitment would still apply.

2   *Direct contact with schools, colleges and universities*   Many businesses maintain links with educational establishments. This can provide them with an initial screening service in that many such places will only recommend people who will reflect credit to their organisation or will use their own knowledge of students to select those who have the required skills and personal qualities. A personnel manager wishing to recruit a school leaver might find it worthwhile to phone the careers teacher in four or five secondary schools, state their requirements in general terms, fix a time for interview and be sure of having a number of good applicants for the job. Over a period of years it is possible that good links are established and this method can become an extension of personal recommendation.

3   *Job Centre/Careers Office*   Both services are run by the Training Agency to provide a centre for those looking for applicants and those seeking employment. Job Centres are for all unemployed whilst the Careers Service is designed for the school leaver.

4   *Advertising*   This method is likely to produce the largest number of applicants but it is expensive both in terms of the cost of the advertising and in the processing of a large number of applicants. Advertising also presents problems in terms of choosing the media to be used. Advertising for specialist staff might be more effective in technical journals. A mistake can be expensive.

5   *Trade unions may recommend people for specific jobs.*

6   *Private employment agencies may also be used*   Although they will charge for their services they will still have the advantage to the business using them of undertaking the preliminary survey of applicants thus saving costs in the business itself.

7 *'Head hunting'* This is a colloquial term used to describe the activities of specialised private agencies acting on behalf of their principals in seeking out highly qualified staff who may not be actively looking for a job. The person approached is likely to be offered an attractive salary and benefits package as an inducement to change her/his job.

8 *Professional Bodies Appointments Services/Ex-service organisations* These bodies offer a specialised service for groups of people with specific skills and experience. Public services such as the police force and the armed forces whose members may retire earlier than the rest of the working population have an employment service as part of their own personnel policy.

SELF ASSESSMENT

1 Give three factors in favour and three against internal recruitment.
2 List three types of organisation that may be of help to a business in the recruitment process.

Selection

By the time this stage has been reached the business should be aware of the job to be filled, has sought applicants using the methods listed and must now match the information provided by the applicant against the recruitment profile. This process is known as *shortlisting*. Applicants who are considered unsuitable or who have a lower level of skills than the rest of the group are discarded. Those who are left are called for interview.

Interviews are useful in that they provide the opportunity for applicants to ask questions about the job and the business and find out information which may not have been available to them before. A good interview will also allow candidates to see the place in which they will be working. There is research evidence to suggest that a failure to do this can lead to early resignations. For example, some people might have very strong feelings about working in an open plan office – either for or against. Interviews also give the business the chance of assessing the personality of the person applying for the job in the light of the people she/he is likely to be working with.

The process of selecting people will vary according to the business and the type of job involved. There may be two or even three shortlisting exercises undertaken, each followed by an interview. At each stage the number of applicants will be reduced. This may take place over a period of as long as six months.

Interviews can vary from a short formal session to a period of several days which might include a formal interview, informal sessions and the use of selection tests to judge aptitudes and attitudes. In general the more responsible and complex a job the more complex and extended the selection procedure is likely to be.

Job offers

The offer of a job may be oral in the first instance and then confirmed by letter. The Employment Protection (Consolidation) Act of 1978 states that all employees must be given a written statement of their conditions of service within twelve weeks of the beginning of their employment. This statement may be separate from the job offer or it may be incorporated into it. The latter procedure has the advantage of informing the new employee of the exact conditions of service at an early stage, and thus reduces the risk of expensive mistakes.

Selection of recruitment method

A large organisation is unlikely to use a single method of recruitment. The method selected will depend upon the circumstances in which the organisation finds itself and its experience of the effectiveness of different methods.

Methods of recruiting can be assessed as shown below:

1 In Chapter 6 ('Accounting'), we studied the use of ratios in management accounting and stated that the technique could be used to judge the efficiency of other areas of business activity. Ratios can be used to estimate the value of different methods of recruiting staff.

    Number of interviews : Number of offers made

    A high level of interviews compared with the number of offers made could suggest that the selection procedure is at fault.

    Number of offers made : Numbers starting work

    If people are not accepting the offer made to them there is the possibility that the information they received from the literature published by the business was misleading.

    Number starting work : Number considered satisfactory

    Again this suggests a mismatch between the skills required and the ones considered to be required by the recruiter. Perhaps a more careful job analysis or a more precise recruitment profile might be required.

    Cost of exercise : Number starting work

    The aim of a good recruitment procedure is to get the best possible work force at the lowest cost of recruitment.

2 The state of the labour market will influence the recruitment method chosen. If the local market is buoyant, with a large number of job opportunities but a low number of unemployed, a business that has traditionally advertised locally may be forced to advertise nationally to fill its vacancies. In a situation of high unemployment a business might find sufficient suitable applicants by the use of the different types of personal contact rather than undertake the expense of advertising.

3 The type of staff being recruited can be an important factor in deciding the method of recruitment. People with high level skills in short supply may be head hunted. In extreme cases, for example where the skill is in a new technology, the labour market may be international.

The importance of good selection procedures must be emphasised. In Chapter 12 ('People and business'), and throughout the first part of this chapter, the emphasis has been on the business acquiring a labour force which has the skills and personal qualities to suit its needs. However, it should not be forgotten that the activity of selecting employees will depend on a number of factors, some of which may be beyond the control of the business. A shortage of labour might require the re-design of jobs so that they can be performed by people with a lower level of skill. Good selection procedures will contribute to the efficient working of the production, marketing and financial functions of a business, but its ultimate success could well depend on the state of the economy, the type of market in which it is operating, the state of that market and, in some circumstances, the attitude of the government towards the type of business.

These external constraints can also affect the labour supply available to a business. Bad publicity concerning safety regulations in an industry can limit the supply of labour to a firm in that industry no matter how effective its own safety procedures might be. People concerned about job security are unlikely to take a job in a declining industry unless their choice of job is restricted. It has been pointed out earlier in this chapter that the labour market in which a business is operating will affect its decisions. A business operating in a declining industry is unlikely to be able to offer wages competitive with more prosperous firms.

SELF ASSESSMENT

1 State briefly the stages in a selection procedure.
2 Explain the value of two methods of assessing recruitment procedures.
3 Give one advantage and one disadvantage of the interview as a selection procedure.
4 A business advertises nationally for unskilled labour. Give one reason why this might be necessary.
5 A business is having difficulty in recruiting. List and explain three reasons for this state of affairs.

Training

Training is the term used to describe all the activities involved in bringing a person to a desired degree of proficiency in the skills, attitude and knowledge required for a job.

Like all other business activities training should follow a *plan* and is limited by the equipment, finance and personnel available in the business and also by the state of the economy, government intervention and the attitudes of society as a whole.

Figure 14.4 illustrates the steps involved in organising training. In a small business it may outline the mental processes of the owner of a business when recruiting a new member of staff. In large businesses it may be a formal process resulting in a written document that will contribute information for a training budget. The background to such steps will involve the following factors:

1 *Establishment of objectives* The most important objectives will be those of the business. From these and the manpower plan derived from them, it will be possible to draw up priorities concerning the types of training most needed. Following this analysis of jobs, the standard of expertise required and the expertise of the existing workforce will be necessary information before the objectives of the training department can be formulated. A business operating in a high cost, high quality market is likely to require highly skilled labour. If,

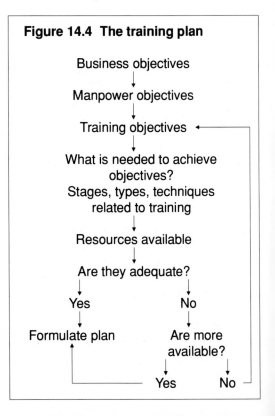

Figure 14.4 The training plan

Business objectives
↓
Manpower objectives
↓
Training objectives ←
↓
What is needed to achieve objectives?
Stages, types, techniques related to training
↓
Resources available
↓
Are they adequate?
↓   ↓
Yes   No
↓   ↓
Formulate plan   Are more available?
↑   ↓
                Yes   No

in addition, they are operating in an environment of rapidly changing technology the plan may need to make provision for a constant up-dating of skills.

2   *Necessary steps to reach the objectives* At this stage the business draws up an outline programme of training. This might include a statement of the stages in the training programme and the appropriate techniques that might be used.

3   *Resources* Having decided what it *should* do the business must then decide what it *can* do. It must see what resources it has to achieve the programme in terms of personnel, equipment and finance. It should also take into account external resources that might be available to it. In Chapter 10 ('Background to production'), we saw that a local college of further education can be seen as an external economy of scale. It will charge for its courses but the fees are likely to be lower to a business sending five students than it would be to employ somebody to educate those students and provide the equipment. The five students will be, perhaps, a third of the final class. Government grants can be used to finance training and we will look at these in more detail when we consider the Training Agency schemes such as Youth Training and Open Tech.

4   *Modification* If the original plan cannot be funded by available resources then it may have to be modified.

5   *Evaluation* Like all plans the training plan must contain monitoring systems, that is methods of gathering statistical and financial information to check the success of the scheme.

Many employers consider training to be an expensive, time-consuming exercise with the prospect of well-trained employees resigning for better-paid occupations. What are the advantages of training to the employer?

1   Well-trained workers give greater profits. A skilled craftsperson is likely to be able to work faster, more accurately and with less waste than somebody with a lower level of skill. As a result his productivity will be higher and production costs lower. A shop assistant who has been trained to present the right attitude to a customer, who knows the stock available and is prepared to discuss the customer's requirements is more likely to make a sale than an assistant with no interest in stock or customer.

2   A well-trained person needs less supervision. This will reduce costs by widening the span of control possible and reducing the number of supervisors needed. It can also act as a motivator. In Chapter 12 ('People and business'), we discussed the role of job enlargement as a motivator. To make a contribution to job enlargement the person concerned will need extra training.

3   Training can also reduce the accident level in a business by drawing attention to the danger areas and, by improving skills, knowledge and attitudes, reduce the possibility of them occurring.

4   Well trained staff are more versatile and this can be important in times of rapidly developing technology when the skills required by the business are likely to change.

5   A good training programme will raise the prestige of the business and attract good applicants for its jobs. The products of a good management training programme are more versatile than people whose training has been designed for one industry.

Education and training

Education can be defined as a programme of activities designed to develop the mental, physical and social skills of individuals without reference to a specific job. Training is a programme of activities directed to the acquisition of skills for a specific job. It may also contain elements in the programme designed to improve the general level of physical, mental and social skills of the people concerned. This, it is hoped, will improve the ability of the individual to cope with change. In many cases it will do so but education is a co-operative effort between student and teacher or lecturer. If either party approaches the exercise with attitudes antagonistic to education the hope is unlikely to be realised.

Methods of training

1   *On-job training* is the oldest in human history. In its simplest form the person being trained learns the job by working alongside somebody who has already acquired the skills. It is cheap because there is no need to set up special training facilities and the person being trained will learn in the conditions in which the work will be performed. This can be important in jobs where the working conditions might be stressful and unpleasant. On the other hand trainees are likely to spoil materials and make mistakes which will take more experienced people time to rectify. They may learn bad working habits which can be inefficient and unsafe. The person doing the training may be unsuitable, lacking the communication skills essential for good teaching. She/he may also be unwilling to slow the work pace – particularly if pay is dependent on output.

On-job training is an integral part of most training programmes. Even in situations where the skills and knowledge are taught separately there will come a time when the trainee needs to apply acquired knowledge in a real business. The academic qualifications for most professions can be gained in institutes of higher education, whether universities, colleges or polytechnics. But before people can be accepted as professionally qualified they must be able to produce evidence of work experience in a professional environment. A deck officer in the merchant navy must be able to produce evidence of a specified amount of sea time before being allowed to take the professional examinations of the Department of Transport.

2   *Off-job training* may take place in specialist training areas or establishments within the business or, where there is sufficient local demand from several businesses, at a college of further or higher education.

Off-job training has the advantages of specialist instructors who usually have actual experience of the job concerned. The trainees are without the pressures of a working environment and can therefore increase their speed and accuracy to a high level following a carefully planned programme. It is easier to estimate the costs of the exercise and also easier to monitor the progress of the trainee. When the business provides the facilities off-job training can be expensive. It can also pose problems when the trainee is required to transfer learned skills to the working environment, particularly if the equipment used in training is different from that used on the shop floor. If off-job training is provided by colleges belonging to the state sector of education the business may benefit from external economies of scale.

3 *The Training Agency* is a government body which is designed to implement training for a variety of needs according to the perceived needs of the UK in the medium term. Youth Training is intended to provide young school leavers with an opportunity to 'taste' a variety of occupations and select the one to which they are most suited while giving them the chance to learn 'life-skills' – how to apply for a job, interview well, live independently of parents, etc. – which they may lack. 'Open Tech' gives individuals and people seconded by businesses the chance to update their existing skills under the guidance of a college tutor.

Types of training

1 *Induction* The purpose of induction training is to introduce new recruits to the business, the objectives, methods, organisation and the people they will be working with. The length of time devoted to an induction course can vary from a few hours to several months, depending on the job. The first six months of training for a student nurse might be classified as induction training. This will involve experiencing different types of nursing in a variety of institutions. The induction course for a clerical worker may take no longer than an introduction to the supervisor and ensuring that somebody will take care of the newcomer for the first few days. In recent years the importance of induction training has become appreciated particularly for its effect on reducing labour turnover.

2 *Training in attitudes* is a long-term process and less easy to evaluate than other forms of training. In Chapter 12 ('People and business'), we saw that the attitudes of an individual are formed by their experience. Attitudes are difficult to change. Attitude training might be on-job with the encouragement and example of a person judged to have the right attitudes, and off-job using roleplay, case studies and similar simulations followed by group discussion. The purpose of the exercises is to extend the experience of the individual in a relatively controlled environment.

3 *Training for promotion* Depending upon the type of job, training for promotion will use a mix of the techniques given above. A person about to be promoted to supervisor might need knowledge of health and safety legislation (short courses or lectures) and will also need to develop skills in staff management (simulated exercises or case studies).

4 *Training for change* Organisational and technological change will require training programmes. A change in technology may mean that all the skilled operatives employed in a business will need familiarisation with new equipment and techniques.

Evaluation of training

The effectiveness of training can be judged in terms of the following:

- the number of accidents and their causes.
- the rate of labour turnover. Induction training was given a more important place in the training programmes of business when it was realised that a high proportion of resignations occurred in the first few months of employment because people found a workplace strange and unwelcoming.
- the number of suitable candidates for internal promotion.
- the quality of the work produced, the number of rejections, the amount of waste and the level of productivity.

In each of these areas, of course, a business will have acceptable levels. To aim at perfection would be expensive and the effectiveness of training is judged against its cost.

SELF ASSESSMENT

1   Why should training be a continuous process?
2   State two reasons why on-job training might be more effective than off-job training.
3   A period of economic recession results in a widespread cut in the training budgets for businesses in a certain industry. Later expansion of the economy reveals a shortage of skilled labour in that industry. Give two possible reasons for the original decisions to reduce the level of training. Outline two problems the industry will face as a result of the decisions.
4   Explain briefly the implications for training of a change in technology.
5   What is the difference, if any, between education and training?

Appraisal

The English language contains many words whose interpretation depends upon the attitude of the listener. *Appraisal* is one of them. According to the dictionary it implies the existence of an expert who reviews the progress, appearance or capability of a person or thing. A dealer appraises an antique for its provenance and value. A teacher appraises the progress of pupils.

Appraisal of staff is necessary for the following reasons:

☐   to select the people who are suitable for promotion.

☐   to check the efficiency of the recruitment, selection and training practices.

☐   to improve the way in which people are doing their jobs.

☐   to make individuals aware of the objectives of the business.

Appraisal takes place each time a manager checks on the work of a subordinate, discusses that work and indicates how it could be improved. Appraisal is part of the job of any person who is responsible for the work of other people. Some large organisations have introduced formal systems of appraisal. This usually involves a standardised appraisal form and an interview at regular intervals. This can lead to a number of problems:

☐   people become resentful if they feel their work is being criticised. This can result in less efficiency rather than greater efficiency as working relationships deteriorate.

☐   badly designed forms can require subjective judgments on a person's ability.

☐   the existence of an appraisal form and a set time for an appraisal interview can tempt managers to leave the task of appraisal to the time designated. Appraisal should, of course, be ongoing and directed towards improving performance. The formal interview should be no more than a summary of previous discussions.

☐   some jobs are more difficult to appraise than others. The more complex the job the greater the difficulty in judging the efficiency with which it is done and the greater the difficulty of finding somebody capable of analysing problems and offering constructive support.

Redeployment and transfer

We have already stated that organisational and technological change can make it necessary for a business to transfer workers from one department to another. This may also be done as a deliberate move in staff development, that is to widen the range of experience of staff and make them more suitable for promotion. It may be part of a job enrichment or enlargement scheme. Employees may also request transfer for personal reasons. They may believe that experience in a particular department will enhance their promotion prospects. They may dislike the people with whom they are working. In a large organisation, they may request a transfer to another part of the country because their partner has taken a job there.

Employee-instigated transfers and those which are clearly seen by the staff to have personal advantages, present few problems, inability or unwillingness on the part of the business to agree to the transfer being the major one in that it can lead to dissatisfaction in the person refused. Transfers instigated by the business for organisational reasons are potentially more difficult in that the person concerned may feel threatened in job security and status. The majority of people do not enjoy the experience of a totally new environment. Job change is an acknowledged cause of stress.

Resignation, redundancy and dismissal

Resignation

The relationship between employer and employees is defined by law. In the section on recruitment we saw that an employer was required to give an employee a written contract of employment within twelve weeks of the date when work started. Resignation is the decision on the part of the employee to terminate the contract of employment. The notice of an intention to do this may be included in the contract of employment or it may be based on the customary practice for that occupation.

It may be customary in certain occupations for the length of the notice required to coincide with the periods in which people are paid. A person paid weekly may give a week's notice. A monthly paid employee may need to give a month's notice. In education, where employees are paid monthly and the organisation of schools and colleges is on a term basis, dates may be specified by which a resignation must be given. These will be designed to coincide with the payment periods and to minimise disruption to the work of the school or college during a term.

The practice of making the period of notice correspond to the payment period reduces the risk of dispute over the amount of money due to the employee, although holiday pay and bonuses due can still cause problems. The greater the degree of disruption an employee could cause by resignation the more likely it is that termination of contract will be a clause in the written contract of employment. Where a highly specialised employee is concerned she/he may be required to complete specific tasks before employment can be terminated rather than be tied to a time period too rigidly. A scientific research worker whose contract requires three months' notice may be released after one month if a project has finished, rather than allowed to start on another piece of work which another person would then have to take over.

Dismissal

The ability of employers to dismiss staff was limited by the Industrial Relations Act and confirmed by the Trade Union and Labour Relations Act of 1974. The grounds for fair dismissal are:

1   *Inability to perform the work required*   The employer has a legal responsibility to ensure adequate training is given and to warn the employee of the unsatisfactory nature of her/his work. If a business finds this a problem then it should revise its recruitment and training procedures.

2   *Misconduct*   The employer must be able to show that warnings suitable to the gravity of the offence have been given. Summary dismissal, that is dismissal without notice, may be justified if an employee has endangered lives, perhaps by drunkenness. For other offences an established pattern might include:

□   several informal warnings by the supervisor.

□   if the offence persists, a formal oral warning by the manager with supervisor and a trade union representative present.

□   a written warning which may be handed to the person with the same degree of formality.

The Advisory, Conciliation and Arbitration Service (ACAS) has drawn up a code of practice relating to dismissals. It states that employees should be aware of the disciplinary procedures of the business, that there should be a system of warnings similar to the one outlined above and an appeals procedure should be in operation.

3   *Redundancy*   A dictionary defines the word 'redundant' as meaning superfluous or characterised by an excess. Under the terms of the Employment Protection (Consolidation) Act of 1978 a person can be made redundant if the employer can show that the type of labour offered by the employee is no longer required (superfluous) or that the need for it has decreased (some employees are in excess of requirements).

4   *There may be legal restrictions on employing a certain category of person*, for example children under a certain age.

The law relating to unfair dismissal is open to interpretation, and employees who believe themselves to have been dismissed unfairly on grounds such as their right to join a trade union, the right to strike, discrimination under the provisions of the 1976 Race Relations Act and/or the 1975 Sex Discrimination Act have the right of appeal. They would take their case to an industrial tribunal which, if it finds in the favour of the employee, can order re-instatement, re-engagement or compensation. The choice lies with the employee.

Redundancy

The definition of redundancy given in the previous section should be sufficient to make clear that it is an unpleasant experience for the person concerned, even when accepted voluntarily. It can attack the status and security needs of the individuals concerned and, in extreme cases, undermine the lifestyle of the person and her/his family. Because it can affect individuals dramatically it can also have serious problems for the business making the redundancies:

1   It is expensive, and the better organised and more powerful the labour force the more expensive it is likely to be. If redundancy proposals are opposed by the trade unions concerned there could be industrial action which would further disrupt production with the resultant loss of output and possibly sales. When redundancy is not opposed the trade union may be able to negotiate terms which involve redundancy payments above the legal minimum. These costs may be considered short term by the business and can be offset against savings as the result of greater efficiency in the long term.

2   Rumour and fear of redundancy can affect the morale of existing employees. Assurances of no further plans to make people redundant may be disbelieved and the business may experience problems in maintaining output and quality. They may also lose valuable staff.

'I am getting out. They've got 1500 men to get rid of in the next two years. They tell me my job is safe but I can't take any chances. There is the mortgage to pay and the kids to keep.'

The man speaking had no difficulty in finding another job with a firm he considered more stable. Given his qualifications and experience it was unlikely that he would have been made redundant but he felt too insecure in an atmosphere of threatening redundancy to take the risk.

3   The image of the business is likely to suffer. This in turn could affect recruitment and a business might find it difficult to attract good employees, even in areas where redundancy is unlikely. Redundancy, even as a result of re-equipping plant with advanced technology, carries with it the implication of failure.

4   When a business follows a policy of voluntary redundancy they take the risk of losing skilled and versatile staff who see a generous redundancy payment as a way of financing their future plans.

5   Redundancy may be against the declared policy of the business. In this case the need for redundancies will reflect on its public image. It can also lead to conflict at managerial and board levels.

In theory, redundancy should not be necessary if the business has a good manpower plan. In practice, the rate of change of technology and changes in the market can make it difficult for a manpower plan to project very far into the future. To some extent the industry in which a business operates and the type of materials it uses will affect its ability to forecast its staffing requirements with any degree of accuracy.

Where a business can identify a future problem it may review its marketing policy. Can it increase sales by changing its advertising and pricing strategy? Is it targeting its efforts on the right market segment? Could a change in distribution methods help? Is the packaging right? Could sales promotion increase revenue?

This approach will be most helpful when redundancies are caused by declining sales. When redundancies are the result of a change in technology, the marketing department may already be efficient. In this case a marketing drive will only have a marginal effect on redundancies.

Redundancies may also be avoided by cutting down on part-time work, subcontracting and overtime. Work-sharing could also be introduced and, in occupations with a pension scheme, early retirement can be encouraged.

So far in this chapter we have looked at people management in terms of the natural life of an employee within the business from the time of employment, through training and job changes to the point where the contract of employment is terminated by either the employer or the employee. In the next sections we shall be looking at the responsibility of management during the period of employment; the *need* to motivate and the *responsibility* to provide working conditions which take account of the health and safety of employees.

SELF ASSESSMENT

1 A manager is preparing to dismiss an employee. State two reasons why she/he may be reluctant to do so.
2 Redundancy can lead to a feeling of insecurity in the remaining employees. What effects might this have on the production manager?
3 Distinguish between appraisal and management by objectives (page 289).
4 Give two ways in which redeployment can lead to insecurity in a workforce.
5 Outline three ways in which a business might avoid issuing redundancy notices.

Motivation

A business needs to motivate its workforce if it is to make the best possible use of the financial and material resources at its disposal. In Chapter 12 ('People and business'), we examined the theory of human motivation. In this chapter we will look briefly at the practical ways in which a business might attempt to motivate its employees.

Remuneration

Most people have to work in order to survive. An attractive salary is likely to be one of the features that persuade people to apply for a job. In the market for labour it is reasonable to suppose that successful businesses can offer higher salaries than their competitors, and so attract well qualified workers. Logically this should mean that these businesses will continue to be successful because the quality of their decisions in finance, marketing and production and the resulting product offered to the market will continue to be better than those of their competitors. In practice there is some debate about the continuing importance of money as a motivating factor. People's perceptions of what constitutes a good salary may change. Someone who is employed in a new job at a salary 10 per cent higher than before might be pleased initially, but when the new salary is compared with those of colleagues she/he may be less satisfied.

   The way in which people are paid can also help determine whether or not money can act as a motivator.

Payment by results
This term covers schemes based on measurement of the work done, and the amount paid is related directly to the amount of work completed. It can include piece rates, commission and bonus incentive schemes. F. W. Taylor laid down the principles for a successful scheme of payment by results in terms of good job design, careful selection of the workforce and good training. It can be expensive for a business to operate in terms of the clerical work associated with records and changes in technology or working practice might make it progressively easier for people to reach the targets set and achieve high bonuses. This erodes any advantage to the business of introducing new methods and any attempt on the part of the business to redefine standards is likely to be met with considerable opposition from the workforce. In other words the scheme is a potential source of conflict. This conflict is not necessarily between management and workforce. Payment by results can also lead to inter-group conflict where one group of workers perceive the targets set for them as being

high compared with targets set for other groups in the organisation. The use of payment by results as an incentive to work more productively can also be limited:

- ☐ by the complexity of the scheme. If it is unintelligible then there will be less incentive to work more productively as people will not have a clear concept of the relationship between effort and payment.

- ☐ working groups may establish a group norm in relation to production standards. Pressure may be brought on people working more productively to conform to the standards of the group.

- ☐ proposed change of technology and/or working practice will be met with suspicion as people will see it as an attempt to erode their wages.

Participation

Involving employees in the decision making processes of a business reduces the feeling of alienation which may be present and increases employee commitment to the achievement of objectives. Participation may be as simple as a suggestion box with financial rewards for cost-reducing suggestions. It may consist of an elaborate system of meetings of employee representatives or it may be merely meetings between management and employee representatives to inform the employees of decisions already taken.

Participation can be time-consuming, and some employees will take the view that they are not paid to make decisions – that is the job of management. The past history of the business will also influence the success of a participation scheme. A business with a tradition of autocratic management will find implementation more difficult. Employees will not be accustomed to making decisions and there may be suspicion and resentment.

Employee shareholding is seen by some people as an extension of the idea of participation, with advantages in motivating the workforce. The argument is simply that if people have a financial stake in a business then they have a greater reason for working more productively and making sure the business is a success. Privatisation of nationalised industries with priority in buying shares given to employees, and management buy-outs with employee investment have led to an increase in shareholding amongst employees. Critics of this point of view argue that the shares will eventually be sold for a profit and in the long term the increase in employee shareholding will be negligible. At the moment tax advantages make it profitable for the shares to be held for five years. It is too early to say what will happen when the majority of schemes have been in existence this long. Much of the discussion on the value of employee shareholding tends to be coloured by political thinking, which makes it more difficult to evaluate.

Job rotation, job enlargement, job enrichment, training and promotion prospects all have a place in determining the level of motivation within a workforce. So also does the leadership style, the relationship both within and between groups and the environment within which a business is operating. In Chapter 12 ('People and business'), we discussed the idea of the complex person. If the workforce are to be motivated their needs must be met, but those needs are changing and are varied according to the individual. To design motivation schemes to suit all workers at all times would seem an impossible task.

Poor motivation can lead to a high rate of labour turnover, high absenteeism, poor quality products, low productivity and poor industrial relations.

Monitoring personnel policy

The effectiveness of a personnel policy can be judged by a number of measures:

- □ the safety record of a business;
- □ the level of absenteeism;
- □ recruitment records;
- □ the rate of labour turnover;
- □ the level of productivity;
- □ the quality of the work produced and the level of wastage.

Problems in any of the above areas will indicate a personnel problem. The degree of control the business has over the problem will vary according to the environment in which it is working and over time. Labour turnover is likely to be high for a boring job in a period of full employment. A business employing innovative technology might find it difficult to recruit people with experience in the technology and, for a time, have high levels of labour turnover together with low productivity and wastage.

Protection

Work is a dangerous activity. Over the years a body of legislation has grown up regulating the workplace and the way in which people work to ensure the health and safety of the workforce. Some of these Acts refer to specific industries, for example the Factories Act of 1961 and the Offices, Shops and Railway Premises Act of 1963. The Health and Safety at Work Act of 1974 placed a general responsibility on all employers and employees to maintain a healthy and safe working environment. Under the Act employers are required to:

- □ prepare and distribute to their employees a written statement of safety policy.
- □ educate and train their workforce in the need for safe working practice.
- □ ensure that working practices are safe, all products are safe and, if necessary, clear instructions are issued for safe use.
- □ consult and co-operate with employees' representatives.

The laws are enforced by inspectors, either employed by the Health and Safety Executive or by the local authority. Businesses must co-operate with the inspectors, allowing them to collect evidence and to close down if so instructed.

Conclusion

The people involved in business can be seen as the most important resource of that business. Finance, production and marketing are, after all, only words given to a group of tasks performed by people. The success or failure of each will depend largely on the quality of the people undertaking the task, the motivation and commitment. It could be argued that Chapters 12 ('People and business') and 13 ('Business organisation and communication') are the most important chapters in this book, and the implications of the subject matter stretch far beyond the immediate concerns of the personnel department.

REVIEW

1 Forsythe plc produces large industrial equipment. The company has a history of poor industrial relations dating back to the mid-1960s, and the situation was not improved by the economic recession of the 1970s and 1980s. To make matters worse there was world over-capacity in the market and the major foreign competitors – West Germany, Japan and Korea – were all more cost-effective than Forsythe. In order to survive Forsythe's management invested in new equipment and proposed changes in working practices: rigid demarcations between jobs were to be abolished; all employees, including skilled workers, were to take their turn in 'service' jobs, e.g. cleaning and painting. Working hours became more flexible. It was expected that these measures would be met with considerable opposition from the workforce and expressed through the trade unions.

   a What steps might the management of Forsythe's take to ensure the success of their proposals?

   b What external factors might contribute to the acceptance of these proposals by the workforce?

2 Peter Jackson has just been appointed production manager at a small clothing factory. Within a short time of taking up his job he is aware that morale in the factory is low and, judging by the number of complaints on file, quality control is poor. He decides to introduce a system of quality circles – that is a small group of employees who meet regularly and voluntarily, to discuss technical problems associated with their work and decide on ways in which these might be overcome. The scheme met opposition both from employees and from other members of the management team.

   Shop steward: 'It's pointless, isn't it? Sitting round talking when we should be getting on with the job. My members are paid by results. Wasting time talking will just reduce their pay. Besides it is the management's job to sort out problems – that's what they are paid for.'

   Managing director: 'A waste of time. Most of them are uninterested in working. If we paid them time rate they would just sit talking all day. Giving them time to meet to discuss problems will just be an extended tea break to them.'

   Peter Jackson persevered with his idea and won reluctant permission for his experiment from both management and the shop stewards. By the end of six months there was a perceptible improvement in quality, costs were down and the production flow had improved.

   a From your knowledge of the advantages of participation explain why the quality circles in this instance were successful.

   b Outline the arguments used by Peter Jackson:

     i to the managing director

     ii to the shop steward

     to persuade them that the experiment was worth making.

   c What conditions would have to be satisfied to ensure the success of quality circles?

3 A small manufacturing company is proposing to appoint a personnel manager for the first time.

   a List the functions of a personnel manager.

   b For each function state who is likely to be performing that function before the appointment of the personnel manager.

   c What organisational advantages and disadvantages might arise from the appointment?

Activities

1 Interview a person who is employed in an area in which you have a special interest. Analyse the job from the results of the interview and draw up a checklist of personal characteristics, skills and experience that are needed.

2 Interview a number of people on their attitudes to work and working conditions. Analyse the results of these interviews. Do they suggest any problems in motivating workers?

Suggested projects

1 Should business X employ a safety officer?

2 A critical evaluation of the payment system in plant Y.

Essays

1 Define job evaluation and assess its utility to a business enterprise.

2 Outline and comment on the impact of current employment protection legislation on a business enterprise.

3 Discuss the ways in which a manager might attempt to improve the morale of the workforce.

4 The personnel function is fundamental to the success of a business enterprise. Discuss.

5 Analyse the essential principles of a good training programme.

6 The head of a school/college will be interviewing a shortlist of three candidates for the post of A-level business studies teacher. Candidate A is professionally well qualified, has worked in industry but has no teaching experience. Candidate B is moderately qualified and has two years' successful teaching experience. Candidate C has just qualified as a teacher of business studies. Suggest factors which might influence the head's choice and consider:

a how the head might brief himself for the interviews.

b the questions he might ask each candidate.

c the information she/he might seek before making a decision. (25) 1986 (CLES)

15 Decision making in business organisations

When you have studied this chapter you should be able to:

☐ Explain what is meant by decision making and why it is necessary.

☐ Identify the stages in the decision making process.

☐ Distinguish between different types of decision.

☐ List the influences on decision making style.

☐ Discuss the influences on decision making style.

☐ Classify the different types of business problem.

☐ Define management science.

☐ Identify the stages in the scientific approach to decision making.

☐ Understand the element of risk in decision making.

☐ Define the nature of forecasting.

☐ Identify the major components in forecasting.

☐ Define a moving average and a weighted moving average.

☐ Calculate moving averages using simple data.

☐ Evaluate the limitations of the technique.

☐ Calculate an index number from given data.

☐ Understand and use a simple weighting system.

☐ Appreciate the problems associated with the compilation of index numbers.

☐ Distinguish between the Laspeyre index and the Paasche index.

An underlying theme throughout this book has been the need for a business to take decisions. This derives from the fact that:

☐ all resources are scarce and that the business must select the most profitable use for them.

☐ there may be several ways of achieving the desired objectives and the most profitable way needs to be selected.

To recap briefly, it is necessary for a business to take decisions in relation to the use of financial, staff and technical resources which will in turn affect the financial, marketing and production activities of the business.

In previous chapters some decision making practices and techniques have been introduced as an integral part of the chapter, for example DCF, break-even charts and the need for planning to implement decisions. It is now time to look at the decision making process and the types of decision a business needs to take in more detail.

Types of decision

The type of decision a business makes can be classified according to the number of unknown variables which may have an influence on the outcome of a particular course of action and the type of problem involved.

Decisions and constraints

The overall objectives of a business are long term and are therefore subject to constraints imposed by competitors, governments and society in general. The decision as to whether or not to pitch prices at a high level compared with those of potential competitors (*skimming*), or a low level (*penetration*), will depend on the judgment of management about the potential behaviour of competitors; e.g. the decision to invest in North Sea oil, with its high production costs, depended on a reading of the future market for oil and its potential world market price.

In general these decisions relate to the *profitability* and, ultimately, the *survival* of the business in its present form. They have become known as *strategic* decisions.

Most decisions in business can be described as *tactical*. There are a limited number of options open to solve any problem, and solutions tend towards the routine. When tactical decisions have to be taken on a day-to-day basis they become *recurrent*, that is they happen over and over again. There is a danger in this. Many different problems can display the same symptoms. A high rate of absenteeism, for example, might have its origins in recruitment, training and remuneration policies. It could also be the result of a poor working environment which reflects on the organisation of the production function, or may be out of the control of the business. A workforce unaccustomed to rigid working hours may not see the need for regular attendance. In this case the high level of absenteeism might become a routine problem, accepted as the norm, with no attempt to analyse the problem, although it could become a serious internal constraint upon the achievement of strategic objectives.

Making decisions

The process of making decisions is the same regardless of the type of decision being made. In routine decisions the process may be formalised with set procedures to be followed. In 'one-off' decisions the process may be more apparent and could take months or even years. A decision as to whether or not to go ahead with a major civil engineering project will be taken only after the results of a prolonged feasibility study are known and have been evaluated. The process can be summarised in the following stages.

1   State the objectives to be achieved.

2   Define the problem to be solved. We have already suggested that this may not be as easy as it appears. A product which is not reaching the predicted level of sales might be over-priced, carry a bad reputation for quality or have the wrong distribution channel.

Figure 15.1 The decision making process

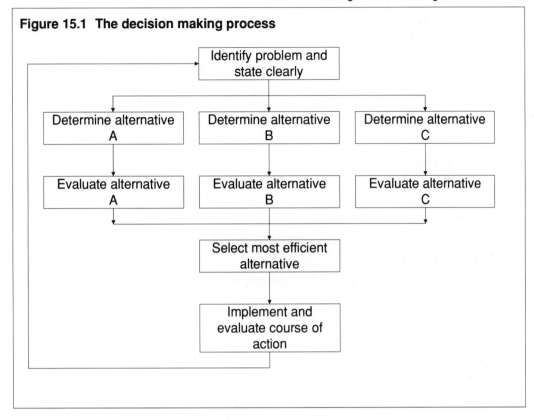

3   Collect available information. This will determine the internal constraints (staff, availability of finance, production capacity, etc.), and the external constraints (the economic environment, the market in which the business operates, any legal limitations) on the course of action.

4   Draw up alternative solutions to the problem. It is very rare for there to be only one solution available. At this point it is necessary for the business to consider its objectives. Some courses of action are more likely to achieve these objectives than others. This process involves the analysis and evaluation of the different courses of action. We have already seen some of the techniques that might be used to find and analyse information. However, decision making also involves risk and mathematical techniques to evaluate risk, such as decision trees, might be used.

5   Once a decision has been reached then it is implemented using the planning procedures outlined in previous chapters. You should remember that this process involves the collection of information to evaluate the progress of the plan. The same information will contribute towards the evaluation of the effectiveness of the original decision.

The stages in the decision making process are illustrated in Figure 15.1.

The way in which decisions are made are not quite as straightforward as this outline suggests. A manager's approach to decision making is likely to vary according to the type of decision being made, the personality and experience of the manager and the circumstances in which the decision has to be made. These influences are illustrated in Figure 15.2.

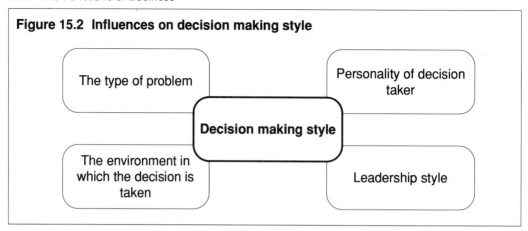

Figure 15.2 Influences on decision making style

The type of problem

Personality of decision taker

Decision making style

The environment in which the decision is taken

Leadership style

The resources in time and money a manager is prepared to devote to a problem will depend upon:

☐   the type of problem, for example whether it is a routine situation which can be solved by experience.

☐   the clarity of the problem.

☐   the resources available.

☐   the importance of the decision to the manager's career. A person who is clearly responsible for a decision is likely to take more time and trouble in making it than a person whose accountability is less clearly defined.

☐   the personality and experience of the manager. Some people are more willing to accept risk than others.

☐   whether or not the decision can be easily changed.

The final result will depend on the balance between the importance of the decision and the desire of the decision maker to get it right with the reluctance to devote too much effort to the problem.

SELF ASSESSMENT

1 Give two reasons why decision-making is an unavoidable business activity.
2 Distinguish between strategic, tactical and recurrent decisions.
3 Identify one danger of recurrent decisions.
4 Explain briefly the relationship between decision making, objectives and constraints.
5 Give two ways in which the decision making process can be influenced by the decision maker.

Business problems

To each owner or manager of a business it might appear that her/his problems are unique. To a certain extent this is true. Each business is a unique organisation. It has evolved out of a set of circumstances that are unique to its experience. On the other hand it is possible to group problems into major areas which have appropriate techniques to contribute to the solution of the problem.

1 *Resources problems* Accepting that all resources are scarce compared with the demand for them, the existence of competing uses for the available resources of a business leads to the need to decide how they shall be allocated. The business is faced with problems concerning the use of time, staff and production capacity. Which product should the resources be devoted to? What proportion of the resources of a business should be allocated between departments? Which is the most important at the present time? Marketing? Research and Development? Information for the solution of these problems is derived from market research as well as the internal records of the business. At this level deciding on the allocation of resources may involve the use of different costing techniques, contribution analysis, market research and staff planning.

Resource allocation is not only concerned with the allocation of resources to different business functions. Given that the equipment available in any one department is limited the problem arises how best to use that equipment.

A small factory produces a range of engineering components all of which have to be processed through Machine A. There is only one of these machines in the factory, and the possibilities of sub-contracting are limited. Theoretically Machine A has the capacity to process all the components in the time allowed. In practice the machine has become a bottleneck. The business is finding difficulty in meeting orders for the fastest moving components whilst stocks of other components are building up.

Machine A is a limited resource. The evidence suggests that it is not being used efficiently. It also suggests that priority should be given to the more popular components while less popular items could be processed at a more leisurely rate which would have the advantage of reducing the stocks of high-value finished goods. In this example there is no evidence to support the installation of an additional machine; therefore there are no additional demands on the total resources of the business. The solution might lie in a coding system to give priority to the fast-moving components. This is likely to have implications for the use of staff, e.g. changes in working practices and priority for Machine A by the maintenance departments. Taking this problem from the point of view of the components it can also be interpreted as a *queuing problem*.

Where a variety of resources are needed for several projects which need to be completed in sequence, or where a business has control over resources which can be used in a variety of projects then a technique known as *critical path analysis* (CPA) can be usefully employed. Critical path analysis is a collection of techniques designed to find the lowest-cost method of completing an operation. If resources are kept idle because other stages of the project have not been completed then this will increase the costs of the project. A small builder will plan a job from experience, and will estimate the time each activity will take and make arrangements to hire any additional equipment needed to fit in with the time sequence of the job. A mistake in these estimations might cost additional hire fees. Where a task has been sub-contracted, the builder might make plans to do another, shorter, job in the time available. The builder is using a rule of thumb critical path analysis. In more complex jobs a network will be drawn up before the work begins, indicating the sequence of activities, their dependence on each other and the degree of flexibility in the use of scarce resources (*float*).

2 *Replacement problems* Unfortunately equipment has a limited life and at some stage a business has to decide whether or not to replace obsolescent or worn out machinery. This decision will be made on the basis of the estimated market for the final product, e.g. the expected life cycle of the product, the cost of the machine and alternative uses for the resources.

Maintenance also generates replacement problems. The failure of a machine might cause hold-ups and delays in the work process. On the other hand the activity involved in repairing or replacing that machine might cause greater hold-ups. This is a costing problem. Which alternative involves the least cost to the business concerned? A business employing outside contractors to service its office equipment at a fixed service charge per call plus an hourly rate for the work itself might find it cheaper to leave the repair of routine equipment until it has several tasks to be done. On the other hand the same business might be prepared to call in the contractor if the equipment to be repaired is essential for the operation of the whole system.

3   *Location problems* On page 219 we outlined the factors a business would take into account when deciding where to locate a factory. It was also indicated that each factor would have a different degree of importance in each decision and this can be translated into costs. For example if a factory serves five customers in a given area, which site would reduce transport costs by the greatest amount? The same basic problem is involved in the setting up of service departments within a business with several factories. One solution to this problem involves the use of a transportation matrix which can be solved by the use of linear programming.

4   *Inventory problems* The techniques which might prove useful for a business in this area include costing, statistical analysis of the problem, and the results of market research.

Parts queue to be processed by machines, customers queue to take their turn at the checkout counter of a supermarket. It makes sense in terms of low costs and customer satisfaction to reduce the waiting time as much as possible with the minimum use of additional resources. In a small shop the problem will be solved by observation. Tuesday morning and Thursday morning might be busy times for a sub post office with a large number of pensioners registered with it. It will also attract custom for the general shop next door. Common sense will tell the owners of both whether or not they will need additional staff on those mornings.

Where trade is less certain it becomes more difficult to assess the requirements. When trade is random the business will be interested in how often an event occurs in a given unit of time. In other words how many customers are likely to need service between 9 a.m. and 12 noon on a Tuesday morning? The *Poisson distribution*, which is derived from the binomial distribution, can provide a useful approximation for these purposes (see Chapter 5 'Statistics'). If the average rate of arrivals at a checkout counter is ten per hour, it would be possible to calculate the probability of an unacceptable number of customers arriving; unacceptable, that is, in terms of the length of time they would have to wait and the damage this might do to the future trading prospects of the business.

5   *Marketing problems* Marketing problems must also include production problems. The product mix, quality control, distribution channels and pricing are likely, in larger businesses at least, to be based on the analysis of historical data using statistical techniques outlined in Chapter 5 ('Statistics'). Linear programming can also be used to determine the optimum product mix.

When marketing their products businesses will also be concerned with the reactions of their competitors. This relates to the question of market power we discussed in Chapter 3 ('Markets'). When a major oil company reduces the price of petrol it is likely that its competitors will follow suit in order to retain their share of the market.

1 Classify the following situations according to the problems listed above. You may put each situation into two categories if you believe your decision to be valid. Give reasons for each of your choices.
  a A company launches a takeover bid for a business that supplies it with an important component.
  b A small business investigates the possibility of investing £5000 in market research.
  c A business identifies a bottleneck in its production flow.
  d A stores manager discovers that the business is carrying an excess number of one component.
  e A business loses an order because of the breakdown of an important machine.

Management science

This is the use of a scientific approach to decision making. It is a systematic and logical approach to problem solving that, by clarifying the situation, can help a manager make better decisions. Note the use of the word 'help' in the last sentence. The decision making techniques that have been developed do not make the decision, they provide the manager with more information. Figure 15.3 is an outline of the management science process.

A model in management science is usually expressed in terms of mathematical relationships. Figure 15.4 illustrates some of the techniques used in management science and the type of problems they can be used to solve.

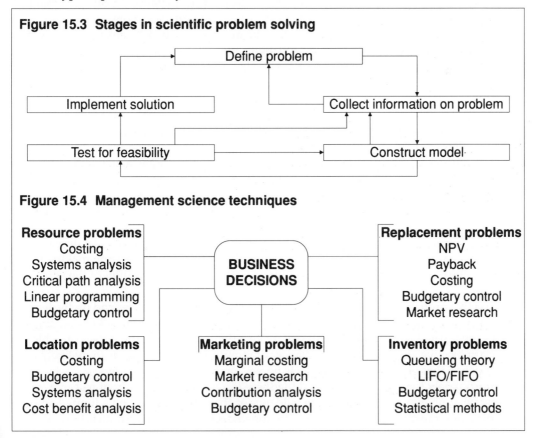

Figure 15.3 Stages in scientific problem solving

Define problem → Collect information on problem → Construct model → Test for feasibility → Implement solution

Figure 15.4 Management science techniques

Resource problems
Costing
Systems analysis
Critical path analysis
Linear programming
Budgetary control

Replacement problems
NPV
Payback
Costing
Budgetary control
Market research

BUSINESS DECISIONS

Location problems
Costing
Budgetary control
Systems analysis
Cost benefit analysis

Marketing problems
Marginal costing
Market research
Contribution analysis
Budgetary control

Inventory problems
Queueing theory
LIFO/FIFO
Budgetary control
Statistical methods

People and risk

Risk occurs when there is more than one possible outcome from a decision, some of which are less desirable than others. The way in which people react to this situation has been the subject of study by psychologists. What makes someone willing to make a particular decision when colleagues are urging caution? Why does a person take an apparently irrational decision – one which, on the surface at least, is unreasonable given the available evidence?

In Chapter 12 ('People and business'), we developed the idea that people had their own unique 'bundle' of objectives and personality traits which would influence their behaviour in any one situation. Freud suggested that some of the motives which influence the way in which people act were in fact subconscious. His argument was that if we knew what these subconscious motives were then irrational decisions would appear rational in the light of additional information.

During the 1940s and 1950s psychologists continued to study this question. Their main interest was whether or not people tried to maximise their satisfaction from any decision they made. This personal satisfaction might include monetary reward, but only as one of their motives. We discussed this in Chapter 12 ('People and business'), when we looked at the role of money as a motivator. The *utility* of a decision to an individual – that is the extent to which it satisfies the desires of the individual – is *subjective*. In other words it is the perceived utility that is important to people.

Any event has an actual (*objective*) possibility of occurring. If you toss a fair coin there is a one in two chance it will come down heads – assuming the way in which it tossed each time does not vary and it does not land on its edge. The word 'fair' is used to indicate that the coin is balanced and normal, i.e. not double headed for instance. In decision making, therefore, the logical thing to do is select the decision that will lead to the outcome with the highest probability of occurring and will give the maximum utility. There is some evidence to suggest that people use subjective probability when making decisions even when the actual probabilities are known. The coin tossing example is a case in point. No matter how often the coin is tossed the probability of it showing heads as a result of the next toss remains one in two, i.e. 0.5. If you toss the coin ten times and each time it showed heads many people would argue that there was a greater chance of it showing tails on the next toss. This is not true. A subjective rather than an actual probability is being applied and may be justified in terms of 'Well, it's the law of averages'. This judgment of the situation is based not on numbers, but on an intuitive understanding of the probability. Eleven heads in succession does indeed have a low probability. It is in fact 0.5 raised to the power 11, or approximately 0.00049. However, by the time the coin has landed heads 10 times, half the miracle has already occurred. To argue otherwise would be to assign to the coin a memory of what happened to it previously.

To summarise the argument so far we are saying that people tend to make decisions on the *subjective expected value* of its outcome; a long phrase to describe decision making based on subjective estimates of probability combined with the subjective utility of the perceived outcome.

Subjective probability is not only a matter of intuition. It will also depend on the level of knowledge and experience of the people concerned. Someone who follows horse racing and studies the form of horses closely will still make a final selection of the horses on which to bet by a subjective judgment of their chances of winning, but the choice is more likely to be accurate than that of someone who selects horses on the basis of their names.

Unfortunately for good decision making there is a considerable body of research which suggests that people do not use all the evidence at their disposal. Given a limited amount of information most people make a good, reasoned decision. When the data is too extensive there is a danger that much of it will be ignored. This is sometimes known as information overload. Individuals will select the information that, in their subjective judgment, is the most important.

Given the fact that in many business decisions information is incomplete, either because the cost of collecting it is prohibitively expensive or because the information is not available, it is not surprising that the record of a management team for making good decisions is taken into account by investment analysts when attempting to forecast the future potential of a company.

Management science techniques

Forecasting

A forecast is a prediction of what is expected to happen in the future. These predictions are based on past experience. This may be summarised in terms of statistical or accounting data, or it may be the less quantifiable experience of the management involved in making the decision.

In planning businesses must forecast what they think is going to happen – future sales, expected production, changes in interest rates, availability of investment funds, the amount of stock to order, etc. Some of these forecasts will be for a relatively short period of time; no longer than a month. Others, for example those used in preparing an annual budget, will be for periods of up to a year. Forecasts to be used in investment decisions may need to predict market changes for the expected life of the project. The longer the time period involved, the greater the chance that circumstances on which the forecast was made will change.

Apart from the time period for which the forecast is made the forecast must also take into account any obvious patterns that appear in the original data. Look carefully at Figure 15.5 which shows the sales of a business over a twelve-month period.

The sales have an upward trend, that is there is a general tendency for them to rise during the year. In some months the sales are lower than the month before. If this tendency is repeated in each year's statistics then the sales are said to be subject to seasonal variations. However if this pattern is the result of changes in the market which do not necessarily repeat themselves at the same time every year, for example a change in interest rates, then it is known as a cycle.

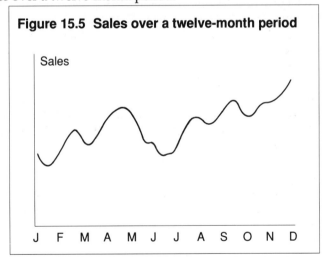

Figure 15.5 Sales over a twelve-month period

Time series analysis

Time series methods are those which take into account changes in data and project the findings into the future to help with planning. In this chapter we will deal with the *moving average* and the *weighted moving average*.

The moving average

A moving average smooths out the variations in data caused by seasonal and cyclical fluctuations, and so allows the general trend to become clear. It is quick, easy and cheap to calculate and useful for short-term predictions. However, it does not give weight to the reasons for the existence of the trend and should therefore be treated with caution. Forecasting based on the calculation of a moving average assumes that the reasons for the trend have not changed. This method may be used for forecasting future short- and medium-term (up to one year) demand for supplies and the final product to help in budgeting, medium-term investment decisions, stock control and staff planning.

JACK'S LUNCH SERVICE

Jack Reston began his lunch service as soon as he finished his business studies course at college. He thought he had researched his market thoroughly, but his first three months of trading were disappointing. Jack had no doubt about the reason. He was the only lunch service in the area that would deliver good food to homes and places of work, but if he could not meet the demand for his top-selling line, a well presented plate salad using organically produced foods, his total sales fell. He decided he needed more accurate estimates of the demand for his product. From his sales records Jack draw up the information for sales in the first three months of trading, shown in Figure 15.6.

Jack decided to calculate a three period moving average for the data, that is an average of three weeks in sequence. Thus his moving average for week 2 was calculated as follows:

$$\frac{20 + 25 + 40}{3}$$

= 28.34 orders per week

The moving average for the next period, that is from week 2 to week 4 he calculated as follows:

$$\frac{25 + 40 + 43}{3}$$

= 36 orders per week

Jack continued until he had drawn up the table shown in Figure 15.7.

From this table Jack can make a forecast for orders for the 13th week. He will simply take the last average calculated above (66.7) and cater for that number of lunches – or, more likely, he will cater for 67 lunches.

Figure 15.6 Sales of plate salads

Week	Sales
1	20
2	25
3	40
4	43
5	47
6	53
7	50
8	52
9	60
10	59
11	66
12	75

Figure 15.7 Three period moving average for sales

Week	Sales	Moving average
1	20	
2	25	28.34
3	40	36.00
4	43	43.33
5	47	47.66
6	53	50.00
7	50	51.67
8	52	54.00
9	60	57.00
10	59	61.66
11	66	66.67
12	75	

In this example a three period moving average was calculated. Depending on the amount of data available and the degree of accuracy required a business will select three, four, five, six, ten or fifteen period moving averages.

If Jack had wanted to forecast further into the future he would have had to study his table of moving averages more carefully. He might have looked for:

☐   a pattern in the trend, for example a percentage increase in the number of sales over a period of time.

☐   changes in seasonal sales.

The information he has shows an upward trend in sales which will give him the confidence to increase his production but little else. It would be more valuable to him if he gave greater importance to the more recent sales figures – after all they are the ones that reflect most closely the way his clients feel about his service now.

Weighted moving averages

Jack wants to give more importance to his most recent sales information. Let us assume that he believes the sales information in week 11 is three times more important than the information for week 9. His calculations would change as follows:

$$\frac{(66 \times 3) + (59 \times 2) + (60 \times 1)}{6}$$

$$= \frac{198 + 118 + 60}{6}$$

$$= 62.67$$

Note that instead of dividing by three, the period, in this instance we have divided by the sum of the weights (3 + 2 + 1 = 6). The forecast is also slightly lower than the one using the unweighted moving average.

In this example the weights vary from 3 to 1. If you were using a five period moving average then you could use the figures 1 to 5. This is the simplest example of weighting. Further information might indicate that greater weight should be given to the later figures and a much lower weight to earlier figures, but this goes beyond the brief of this chapter.

SELF ASSESSMENT

1 List the three main components of time series data.
2 Distinguish between a six and an eight period moving average.
3 Plot a graph of the information given in Figure 15.7.
4 If Jack wanted to predict his sales for the rest of the year what assumptions would he have to make if there was no further information available to him?
5 Calculate a four period moving average for the information given in Figure 15.6. What differences can you observe between the two sets of data?

Index numbers

An index number is a convenient way of comparing changes in sets of data over time. It is a useful way of showing trends in prices and quantities that is easy to understand. Because index numbers can be calculated in different ways it is important that the same method is used for any series otherwise the figures within that series are not comparable and lose all value.

Figure 15.8 shows the production index of a business:

□ the list of numbers is known as the *series*.

□ 1982 = 100. This is the *base year*. The base year is the period with which all other years are compared.

Calculation of index numbers

The simplest way of calculating a series of index numbers is to express the quantity or value of each year as a percentage of the quantity or value of the base year. The following figures refer to the production of a business over a period of five years.

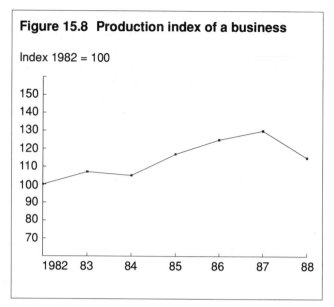

Figure 15.8 Production index of a business

Index 1982 = 100

	1984	1985	1986	1987	1988	1989
Output (tonnes)	1000	1126	1148	1190	1210	1240

Assuming we select 1984 as the base year:

$$\text{Index number} = \frac{\text{Quantity for year X} \times 100}{\text{Quantity for base year}}$$

$$= \frac{1000 \times 100}{1000}$$

$$= 100$$

The index number for 1985 can then be given as:

$$\frac{1126 \times 100}{1000}$$

$$= 112.6$$

That for 1986 will be:

$$\frac{1148 \times 100}{1000}$$

$$= 114.8$$

The annual percentage increase between 1985 and 1986 will be:

$$\frac{(114.8 - 112.6) \times 100}{112.6}$$

$$= \frac{2.2 \times 100}{112.6}$$

$$= 1.95$$

This is a simple example. The production output is given in tonnes. It can be assumed that the business has only one product. What about a business that has a number of products? The output of one might be far more important to the business than the other products, but this is not reflected in the index number.

The answer to this problem lies in weighting. This assigns to each element in the production figures for one year a figure that reflects its relative importance to the business. If we assume that the business in the above example has three products X, Y and Z, and that X brings in three times the revenue of Z, while Y earns twice the revenue of Z, we can allocate weights as shown in the table.

Output in 1985	1148	
Product X	254	x 3
Product Y	500	x 2
Product Z	394	x 1

The new index number would then be:

$$\frac{[(254 \times 3) + (500 \times 2) + (394 \times 1)] \times 100}{1126}$$

$$= \frac{(762 + 1000 + 394) \times 100}{1126}$$

$$= \frac{2156 \times 100}{1126}$$

$$= 191.5$$

This is a significant change from the original figure of 114.8!

The selection of weights is not quite the simple process it appears here and the organisation compiling index numbers will use other statistical and accounting data to determine the importance of the different items in a package of goods to be included in the series.

Problems in the construction of index numbers

1   *The information available*   This can influence the period for which the index number is constructed and the items that can be included in it. If a certain type of information is not available monthly then it may have to be excluded from a series drawn up on a monthly basis. This will affect the validity of any comparisons made using that index number. Again, if the information is based on sample data there are additional problems related to the possibility of sampling error.

2   *The information to be included*   There are a large number of items that could be included in a series designed to measure changes in the cost of living. The problem is to select the items most representative of the whole population. A significant rise in the price of expensive cars would affect the cost of living of one part of the population but would have no effect on the majority of people. Once items have been selected the wide range of brands available in most consumer goods makes it impossible to include all of them. Those selected should reflect the general price movements of the class of good.

3   *The selection of a base year*   The base year is the point of reference for the rest of the series. The year selected should not contain any distortions. A major strike that suppressed production in a base year would make the comparisons for following years look

unusually favourable. The most important thing in selecting a base period is to make sure that prices and quantities have a reasonable relationship to each other, i.e. it should reflect their historical relationship.

4 *The selection of weights* This can be seen as an information problem. The importance of any item included in an index can be decided only on the basis of the data available. This data may have been collected for the purpose of constructing an index, but it may have been collected as part of the accounting control system of the business and may therefore not be suitable. It is also important that the weights used from a sample reflect the importance of the whole range of goods. Thus the weight given to leisure in a cost of living index should reflect the importance of all leisure activities in spending patterns. This could involve problems in the definition of leisure activities.

5 *The time period over which comparisons are made* The longer the time period the greater the probability that the weighting given to different items will change. Comparisons over long periods are not, therefore, reliable. In order to overcome this problem the *Paasche index* uses updated weighting factors, in contrast to the *Laspeyre index* which uses the weights for the base year throughout the series.

SELF ASSESSMENT

1 What is the base period as used in the compilation of index numbers?
2 Given the following information calculate a simple time series.

Year	Output in tonnes
1985	900
1986	1500 (base year)
1987	2560
1988	2970
1989	3650

What was the annual percentage increase 1986–1987? Show your calculations.
3 What is a weighted index number?
4 Explain briefly the importance of each of the following in the construction of index numbers:
   a The choice of items
   b The base period
   c The method of weighting.
5 Give one reason for selecting the use of Paasche index rather than the Laspeyre index.

REVIEW

1 Best for Baby Ltd is a new business supplying and delivering toiletries and foods for children aged 0–24 months. The target market is families and very small businesses, such as childminders, within a ten mile radius of the depot, who find it difficult to reach normal retail outlets. There are a number of excellent supermarkets in the area and, in order to

remain competitive, Best for Baby has set very high standards of customer service. In order to achieve this the two directors want to be able to forecast the number of orders that will be placed in the next month so that they can make sure they have enough vans and drivers to make the necessary deliveries on time.

From the existing records of the business they have drawn up the following data on the deliveries made in the first twelve months.

Deliveries made in the first year of operation: Best for Baby Ltd

Month	Deliveries made
January	90
February	120
March	135
April	125
May	130
June	110
July	105
August	80
September	95
October	100
November	115
December	130

a Construct a graph showing the pattern of deliveries for Best for Baby Ltd.
b State and explain two possible reasons for the pattern of deliveries shown in the graph.
c Calculate a three month moving average for the data given.
d State the forecast for the next month in the sequence.
e What additional information would be required in order to calculate a forecast for more than one future period?

2 The data below shows the number of cars of a given model a dealer sold in a month.

Month	Cars demanded
January	8
February	6
March	7
April	10
May	11
June	15
July	20
August	50
September	35
October	30
November	18
December	9

a On a graph show:
  i   The actual demand for cars over the twelve month period.
  ii A three month moving average.
  iii A five month moving average.
b Identify and explain any patterns in the original demand.
c Comment on the value of using a moving average to analyse demand in this case.

3 a What is an index number?

b Give three circumstances in which the calculation of an index would be useful for a business.

c State and explain one reason why weights are used in the calculation of index numbers.

d From the information given below calculate a weighted price index.

Item	Year 1	Year 2	Year 3	Weights in year 1
Loaf of bread	38p	45p	50p	10
Gallon of petrol	76p	185p	196p	6
Rent per day	200p	220p	250p	5

4 The information given below was taken from the *Economic Progress Report*, August 1987.

The retail prices index (RPI) is the most commonly used measure of inflation. It measures the changes in the prices of practically all the goods and services which people buy. As such it provides a good guide to the changing purchasing power of the 'pound in people's pockets'.

The RPI takes account of taxes on goods and services (VAT, tobacco and alcohol duties) as these are parts of retail prices. It does not take account of changes in income tax and national insurance contributions. However, these are combined with the RPI in the tax and prices index (TPI) which tells taxpayers what on average they need in pay rises to maintain their own spending power.

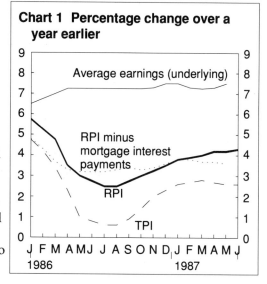

Chart 1 Percentage change over a year earlier

a Define the term 'index' as used above.

b State and explain any patterns you can observe in Chart 1.

c Outline three ways in which the information given above could be useful to a business manufacturing consumer durables.

5 Parkside Plastics employs 1000 people, the majority of whom are engaged in repetitive tasks. Over the past two years absenteeism and labour turnover have increased. The management tended to regard this deterioration as inevitable given the improved job opportunities in the area and the boring nature of the work. Recruitment, selection and dismissal decisions were taken on a routine basis.

In 1989 a new personnel manager was appointed, and she took a very different view of the situation. As this manager, write a formal report to the managing director covering the following points:

a The relationship between strategic and tactical decisions.

b The research necessary to define the problem.

c The investment that might be required to solve the problem.

Activities

1 Record the changes over a period of time in the value of the shares of a company quoted on the Stock Exchange.
   a Calculate several weighted moving averages of the data you have collected.
   b Use the moving averages to prepare a short-term forecast of changes in the share price.
   c Evaluate the results of your activity.
2 This activity should be completed with the co-operation of a manager you are work shadowing.
   a Classify all decisions the manager makes under the headings 'strategic', 'tactical' and 'routine'.
   b Discuss your classification with the manager at the end of a few days. You may find that decisions you classified as routine only appeared to be so because of the experience the manager had in decision making.
   c Repeat the classification process at intervals throughout your placement. To what extent did your insight into the decision making process improve during this time?

Essays

1 Identify and comment on the ways in which internal and external constraints affect the development of a business.
2 Discuss the relationships that exist between long- and short-term decisions.
3 'There is no such thing as a routine decision. A problem is a symptom and, like the symptoms of a disease, can have a variety of causes.' Discuss.
4 'Forecasting is fraught with difficulty and should be used with caution.' How far do you agree with this statement?
5 'The expansion of information technology will not necessarily improve decision making. In fact it could make it worse.' Comment on this statement.

16 Tools for decision making

When you have studied this chapter you should be able to:

- Define linear programming.
- Identify the type of problems in which this technique is useful.
- Solve simple problems using linear programming.
- Identify the type of problem to which a transportation matrix can be applied.
- Solve a simple transportation problem using the northwest corner method.
- Solve a simple transportation problem using the minimum cost method.
- Understand the importance of network analysis in planning and cost control.
- Distinguish between CPA and PERT.
- Construct a simple network diagram from information given.
- Analyse a network to determine the critical path.
- Determine the earliest and latest start times in a given network.
- Define the term 'float' and outline its usefulness.
- Understand the purpose of cost benefit analysis.
- Distinguish between a probability tree and a decision tree.
- Understand the difference between objective and subjective probability.
- Calculate the expected value of an event.
- Construct a simple decision tree.

By reducing complex problems to a simplified model, the techniques of management science allow the decision maker to clarify the issues involved. This makes it easier to choose the alternative that will contribute most effectively to the objectives of the business.

Linear programming

This method can be of assistance in problems involving:

- the product mix;
- an investment portfolio;
- ingredient mixtures;

☐   choosing an advertising medium;

☐   minimising transport costs;

☐   location.

Linear programming evolves from the way in which numbers are represented graphically, and the fact that for any two numbers – say x and y – one and only one of the following statements is true.

either x is less than y

or x is equal to y

or x is greater than y

Symbolically these statements are written:

either $x < y$

or $x = y$

or $x > y$

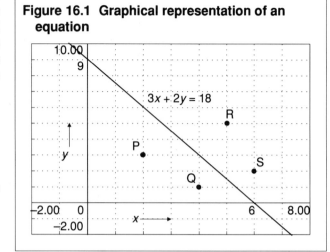

Figure 16.1 Graphical representation of an equation

To distinguish < from > note that the 'jaws' open towards the larger quantity.

Look at the graph illustrated in Figure 16.1.

To represent the equation $3x + 2y = 18$ we have joined all the points (x, y) which satisfy the equation. For example, when $x = 0$ and $y = 9$ then:

$3(0) + 2(9) = 18$

Other points for which this equation holds true are (4, 3), (6, 0), and so on. These points, in this case, lie on a straight line. All the equations we will be dealing with in this section have straight line graphs – hence the name *linear* programming. Because the graph is a straight line we only need two points to fix it. In this case (0,9) and (6,0) seem the most obvious.

So every point on this line represents a value of x and a value of y for which $3x + 2y = 18$. We have done more than that. Look at the point P. Here $x = 2$ and $y = 3$, so $3x + 2y = 12$.

At Q, $x = 4$, $y = 1$ so $3x + 2y = 14$

At R, $x = 5$, $y = 5$ so $3x + 2y = 25$

At S, $x = 6$, $y = 2$ so $3x + 2y = 22$

So at P and Q $3x + 2y < 18$. This is true for all points below and to the left of the graph. Similarly at R and S and all points to the right and above the graph $3x + 2y > 18$.

If you cannot see this select your own combinations of x and y for the values given and substitute them into the equation.

We will now turn this example into a business problem. Let us assume that the 18 in the equation is the total amount of raw material available to a two product business (product X and product Y) for a week's production. The raw material is used in both products. If the business decides to use all the raw material on product X it can manufacture six. If all the raw material is used on product Y then the maximum output will be nine. In most weeks the business needs to produce some of product X and some of product Y. Let us say that it produces x of product X and y of product Y, then it can produce any combination of x and y that lies on the line of the graph.

It can also produce any combination of products X and Y that lie below or to the left of the graph. This would not be a good idea. As we have already seen, combinations of x and y in this region are less than 18 so some of the raw material would not be used and the business would not be making the maximum profit. In other words these combinations would not be contributing to its objectives. Combinations of x and y above and to the right of the graph are impossible for the business to achieve – it does not have that much raw material.

So far we have accepted the equation as given, but why have we used $3x$ and $2y$? The answer is very straightforward. The business has 18 tonnes of raw material. Product X requires 3 tonnes and product Y requires 2 tonnes. So the business needs to know all the different ways in which it can combine $3x$ and $2y$ within the limits imposed by the 18 tonnes at its disposal. The amount of raw material is a constraint on the decision.

One further point. By introducing the idea of products into the problem, we have automatically introduced two other constraints. It is not possible to produce a negative amount of a product, consequently neither x nor y can be less than zero.

Linear programming with two constraints

JRG Ltd is a garment manufacturing company about to launch its spring range. In one small part of its factory it intends to produce two lines in women's blouses. The materials and labour used in both are identical, but one blouse is more elaborate in design and uses more labour but less material. Market research has shown that this blouse can be sold at a higher profit per unit.

We can analyse this case as follows:

☐ *the problem* How many of each blouse to produce?

☐ *the objective* To make the maximum profit.

☐ *the constraints* The materials and labour available.

Each blouse uses the amount of resources shown in the table. Suppose the business makes a of blouse A and b of blouse B. Look at the labour constraint first. The total labour used is:

Product	Labour (hours)	Materials (metres)	Profits (£s)
Blouse A	2	6	4
Blouse B	5	5	5

$2a + 5b$

Unfortunately the business is limited to a maximum of 80 hours of labour per week. This can be expressed as:

$2a + 5b <$ or $= 80$, i.e. $2a + 5b \leq 80$

Figure 16.2 shows the range of possibilities open to the business from using all its labour resources on blouse A to using all its labour resources on blouse B.

In any week the business expects to have a maximum of 120 metres of material to make the blouses. The material constraint is therefore:

$6a + 5b <$ or $= 120$, i.e. $6a + 5b \leq 120$

This constraint is shown superimposed on Figure 16.2 to give Figure 16.3. If you look at the shaded area in Figure 16.3 you can see the possible production taking into account both constraints. This is called the *feasible solution area*. All product combinations in that area are possible. The business has not yet solved its problem. It has still to discover the combination of products that will give the maximum profit.

We know that blouse A will make a profit of £4 and blouse B a profit of £5 per blouse sold. Assuming all production is sold, Figure 16.4 shows the possible profit combination lines when total profits for the week are £20, £40, £60, and £80. These lines are based on the equation:

$$4a + 5b = \text{total profit, P, in £s.}$$

For example, if the profit is to be £40 and all resources are devoted to blouse A then the business will need to make 10. If all resources are devoted to blouse B then it will only need to make 8.

Take careful note of the following:

□ the lines are parallel to each other because their gradients are defined by the ratio of the profits derived from each blouse.

□ the further the lines are from the origin the greater the profit the business receives, i.e. the greater the value of P.

How does the business know at which point it will maximise its profits?

Figure 16.2 The labour constraint

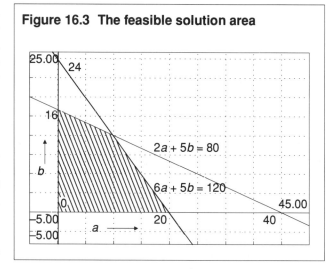

Figure 16.3 The feasible solution area

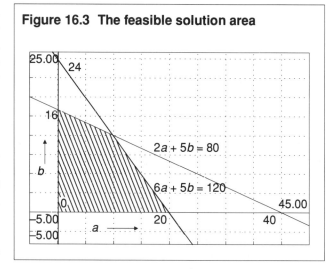

Figure 16.4 Possible profits on blouses

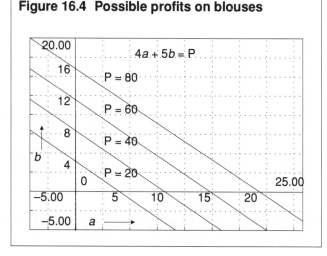

Look carefully at Figure 16.5, which consists of Figure 16.3, plus the line for which P = 40 from Figure 16.4. There must be other lines, parallel to the P = 40 line, further from the origin (P > 40), but which still intersect the feasible area. You can probably see that the one furthest from the origin (Maximum P) must pass through the point C. At C, a = 10 and b = 12. By making 10 of blouse A and 12 of blouse B a maximum profit of £(4 x 10) + (5 x 12), i.e. £100, can be achieved.

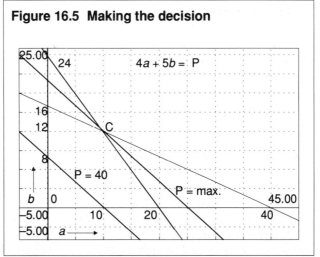

Figure 16.5 Making the decision

It must be stressed that this is only a potential maximum profit because it depends upon:

- ☐ 80 hours of labour being available;

- ☐ 120 metres of material being available;

- ☐ all production being sold.

Profit lines to the left of C will mean that some materials and labour are not being used therefore profits are not being maximised and the objective of the business is not being achieved. Profit lines to the right of C cannot be achieved because the business lacks the necessary resources. Only by increasing available resources or by improving productivity can these be reached.

In this example the business was aiming to maximise. Linear programming can also be used in decisions when the object is to minimise, e.g. producing goods with the minimum of cost. In this case the feasible solution will be to the right of the constraint boundaries and the point selected will be the one where the cost line is as close to the origin as possible.

SELF ASSESSMENT

1 Explain briefly how a linear programming approach could help in the solution of the choice of an advertising medium. State:
   a a possible objective in this situation.
   b two constraints.

2 Express the following in words:

   a $x > y$ **b** $y > x$ **c** $y = x$ **d** $x < y$

3 Distinguish between a maximisation and a minimisation problem in linear programming.

4 A business has £10 000 to spend on advertising. This will buy 20 hours advertising with a regional radio station or 50 hours advertising with a local radio station.
   a Construct an equation to show the constraints on the business in making the decision.
   b What other information would the business need before it could construct a linear programming model?

5 Explain why an increase in productivity would move the profit line away from the origin in the case of JRG Ltd.

Transportation models

The transportation model is a form of linear programming that takes its name from the problems it is designed to solve. It is used in the following circumstances.

- ☐   A product is to be transported.
- ☐   The cost must be minimised.
- ☐   There are a number of sources for the product.
- ☐   There is a fixed supply from each source.
- ☐   There is a fixed demand at each destination.

There are a number of methods of solving transportation problems that satisfy these criteria. We will concentrate on the method known as the *northwest corner method*. This name is taken from the way in which the problem is approached.

The northwest corner method

A business purchases the raw material used in its three factories from three different suppliers in Birmingham, Bristol and Manchester. The factories are sited in Liverpool, Preston and Slough. The following information is given:

Factory	*Demand for raw material per month (tonnes)*
A Liverpool	700
B Preston	400
C Slough	800

Suppliers	*Maximum supplied each month (tonnes)*
X Birmingham	500
Y Bristol	800
Z Manchester	600

Transport costs of one tonne of raw material from supplier to factory.

Supplier	*Factory*	*A*	*B*	*C*
		Liverpool	Preston	Slough
X Birmingham		£5	£7	£9
Y Bristol		£9	£11	£10
Z Manchester		£3	£3	£11

Figure 16.6 shows the transportation matrix for the information given above. We now have to allocate supplies to the different factories starting with the northwest (top left-hand) corner of the matrix. In this case we have Liverpool demanding 700 tonnes but Birmingham can supply only 500 tonnes. We place 500 in the box for Liverpool and Birmingham (A,X) and cross out the other two boxes on this line. All Birmingham's supplies for the month have been used to supply Liverpool. This is illustrated in Figure 16.7.

Liverpool is still in need of more supplies. We go to the next square (A,Y), in this case the one directly below. Liverpool needs another 200 tonnes. This can be supplied by Bristol. So

200 is inserted in that square and the box below is crossed out. Liverpool's needs have now been filled. Bristol still has 600 tonnes of raw material (800 – 200 supplied to Liverpool). We go on to the northwest corner that has not had any figures allocated to it (B, Y). Preston wants 400 tonnes. So Bristol can supply these and still have 200 tonnes left over. Figure 16.8 shows the state of the transportation matrix now.

Note that the box B,Z has also been eliminated, so our next northwest corner is C, Y. Slough requires 800 tonnes. It can get 200 from Bristol (C,Y) and 600 from Manchester (C,Z). The completed allocation is shown in Figure 16.9.

The total cost of transport can then be calculated by multiplying the amount allocated to each box by the transport costs in the top right-hand corner of the box and adding the results.

The northwest corner method allocates supplies to the factories but does not attempt to minimise the cost of transport. The basic matrix can be adapted to take account of this. Instead of allocating to the northwest corner the initial supplies are allocated to the box with the lowest transport costs. An example is given in Figure 16.10.

SELF ASSESSMENT

1 Give 3 conditions that must be met before a transportation matrix can be used.
2 What are the two constraints in any allocation decision?
3 Distinguish between the northwest corner and the minimum cost methods.

Figure 16.6 The transportation matrix

From \ To	A	B	C	Supply
X				500
Y				800
Z				600
Demand	700	400	800	1900

Figure 16.7 Initial stage in solution of problem

From \ To	A	B	C	Supply
X	500			500
Y				800
Z				600
Demand	700	400	800	1900

Figure 16.8 The next stage

From \ To	A	B	C	Supply
X	500			500
Y	200	400		800
Z				600
Demand	700	400	800	1900

Figure 16.9 The final allocation

From \ To	A	B	C	Supply
X	500			500
Y	200	400	200	800
Z			600	600
Demand	700	400	800	1900

Figure 16.10 The minimum cost method

To From	A	B	C	Supply
X	100 ⌐5⌐	400 ⌐7⌐	⌐9⌐	500
Y	⌐9⌐	⌐11⌐	800 ⌐10⌐	800
Z	600 ⌐3⌐	⌐3⌐	⌐11⌐	600
Demand	700	400	800	1900

Network analysis

A network is a system of interrelated events through which an item or items move in order to achieve a given objective. The ingredients of a cake, for example, go through the stages of assembly, processing, baking and decorating before the cake is ready for sale and consumption. This is illustrated in Figure 16.11. The arrows represent the activities involved in making the cake. The circles are called nodes and represent events, the starting and finishing of an activity.

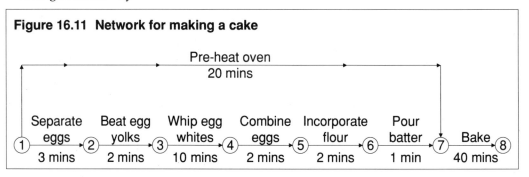

Figure 16.11 Network for making a cake

Network analysis can be used in a variety of business situations. It is particularly useful in complex activities when it can help minimise:

☐ loss of time, by ensuring that the transition from one process to another takes place as smoothly as possible.

☐ cash flow problems, by ensuring that materials are bought when they are needed and are not bought too soon.

☐ material wastage, by cutting down on the risks of spoilage and pilfering.

☐ capital equipment required, by ensuring maximum utilisation of the capital stock.

A major advantage of network analysis is the fact that it produces a picture of the system which is relatively easy for managers to interpret.

Network analysis has a number of techniques associated with it. The most commonly referred to are critical path analysis (CPA) and project evaluation and review technique (PERT). Using CPA certain times are calculated – an activity will be given a definite date on which it will be completed. PERT uses activity times calculated on probability. At first sight the PERT approach appears to be more realistic. If network analysis is being used in planning then it is concerned with future events and there are, inevitably, unknown variables. However there are some theoretical difficulties associated with PERT analysis – such as the tendency of users to make optimistic estimates of completion dates. This book will concentrate on the CPA network.

Constructing a network

The owner of a small shop is planning an extension to take advantage of its growth in trade. The network for this project has three main activities. These are shown in Figure 16.12. Take careful note that:

- □ the nodes are numbered.

- □ the arrows show the order in which the activities will take place. It is obviously not sensible for the owner to start laying the foundations until the plans have been drawn up and approved. It is equally obvious that the shop cannot be fitted until it has been completed.

- □ the times on the arrows give the length of time each activity is expected to take.

Figure 16.12 Network for extending a shop

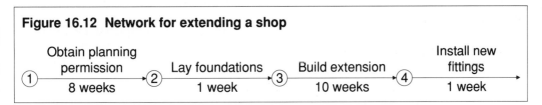

This network shows the major activities involved in this project. It gives an outline plan of the order in which things can be done. We can now expand it to examine the problem more closely. The major activities can be listed as follows.

	Activity	Expected time (weeks)
A	Design the extension	12
B	Obtain planning permission	8
C	Lay foundations	1
D	Order materials	1
E	Build extension	10
F	Design interior	4
G	Order new fittings	3
H	Install new fittings	1

Look at Figure 16.13.

1   Activities A and B – the design of the extension and obtaining planning permission – must take place before any other activity can be started.

2   Activities C and D can be done during the same time period. These activities branch away from node 3. Both these activities have to be completed before work can start on activity E. In CPA activities cannot share the same starting and finishing nodes; this is shown in Figure 16.14.

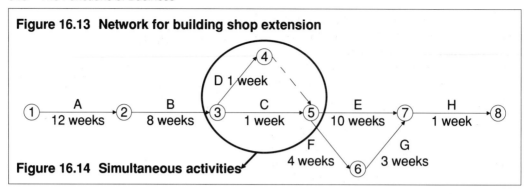

Figure 16.13 Network for building shop extension

Figure 16.14 Simultaneous activities

Simultaneous activities branch from the previous activity but one will be linked to the subsequent activity with a dummy line. This is a dotted arrow. It does not have any time penalty.

3 The total amount of time needed to complete all these activities is 40 weeks, but we know that some of them are going to happen simultaneously so the final time will be less.

The network has been constructed, it has now got to be used. It can give help in:

☐ determining the minimum time in which a project can be completed, i.e. its critical path.

☐ timing the start and completion of each activity, i.e. scheduling.

Determining the critical path

The shortest time in which the job can be done is determined by the longest path through the network. In our example there are several paths. These are illustrated in Figure 16.15.

The first path is the longest and so it is the critical path. You should note that it is eight weeks shorter than the original time suggested.

Figure 16.15 Paths through the network

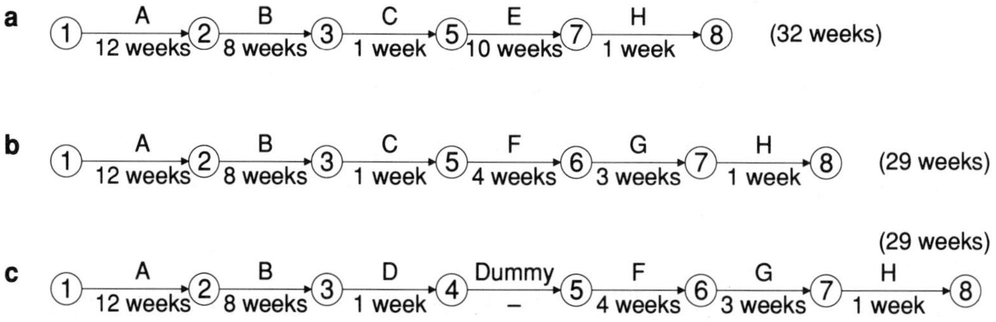

a ① A 12 weeks ② B 8 weeks ③ C 1 week ⑤ E 10 weeks ⑦ H 1 week ⑧ (32 weeks)

b ① A 12 weeks ② B 8 weeks ③ C 1 week ⑤ F 4 weeks ⑥ G 3 weeks ⑦ H 1 week ⑧ (29 weeks)

c ① A 12 weeks ② B 8 weeks ③ D 1 week ④ Dummy – ⑤ F 4 weeks ⑥ G 3 weeks ⑦ H 1 week ⑧ (29 weeks)

Scheduling

Scheduling is making a timetable of when things are going to happen. The shop owner will want to know when the dividing wall between the new building and the original shop is going to come down so that the business can be planned around that time. She/He may have to move shelves, counters and other fixtures to give the builders clear space, and may have to close the shop – in which case customers will have to be given notice. To help in this planning and to help the builders with decisions such as what equipment will be required and when, the network needs to be analysed to find the starting and finishing date for each activity. Of course, unforeseen things might happen but at least the earliest start time and the latest finish time of the preceding activity can be calculated. The way in which this is shown on the diagram is shown in Figure 16.16.

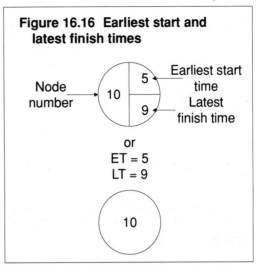

Figure 16.16 Earliest start and latest finish times

Calculating the earliest start time

To calculate the earliest start time of each activity it is necessary for us to calculate the critical path through the network to the node at the beginning of the activity. Looking at Figure 16.15 we can see that the earliest start time for node 5 is:

A + B + D

12 + 8 + 1 = 21

If two activities end at the same node, in other words there are two activities to complete before the next stage of the project can start, then it is the longer of the two activities which determines the earliest start time of the next activity.

Latest finish time

The latest finish time is the latest time an activity can finish without delaying the start of the next activity and the completion of the final project. In determining the earliest start time we started at the beginning of the project and worked our way forwards. In determining the latest finish time we work the opposite way. Using Figure 16.15:

1   Write down the time at node 8. This is 32 weeks.

2   Subtract from this the time taken by activity H, that is 1 week.

We now have 31 weeks as the latest time at which node 7 must be reached. Continue this exercise for each activity until you have worked your way through the network.

The float

In any project there will be some activities that can overrun the time calculated for them without delaying the start of the next activity. In our example activities F and G have a total time of 7 weeks, but activity H cannot start until activity E (10 weeks) has been completed. This is known as the *free float*. The *total float* is the difference between the earliest start time of an activity and the latest start time.

This free time can be very useful in planning projects. Let us imagine a building contractor has the equipment and the trained labour for installing a silicon injected damp proof course in a house. There are three house renovation projects. In the initial planning the installation of the damp proof course in house Z was scheduled for 31 March, and that in house Y for 5 April. The work on house Z was expected to take two days, plus a day for packing and transporting the equipment. Unfortunately the work on house Z is running behind schedule. It will not be ready for the damp proof course until 4 April, so work on house Y cannot start until 7 April. The contractor can:

- ☐ delay the work on house Y until house Z is finished, and so risk two dissatisfied customers.

- ☐ delay the work further on house Z but complete house Y on time. There will only be one dissatisfied customer, but that one is more seriously dissatisfied.

- ☐ hire the necessary equipment and additional labour to get both jobs done. The problem with this is that the contractor might not be able to keep control over the installation of the damp proof course.

The existence of a three-day float on house Y would mean that the contractor could do both jobs without further delaying house Z and delaying house Y. In other words, knowledge of the presence of a float and its duration can increase the flexibility and efficiency with which a business can use the resources at its disposal.

SELF ASSESSMENT

1 Distinguish between the use of nodes and arrows on a network diagram.
2 Give two reasons why network analysis is more useful in complex than in simple operations.
3 Distinguish between CPA and PERT as methods of network analysis.
4 Using the information in Figure 16.15 and the activity times given above, calculate the earliest and latest start times for all activities.
5 Explain how determining the critical path and the scheduling of a project could save a business both time and money.

Cost benefit analysis

Businesses are part of the community and some commercial decisions made by a business will affect the general well-being of a community. The most obvious example is, perhaps, pollution as the result of industrial processes carried out by a business. Many of these decisions will be internal to the business and implemented within a known legislative framework, for example the Clean Air Act of 1956.

In other cases the consequences of business decisions are less clear-cut. A business applying for planning permission to build a factory on a particular site might argue that it is bringing employment into the area, boosting the revenue of the local authority by paying rates and improving the appearance of the area by building a modern factory with landscaped grounds on what was previously a derelict area. Weighed against this might be the arguments of the local residents concerned about congested roads, pollution and noise.

Local authorities and central government face a similar conflict of interest when undertaking projects concerning the provision of services and the improvement of the infrastructure of an area. Will a by-pass designed to take traffic from the centre of a market town assist the development of the town by reducing congestion and noise – or will it contribute to the decline of the town by taking away passing trade and making it easier for local residents to travel to a better shopping centre some miles distant? Will closing an uneconomic branch line of the railway system or axing a loss-making bus service destroy local community life – and what other hidden costs will be incurred by the decision and who will bear them?

The distinction can be made between the *private costs* of any decision – that is the cost to the individual or organisation responsible for the decision and which is usually reflected in the production cost of the business, and therefore in the price of the product – and the social costs (sometimes called *externalities*) which are borne by the community as the result of that decision. This implies a conflict of interest in many decisions between financial criteria and social or political criteria. Cost benefit analysis is a collection of techniques which attempts to find an objective measure of the utility of a proposal based on the range of people's values in a community, and to measure these values on a common monetary scale. The list here gives an imaginary cost benefit analysis used in the selection of a site for the dumping of industrial waste.

Costs	Benefits
New roads	Increased employment
Heavier traffic	Landfill and reclamation
Loss of amenity land	Revenue from dumping
Local ecology	Cleaner environment

SELF ASSESSMENT

1 Define cost benefit analysis.
2 Distinguish between private costs and externalities.
3 A by-pass is proposed for a picturesque village in an area of outstanding natural beauty. List the possible costs and benefits. Explain briefly some of the problems that will be involved in allocating monetary values to these.

Decision trees

A *tree diagram* plots the possible outcomes of an initial decision over a period of time. If you look at the outline of the diagram in Figure 16.17 you will see that it takes its name from its branching appearance.

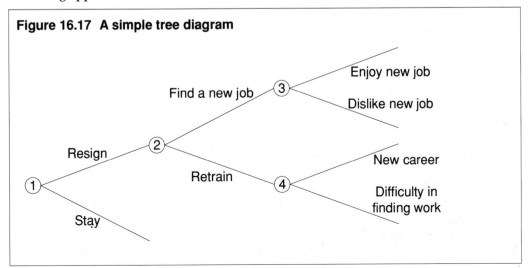

Figure 16.17 A simple tree diagram

8-til-late is a small chain of supermarkets. Its shops are located in small suburban shopping centres. G and HJ Efstathiou are the managers of one of these stores, and they are not pleased when they discover that Toptill, a national supermarket chain, plans to open a store less than one hundred yards from their own. They draw up the tree diagram given in Figure 16.17 to estimate the possible effect of the opening of the Toptill store on their customers.

The diagram is useful but it does not go far enough. To be of real value to the Efstathious it would have to tell them the likelihood of each of the events occurring. For example, what is the likelihood of a customer who switches to Toptill in the first month of its opening returning to the Efstathious' 8-til-late in the following month?

To make a tree diagram more useful we have to turn it into a *decision tree*, by incorporating the probability of the occurrence of each event. To do this we need to look carefully at two terms:

☐   probability;

☐   expected value.

Probability

If we toss a coin it will come down heads or tails. This is a part of a probabilistic experiment and the outcome (heads or tails) is known as an *event*. In this instance we know that it is equally likely that it will come down heads or tails so we can say that the probability is one in two. We can also express it as:

☐   50 per cent.

☐   1/2.

☐   0.5.

In this case we know the probability. When this happens we say the probability is objective.

In many business contexts the probability of an event is not so clear. It may be possible to use past records of the business to estimate the possibility of an event occurring, or managers may have experience of similar situations and use this and personal belief to assign a subjective probability to an event. 8-til-late might have experienced similar circumstances in other stores and draw on their sales records to find out what happened. The Efstathious may have managed a store that encountered the same problem and use their experience to make their own estimates. However they reach their conclusions they are now in a position to assign probabilities to their tree diagram.

You should note that the probabilities from each starting point always add up to one. If percentages were used then the probabilities would always add up to 100 per cent.

Expected value

The expected value of an event is the probability of it occurring multiplied by the benefit the business can expect if it happens. For example, a business is deciding whether or not to invest £100 000 in an advertising campaign. The campaign has a 0.6 probability of success. The expected value from a successful campaign, therefore, is:

0.6 x £100 000 = £60 000.

The decision tree

So far we have looked at probability trees and the idea of expected value. The manager using this technique in making a decision wants to know which course of action will be best. Faced with the problem the analysis takes the following course:

- ☐ identify the courses of action open to the business.
- ☐ identify the possible results of the action.
- ☐ assign probabilities to each of the results.
- ☐ calculate the expected value of each result.
- ☐ select the course of action with the highest expected value.

Look at the decision tree in Figure 16.18. Notice the following points:

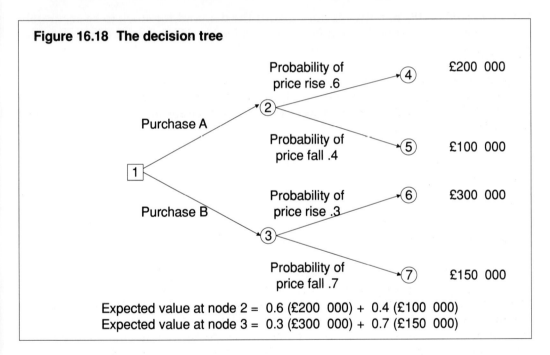

Figure 16.18 The decision tree

Expected value at node 2 = 0.6 (£200 000) + 0.4 (£100 000)
Expected value at node 3 = 0.3 (£300 000) + 0.7 (£150 000)

- ☐ the square represents a decision point.
- ☐ the circles mark the probabilistic alternatives.
- ☐ the decimals on the lines are the probabilities of that event occurring.
- ☐ the values (£s) represent the income to the business if that event does occur.

The expected value at one node becomes the starting point to calculate the expected value for the next node.

Simulation

This is a method of analysing a problem by building a mathematical model that describes the state of the real world and the relationships that exist within it. This allows the manager to experiment with a variety of solutions to the problem with a minimum of expense and without the risks of loss that the real world involves. Simulation is particularly important in those industries where experimenting in the real world is impracticable (for example, by the construction of prototypes). It is also used when a problem has a large number of variables each of which can significantly affect the final outcome.

Uses of simulation

1   *Problems involving queuing*   The supermarket checkout, pumps at the petrol station, and different parts waiting for processing by the same machine are all examples of this.

2   *Stock control*   It is not always possible for the demand for stock to be accurately determined. There may be random factors involved in which case simulation can give information on the possible patterns of demand the business might face.

3   *Cash flows*   Although projected cash flows are based on information already possessed by the business, the final cash flow is the result of variables outside the control of the business. By simulating the different cash flows generated by different sets of circumstances the business is able to plan more flexibly.

4   *Training*   The use of business games in management training provides the trainees with the opportunity to encounter complex problems that in the real world they could not be allowed to experience.

5   *The environment*   Major civil engineering projects can have so many repercussions that it is impossible to analyse them without simulation. The construction of a barrage across an estuary will have implications for the ecological and socio-economic balance of the area.

Simulation is a relatively inexpensive way of testing the possible outcomes of complex situations. The improved access to computer technology has increased its viability and extended its power as a management tool. However it is still a tool, and the efficiency of the final system will depend on the skill and care with which the model of the system was constructed. The fact that a simulation system has to be created for each problem places a burden of creativity on the designers. Although they are relatively inexpensive, good systems require a major investment in time and expensive manpower to construct.

Conclusion

The use of operational research techniques is expanding. It must be remembered that they are only part of the decision making process. The techniques are limited by the fact that they rely on quantitative analysis. The social, ethical and cultural environment in which a business operates will also have an important weighting in a final decision. These considerations can often be built into simulation. It should be remembered that the apparent certainty of the quantitative statement disguises the value judgments that have taken place.

REVIEW

1 Juskids Ltd manufactures two electronic toy products. The major processes for the production of both are pressing, assembly and packaging. Toy A has a contribution of £7 and toy B a contribution of £5. The cancellation of an order for another product made the following spare capacity available in the different sections of the factory. This spare capacity, and the capacity requirement per toy, are shown in the table.

Spare capacity	
Pressing	72 hours
Assembling	231 hours
Packing	105 hours

Capacity requirements		
	Toy A	*Toy B*
Pressing	1 hr.	4 hr.
Assembling	7 hr.	11 hr.
Packing	7 hr.	2 hr.

  a What do you understand by the term 'linear programming'?
  b Express the above constraints in the form of inequalities.
  c Demonstrate this problem graphically.
  d What is the optimum use of the spare capacity for the production of these toys?
  e State and explain any assumptions you have made in your answer to **d**. .

2 A company owns two mines both producing iron ore. The ore is extracted and then separated into one of three grades; low, medium and high.

  The company has a contract to supply 40 tonnes of high, 100 tonnes of medium and 120 tonnes of low grade ore per week to a smelting works. The rates of extraction and separation, in tonnes per hour, at the two mines is given in the following table:

Rate of extraction and separation		
Grade	*Mine 1*	*Mine 2*
high	1 t/hr	2 t/hr
medium	5 t/hr	2 t/hr
low	4 t/hr	3 t/hr
Running costs		
	£600 per hour	£1000 per hour

If running costs are as shown above, for what periods each week should each mine be worked so as to fulfil the contract at minimum cost?

3 a Distinguish between CPA and PERT.
  b Outline briefly the operational research approach to problem solving.
  c State and explain two circumstances in which network analysis can be used.
  d In the table are the ten activities needed to complete a civil engineering project. Draw the network for the project.
  e Calculate the earliest start time and the latest finish time for each activity.
  f What is the float for each activity?
  g Define the critical path in terms of the nodes through which it passes.
  h What is the expected duration of the project?

Activity	Must be preceded by:	Time (days)
A	–	3
B	–	8
C	–	9
D	A	8
E	B	5
F	C	5
G	E	4
H	F	5
I	D and F	7
J	G and H	6

4 The Prescot Construction Company plc is a multinational, civil engineering organisation. It has tendered £100m for a contract to develop mineral deposits in the UK. The company calculates it has a 70 per cent chance of winning the contract. If it fails to win the contract it will invest its resources in an alternative project with a guaranteed profit of £50m.

If the business is successful in winning the contract it is considering developing a new mining process, the result of research by its R & D department. The alternatives to this are using existing methods, which are not as efficient as the new process, or subcontracting the work to other businesses.

The expected outcomes are as follows:

	Outcomes	Probability	Profit (£m)
Develop new process			
	Success	.40	700
	Moderate	.50	400
	Failure	.10	−100
Use existing process			
	Success	.60	400
	Moderate	.20	200
	Failure	.20	−30
Subcontract			
	Success	1.00	300

a On the basis of the information given above, construct a decision tree for this problem.
b What course of action should the business take? Give reasons for your answer.

Activities

1 With the co-operation of a small business (a craft workshop would be ideal), devise a linear programming model to determine the allocation of its resources between product lines. Make a careful note of any problems you experienced, for example in determining the constraints. Why did you experience these problems? What decisions did you take? On what assumptions did you make these decisions?

2 Design a questionnaire to be distributed to fifty local businesses. The purpose of the questionnaire is to discover which businesses regularly use operational research techniques, and for what purpose. You should consider the type of business you would include in your survey and why; the techniques you are interested in and the reasons for the use of operational research.

Essays

1 What is operational research? Comment on the use of operational research techniques as an aid to decision making and control in enterprises.

2 'The value of operational research techniques is limited by the accuracy of the information on which they are based.' To what extent do you agree with this statement?

3 What do you understand by the term 'critical path analysis'? Outline the main methods used and comment on their use in project control.

4 Define the term 'linear programming'. Examine critically its uses in a business organisation.

5 Comment on the view that the use of operational research techniques in a business enterprise can contribute to information overload.

Part 3 Business in society

17 Business and the economy

When you have studied this chapter you should be able to:

☐ Understand what is meant by the term 'the level of economic activity'.

☐ Identify the major elements of a simple economic system.

☐ Define and identify injections and withdrawals.

☐ Appreciate the impact of changes in injections and withdrawals on the business community.

☐ Outline the factors contributing to inflation.

☐ Identify the effects of inflation on business.

☐ Describe the balance of payments.

☐ Identify the major international agencies regulating foreign trade.

☐ Appreciate the role of business and government in promoting economic growth.

☐ State the economic objectives of government.

☐ Outline policies used by governments in attempting to achieve these objectives.

☐ Appreciate the impact of these policies on the business community.

In Chapter 2 ('The business as a system') we examined the business community as part of the economic system of the UK. Now we will explore this idea further by concentrating on the impact on business of a change in the behaviour of the economic system and the possible effects of governmental attempts to control the system. To simplify a very complex pattern of relationships we will divide the chapter into the following parts:

☐ the level of economic activity.

☐ changes in the value of the currency both within the country and in the world.

☐ the competitive position of the country in relation to the rest of the world.

☐ improvement in the material standard of living within the country and the rest of the world.

These aspects of an economy are interdependent. Rapid inflation can change the overall competitiveness of British goods against their international competition, and make it more difficult for British exports. This in turn can lead to higher levels of unemployment. This position is likely to be made worse if inflation causes cash flow difficulties for businesses leading to an increase in the number of bankruptcies and company liquidations.

It is important to remember that this is an overall view of the way in which the economy can affect business. The theory on which it is based is still a matter of debate amongst economists. The emphasis therefore will be on what *might* happen in certain circumstances, rather than what *will* happen. A great deal will depend on how the rest of the system reacts and, as that will depend on the decisions people make, it is likely that the response to the situation will change over time. These decisions will have ideological, social and political dimensions as well as reasons that could be considered purely economic. Some of these influences have been considered in Chapter 12 ('People and business') and will be further developed in Chapter 18 ('Business and society).

The level of economic activity

At any given time a community will possess a finite number of resources with which to produce the goods and services it needs. If the people in that community are to enjoy the best possible standard of living that the resources can produce then *all* the resources must be used as *efficiently* as possible – that is the highest possible output must be obtained from the lowest possible input.

When some of the resources in an economy are not active, i.e. not employed, then *unemployment* is said to exist. When resources are employed but not as fully as possible, we speak of *underemployment*. When all resources are fully and efficiently employed the economy is said to be enjoying *full employment*.

None of the terms defined in the previous paragraph are absolutes. They are all open to debate and, on occasions, acrimonious political argument. In a market economy employment statistics will always show some people as unemployed. Employment statistics are based on the number of people registering for work. Even in a booming economy there will be people registering as unemployed while they change jobs, and other people who have a limited choice of the work they can do through mental or physical disability.

Full employment in statistical terms can disguise underemployment. Businesses might continue to employ people they see as key workers when demand for their products drops, to avoid the costs involved in recruitment. This will be a short-term measure but will lead to a time lag between the onset of a *recession* (a general decline in the demand for goods, in profits and in investment) and the resulting unemployment. This time lag can be lengthened by employment protection legislation and trade union activity.

Some economists (and politicians who agree with their theories) argue that it is impossible for an economy to work efficiently if there are vacancies for everybody who wants to work. To them full employment is that level of employment at which the economy works most efficiently with, perhaps 5 per cent unemployed, compared with the levels of 1 per cent and 1.5 per cent that were achieved in the late 1950s and 1960s. In contrast to this view other politicians argue that people have a right to work and jobs should be created in sufficient numbers for everybody who wants one.

At any particular instant, there will not be complete agreement on either the level of economic activity that is being achieved – criticism of the statistical methods of the government – or on the level that is considered desirable. There may, however, be consensus that the level of activity is generally too high or too low. It is the causes and consequences of this general situation with which we will be concerned for the rest of this section.

A simple model of the economy

There are many small, rural communities in the world that are virtually self-sufficient. People grow the crops and gather the wild produce of the surrounding countryside to provide themselves with the basic necessities of food, clothing and shelter. We can classify these activities into the *producers* of goods and services (*businesses*) and the *users* of goods and services (*households*), although the activities themselves may be carried on by the same people in the same building. A father and son working as glove-makers in a mediaeval town would have a workshop within the family home. As members of that household they would use the goods and services provided by their own business and other businesses for which they would pay. Also as members of the household they would sell their services as glove-makers to the business for which they would receive payment. This relationship is presented more generally in Figure 17.1.

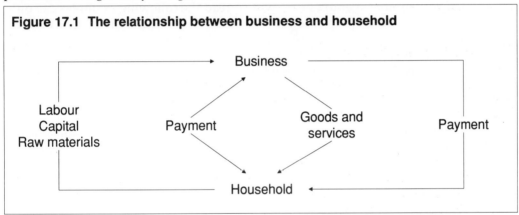

Figure 17.1 The relationship between business and household

Provided all the goods and services produced are bought and all the money received by households is spent then the level of activity in this economy will stay the same over time. We say that it is in *equilibrium*. Of course, not everybody might be involved in this economy. Equilibrium does not necessarily mean that there is full employment, only that the level of economic activity remains the same. If the level of activity in this simple economy is to change then there must either be an increase in the resources available to it, that is an *injection* into the economy; or a decrease in the resources available to it, that is a *withdrawal* from the economy.

The simple economy has served its purpose in establishing the basic relationship between households and business. In examining injections and withdrawals we will be concerned with more complex economic systems.

SELF ASSESSMENT

1 Distinguish between unemployment and underemployment.
2 Explain simply how one person can be a producer, a consumer and contribute towards government policy.
3 Give two reasons why employers hesitate to reduce the workforce at the start of a recession.
4 Explain, with the aid of diagrams, why reducing the level of unemployment benefits could lead to an apparent fall in the number of unemployed.
5 Distinguish between injections and withdrawals.

What are injections?

Injection is an economic term used to describe a flow of resources into an economic system. All injections fall into one of the following categories:

Government expenditure

Central and local government spend money on the provision of the goods and services to which they have a political commitment. Some of this money is spent directly. The maintenance of a civil and local government service requires the purchase of paper and office equipment as well as the purchase or lease of buildings. In this area the government is also a major employer of labour with a wide variety of skills. Central and local government both have responsibilities for the provision of health and education services as well as the maintenance of the infrastructure of the community – roads for example. Because the influence of government spending is so widespread the following examples can only indicate the possible effects of expansion or contraction on different sections of the business community.

1   The construction industry is very dependent on government spending. Most major civil engineering enterprises need some financial support from government, e.g. a projected river barrage on a tidal estuary to generate electricity using hydro-electric power. It has been estimated that the market for privately owned housing is nearing saturation point and therefore any further expansion in house-building will be in the public sector. Expansions in education and health services will also affect the construction industry.

2   Increased spending on social security is likely to benefit those businesses which provide low cost goods and services for low income groups. Businesses providing goods and services that might be classified as luxuries could also benefit. Renting a colour television and a video recorder provides cheap entertainment for a family that people enjoying a higher income and therefore a wider range of options might forego.

3   Spending on scientific research creates jobs for scientists and demand for equipment. Indirectly it lowers the production costs of business and makes them more competitive by providing them with the expensive research, essential if they are to develop new products.

4   All government spending provides additional demand for businesses that service the main industries involved. Publishers, paper makers, the manufacturers of computers, cars, steel, electrical equipment, radars, aeroplanes, furniture and food will experience an increase or decrease in demand depending upon the level of government spending. The importance for an individual business will depend on its own degree of competitiveness in its own market.

Indirectly, and subject to the same market constraints, the suppliers of consumer goods will experience a change in demand. The market constraints are important and you should remember them. Later in this section we will be discussing imports. When imported goods are more competitive than domestically produced goods, or when the home market cannot supply the goods and services people want to buy, any benefits from an increase in government spending will be withdrawn from the domestic economy and become an injection into another economy as an import.

In general government spending tends to be labour intensive (think of activities such as teaching, nursing, maintenance, cleaning and construction). Wages per individual tend to be low but the total wage bill is high and is quickly converted into spending power. This is useful in a stagnant economy with a low level of costs and little international trade because any increase will fuel the domestic economy comparatively rapidly. In an economy with a high level of foreign trade, a level of inflation greater than that of its major international competitors and an aggressive international market this may not be a valid option to boost the level of activity in an economy. Why this should be the case will become clearer as you work through this chapter.

Exports

Exports act as injections because home produced goods and services are sold abroad for their costs plus profit and provide an increase in the wealth of the economy. When a country exports it can benefit from specialisation. The UK can only grow oranges at an enormous cost compared with countries with a more favourable climate. In the eighteenth and nineteenth centuries superb – and enormously expensive – hothouses provided the rich with semi-tropical fruits. The expansion of trade has made a much wider range of fruit and vegetables available to a greater proportion of the population. On the simplest level foreign trade is a matter of exchanging what you have for what you want. Without foreign trade the potential standard of living would be lower.

The West German economy expanded rapidly in the years following the Second World War, in part because of the favourable conditions which existed in international markets for its exports. This *export led* growth encouraged investment in exporting industries and fuelled demand in the domestic market thus encouraging further investment.

The import and export of goods (*visibles*) and services (*invisibles*) depends, in a free market economy, on the buying decisions of individuals and organisations. To export, a business must be able to compete with foreign businesses in terms of cost, quality and service. The overall exports of a country will depend on the general level of competitiveness of individual businesses. Governments attempt to help in this by providing *subsidies* to exporting firms. A subsidy is a payment made to a business to prevent an increase in price (an example of government expenditure) or to help businesses lower prices which are seen as uncompetitive. Subsidies may be made to businesses operating in the domestic as well as foreign markets. Subsidies to exporting businesses can cause friction between governments. Claims that goods are being sold abroad at less than cost price (*dumping*) may lead to the imposition of trading restrictions on imported goods by another country and the loss to the exporting country of that foreign market.

Exporting businesses bring more money into the economy which generates further income and demand in the home market for other goods and services. For the moment this statement is satisfactory but when we look at international trade and the balance of payments in more detail the complexities of the situation will become more apparent.

Investment

Investment is the organisation of resources saved from a previous time period to produce *capital goods*. These are goods which will be used for the production of other goods and services for sale. Some of this investment will be to replace worn out or obsolete equipment. Other investment will be to extend the range of activity of a business.

Replacement investment alone will maintain the existing level of economic activity. Investment in addition to this (*net investment*) will raise the level of economic activity in a country by creating additional demand for capital equipment and labour.

Business managers, as you should by now be aware, are not inclined to invest unless they can see the possibility of profit. The level of net investment in a country will depend upon the way in which the majority of owners and managers are confident that there will be a sustained and effective demand for the goods and services they produce. The total level of net investment will therefore depend on the investment decisions made by individual businesses using the criteria discussed in Chapter 7 ('Finance').

SELF ASSESSMENT

1 Classify each of the following under the main groups of injections:
   a The Ministry of Defence pays for a new submarine built by a British shipyard.
   b A private company builds a new plant.
   c A West German business buys a consignment of components from a British firm.
2 What effect does an increase in injections have on the level of economic activity in a country assuming all other things stay equal?
3 List three ways in which government spending could affect a business in:
   a the primary sector.
   b the secondary sector.
   c the tertiary sector.
4 Explain why dumping is considered an unfair trading practice.
5 Give two ways in which the government can attempt to influence business decisions in order to increase the level of exports and investment in a country.

What are withdrawals?

Withdrawals are the opposite of injections and the terms used reflect this.

Taxation

Taxes are payments made to central and local government in order to finance the activities of government on behalf of the community. Money is therefore withdrawn from the circular flow of income by this activity.

It is necessary to understand the different ways in which taxes are levied in order to appreciate their potential impact on business. It is also important to remember that this is an area of some controversy.

1 *Direct taxes*   are paid directly to government by individuals or organisations. These include income tax and corporation tax.

2 *Indirect taxes*   such as value added tax (VAT), import duties and excise duties on alcohol, tobacco and oil are paid on the quantity or value of the goods and services being taxed.

3 *Progressive taxation*   is a tax system designed to take a greater *proportion* of the income of the rich compared with the income of the poor. Income tax is designed as a progressive tax.

4 *Regressive taxation*   takes the same amount of tax from everybody, irrespective of ability to pay. Regressive taxes are usually levied on goods and services when people can choose whether or not to pay the tax. If the tax payable on a washing machine is £100 the person with an income of £8000 per year will pay the same tax as the person with an income of £40 000 per year, though the sacrifice of the person on the lower income will be greater. The community charge is an example of a regressive tax.

Some of the effects of taxation on business are listed below:

1   It has been argued that a high rate of progressive taxation on income can act as a disincentive to work and risk taking. People on a high income with a wide range of leisure activities open to them may opt for leisure rather than work when taxation rates are high. For example a person whose union has negotiated a productivity agreement might find that she/he can earn enough money to satisfy her/his needs by working a four day week. By working a fifth day she/he could earn an extra £100, but 50 per cent of this would disappear in tax. She/He makes a personal decision that the extra £50 is not worth the sacrifice of leisure. This type of absenteeism could cause problems in production organisation for a business, reduce production levels and increase costs.

   The argument against this is the fact that money can act as a motivator. People will tend to work to a given 'take home' pay. When increased taxation reduces the amount of money they have to spend then they will look for opportunities to increase their income. High taxation can be seen as an incentive to work.

   A business will take corporation tax into account when estimating the profitability of an investment project. High taxation will reduce the Net Present Value of cash flows. The greater the perceived risk of the investment the greater the disincentive effect of high taxation.

2   High levels of direct taxation can also affect the demand for the products of some businesses. Luxury goods with a high income elasticity of demand will suffer from a sharp increase in the level of income tax and benefit from a fall.

3   A tax on a good or service can be seen as an increase in the production costs of the business. It therefore has the effect of shifting the supply curve of the industry to the left.

Figure 17.2 shows the effect of the same tax on an industry but with different demand curves. In Figure 17.2a the demand curve is relatively inelastic. Most of the tax is passed on to the consumer in terms of higher prices. In Figure 17.2b the relatively elastic demand curve forces the industry to absorb most of the tax itself. A business operating in the situation illustrated in Figure 17.2b might be forced out of business by the tax if its profit margins were already low. In both cases the business will have to absorb some of the tax which will lower profit margins and, possibly, be taken into account when considering future investment plans.

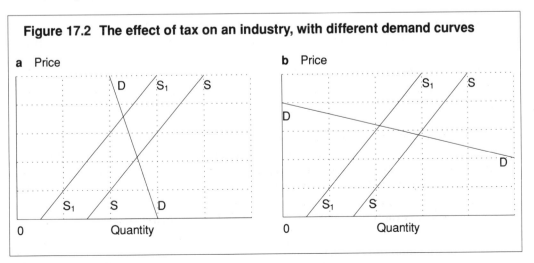

Figure 17.2 The effect of tax on an industry, with different demand curves

a   Price

b   Price

Imports and savings

Imports take money out of the economy. They compete with domestically produced goods and services. Saving is the result of a decision of a person or an organisation not to consume or invest. In defining injections and withdrawals there are two things you should remember.

1   A flow of money into and out of the economy is defined as an injection or withdrawal depending on its immediate effect. Thus taxation is defined as a withdrawal. The money does not become an injection until the government makes a decision to spend it. Saving is a withdrawal although businesses may decide to use their savings for purposes of investment. It is possible for a government to decide *not* to use all its tax revenue, in which case the level of activity in the country will fall *unless* there is a corresponding increase in the amount of private investment undertaken and/or in the level of exports.

2   Government expenditure and taxation have been given more attention in this section than the other injections and withdrawals. This does not mean they are more important. The decision to save is implicit in all purchasing and investment decisions made by individuals and organisations. Chapters 7 ('Finance') and 8 ('Marketing') indicated the factors which affect the consumption, saving and investment decisions of individuals. Chapter 7 also described the way in which savings can be made available for investment through the workings of the money and capital markets.

Exports and imports will be analysed in more detail later in this chapter. The emphasis on government spending and taxation here is a matter of convenience rather than principle.

Summary of the circular flow of income

☐   When injections and withdrawals are exactly the same over a period of time the level of activity in an economy will not change.

☐   An increase in the level of injections and/or a decrease in the level of withdrawals will lead to an increase in the level of activity in the economy.

☐   A decrease in the level of injections and/or an increase in the level of withdrawals will lead to a decrease in the level of activity in the economy.

SELF ASSESSMENT

1   What are the major withdrawals? Why are they given this name?
2   Outline one way in which the following tax policies could affect the business community. What type of business would be most affected? Give a brief explanation of your answers.
   a   A reduction in the basic rate of income tax.
   b   Exemption from corporation tax for businesses investing a given proportion of profit.
   c   The extension of VAT to all goods and services.
   d   A shift from progressive to a regressive taxation policy.
3   Imports withdraw money from the economy. Give two reasons why they are necessary.
4   Why is the decision to save or not to save implicit in all purchasing decisions?
5   Assuming all other things stay equal, what is the likely effect on a business producing consumer goods of the following:

   a   An increase in imports?
   b   A decrease in the rate of VAT?
   c   An increase in government spending on education and the health service?
   d   Subsidies for exporters?
   e   A government drive to increase saving?

Changes in the value of money

The value of a currency can change internally by inflation or deflation and externally by appreciation or depreciation. The internal and external values of a currency are interrelated.

Inflation

Inflation is a *general* rise in the price level of a country and a fall in the purchasing power of the unit of currency. A rise in the prices of one industry does not constitute inflation, although it may contribute to it, particularly if the industry is an important one in the economy.

The precise causes of inflation are a matter for debate. The list that follows states the potential causes of inflation without attempting to give any weight to their significance. To a business manager the most important thing about inflation is that it exists.

1   *Cost push inflation* is the result of a general rise in the costs of production. A general increase in wage levels in excess of increases in productivity, an increase in commodity prices on the world market and an increase in the cost of capital as a result of high interest rates in the international money markets could fuel inflationary pressures in an economy.

2   *Demand pull inflation* is the result of an excess of demand over production.

The *inflationary spiral* is the term used to describe the relationship between cost push and demand pull inflation. Let us assume that in a particular year a number of trade unions in key industries reach agreement with their managements on wage increases greater than the agreed increases in productivity. The increase in production costs resulting from this would be passed on to the customer at least to some degree. Individuals would begin to find their income inadequate to purchase the goods and services they saw as essential to their lifestyle. This in turn would lead other unions to press for wage claims to keep up with the increase in the cost of living. If these wage claims were not linked to productivity agreements this would result in a further increase in costs. Competitiveness between groups of workers could make the situation worse. The desire to preserve wage differentials between skilled and unskilled workers and the attitude of 'If they can get it why can't we?' between workers in different industries can add to the inflationary effect. At the same time the increase in purchasing power – which is not accompanied by an increase in the quantity of goods available – leads to the situation of 'too much money chasing too few goods'. Businesses find that even if their costs have increased so also has the price people are prepared to pay for the goods they produce. Soon the gains from the original round of pay bargaining are lost and the process begins again.

It is unfair to place all the blame for inflation on the bargaining process between trade unions and employers. In 1960 the Organisation of Petroleum Exporting Countries (OPEC) was established by the major oil producing and exporting countries accounting for approximately 90 per cent of the world's oil exports; a situation which gave OPEC considerable market power. Oil was cheap during the 1950s and 1960s and is an important industrial commodity – not only as a source of fuel (electricity generation and smelting) and power (petrol) but also as a raw material in industries as diverse as plastics and synthetic fibres. In 1973 the member countries of OPEC agreed on a massive increase in oil prices supported by agreements to limit output. The reliance of industry upon oil meant the effects were immediate, dramatic and inflationary in the industrialised economies.

Governments can also cause inflation. A government has the ability to create money. An increase in the money supply of an economy will increase the overall level of demand but will not necessarily lead to an increase in levels of production. A classic case of too much money chasing too few goods.

Inflation and business

Some factors in this relationship are examined below.

1   Temporary demand inflation can persuade businesses to invest. Prices rise and money profits rise with them. Investment increases productivity and sustains demand so the inflationary spiral is wiped out. This is possible after a period of stable prices. Economists argue that once inflation is accepted as part of the economic system individuals and organisations budget for sustained inflation. Wage claims are made, not on the present level of inflation, but on what it is expected to be. If the rate of inflation has been rising at 1 per cent per annum for five years then wage claims will be made on a minimum of the existing rate of inflation plus 1 per cent.

2   Inflation can cause problems in the accounting procedures of a business. When assets are valued at historic cost and profits at present cost, the profits, and therefore the taxation position of a business, can be overstated. The introduction of current cost accounting was an attempt to rectify this situation.

3   When inflation is constantly eroding the value of incomes and when a significant proportion of taxation is based on income, the purchasing power of consumers can be eroded in spite of major income rises. A wage increase of 20 per cent might compensate for inflation but if it takes people into a higher tax bracket it could still reduce their purchasing power. For people on low incomes this is further complicated by the loss of government transfer payments. A married person with a family but on a low income, who then receives a substantial rise in pay, might still find it inadequate to support their previous purchasing pattern if it takes them into the tax paying category and they lose state benefits. This *poverty trap* will also have implications for businesses selling to this section of the population. The importance of this will depend on the number of people involved and the total value of the purchases.

4   Inflation increases the importance of the management of working capital. Borrowing becomes more expensive, and credit extended to customers loses money value so it is in the interest of customers to delay payment and stocks valued at purchase price have to be replaced at a higher price.

5   Persistent inflation can erode business confidence. When faced with an investment decision a business manager might decide not to reinvest, particularly if money markets are offering a high rate of interest. The temptation might be to invest in capital intensive technology. A widespread trend in this direction can lead to unemployment, a decline in demand and a decrease in the level of economic activity within the economy.

Deflation

Deflation is a reduction in the general level of prices. The effect on business will depend upon whether costs fall more rapidly than the price of the products. A rapid reduction in essential commodity prices can lead to higher profits if market prices for finished goods are maintained.

Deflation may also come about as a result in the decline of the general level of economic activity in the country. Higher levels of unemployment will lead to a reduction in the demand for goods and services and therefore for the factors of production used to make the goods and provide the services. This may be the result of deliberate policies on the part of a government to counteract inflation.

Inflation and foreign trade

Inflation within an economy will change the pattern of competition as some sectors of the economy will be affected more than others and some businesses will be more efficient in responding to the problems caused by inflation than others. If the inflation rate within a country is high compared with that of its major foreign competitors, this can have serious consequences for the economy, making the goods and services it produces more expensive than foreign goods and services both in the domestic economy and in world markets.

The exchange rate

The exchange rate is the value of a currency measured in terms of other currencies. On one particular date in 1990 the value of the £ sterling expressed in terms of foreign currencies was:

France	9.94 francs
Germany	2.97 Deutschmarks
United States	1.90 dollars

A good produced in England for £1 – assuming no other costs, for example transport or import duties – would sell in France for 9.94 francs, in Germany for 2.97 DM and so on. The reverse would also be true. West German products produced at a cost of 2.97 DM would sell in this country for £1.

The exchange rate of a currency can be seen as its price, and this is determined by he interaction of the supply and demand for that currency. When the value of sterling rises the value of other currencies in relation to it will fall. £1 sterling might then be exchanged for 5 DM. You need more of other currencies to 'buy' £1. When the value of sterling falls fewer units of another currency will be needed to buy £1.

A rise in the value of sterling will make British goods less competitive in West Germany and any other country whose currency has fallen in value compared with sterling. Goods which had been sold in West Germany for 2.97 DM will now cost 5 DM. On the other hand West German goods sold in the United Kingdom will be cheaper and more competitive with home produced goods.

Inflation can have the same effect of making British goods more expensive abroad. If we assume that the price of British goods doubles as the result of inflation, the exchange rate stays the same and West Germany experiences no inflation then the real price of British goods being sold on the West German market will double. The prices of West German producers will be more competitive.

In theory the fact that British goods are less competitive in international markets should shift the demand curve for sterling to the left and lead to a fall in the value of sterling until the effects of inflation have been wiped out. In practice other variables come into play that stop this happening.

Inflation and movements in international currency markets are not the only things that make British produced goods uncompetitive on world markets. Design, efficiency and service will play their part. Inflation and currency movements will always remain important.

Changes in the exchange rate and the effects of inflation will not have a uniform impact on all sectors of the British economy. When the pound is weak exporting firms may have a competitive advantage but businesses which rely on imports for raw materials or components will find their costs rising. This may make them less competitive in both domestic and foreign markets. The final impact on an individual business may well depend upon the flexibility of its response in terms of production and marketing.

SELF ASSESSMENT

1 Distinguish between inflation and deflation.
2 The level of inflation in an economy is 10 per cent. A union puts in a wage claim for 12.5 per cent. Explain the reasoning behind this. What are the implications for the businesses concerned?
3 During a period of inflation a business follows a policy of paying creditors as late as possible but keeps a very close check on its debtors. Explain the reasoning behind this policy.
4 Give three ways in which deflation will affect a business.
5 In an effort to correct a deficit balance of payments a government increases the rate of interest of an economy. Explain how this policy will affect:
   a The exchange rate.
   b The level of inflation.
   c The demand for goods and services.

Foreign trade

In the previous section we looked at the way in which changes in the value of the exchange rate and inflation could affect the competitiveness of British business. In this section we will look at the way in which the overall trading position of a country can affect the general level of prosperity of the country. We will also examine some of the organisations which exist to facilitate and regulate trade between countries.

The balance of payments

The balance of payments is a summary of all transactions between individuals and organisations in the UK and the rest of the world. It is compiled from information provided by participating organisations. Like the accounts of a business the information needs to be compared over time and interpreted, to be valuable.

It is divided into the following sections:

1 *The balance of trade,* which is concerned with the import and export of goods (*visibles*).

2 *The balance of trade on current account,* which includes the balance of trade and invisibles, that is income received from or paid for the selling of services e.g. tourism, banking, insurance, shipping and royalties from books, films and patents.

3 *The capital account,* which is concerned with the movement of private and government investment capital into and out of the United Kingdom.

A surplus on the balance of payments is an injection of income into the economy. When the level of economic activity is low this can lead to an increase in employment – export led growth. If the economy is already at or approaching full employment a surplus on foreign trade, by adding more income, can lead to demand pull inflation.

A surplus on the balance of payments also means that the demand for sterling is high in relation to available supply and the value of the pound will rise.

An overall deficit on the balance of payments means that income has been withdrawn from the economy, which can lower the level of economic activity and weaken the pound.

The International Monetary Fund (IMF)

Trade between nations is essential in the modern world economy. It allows specialisation, larger markets with the advantages of economies of scale, and increases the range of goods and services available to the consumer. As in all free economies not all countries are equally competitive and a pattern has emerged in which some countries are more likely to have a surplus or a deficit on the balance of payments than others.

Faced with a consistent pattern of deficits it is tempting for a government to try to export the unemployment thus caused by imposing duties and quotas on imported goods. This will have varying effects on the business community. Consumers might still prefer to buy imported goods regardless of the increase in price (inelastic demand) and so the benefit to home producers might be negligible. On the other hand efficient exporters might find their overseas markets blocked by the retaliatory measures of foreign governments. Unemployment might be shifted from one sector of the economy to another and, if the trend towards protectionism becomes worldwide, the world economy is likely to move into recession. That is the overall level of world economic activity would fall and the less competitive nations would be the worst affected.

This pattern of protectionism did emerge during the 1930s and contributed to the economic problems of the time. To prevent the same thing happening after the Second World War the Bretton Woods Agreement established the International Monetary Fund. Member countries contribute money to the fund, the precise amount depending on the importance of foreign trade to the economy of the country. Countries with a temporary balance of payments problem can draw on the fund to cover their debts and are thus enabled to go on trading. Conditions of the loan vary, but usually include a requirement for the country to deflate its economy. A lowering of the level of injections or a rise in the level of withdrawals will reduce the level of economic activity and so reduce the demand for imports of both raw materials or components and finished goods. It is rather like a bank manager telling an overdrawn client to cut down spending.

John Maynard Keynes, a British economist involved in the conference that led to the Bretton Woods Agreement, wanted a complementary system of penalties to apply to countries which were consistently in surplus, arguing that they, too, contributed to international payments problems, but this was not adopted.

The General Agreement on Tariffs and Trade (GATT)

This was established in 1947 with the aim of promoting world trade by reducing tariffs and, through negotiation, the removal of non-tariff barriers to trade such as quotas and subsidies.

There are a large number of organisations that co-ordinate the movement of funds between countries and contribute to research into the behaviour of international markets. The IMF and GATT have been included here because they are most likely to have a direct impact on business. Organisations such as the World Bank and the Organisation for

Economic Co-operation and Development (OECD) can help expand world markets by investing in countries and, by raising the standard of living, increase the total demand for goods in the world.

The European Community (EC)

The EC was established by the Treaty of Rome in 1957. At that time there were only six members – France, West Germany, Italy, the Netherlands, Belgium and Luxembourg – but since then the number has expanded to include the United Kingdom, Eire, Denmark, Greece, Spain and Portugal. Political union between member states is a long-term objective of the EC but the vast majority of its activity is commercial.

The objectives of the EC can be given as:

1   To provide a large common market by removing restrictions on trade, including tariffs, quotas, subsidies and restrictions on the movement of labour and capital. The existence of this market would provide the incentive for specialisation and the growth of large-scale businesses and the benefits of economies of scale.

2   To co-ordinate national policies in agriculture, transport and industry.

3   To standardise commercial legislation regulating such things as monopoly.

By far the greatest proportion of the funds available to the EC are absorbed by the Common Agricultural Policy and for this reason we shall use it as an example of the way in which the EC can affect British business.

The Common Agricultural Policy (CAP)

The Common Agricultural Policy works to support agriculture in two main areas:

☐   by supporting the income of farmers through intervention in the market.

☐   by improving agricultural productivity by the availability of improvement grants.

Target prices are set for a range of product including cereals, milk and beef. Should the market price start to fall below these target prices the Community buys up the surplus and stores it against future scarcity. At the same time European prices are protected against the effect of low world prices by the imposition of import levies which raises the price of imported foods to slightly above the target price.

If you study Figure 17.3, you can see that the Community imposes a minimum price on agricultural products. This leads to an excess of supply over demand. It is this excess which is bought up by the Community at the target price.

The stocks accumulated by the Community have given rise to 'milk lakes' and 'butter mountains' and this in turn has led to considerable criticism of the CAP for waste of resources.

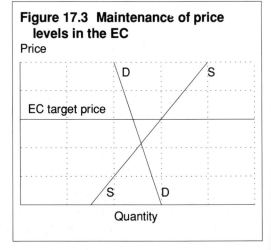

Figure 17.3 Maintenance of price levels in the EC

The potential impact on business varies according to the type of business and the geographical area in which it operates.

1 Guaranteed prices above the level of the world market mean that farmers receive higher incomes and this improves the general prosperity of rural areas and the businesses which serve them.

2 Improvement grants generate demand for farming equipment and so benefit businesses supplying farmers.

3 Changes in the EC support system, for example reducing the quotas of milk farmers are allowed to produce, can lead to changes in the product mix of farming. When this happens suddenly it can cause investment problems, particularly for the small farmer.

4 It is argued that the prices set by the EC discourage efficiency in the farming industry. Farmers produce the crops that will give them a maximum income rather than the crops to which the land and climate is most suited.

5 EC policy results in higher food prices. This means that people have less money to spend on other goods and services. This is particularly true of lower income groups who spend a higher proportion of their income on food than other people.

SELF ASSESSMENT

1 Give three international organisations whose policies could have an effect on British industry.
2 State three ways in which membership of the EC affects British business.
3 Outline three reasons why the management of a business manufacturing consumer durables would be concerned if there was a persistent balance of payments deficit:
   a in the country in which it is located.
   b in a country to which it exports.
4 In what way does a country with a persistent balance of payments surplus contribute to problems in world trade?
5 In what ways can GATT lead to an increase in world prosperity?

Economic growth

The term 'economic growth' describes a situation in which the standard of living in a society improves over time. Net investment has an important part to play in this but there are other factors which are less easy to quantify. Trade unions, poor management, inflexible institutions and inadequate education and training have all, at one time or another, been set up as scapegoats for Britain's relatively low rate of growth compared with its international competitors. As usual, there is no easy answer.

Business and economic growth

Businesses benefit from a general growth in the economy in terms of increased demand for their products and higher profits. Sustained growth is also conducive to the adoption of long term planning strategies and, therefore, the ability of the business community to ride out short-term variations in the level of growth. It can also lead to complacency and a lack of preparation for fluctuations in the level of economic activity. Figure 17.4 illustrates some of the ways in which the business community can respond to a period of economic growth.

Different economies experience different rates of growth. Figure 17.5 shows the internal and external constraints on achieving a high rate of growth.

Figure 17.4 Responses to economic growth

The positive approach	Growth	The negative approach
Increase training		Increase overtime working
Improve working conditions		Introduce or extend shift working
Extend product range		Rely on increased spending power to improve profits
Increase advertising		
Spend money on 'image'		No excessive investment in plant
Increase capital investment		No additional investment in new technology
Improve productivity		
Extend production facilities		Paddle on as always!
Increase spending on R & D		

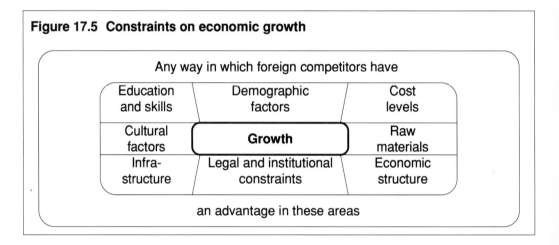

Figure 17.5 Constraints on economic growth

Any way in which foreign competitors have

Education and skills	Demographic factors	Cost levels
Cultural factors	**Growth**	Raw materials
Infra-structure	Legal and institutional constraints	Economic structure

an advantage in these areas

The multiplier effect

So far we have treated the relationship between an increase in the level of injections or a decrease in the level of withdrawals as having a once and for all effect on the general level of economic activity. An injection into the economy is likely to encourage further injections. Take as an example a small town with a limited range of shops designed to appeal to and serve the local community. The local economy has an unemployment level of 15 per cent. A factory is built on the edge of the town employing local labour and external capital. There is an *injection* into the economy. Incomes rise, business improves and local shopkeepers are persuaded to expand using hitherto unused capital. They, in turn, employ more people. Other inhabitants in the area begin to see business opportunities. A restaurant is opened, new houses built and people offering professional services such as accountancy and law begin to move in bringing their own injections of capital with them. That initial injection might lead to double or treble its amount in terms of increased income. The ratio between the initial capital injection and the final level of income is known as the *multiplier*. So if £1m leads to £2m increased income the multiplier is said to be 2.

Of course it is not as simple as that. If a person earns an extra £30 a week as a result of the expansion in the local economy not all of that money will go back into the economy. Some of it will be saved, some will be spent on imported goods and some will be withdrawn by taxation. The proportion of any increase in income which will be withdrawn from the economy is known as the *marginal propensity to withdraw*. It does not take much thought to see that if everybody saved all their additional income the level of economic activity would stay the same. The final multiplier effect will therefore depend on the marginal propensity to withdraw in the economy. The multiplier can be calculated as follows:

$$\frac{1}{1 - w}$$

where w is the marginal propensity to withdraw.

In a situation where a country is not competitive internationally, an increase in government spending might be siphoned out of the economy by a high marginal propensity to import.

SELF ASSESSMENT

1 Define the multiplier effect.
2 Of every extra £1 in income 40p is spent on imported goods, 20p is saved and 25p is taxed. Assuming all other things remained equal what would be the effect on national income if the government increased its expenditure by £100m?
3 State and explain three ways in which sustained growth in an economy can:
   a benefit
   b cause problems for
   the business community.
4 Give three external factors which can limit the growth of an economy.
5 Explain why a low level of investment in training will limit the scope of an economy to grow.

Managing the economy

Since 1945 it has generally been accepted that the major economic objectives of government are:

☐ the maintenance of full employment;

☐ the maintenance of a stable currency;

☐ a sound balance of payments;

☐ economic growth.

Employment

Although these are the main objectives of any government, the priority given to any one of them will depend on the economic environment in which the government is operating, the political philosophy of the government and the relative importance given to the achievement of an objective. The methods used to achieve these objectives will also vary according to the economic environment and economic analysis of the way in which the economy behaves.

It has already been pointed out that the term 'full employment' can be interpreted in a variety of ways, and the official level of unemployment depends on the number of people who register for work. Many people may be actively looking for work but fail to register because they may not be eligible for unemployment benefit. On the other hand there are people registered for work who have only a limited number of jobs available to them. Whatever the level of employment the government is aiming for, the methods used to achieve it must relate to the causes of unemployment. At any one time the number of people unemployed will be caused by a combination of the following factors:

- frictional unemployment.

- structural unemployment.

- technological unemployment.

- cyclical unemployment.

Frictional unemployment

This describes the period of unemployment that occurs in the interval between leaving one job and finding another. Frictional unemployment can be made worse by geographical immobility. There may be an excess of vacancies over applicants in one part of the country and a reverse situation in another part of the country. Lack of information can also worsen the problem. Governments can help reduce frictional unemployment by improving information about job vacancies through the Careers Service and Job Centres, by giving people financial incentives to move from one part of the country to another, and by retraining schemes. Successful government policies to combat frictional unemployment can reduce the recruitment costs of business, reduce training costs and limit the loss of production through recruitment problems.

Structural unemployment

This describes unemployment which arises out of a change in the industrial structure of the country – the decline in importance of an industry for example. Steel, shipbuilding and textiles have all declined in importance over the past thirty years in the British economy. When the decline is relatively slow the unemployment caused may be described as frictional. Rapid decline and a lack of other job opportunities can contribute to *regional unemployment*, a situation in which one part of the country has consistently higher levels of unemployment than the national average. Regional and structural unemployment are not synonymous – there may be political and geographical considerations contributing to regional unemployment in addition to the decline of industries – but there is a high level of correlation between the two.

Government (including local government) may attempt to combat structural unemployment by giving grants, low interest loans, and exemption from rates to businesses establishing themselves in areas with a high level of structural unemployment combined with regulations to discourage or forbid industries to establish themselves in areas with an excess of vacancies over applicants. Such policy measures can reduce the costs of the businesses concerned but also increase their costs if the desired locations are too far from the market and the transport system is inadequate. An important part of policy then is to improve the infrastructure of the region concerned. For example a multinational company supplying the car industry with equipment was refused permission to open a factory in the Midlands in the early 1960s. Instead it was offered an attractive financial package to locate in the north east, Merseyside, Scotland or Northern Ireland. Merseyside at that time had the largest concentration of car factories in the country outside the Midlands. The closure of another factory had released people for employment with similar skills to those required by the new firm which in turn reduced training costs. The existence of the port and rapid access to the national motorway network decided the matter as far as the company was concerned. Some people argue that incentive packages to industry to locate or relocate in depressed areas are exploited by footloose industries.

When the decline of an industry is attributed to foreign competition a government may respond by imposing import duties or quotas but this may lead to retaliation which is likely to be aimed at strong exporting industries of the country rather than the declining industry. Further international complications come from membership of GATT.

Technological unemployment

This can be the result of a switch on the part of a company to capital intensive methods of production. This may be done to avoid high labour costs, improve quality or avoid industrial disputes, or it may be the result of a radical change in the type of technology used by a society. The remedies for technological unemployment centre on retraining schemes, particularly in the latter case where businesses may be short of the required types of skills. It may also involve changes in educational policy with implications for businesses that supply this sector of the economy. It is unlikely that a major change in technology would be on a national level only. It may be taking place in response to international trends and the need to remain competitive can be a driving force in government support in this matter.

Cyclical unemployment

This derives its name from an observed tendency in industrialised economies to experience successive booms and slumps in the level of economic activity known as the *trade cycle*. Theories to explain this phenomenon are still being developed. They can be summarised as those which emphasise the importance of the total demand for goods and services in an economy, *demand deficient* unemployment, and those which emphasise the importance of *supply*.

Keynes, in his *General Theory of Employment, Interest and Money* published in 1936, gave added impetus to the demand deficient theories. He summarised, synthesised and added to the work of previous economists to suggest that unemployment was the result of a low level of demand and, in a situation where private enterprise was unable or unwilling to make good this gap, it was the responsibility of governments to do so. After the Second World War Keynesian economic theory was applied by governments and a number of standard economic policies were developed:

☐ increased government expenditure on labour intensive industries and occupations, e.g. civil engineering, which would have the added advantage of improving the infrastructure of the economy to support business activity.

☐ incentives, information and support for exporting businesses to improve the level of injections.

☐ incentives to investment for all industries in the form of tax exemptions, grants, etc.

☐ reduction in the level of taxation to increase the level of disposable income in households and generate demand for consumer goods and consumer durables.

Keynes was writing in the 1930s, which was a period of sustained deflation. The policies worked well immediately after the Second World War and led to a period of continuing growth in the western economy. Towards the end of the 1950s economists were becoming concerned about the possible results of stop–go policies. A stop–go policy implies that spending to maintain the level of employment leads to inflation, and balance of payments problems result as the level of imports rises. Within the space of a few years this would be followed by deflationary policies to correct these problems.

This could not be seen as an ideal climate for sustained business growth. The period of boom saw an increase in orders but there was little incentive for businesses to invest in new plant and equipment when they expected a government inspired recession within a few years. Instead, it was argued, the tendency was for businesses to allow their order books to lengthen, the resulting backlog helping them to ride the expected recession. This did not do a great deal for the reputation and competitiveness of British industry on international and domestic markets.

Other economists, notably Milton Friedman of the University of Chicago, expressed increasing concern about the long-term effects of these policies. *Deficit budgeting*, that is a situation in which government expenditure exceeded revenue from taxation, meant that the gap between government spending and revenue from taxation had to be financed by borrowing. When this borrowing drew on the unused savings of the private sector the problem was relatively small. Inflation would result but it would be minor and tend to be wiped out as production increased. On the other hand when government spending was financed by the creation of new money through the banking system it had an immediate effect on the economy but the inflation generated was longer term with the problems for business that we have already discussed.

The *stagflation* – a stagnant economy in terms of growth and a rising level of unemployment combined with inflation – of the late 1970s should not have happened, according to the original Keynesian model. Inflation should only occur when the economy is reaching the level of full employment and there is competition for resources. Economic opinion swung towards *monetarism*, which advocated controlling the money supply, allowing it to grow by only a sufficient amount to finance growth in the economy, and an increased emphasis on promoting supply.

This is a more sophisticated version of *Say's law* – supply creates its own demand. In the UK there was greater reliance on the working of a free market economy to promote efficiency through competitiveness, and an attempt to reduce the role of government in the management of the economy.

It is too early to draw firm conclusions concerning the success or failures of these changes in economic and political attitudes. Some consequences and implications for the business community can be observed but whether or not they will be long- or short-term trends it is impossible to say.

1   The attempts on the part of the government to control the public sector borrowing requirement (PSBR) resulted in an immediate decline in demand for those businesses which supplied the public sector.

2   An unemployment level of over 3 per cent, which some economists would argue is necessary to keep the rate of inflation low, meant an inevitable reduction in the level of actual demand for goods and services compared with the potential demand.

3   The fall in the rate of inflation from 10 per cent in 1982 to less than 5 per cent in 1986 stabilised the position of businesses in the management of cash flow. Major international competitors such as Japan and West Germany are experiencing lower rates of inflation with the consequences for British international competitiveness outlined in the section on inflation and exchange rates.

4 It is claimed that an increase in unemployment combined with legislation that limits the activities of trade unions has resulted in decreased militancy and an improvement in industrial relations.

5 Privatisation, the transfer of ownership and control of a nationalised industry from the public to the private sector and the opening to private tender of services formerly supplied by central or local government, have been pursued by the government in a belief that the introduction of market forces will improve efficiency. Critics argue that the transfer of ownership of state monopolies to the private sector will simply create private monopolies which will be less accountable for their actions. This could have important results for businesses who use their services by reducing their power.

The general thrust of government policy between 1979 and 1989 was the freeing of the economic system combined with policies to reduce the level of inflation as the prerequisites for economic growth and, therefore, long-term and stable growth in the level of employment. The one thing that can be predicted with certainty about government economic policies is that they will lead to change in the business environment – the general problems of which for the individual business manager are dealt with in the next chapter.

Inflation

Standard policies to reduce the level of inflation in an economy are directed towards the control of the money supply, a reduction in the level of injection or a rise in the level of withdrawals, and a decrease in demand. High interest rates to encourage saving also discourage investment. Increases in taxation will also reduce demand although some people argue that it is more likely to reduce savings as consumers maintain their lifestyle at the expense of savings. As a result the overall level of withdrawals may not rise by the increased rate of taxation. Controls on hire purchase and the availability of credit may be imposed to the detriment of industries the purchase of whose goods are financed in this way.

The balance of payments

Policies designed to improve a deficit balance of payments will concentrate on improving exports by subsidies, loans and services offered by the government to private business. High interest rates will also help with this by attracting foreign capital into the country and increasing the earnings of the banking and financial services sector of the economy. When import controls can bring retaliation the reduction of the level of imports can only be achieved by reducing the general level of demand in the country – so increasing unemployment.

SELF ASSESSMENT

1 Define stagflation.
2 Give one example from your own knowledge of each of the types of unemployment listed above.
3 Distinguish between structural and regional unemployment. Do they have anything in common?
4 Why are footloose industries able to exploit incentive packages to relocate in areas of high unemployment?
5 What is deficit budgeting? What effect would it have on unemployment in the short term?

Conclusion

The economy is a complex system and, like all such systems, attempts to alter the way in which it works can have unforeseen consequences. This chapter has done no more than outline the way in which the economy works.

- ☐ The balance between injections and withdrawals determines the level of economic activity.

- ☐ The working of the British economy is affected by foreign economies and international organisations of which the UK is a member.

- ☐ Government policy will determine priorities of economic objectives and this will influence the level of economic activity in the economy.

- ☐ The importance of the general state of the economy as a constraint upon the decision making processes of individual businesses.

REVIEW

1 A government wishes to raise the level of activity within the economy. The following suggestions have been made by a political adviser:
   - ☐ a reduction in income tax.
   - ☐ a reduction in the general level of taxation balanced by a reduction in public spending and an increase in borrowing.
   - ☐ an increase in the level of import duties with quotas on imported foreign goods.
   - ☐ tax allowances against all investment projects in industry.
   - ☐ the abolition of National Insurance contributions.
   - ☐ an increase in training schemes such as YT, combined with generous allowances to persuade people to start their own businesses.
   a For each of the above options state what additional information you would require before you could judge whether it was valid.
   b For each of the above options state the potential effects on British industry.

2 Outline the possible effects of each of the following on a business producing consumer goods and a business producing goods for an industrial market.
   i A fall in the value of sterling.
   ii An increase in interest rates.
   iii Rapid fluctuations in the level of interest rates.
   iv A rapid change in the technology used by industry.
   v A rise in the general level of unemployment.
   vi An increase in the average wage rate of 3 per cent combined with an inflation rate of 5 per cent.

3 Agricultural support policies are increasingly coming under attack. Developed countries are using a variety of measures to protect domestic agriculture:
   - ☐ the imposition of a minimum price and a guarantee that the government will buy surplus produce at this price.
   - ☐ quota systems under which farmers are granted permission to produce a limited quantity of a crop.
   - ☐ payments made to farmers to make up the difference between the market price and the guaranteed price for the crops.
   - ☐ controls on the resources that can be used in farming, for example limiting the amount of land that can be cultivated.

These domestic policies usually result in higher food prices for the consumer. To limit competition from developing countries, which often have cost advantages in production, they are accompanied by trade policies which impose tariffs and quotas on imported produce and, when support policies result in a surplus, subsidised exports.

The economic effects of these policies can be divided into four separate areas:

- income is redistributed from urban, industrial consumers to the rural economy.
- high food prices encourage farmers to produce more and so use a greater proportion of national resources than they would otherwise have done.
- high food prices are in competition with other consumer goods.
- developing countries face a falling demand for their agricultural products.

The following extract is adapted from the article 'Agricultural protection in industrialised countries' published in the *Economic Progress Report*, September/October 1986.

A study carried out by the World Bank constructed a model of supply and demand for grains, livestock products and sugar (which accounted for about three-quarters of world agricultural trade in 1980–82) across all major countries or country groups. The model was used to quantify the effects of agricultural protection (both domestic and trade policies) by comparing the current system of protection with more liberal regimes.

As with any results based on a model of this kind, the exact estimates of the effects of protection should not be regarded as precise. Also the consequences for the agricultural sectors, which account for a significant proportion of economic activity and employment in industrialised countries, and the consequent dynamic effects, are not spelled out in detail. Nevertheless the results are striking. They indicate that the liberalisation of agricultural protection would generate a marked shift in agricultural output away from industrialised countries and towards developing countries, as well as causing a net increase in world food prices. There would be a marked transfer of income away from farmers in industrialised countries, but this would be more than offset by gains to consumers and taxpayers as a result of overall gains in economic efficiency ... If developing countries liberalised their agricultural sectors at the same time as industrialised countries, both groups of countries would be better off. Only the centrally planned economies, who are the main beneficiaries from current policies, would lose. Overall, the world economy would gain in terms of economic efficiency to the tune of over $40 billion.

a Explain, using diagrams where appropriate, the effects of agricultural support policies on market price and quantities produced.

b Outline the arguments a government of an industrialised country might use to justify agricultural subsidies.

c Explain how the liberalisation of agricultural trade might help producers in the secondary and tertiary sectors of the economy. Are there any sub-groups in these sectors who might suffer as a result of liberalisation?

d You are a livestock hill farmer (both conditions qualify for subsidy). Discuss the marketing and production strategies you might consider in the event of liberalisation. The discussion should be in general terms of marketing and production principles.

4 The following passage is adapted from 'Business Brief' (*The Economist*, 29 October 1983). Read the passage carefully and answer the questions which follow.

The recent decision of Nissan's chairman to drop his opposition to building cars in Britain means that a formal announcement of the controversial investment is only weeks away. Arriving at that decision took three years of indecision. This was caused by anxieties over:

1. The duration of the recession in the UK economy.
2. The amount of UK manufactured components to be used in Nissan's cars.
3. Whether or not Britain would continue to be a member of the Common Market.
4. The number of unions Nissan would have to deal with. It would prefer to work with only one negotiating body.

N.B. Nissan is a multinational company.

a Define the term 'multinational company'. (2)
b State and explain
  i two reasons why a multinational might be welcomed by the host country.
  ii two reasons why a country might be suspicious of a multinational's wish to invest in it. (8)
c Explain why the four anxieties of Nissan listed in the passage made the company reluctant to invest in the UK. (15) 1985 (AEB)

Activities

1 Interview two farmers, one who produces subsidised or controlled goods, the other who works in an unregulated sector of the agricultural economy. From the results of the interview comment on the effects of agricultural support policies on business planning.
2 Investigate the impact of a rising or falling level of unemployment on the recruitment procedures of a business.
3 Select a trend in the national economy which is widely reported in the press. Collect as much evidence as possible concerning the effect of this trend on the business community. Your evidence may be from primary sources – for example by interview with local business managers or consumers – or from secondary sources. Analyse the information, paying particular attention to the diversity of response. In what ways and why does your analysis differ from that of an economist?

Suggested projects

1 A study of the impact of rising local unemployment on the business community of a small town.
2 The effects of government regional policy on local small business opportunities.

Essays

1 Comment on the impact of rising unemployment and inflation on a manufacturer of consumer goods.
2 Outline and discuss the effects of changes in the value of sterling on manufacturing industry.
3 A government has the control of inflation as a priority in its economic policy. Comment on the effect on the business community of the measures it might take in order to achieve this objective.
4 Representatives of an industry have been successful in persuading the government that the industry is in need of protection from foreign competition. What measures might the government employ to provide the protection? What possible effects could these have on an individual business within the industry:

   a in the short term?

   b in the long term?

5 'We will reduce the level of direct taxation and so increase the incentive to work.' (Prime Minister: the general election 1983) Do you think such a policy would achieve its objectives? (25) 1985 (CLES)

6 **a** 'Marketing managers need to know about elasticity.' Why? (10)

   b If the Bank of England introduced a tighter monetary policy, what, in your opinion, would be the consequences of this for a firm producing video machines? (15) 1985 (CLES)

7 What would be the consequences, for industry, of the chancellor of the exchequer increasing the rates of expenditure taxes? (25) 1985 (CLES)

8 The government is proposing to introduce further credit restrictions.

   a How might this policy be implemented? (5)

   b What effect would you expect these measures to have on:

     i the motor car industry? (5)

     ii builders' merchants supplying the do-it-yourself trade? (5)

     iii the overall level of economic activity? (10) 1986 (CLES)

18 Business and society

When you have studied this chapter you should be able to:

□ List the major external constraints on business activity.

□ Define conflict.

□ Appreciate the sources of organisational conflict.

□ Identify the objectives of trade unions.

□ Outline the organisation of trade unions.

□ Appreciate the constraints on trade union power.

□ Define a pressure group.

□ Understand the constraints a pressure group can place on business.

□ Outline the ways in which society attempts to resolve conflict.

□ Define change.

□ Appreciate the need for change.

□ Distinguish between ethics and values.

□ Appreciate the role of ethics and values as an external constraint upon business.

The social system of each country is unique. At any one time it is the result of the interaction over the years of ideas, ideals and their translation into actions by people and by organisations and institutions.

The social system also interacts with the ecological system of a country. In a developed economy, with the greater proportion of its population living in urban areas, this may not be so obvious. Societies which depend on hunting or agriculture have a social organisation that can be seen to relate to the needs generated by the land, the type of crops they can grow or the animals they can rear. A nomadic people following the herds of a particular animal is probably the most obvious example of this. In urban areas lifestyles, attitudes and group relationships might be affected by the way in which the working day is organised. It can also affect and be affected by patterns of authority and responsibility, the evidence of conflict and the strength of existing institutions.

It is not the purpose of a book on business studies to look too closely at the sociological aspects of a society. Yet business is a part of that society and the general trends which can be observed in the business world at any time will influence the behaviour of society as a whole and will, in turn, be influenced by it. In this chapter we will examine some themes that are often considered the province of sociologists, together with some institutions that have an effect on the behaviour of businesses:

□ conflict in society;

□ trade unions;

□ pressure groups;

□ change;

□ ethics and morality.

Conflict in society

A system is an assembly of interrelated parts that are connected together in such a way as to achieve a stated objective. A society consists of a multiplicity of subsystems, each with its own objectives. Every person within that society will have a personal hierarchy of goals that they hope, with varying degrees of intensity, to achieve. When the objectives of individuals are different from those of the systems in which they operate we say there is conflict. The same is true of the relationship between systems.

The most dramatic result of inter-system conflict is war. Between individuals it is murder. Most conflict does not go to these extremes. It can lie hidden, show itself in anger, or be ritualised through the existence of organisations. It is the existence and impact of inter-group conflict in the business environment that concerns us most.

Sources of conflict in business

Varying objectives

1 *The owners of the business* This person or group of people may have a number of objectives relating to the business itself. We listed profitability, survival and prestige amongst them in Chapter 2 ('The business as a system'). They will also have personal objectives which may or may not conflict with those of the business. In a one person business there is more likely to be a greater identification between personal and business objectives. In large organisations, where shareholder numbers run into the thousands, it is inevitable that the objectives of some shareholders will be at odds with those of the business.

2 *The management* Professional managers should have a primary responsibility to the profitability and survival of the business. This may bring them into conflict with shareholders, who may want larger dividends rather than the allocation of profit to the reserves. Managers are also people. Private objectives of power and prestige might lead them to advocate policies that are commercially unwise. Departmental managers can lose the overview and argue for departmental objectives even when these are at odds with those of the business.

Where there has been insufficient emphasis on the overall objectives of the business and insufficient integration between departments, the different departments may be working at cross purposes. In simple terms the marketing department might launch a major advertising campaign without checking that there is sufficient production capacity to meet the expected increase in demand. Planning and budgetary systems are designed to minimise this type of conflict.

3 *The employees* Most conflict in business is seen as a difference in objectives between those who are employed and want more money or better working conditions, and the

managers and/or the people who employ them. In fact this conflict reflects the conflict between managers and owners and inter-departmental conflict.

4 *The customers* Where a business wants to maximise its profits, customers want to maximise their satisfaction and, if they are also businesses, reduce their costs so that they can increase their own profitability.

Bad organisation

Conflict might arise out of bad organisation. A failure to create the necessary lines of communication or the framework in which teams of people with varying expertise can operate (e.g. design) can mean that people are making decisions on insufficient information. This can lead to misunderstandings and overt conflict, e.g. attempts to allocate blame when things go wrong.

Organisational structure

Conflict may also be generated by the organisational structure. Clearly defined hierarchical structures give individuals a clear chain of command and, usually, an established pattern of career progression. A change to matrix structure, for example, could give an individual several superiors who may not agree on priorities or resource allocation. This problem can be intensified if one or several of the superiors see the ability to command obedience from the subordinate as a matter of prestige. In this situation conflict can be generated at two levels – between departments and also between the organisation's objectives and personal goals of security and promotion.

External factors

The level of conflict generated will also depend on external factors. Employer–employee conflict is likely to be more marked when the employees are members of an active trade union, when there is a tradition of labour militancy in the industry as a whole, where demand for the product is declining and management responds with rationalisation of plant and manpower.

Problems of organisational conflict

Persistent conflict can lead to low productivity, low morale, poor industrial relations, excessive bureaucracy and the involvement of top management in relatively trivial decisions in order to resolve conflict. Conflict implies that there has been a failure to integrate the objectives of individuals with those of the business. In other words a failure to motivate. This can lead to poor quality goods with the expected result on the demand for the products of the firm. Inter-group conflict between management, for resources or prestige, and between shop floor workers in demarcation disputes, is also likely to lead to lower productivity and, in the latter case, disruptive industrial action.

In western culture there is a tendency to see all groups and individuals as being in conflict with each other. Thus conflict is seen as healthy and desirable competition – that by pursuing their own objectives individuals and groups will automatically contribute to the common good. Conflict, in this belief, leads to growth. The extreme form of this argument was put forward by Adam Smith as the 'laissez-faire' system of economic organisation, a free market economy in which there is minimal government intervention.

This approach does not take into account the varying degrees of power possessed by individuals and organisations. One person may be better equipped to dominate in a system of conflict by reason of brute strength, intelligence, acquired skills or personality. There is no reason to believe her/his personal objectives will contribute to the greater good of humanity than a person with less competitive skills. In Chapter 3 ('Markets') we examined the way in which market power might be used by a business to further its own objectives – not necessarily to the benefit of its customers.

The process of developing group cohesion can generate conflict between the group and other groups. The adoption of group identity symbols creates stereotypes that can attract hostility and aggression. This may reduce conflict levels within the group at the expense of external relations with other groups. When people have a close identity with the organisation they work for internal sources of conflict may be ignored in order to increase the business's competitive position. Over the centuries rulers have used aggressive foreign policies to distract the attention of their subjects from problems at home. While their armies are winning battles abroad citizens are more prepared to tolerate conditions at home!

SELF ASSESSMENT

1 State two sources of conflict within a business, and indicate how they might be avoided.
2 For each of the sources of conflict given above state one problem a business might experience as a consequence.

Trade unions

Trade unions are inseparable from the business community, but they are separate organisations with distinct objectives and should therefore be seen as part of the external environment in which a business operates.

Trade unions developed as a response to the changing economic and social conditions in eighteenth- and nineteenth-century England. The increasing urbanisation of the working population, the growth in factory size, and the improvements in communication provided by the railways and cheap postage created the conditions in which combinations of large numbers of workers with common objectives could be organised.

Combinations of workers of a particular trade to protect pay and working conditions were known as early as 1715. They were met with hostility from employers and it was not until 1826 that combinations in protection of labour were made legal. Even after this date other laws were used against them. In 1834 a group of farm workers in Tolpuddle, Dorset attempted to organise a union and were prosecuted for taking illegal oaths. They were sentenced to transportation, seven years in Australia, and the 'Tolpuddle Martyrs' can still provide a rallying cry for the trade union movement and a focus for group identity.

The haphazard growth of the trade union movement to meet changing circumstances has led to the development of several distinct types of trade union.

1 *Craft unions* represent skilled and semi-skilled workers in an industrial trade. They are the oldest form of union, for it was skilled workers who had the economic power, the education and the organisational experience.

2 *General unions* represent a wide range of workers, often unskilled, whose interests are not represented elsewhere, e.g. the Transport and General Workers Union (TGWU). General unions developed at the end of the nineteenth century. Their use of the strike, virtually the only activity open to them in an overcrowded labour market for unskilled labour, led to a period of opposition to the trade union movement that showed itself in restrictive legislation and the increased use of the police and the army to combat strikes.

3   *Industrial unions*   are restricted to the workers of one industry, although they do not necessarily represent all the workers in that industry.

4   *White collar unions*   are the most recent development in the trade union movement, and reflect the increased proportion of the working population engaged in administrative and technical services. The Manufacturing, Science and Finance union (MSF) reflects the sphere of influence in its title. More specialised white collar unions in the public sector are the National Association of Local Government Officers (NALGO) and the Confederation of Health Service Employees (COHSE).

The objectives of trade unions

The general objectives of trade unions may be defined as:

☐   the protection of terms and conditions of employment relating to wages, health and safety.

☐   the protection of job security.

☐   the protection of conditions of entry, e.g. formal qualifications required, training provided, apprenticeship conditions.

The ability of a trade union to achieve these objectives depends to some extent on the number of members it possesses. Union membership provides the trade union with funds and the ability to engage in disputes. To protect that strength it may find itself in conflict with other unions recruiting among sections of the working population it has come to regard as its own preserve.

Employers' associations perform the same protective function for employers that trade unions do for employees. An employers' association will represent the businesses engaged in a particular range of activities, although not all employers will be members and not all industries have such an association. Professional associations, for example the British Medical Association (BMA), fulfil very much the same function as trade unions, but it is extended to cover professional behaviour. Both in their objectives and in some of the tactics they use to achieve those objectives the professional associations have much in common with trade unions.

The existence of organisations with protective functions encourages the development of group stereotyping and the *habit* of hostility towards the opposing group. According to the attitudes or prejudices of any given individual, trade unions may be seen to be destructive organisations working for the good of its own members to the detriment of society at large, or employers can be seen as oppressors and exploiters of the poor. Both attitudes are extremes, but their existence to any degree is likely to lead to mistrust and work against the resolution of conflict.

The conflict of interest between employers and employees has the potential to cause considerable disruption in the workplace. To minimise this the relationships between the two groups are conducted within a framework of rules, that is they are *institutionalised*. The rules will vary from industry to industry, although some will be laid down by law. The process is known as *collective bargaining* and, when legal constraints are non-existent or low, as *free collective bargaining*.

In addition to being used to settle disputes covered by main union objectives, collective bargaining is also used to establish procedural systems designed to prevent the escalation of relatively minor disputes. It takes place on three levels.

1   *National advisory level*   This is concerned with setting guidelines within which collective bargaining can take place. The National Advisory Council (NAC) will include representatives of the Trade Union Congress (TUC), the Confederation of British Industry (CBI) and the government. This is a consultative process and its success or failure can depend on political factors as well as those of the business world. In a time of rapid inflation the TUC might back a voluntary incomes policy and recommend that all wage claims are kept within a given limit. How this is translated into practice will depend on the way in which the negotiators in the industry conduct their negotiations and the circumstances of that industry.

2   *National participative level*   It is this level of bargaining that produces the most dramatic clashes between unions and employers. Participants are national paid officials of the trade union concerned and employers or representatives of employers or the employers' association. Bargaining at national level is concerned with basic wage rates, conditions of service and employment.

3   *Local participative level*   This deals with all the minor disputes, including alleged infringement of procedures, unfair dismissal and matters relating to the individual members of trade unions. Productivity deals may be negotiated at local level, although whether they are possible is likely to be a matter for national negotiation.

Collective bargaining has the advantage of allowing employers and employees to reach agreements that are suitable to their situation, rather than an imposed agreement. This can be useful at a local level where people are likely to have some insight into the causes of disputes and the way in which they could be avoided. It can also be argued that the fewer people involved in a bargaining process the greater the potential for effective communication and the greater the chance of resolving the dispute.

However the conflict still exists and it can be argued that the existence of two clearly defined groups encourages rather than dissipates it. Again the success of one or other group does not depend on the rightness of their cause but more on the relative power of each group. In the next section we will take constraints on the power of trade unions as an example of this but you should remember that the employer involved in collective bargaining will have a similar set of constraints to take into account.

Constraints on trade union power

Constraints on the power of trade unions are listed below:

1   *The market demand for labour*   When a particular skill is in short supply relative to the demand for it, then the union is in a strong bargaining position. In extreme cases workers with the skill may not feel the need for union protection because they are offered satisfactory terms without it. When demand for labour is low the power of the trade union to gain high wages is more limited.

2   *The available technology*   Technological developments have superseded a number of traditional skills and reduced the demand for others. Where the technology can offer a high level of consistent accuracy combined, possibly, with low wastage and a short pay back period it will be preferred to labour – particularly if the industry has a history of bad labour relations.

3   *The market for the finished product*   Labour as a factor of production has a demand derived from that of the finished product. Aggressive competition from abroad, product obsolescence or a poor record in quality and service can make a business or industry less competitive and reduce the demand for labour.

4   *The attitude of members*   Not all trade unions enjoy the same reputation for militancy and cohesiveness. A union whose members have shown a reluctance to engage in industrial action may be thought to be at a disadvantage when it comes to negotiations. On the other hand if such a union were to threaten industrial action it may be thought that they must have a case.

5   *The structure of the labour market*   *Monopsony* (that is where there is only one employer of a given type of labour) restricts union power, particularly if there are several trade unions involved in the negotiations.

6   *The skill of the leadership of both employers and employees relative to each other*   There are varying levels of skill in negotiation and this can be extended to include the handling of public relations and the media, and the projection of personality.

7   *The attitude of government*   Governments provide the framework of laws in which collective bargaining is conducted, and can have considerable influence on the outcome of negotiations in nationalised industries.

8   *The cost of labour relative to other business costs*   If labour is important in the cost structure of the business a relatively small increase in wages could lead to a large increase in costs that will have to be passed on in higher prices. If the market will bear this, i.e. demand for the final product is inelastic, then the union will have greater power than if the market for the final product is elastic.

Need trade unions and business conflict?

Trade unions and the owners and the managers of a business have a common interest in ensuring the survival of the firm. The conflict is rooted in the allocation of the resources of the firm. Whilst trade unions argue for a share for the employees, owners are arguing for higher dividends and managers may be more interested in building up the reserves to increase profits. Profit sharing and share participation schemes have been suggested as ways of tying the interests of employees more closely to those of the firm.

SELF ASSESSMENT

1   The workforce in an industry may be represented by a number of trade unions. On the other hand, a single trade union (an industrial union) might dominate the industry. Give two problems management might experience in each of these situations, illustrating your answer with examples.

2   Using the list of constraints on trade union power as a guide, outline the constraints upon management or owner power when negotiating with a trade union.

Pressure groups

A pressure group is an organisation with objectives that lie within the sphere of politics but without the political power to achieve them directly. The activities of a pressure group may be solely concerned with persuading central and local government to give weight to its views in the decision making process by direct approach, or it may combine this function with practical activities to achieve at least some of its objectives in the short term.

Trade unions, the National Society for the Prevention of Cruelty to Children (NSPCC) and the Royal Society for the Prevention of Cruelty to Animals (RSPCA) fall into the latter category. Organisations such as the Campaign for Nuclear Disarmament (CND), by the nature of their objectives, tend to fall into the first category. All pressure groups devote time and resources to collecting evidence to support their case and, by influencing public opinion, attempt to put pressure on politicians through the electorate. When they are successful their aims may be adopted as policy by a political party.

Pressure groups vary in size, power and organisation. Large national or international pressure groups will have paid employees for administration and research, together with acknowledged links with members of parliament who will present their case in parliament. At the other end of the spectrum a group of parents meeting informally and complaining about the difficulties of crossing a busy main road to take their children to school might put pressure on the local authority to provide a crossing and warning signs by writing letters and staging demonstrations. In this case none of the members of the pressure group will be paid and it will cease to exist when they have achieved their specific objective. They might, of course, discover other things in their environment they object to and, encouraged by success, go on to further campaigning.

The business community can be affected by the activities of pressure groups in three ways:

☐ generally when the pressure group changes the climate of public opinion and there are changes in the law.

☐ specifically when the activities of a pressure group are directed towards a particular industry or firm. This might affect decisions such as siting or could lead to the closure of plants, e.g. the opposition of environmental pressure groups to nuclear power.

☐ incidentally and on a relatively small scale when the activities of a pressure group directed against other organisations interfere with the normal running of a business. The parents in the example given above may picket the road, causing employees to be late.

Where a business is directly affected by the activities of a pressure group it may experience the following problems:

1 The public image of the business will be affected. This may lead to difficulties in recruitment and possibly reduce the demand for products. A sustained publicity campaign about the dangers to health and safety of an industry's production processes can result in more able candidates for jobs failing to apply which can lead to problems in selection and training. A sustained campaign against the political policies of a foreign country combined with an appeal to boycott the products of that country can lower the sales of retailers selling those products and force them to look for alternative suppliers. The effects may be marginal but there is still the potential for an increase in costs. The business will also incur additional costs in improving its own public relations. Advertising to emphasise its value to the community, educational material and improved access for the public in terms of visits may have to be undertaken.

2 When the activities of a pressure group are directed against a specific business and the tactics of the group include the use of legal procedures this will involve the business in legal costs in the employment of solicitors and barristers.

3 In confrontations arising out of production processes, e.g. pollution complaints, the business may have to rethink its production methods and purchase new equipment to minimise pollution with a resultant increase in costs.

4 The activities of a pressure group may also lead to industrial unrest within a business. The trade unions concerned may begin to question working practices, health and safety procedures and compensation for industrial injury or disease.

We have already seen that the degree of success achieved by a trade union or business enterprise engaged in an industrial dispute will depend upon the relative power of the parties concerned. The success or failure of a pressure group also depends on the internal and external constraints on its situation.

- The size, organisation and expertise of the pressure group will affect the outcome. A multinational company with extensive resources would be a formidable opponent for a small group of community charge payers attempting to protect the amenities of their town from a bad siting decision.

- The general economic environment of the area can also influence the success or failure of a pressure group. In an area of high unemployment, maintaining a wildlife sanctuary is likely to be seen as less important than the jobs a factory built on that site would create.

- The existing public image of the pressure group will also influence the outcome. Where the pressure group is perceived as being extremist, public sympathy for the campaign is likely to be low and the impact reduced. When a pressure group has a reputation for exposing dangerous or undesirable practices, public opinion is more likely to be sympathetic.

Trade unions and pressure groups have been selected as examples of organisations whose objectives can appear to be in direct conflict with those of business. Other organisations can also be in conflict with business but their impact is less obvious and less sustained. In Chapters 12 ('People and business') and 14 ('Managing people') we saw the ways in which a business can attempt to integrate the personal goals of its employees with those of the business through a variety of motivational techniques. When this strategy is successful it is likely that the business is satisfying many of the objectives of the trade union movement, and conflict with trade unions will be reduced if not eliminated for long periods of time. Collective bargaining and negotiation between dissenting parties in society cannot resolve all conflicts. When both parties are convinced that they are right, or one party refuses to concede to the rights of others, then a system for resolving conflicts must be established.

SELF ASSESSMENT

1 Define a pressure group and give five examples of pressure groups with different interests which might affect a business enterprise.
2 Outline, with examples, three constraints upon the ability of pressure groups to achieve their objectives and the corresponding ability of owners and managers to resist them.

The resolution of conflict

The oldest method of resolving conflict in society is by drawing up a set of rules governing the relationships between individuals, organisations and the state, by which all citizens must abide. These rules constitute the law of the country. Not all infringements of the law are clear-cut and not all are admitted to. The administration of the law is concerned with deciding who carries the responsibility for a particular action or set of actions. This is done through a system of courts, each of which has limitations on its authority and the decision of each can be appealed against in a higher court, that is one which carries more authority. The final court of appeal is the House of Lords, in all matters of dispute.

The body of law in the UK is divided into *civil law* and *criminal law*. Civil law is concerned with the *law of contracts and torts* (that is *wrongs*, e.g. negligence). Civil law courts settle disputes and award compensation in financial terms for the offence. Criminal law concerns offences which are considered so detrimental to society that the rules are enforced by the state and a code of punishment drawn up for proven offenders. Adulterated food might be a matter for civil law if the adulteration was the result of negligence, and a matter for criminal law if it occurred as the result of deliberate activities on the part of an individual or the business.

Every area of business activity is governed to some extent by the law. The law of contracts is implicit in all buying and selling, including the hiring of labour.

The use of the law courts to settle disputes can be a long and expensive process. To overcome these problems and still enjoy the advantages of impartial, objective decisions a system of arbitration and tribunals has developed.

Arbitration

Provision for arbitration can be the result of a written agreement between the parties concerned, e.g. in a deed of partnership. Such cases are governed by the Arbitration Acts of 1950 and 1975. On the other hand provision may be established by Act of Parliament, e.g. the Advisory Conciliation and Arbitration Service (ACAS) which was established by the Employment Protection Act of 1975. Where arbitration agreements exist they must be adhered to before the parties concerned can use the courts to settle the dispute.

Arbitration has the following advantages:

☐   it is relatively cheap and quick compared with the use of the courts. The speed with which arbitration takes place can also save money apart from legal costs, because normal trading can be resumed sooner.

☐   the arbitrator is selected with the consent of both parties and can be somebody with experience of the problems of that branch of business and can understand the problems.

☐   arbitration hearings can take place in private rather than in an open court.

Once an agreement has been reached under arbitration it is considered valid and binding on the parties who agreed to arbitration, provided it is reasonable, within the scope of the original arbitration agreement and has taken into account every matter referred to it. When a party is dissatisfied with an arbitration agreement it can appeal to the high court on points of law. Failure of one or other party to comply with an arbitration award can lead to legal action for breach of contract.

The structure of ACAS is as follows: the chairperson is assisted by a board of nine members, to which the secretary of state for employment, the CBI and the TUC each nominate three people. It has a staff of civil servants with experience in industrial relations who operate eight regional offices offering conciliation and arbitration services throughout the country. These services include:

- ☐ conciliation in industrial disputes when invited to do so.

- ☐ conciliation between employers and trade unions or individual employees concerning alleged infringements of legislation, e.g. unfair dismissal.

- ☐ advice on procedures and practices relating to personnel and collective bargaining in the form of codes of practice.

- ☐ referring an industrial dispute, with the consent of all the parties concerned, to the Central Arbitration Committee.

- ☐ nominating people to places on the Central Arbitration Committee.

The Central Arbitration Committee can also be specified as the final stage in a voluntary agreement between trade unions and employers concerning the procedures for conducting an industrial dispute.

Industrial tribunals

Industrial tribunals, consisting of a legally qualified chairperson and two members, sit in most parts of the country and have permanent offices in cities. The tribunals are appointed by the government – the chairperson by the lord chancellor and the other two members by the Department of Employment. They are concerned with alleged infringements of the law under such acts as the Equal Pay Act of 1970. Any legal queries arising out of their judgment can be referred to the Employment Appeals Tribunal.

SELF ASSESSMENT

1 You have suffered a prolonged illness as a result of eating contaminated food. There is evidence to suggest that the contamination was the consequence of poor quality control in the business concerned. Assuming the business refused compensation should you seek redress through criminal or civil law?
2 'Arbitration' and 'conciliation' are technical terms used in the field of industrial relations. From your experience give one non-business example of each of the terms.

Business and change

External change

The social system is not static but constantly changing. The time scale of the change will vary from society to society and will depend on:

1 *The nature of society and the receptiveness of its members to change*   This will depend on a large number of interconnecting factors, some of which are extremely difficult to prove. A population weighted towards the younger age groups will, it is sometimes argued, be

more receptive to change than a society with an aging population. If change is seen as disturbing a comfortable way of life or carrying with it too great a risk of failure then it will not be accepted.

2 *The institutions of a society can also discourage change*   Institutions develop to meet a set of circumstances. When society begins to change the patterns of behaviour of institutions may slow the change down.

3 *Rapid change in society*   The rapid growth of population in the eighteenth and early nineteenth centuries meant that the social institutions of the UK were totally inadequate to cope with the new circumstances. The period saw the rapid rise of 'self-help' organisations such as trade unions and building societies, and a radical change in political institutions.

4 *The speed and efficiency of communications*   Good communications spread ideas and make people more receptive to change.

5 *The attitude of governments*   This may be a vested interest. If social organisation suits the governing class then they have a vested interest in preserving the status quo by law or by force. The converse of this is revolutionary change when a government that takes power sees the status quo as positively harmful.

Business as part of society must change with society otherwise it runs the risk of becoming irrelevant and dying. This can be seen as *voluntary* change. The business perceives change in society as a problem and meets it with its normal decision making process. Businesses may also instigate change in order to achieve their own objectives.

There is also an involuntary element in business change. A business is run by people, with people and for people. As the attitudes and ethics of people change so also will the nature of the business. The process might be almost imperceptible, nevertheless it will be there.

To summarise, a business will experience change in:

1 *Personnel*   As people leave a business and others are recruited there will be changes in experience, attitudes and objectives of the employees, which in turn will be reflected in the working groups of which they are members. The more senior the people concerned and the greater the authority and responsibility they carry, the greater the potential for change.

2 *Technology*   A change in technology can lead to changes in production methods, products and the organisation of the business. This will have implications for the recruitment, selection and training policies of the business as well as for marketing and production policies.

3 *Demand*   A change in tastes and preferences can affect the production department but may also require the business to re-examine its marketing methods and distribution policies.

4 *Government*   A change in government policies can have far reaching effects on a business. The introduction of Youth Training has changed recruitment and training policies. Government economic policy may have consequences for the financial and investment policies of the business.

5 *The economic environment* We have already seen the ways in which persistent inflation can affect a business. Recession can lead to changes in debt management and internal reorganisation. The business will react to changes in interest rates and demand with changes in production and marketing strategies.

Internal change

So far we have considered change as something which is forced on a business as the result of changes in the environment in which it operates. These changes have come about because of a large number of individual choices made by people and organisations. The implication was that the business faced with these changes must adapt to them. In doing so the business will need to make decisions. This internal reorganisation can be hindered by an unwillingness on the part of top management to follow through a course of action because of what they see as undesirable side effects. Delegation, for example, might be seen as giving too much potential power to the shop floor and opening management decisions to more informed criticism. The same objection might be made against an improved system of communications. Large organisations which have become too bureaucratised might be particularly resistant to change as might the trade unions and the workforce concerned.

The need for change

The need for reorganisation can be identified in the following circumstances:

1 *Failure to respond to external change* A decline in market share and profitability can indicate a failure in the organisation to respond to changes in the environment. The research and development of the business may not be as innovative as those of its competitors. It may be the recruitment, selection and remuneration policy which is at fault or it could be the result of overloading research workers with administration. To quote a cynical lecturer whose administrative work had been interrupted by the need to take a class, 'If it wasn't for all this teaching we could get on with the job'.

2 *Conflict* The existence of conflict within the organisation might suggest the need for new organisational structures. This is likely to indicate the need for new management structures, improved communication systems and possibly a regrouping of activities when two departments which need to work together are structured separately.

3 *People are trying to do too much* There is nothing wrong with doing a lot of work, but if a person or group of people have so much work to do that jobs are skimped or decisions made without sufficient thought then it can be a sign of poor organisation.

Successful change

Any deliberate change in the way in which people work which is seen to take place will meet with some degree of opposition. In times of high unemployment it is likely that any change will be seen as a threat to job security, irrespective of management reassurance. Working with new people and in new organisational positions requires a relearning process that can induce stress and can lower efficiency. This can reduce job satisfaction as people see their efficiency falling whilst they are working harder as the result of imposed change. For change to be successfully undertaken with the minimum of disruption the following conditions are necessary:

- □ the full support and commitment of top management.

- □ careful diagnosis of the existing problems.

- □ communication of the reasons for change and a willingness to listen to the ideas and opinions of people who will experience the change. This may bring up further problems.

- □ a clear programme and timetable for change which is communicated to all the people concerned. This programme should also include contingency plans for problems that might arise at each stage of the process of change.

- □ all necessary retraining, which should take place before the process of change begins. This will increase the confidence of the people concerned in a situation that invariably attacks security.

- □ systems of control and evaluation, which should be established so that the process of change can respond to new problems rapidly and with minimum disruption.

SELF ASSESSMENT

1 Give two instances in which change in business might be:
  a voluntary.
  b involuntary.
2 Assuming a business experiences a change in technology, give two ways in which this will stimulate change in:
  a personnel.
  b demand.
  c the social and economic environment.

Ethics and business

Ethics are a set of moral principles and values which govern the conduct of individuals and groups within a society. For the majority of people the ethic by which they conduct their life is a set of unwritten and unquestioned rules which they have acquired through the process of socialisation. They are expressed in their attitudes to a situation and in their behavioural response to situations.

It is easy to dismiss ideas as unimportant but the pattern of ethical belief that the majority of people in a society subscribe to will colour their attitudes to what they see as fair and unfair behaviour and have an important influence on the political, social and economic institutions of society.

Attitudes to work

The *work ethic* goes further than the simple need to have a job in order to earn enough money to live. A job is seen as conferring status on an individual, providing both structure and purpose to life. Redundancy or enforced retirement can have disastrous psychological consequences for the people concerned and their families. This attitude to work has caused demarcation disputes between trade unions and organised opposition to the introduction of new technology where it is feared that this will lead to redundancies. It can also lead to overtime bans, work to rules, go slows and, in extreme cases, the sabotage of new machinery.

The word 'Luddite' is often used to describe these activities after the semi-mythical Ned Ludd, who was thought to have led a band of machine wreckers fighting against the introduction of power looms into the textile industry in the early nineteenth century.

How far people's attitudes to work are coloured by the status it is seen to confer, and how far by the need for economic security, is difficult to determine and probably varies from individual to individual. Access to work without discrimination, by e.g. women and ethnic minority groups, has a firm foundation in the need to acquire economic power and a standard of living comparable with the rest of society. It also carries with it the belief that without integration into the economic system the political and social status of these groups also suffers.

Values

The values by which people order their lives form a complex structure and hierarchy that will govern all their actions whether they are operating in the economic, social or political sphere. These values may cover what is seen as acceptable behaviour in terms of honesty, interpersonal relationships and sexual morality, and judgments on the relative value of goods and services compared with education.

The values a society holds in general will affect such things as the responsibility a business is perceived to have towards its customers, shareholders, employees and the environment in which it operates. This can place external constraints on the business in its decision making processes and thus in its allocation of resources. Pressure groups such as the Consumers Association and Friends of the Earth can have a strong influence on the production and marketing decisions of a business, subject to the limitations we have already discussed. The responsibility of a business to its shareholders may conflict directly with its responsibility to its employees. A recent suggestion that above a minimum level pay should be linked with the profits of the employing business illustrates this conflict of interest. If implemented this would align the interests of employees more closely with those of the owners of the business. It has been suggested that carried to extremes this system would encourage existing employees to resist the expansion of employment because it would reduce their own potential earning power. For the same reason they might be against the ploughing back of profits as this would reduce present earnings for the potential benefit of future employees.

The concept of responsibility is inherent in any decision making process. A decision to follow one course of action carries with it the sacrifice of another course of action (*opportunity cost*) and this in turn implies that a course of action which is of benefit to one section of the community may injure another section of the community.

Responsibility carries with it the idea of accountability. In Chapter 6 ('Accounting') we gave a rigid definition of this idea in providing a true and fair account of the way in which a business had used the funds entrusted to it in a given time period. Throughout the book we have implied that a business is accountable under law for a wide range of activities which affect the individuals and groups to which it may be accounted responsible. There is also the additional dimension of ethical and moral responsibility for those activities which are not subject to law. In the short term a business may refuse to accept these responsibilities and refuse to see themselves as accountable. However a long-term change in the ethics and values of a society is likely to be reflected in a change in the ethics and values of the business. Commercial considerations might also force them to conform and changes in the law formalise their accountability.

1 Give two instances in which social values might influence:
   a the marketing decisions of a business.
   b the production decisions.
2 Give two instances in which the values of an individual will affect their response to:
   a a marketing problem.
   b a change in production technology.

Conclusion

This chapter is called 'Business and society', and there is a certain arrogance in that title because it is impossible in a few thousand words to explore the intricacies of the relationship between the business community and society as a whole. The chapter has argued that:

1 Conflict exists in society at all levels and this is reflected in the experience of business. Conflict arises out of differing objectives and the integration of objectives is important in the elimination of internal conflict.

2 Organisations such as trade unions and pressure groups form part of the environment of conflict in which a business operates and the relative power of both is limited by internal and external constraints.

3 The framework of law provides an external system for the resolution of conflict that cannot be resolved by other methods.

4 The whole is influenced by the abstract concepts of ethics and values which are so much part of an individual's personality that it is difficult to form objective conclusions at any moment in time. A failure to appreciate what society or their own peer group accepts as reasonable behaviour has ruined the careers of many a person.

REVIEW

1 In the case studies at the end of Chapter 4 ('Starting and running your own business') we met the Baines family, who were planning to start a nursery. Their plans collapsed when the highways department of the local authority recommended that the planning subcommittee of the council should reject the submission for change of use of the building. The reason given was the possible increase in traffic on a side road giving access to a main road. Joseph Baines submitted his own evidence that the road on which the nursery was to be situated was not, in itself, busy in the mornings and evenings, mainly because access for cars to the main road was so difficult. This evidence was not judged to be adequate.

   With planning permission turned down the Baines began to look for alternative accommodation. This was not easy. Buildings that were suitable carried with them the same disadvantages as the existing site and many had the possible additional disadvantage that there might be objections from neighbours to the change of use. A standard form was issued to all ratepayers by the local authority asking if they had any objection to the change of use of the building. Eventually the Baines found an underused squash court. It was a relatively modern building but the owner was about to close it because the revenue it generated did not cover the cost of its upkeep. There was ample parking space but unfortunately access was to the same road that had caused the original planning submission to be rejected. The Baines negotiated a price for the building and for the conversion work subject to planning permission. In the meantime they had discovered a further complication and were not sure whether it would work to their advantage. The buildings were in the jurisdiction of one local authority, and the road was in the jurisdiction of another. Which one would have the right of veto?

The latest information on the Baines' nursery is a recommendation from the local authority planning committee that they should be given permission for their squash court nursery project.

a In this chapter it was pointed out that a code of laws can prevent conflict arising and help in the resolution of existing conflict. On the basis of this justify the existence of planning regulations:

i in relation to Baines Nursery.

ii in relation to other business activities.

b In the role of adviser to the Baines prepare a statement for the planning subcommittee outlining the advantages of the enterprise to the community.

c Consider the possible costs to the Baines of the rejection of their planning application. What were the costs to the community?

2 A company has acquired a number of acres of land in a rural area. They have reason to believe the land has a quantity of a mineral which they intend to mine using open cast methods. The area is not part of a national park nor has it been designated as an area of outstanding natural beauty. The company does not expect to experience any difficulty in obtaining permission for their mining operations and had given a firm promise to the local authority that, apart from key technical personnel, all recruitment would be done in the area.

The scheme ran into opposition from two distinct groups.

 □ Naturalists, who claimed that the area in question was an important wildlife habitat supporting several rare species of birds and mammals.

 □ Residents who had settled in the villages of the region. Many of these people commuted to a large industrial town thirty miles distant and had elected to live in the country to improve the quality of life.

a Outline the conflict of interests inherent in the above situation.

b State some of the ways in which the decisions of the business concerned may affect the community in which it is located.

c As a representative of the business prepare a list of the arguments you might use in an attempt to reconcile the opposing groups to the mining operation.

d As a leader of one of the opposition groups outline a plan of action to prevent the business starting mining operations.

e What other factors might affect the eventual outcome?

3 Anna Johnson had been employed by a large company for a period of ten years. An active trade unionist, Anna Johnson was aware that she was regarded by certain members of the management as a 'trouble-maker'. She had successfully led an 'equal pay for equal work' campaign within the factory. As part of a reorganisation exercise the company decided to reduce its workforce. Anna Johnson was informed verbally that her employment would be terminated at the end of the following week. She was the only worker in her section to have her employment terminated at that time.

a Anna Johnson considered she had been unfairly dismissed. What grounds has she for this belief and what procedures should she follow?

b In what ways might Anna Johnson's union help her in this matter?
c Apart from legal considerations what other factors might determine the outcome of Anna Johnson's case?

Activities

1 Follow the progress of an industrial dispute. In addition to the causes of the dispute you should also take note of the way in which it is conducted, the tactics used, the interplay of personalities in the negotiators, political considerations, the morale of the workforce, the effects on the community, and short- and long-term results.
2 Study the impact of a large company on the community life of a town.
3 Select a business activity which would require planning permission, for example the construction of a factory on a given site. Do not choose an industrial estate. Investigate the procedures you would have to go through in order to receive permission. Interview local government officials and residents to discover their views on the matter. Analyse the results of your survey and prepare a report on the likely success or failure of the project, giving reasons for your conclusions.

Suggested projects

1 An evaluation of employee attitudes to technical change in company X.
2 What are the effects of legislation on the operations of enterprise Y? (A small business would be more suitable for this project.)

Essays

1 A merger is proposed between two businesses of approximately the same size and producing complementary products. What conflicts may emerge from this situation and how might they be resolved?
2 To what extent can the legal constraints on business activity be seen as counter-productive to the economy as a whole?
3 'The activities of a pressure group are a valid expression of concern by the community in which a business operates.'
'Pressure groups represent minority interests. Their activities increase costs and place unreasonable constraints on the wealth creating sectors of society.'
Reconcile and discuss the above statements with reference to business activity.
4 Consider the statement that all business activity should be made accountable to the society in which it operates.
5 Change and conflict are inevitable accompaniments to life. Comment on the implications of this statement for business organisation.
6 To what extent should a government legislate to control business activity? 1984 (AEB)
7 The manner in which businesses develop is determined by a complex interaction of a variety of forces both internal and external. Identify these forces and examine the ways in which they interact in the conduct of a business. 1985 (AEB)
8 Outline the obligations a business has to its employees and show how they may conflict with its obligations to other groups. 1985 (AEB)
9 Discuss all the implications arising from the introduction of computer technology throughout the administration of a long-established and traditional family business.
10 Argue the case for the reform of British trade unions. 1985 (CLES)
11 You are the managing director of a firm producing telephones. The government has decided to privatise the British telecommunications industry.

a How might the employees of your firm view the decision? (5)

b How might you view the decision, and in what way might your perception of the government's action be:

i similar to

ii different from

that of your employees? (8)

c What short- and long-term financial and organisational issues might the government's decision present? (12) June 1985 (CLES)

12 As leader of a trade union negotiating team which has just had an initial pay claim for an 8 per cent increase in wages (3 per cent more than the current rate of inflation) rejected by the board of directors of a cross-Channel ferry line, prepare a discussion document for other members of your team outlining alternative dispute procedures and their likely effectiveness. (25) 1986 (CLES)

19 Conclusion

No body of knowledge is ever complete. It would be satisfying to claim that if you had worked your way through this book you would 'know' about business. Unfortunately, to make such a claim would not only be untrue, but – worse – the less perceptive among you might believe it.

So what have you achieved? Where do you go from here?

The answer to both questions depends on how you have used the book. For people who know, or think they know, the information and techniques contained in it, the answer is to get out into the world of business, talk to people who do the jobs and begin to appreciate the wide range of interpretations that can be placed on these principles. A textbook can do no more than guide you. Those of you who have already tried some of the activities suggested at the end of each chapter will already be aware of the numerous ways in which each principle can be translated into valid practice.

In business there is no right answer to a problem – the answer will depend upon the internal and external environment of that business. You should also remember that today's decisions create tomorrow's environment.

> In 1984 a local authority created two middle management posts in two separate organisations. The job description was vague and the job specification was non-existent. Both posts were given the same title, the same salary structure and the same job description. Three years later the two post holders met and compared notes. They agreed on the major constraints on their decision making. They gave each other ideas for solving similar problems and commented when the solutions would not be ideal for their situation and also why. The organisational structures of their jobs were very different. Faced with similar problems in differing circumstances they had found different but valid solutions!

The same principle holds true of social institutions such as marriage and the family. One of the major conflicts in life is that of a person moving away from the family circle for the first time and discovering that the values and habits of her/his family are not universally honoured.

If all businesses are unique, how do we make sense of their experiences? At the beginning of this book we attempted to do this in a formal way by looking at the experiences all businesses had in common and by classifying them according to their differences. We can extend this unification by looking at a number of themes that have recurred throughout the main body of the text. Sometimes these themes have been referred to explicitly, sometimes their importance is implicit in the text.

Planning

To plan is to establish future objectives based on present knowledge. We have discussed the business plan in Chapter 4 ('Starting and running your own business') and the plans that are drawn up within the separate business functions in Part 2 ('The functions of business').

Planning, whether formal or informal, is a basic human activity. Individuals make plans all the time. They draw up career plans, and plans for improving their social lives. They submit plans, that is outlines of their objectives and the way in which they intend to achieve them, to the planning department of a local authority when they want to build or alter their own homes.

All human activity can be seen as the process of making plans. Very few people live entirely in the present and, as soon as a person begins to set goals, she/he is planning.

If individuals and organisations establish objectives then they must make decisions as to the way in which they intend to attain those objectives. A course of action must be chosen and this implies that other courses of action are rejected. A sacrifice must be made to which we give the name *opportunity cost*.

If people and organisations are planning in order to achieve their own objectives then it is more than likely that the course of action they select will conflict with the plans of others. We explored this theme in Chapters 12 ('People and business') and 18 ('Business and society'). It is inherent in all business decisions.

Another important aspect of planning is its ongoing nature. Short-term planning objectives may be realised in a matter of minutes, hours, or days. When objectives are not expected to be achieved for a longer period of time then it is necessary to check to see that the plan is on course. This checking process is known as *control*. The information gained might be used simply to correct decisions so that the original objectives will be reached. Where the information suggests that the original objectives are no longer feasible the information may be used to set new objectives.

The scale of business enterprise

The size of a business may be dictated by the market in which it operates, the technology used, the finance available to it, the age of the business and the objectives of its owners and/or managers. A small business may compete successfully in a market dominated by large organisations if it can find a niche in that market to exploit. This, in turn, may limit its capacity for growth. Tolerated whilst it restricts its activities to one sector of the market, it may find the market power of the dominant firms too great to challenge in other sectors.

Praise of small businesses is fashionable at the moment. Compared with larger businesses they require a relatively small amount of start-up capital, they are more amenable to change, communications and human relations can be improved more easily and there is less chance of destructive conflict building up. On the other hand they can often find it more difficult to raise finance, the managers may lack specific areas of expertise and, more important, may not appreciate this lack and employ specialist firms to supply it. Unless the optimum size of that type of business happens to be small they will not benefit from economies of scale.

Of course this is theory. If you have been observing businesses as part of your course and analysing the response of owners and managers to situations you will know that the individual response to the matter of size will vary greatly according to the individual circumstances of the business.

Business accountability is another recurring theme. Individuals are held accountable for their actions. Friends and family can bring social pressures to bear upon them. In extreme cases they have to answer in law. Businesses are also accountable in law. The greater their potential impact on society the greater the number of legal constraints within which they have to operate. Pressure groups formalise social opinion and force a business to conform. Accountability will influence or constrain all business decisions. Chapters 5 ('Statistics') and 6 ('Accounting') introduced the theme of control. All business decisions must be checked to ensure that they support the objectives of the business, their effects must be tested and the information on which they are made should be verified. These activities are undertaken within the organisational framework of the business so that its activities are regulated. Control systems are essential if a business is to be accountable.

The way in which a business develops depends upon the interaction of a wide range of influences and circumstances it encounters from the moment of its launch. Like individuals businesses develop characters of their own. The personality of the original founder may establish behaviour patterns in such things as leadership style, industrial relations and the long-term objectives of the business which may affect the long-term plans of the business years after the founder has moved out of active management. Managers will be selected on their 'fit' to this unspoken ethos of the business.

External influences are also likely to mould the character of a business. Some businesses will react cautiously to changes in the market, the economy and the law. Others will be more adventurous. Different businesses will react in different ways to changes in society and the political environment in which they operate. Some will survive, some will not. All will change, subtly or radically, to meet the changing circumstances. It is this very diversity of business activity which makes business studies so fascinating.

The question posed at the beginning of this chapter might be answered as follows: you have acquired a very basic body of knowledge that will enable you to analyse the business environment. In addition you are aware of the complexity of the subject and the important role business plays in society.

Booklist

Chapter 1   What is business studies?
J.M. Baddeley, *Understanding Industry*, Butterworth with the Industrial Society.
Jim Clifford, *Decision Making in Organisations*, Longman.
David Dyer and Ian Chambers, *Business Studies: an introduction*, Longman.
Tony Hocking and Richard A. Powell, *Investigating Economics*, Longman.
Geoffrey Morse, *Charlesworth's Company Law*, 13th edn, Stevens and Son.
Roger Oldcorn, *The Management of Business*, Pan.

Chapter 2   The business as a system
Peter Donaldson, *A Guide to the British Economy*, Pelican.
Geoffrey Hurd, *Human Societies: an introduction to sociology*, Routledge and Kegan Paul.

Chapter 3   Markets
Alan Griffiths and Stuart Wall, *Applied Economics: an introductory course*, Longman.
E.T. Martin, *Marketing*, Mitchell Beazley.
Peter Tinniswood, *Marketing Decisions*, Longman.

Chapter 4   Starting and running your own business
Colin Barrow, *Financial Management for the Small Business*, Kogan Page.
The Mini Co. Kit, Longman.
M. Mogano, *How to Start and Run Your Own Business*, Graham and Trotman.
Starting a Small Business, Business Guidebooks: Self-help guides for small businessmen.
Gary Jones, *Starting Up*, Pitman.
NatWest Small Business Bookshelf.

Chapter 5   Statistics: an aid to decision making and control
D. A. Bryars, *Advanced Level Statistics*, University Tutorial Press.
A. Green, *A First Course in Statistics*, Stanley Thornes.
D. Gregory and H. Ward, *Statistics for Business Studies*, McGraw-Hill.
Russell Langley, *Practical Statistics*, David and Charles.
Harold Lucas, *Statistical Methods*, Butterworth.
Darrell Huff, *How to Lie With Statistics*, Pelican.
Murray R. Spiegel, *Theory and Problems of Statistics*, Schaum's outline series, McGraw-Hill.

Chapter 6   Accounting: an aid to decision making and control
Peter Corbett, *Accounting and Decision Making*, Longman.
Tony Hines, *Accounting Questions and Answers*, Checkmate/Arnold.
G. Holmes and A. Sugden, *Interpreting Company Reports and Accounts*, Woodhead-Faulkner.
G. Taylor and C. Hawkins, *Accounting for Business Organisations: a practical approach*.
J. Townsley and R. Jones, *Numeracy and Accounting*, Longman.

Chapter 7   Finance
David Myddelton, *Financial Decisions*, Longman.
C.J. Higson, *Business Finance*, Butterworth.
Ray Proctor, *Finance for the Perplexed Executive*, Fontana.
Leon Simmons, *The Basic Arts of Financial Management*, Business Books.

Chapters 8 and 9   Marketing and The marketing mix
Peter Tinniswood, *Marketing Decisions*, Longman.

Nigel Piercy, *Marketing Organisations: an analysis of information processing, power and politics,* George Allen and Unwin.
Gordon Oliver, *Marketing Today,* Prentice Hall International.
E.T. Martin, *Marketing,* Mitchell Beazley.
Tom Cannon, *Basic Marketing – principles and practice,* Holt, Rinehart and Wilson.
Robert G.I. Maxwell, *Breakthrough Marketing,* Pan.
Malcolm H.B. McDonald and Peter Moris, *The Marketing Plan: a pictorial guide for managers,* Heinemann.
Hugh Davidson, *Offensive Marketing,* Penguin.

Chapters 10 & 11　Background to production and Production control
John Powell, *Production Decisions,* Longman.
Keith Lockyer, *Production Management,* Pitman.
H.A. Harding, *Production Management,* M&E Handbooks, Pitman.
R. Hunter, *Production,* Mitchell Beazley.

Chapters 12 & 13　People and business and Business organisation and communication
P. Bryans and T.P. Cronin, *Organisation Theory: the study of human relations within the business organisation,* Mitchell Beazley.
John Child, *Organisations: a guide to problems and practice,* Harper and Row.
Alan Bryman, *Leadership and Organisations,* Routledge and Kegan Paul.
Sandra Dawson, *Analysing Organisations,* Macmillan.
Desmond W. Evans, *People, Communications and Organisations,* Pitman.
Huw Benyon, *Working for Ford,* Pelican.
Pierre Dubois, *Sabotage in Industry,* Pelican.

Chapter 14　Managing people
M.W. Cuming, *Personnel Management,* Heinemann.
M.P. Jackson, *Industrial Relations,* Croom Helm.
K.J. Pratt and S.G. Bennett, *Elements of Personnel Management,* Van Nostrand Reinhold.
H.T. Graham, *Human Resources Management,* M&E Handbooks, Pitman.
Human Factors in Industrial Society, Health and Safety Executive.
Essentials of Health and Safety at Work, Health and Safety Executive.

Chapters 15 & 16　Decision making in business organisations and Tools for decision making
John Powell and John Harris, *Quantitative Decision Making,* Longman.
V.A. Fatseas and T.R. Vag, *Quantitative Techniques for Managerial Decision Making,* Prentice Hall.
J. Curwin and R. Slater, *Quantitative Methods for Business Decisions,* Van Nostrand Reinhold.
Bryan Carsberg, *Economics of Business Decisions,* Penguin.
S.C. Littlechild (ed.), *Operational Research for Managers,* Philip Allen Publishers.

Chapter 17　Business and the economy
Tony Hocking and Richard A. Powell, *Investigating Economics,* Longman.
A.G. Anderton, *Economics: a new approach,* Hyman and Bell.
Frank Livesey, *Economics,* Polytech Publishers Ltd.
Peter Corbett, *The Economy and Decision Making,* Longman.
Terry Price, *Basic Economics,* Pan (Breakthrough).

Chapter 18　Business and society
Gill Palmer, *British Industrial Relations,* George Allen and Unwin.
D.W. Fairhurst, *Business Resources: an economic and social perspective,* Heinemann.
Norman Worrall, *People and Decisions,* Longman.
John Child, *Organisation: a guide to problems and practice,* Harper and Row.

Glossary

absorption costing A method of costing that assigns indirect costs (overheads) to given cost centres.

accountability The responsibility to justify business decisions taken on behalf of other people. Thus the directors of a company are accountable to the shareholders.

acid test ratio The test of a business's ability to pay its debts in the near future. Usually measured by comparing liquid assets with current liabilities.

advertising The paid presentation of information and ideas about products, businesses and institutions. It is used to increase sales, build up an image and create prestige.

advertising elasticity of demand The responsiveness of demand to changes in advertising expenditure.

Advisory, Conciliation and Arbitration Service (ACAS) An independent body set up under the Employment Protection Act of 1974 to help resolve industrial disputes and contribute to the improvement of industrial relations.

after sales service Services to the customer after the purchase of a product. These can include the availability of spare parts, servicing and advice. It can be an important element in the buying decision of industrial goods and consumer durables.

agent Person or business authorised to act (for example, buy and sell) on behalf of another (the principal). The agent receives a commission on the value of the transactions.

aggression Self assertiveness on the part of an individual when experiencing the frustration of a drive.

allocation of resources The method by which the resources available to an economy are divided between the alternative uses. In market economies resources are allocated to those with the financial ability to pay for them. In command economies the allocation decisions are made by the state or agencies of the state.

apathy A reaction of indifference to the frustration of a drive.

appraisal The systematic review of the job performance of an employee to help in promotion, training and job rating.

appropriation account That part of the profit and loss account which describes the way in which net profit has been used.

arbitration The settlement of a trade dispute by an award made by a third party.

articles of association A document stating the regulations covering the internal organisation of a company. This document must be submitted to the Registrar of Companies as part of the process of registration.

assets The possessions of a business that contribute to the value of the business.

attitudes The semi-permanent pattern of responses shown by individuals to given situations.

audit The scrutiny of the accounts of a business by a qualified third party to ensure they give a true and fair view of the state of the business.

auditor The person who carries out an audit.

auditor's report The report prepared by the auditor on the accounts of a business. Company law requires that an auditor's report is attached to the accounts of a company when they are presented at the annual general meeting. The report should contain explanations of ambiguous statements.

authority The right of a person to use power to ensure that the duties entrusted to them are carried out.

autocratic leadership The exercise of authority without consulting subordinates.

average fixed costs Total costs divided by output.

balance of payments The summary of all transactions between the residents of a country with the residents of other countries.

balance of trade The summary of all payments and receipts from the buying and selling of goods between the residents of a country and those of other countries.

balance sheet A statement summarising the assets and liabilities of an organisation.

bar chart An illustration of a distribution by means of (horizontal) parallel bars of equal width, whose lengths are proportional to the frequency.

barriers to communication Any circumstance that impedes clear communication.

barter The exchange of goods and services for other goods and services.

batch production A method of production in which a number of items are processed at the same time.

bill of exchange An unconditional order in writing from one person to another, signed by the person making it, requiring the person to whom it is addressed to pay a given sum, on a given date to a named person or the bearer.

bonus payment A payment above the agreed basic pay of an employee for achieving set targets in, for example, output, punctuality, attendance.

brand loyalty The tendency on the part of customers to repeat buying of the same brand.

branding Giving a name, other than the name of the business, to a product or group of products to differentiate them from similar products.

break-even point The level of output at which the revenue generated by a business is just sufficient to cover its costs.

budget A detailed plan showing how a business or part of a business intends to reach its financial goals.

buffer stock The minimum stock level held by a business to ensure it can cover contingencies.

bulk discount A discount from the quoted price for buying large quantities of stock.

business An organisation that buys in goods and services which are then used to produce different goods and services to be sold at a profit.

capital The total stock of wealth (as opposed to income) owned by a business.

capital account The summary of the inflows and outflows of capital to a country recorded in the balance of payments.

capital expenditure Money spent on the purchase of fixed assets.

capital structure The different types of loan and owner capital by which a business is financed. It is usually measured by ratios comparing each type of financing with the total capital in use.

cartel A formal agreement between a number of businesses establishing accepted prices for their product. It is usually accompanied by investment agreements and quotas on production.

cash flow The money that flows into and out of a business over a given period of time. A projected cash flow for a future period is known as a cash flow forecast/cash flow budget.

centralisation A situation in which the authority in a business tends to be concentrated at higher management levels.

certificate of incorporation Certificate issued by the Registrar of Companies to a business that has satisfied the requirements for incorporation and is therefore permitted to trade as a company.

chain of command The hierarchical relationship between roles in an organisation defined in terms of authority and responsibility.

chain of production The progress of goods from the primary sector, through the secondary and tertiary sectors until the end product reaches the final consumer.

channels of communication The paths by which instructions in a business move from the higher to the lower levels of the hierarchy.

channels of distribution The organisations through which goods are passed before they get to the final customer.

charismatic leader A leader who derives authority from attributes of personality.

circular flow of income A term used in economics to describe the major income flows within an economic system and between economic systems.

class A group of values of a variate.

class limits Numbers (not necessarily values of the variate) that form the boundaries between classes.

class width The difference between the upper and lower class limits.

classification The grouping together of items, people, industries, etc., according to common characteristics.

collateral Assets offered in security for a loan.

collective bargaining Bargaining between the representatives of the owners of a business and the people employed in that business with the aim of settling differences, for example pay, conditions of work. Free collective bargaining is not constrained by law.

collusion A secret agreement for an illegal purpose.

command economy An economy in which decisions relating to the allocation of resources are made by the state. *See also* planned economy.

commodity markets The transactions of merchants dealing in commodities such as tea, wool, cotton, rubber and tin.

Common Agricultural Policy (CAP) A support system for agriculture involving quotas and subsidies for certain products, operated by the European Community.

communication The process by which information, ideas, attitudes and emotions are transmitted from one person to another. The extent of understanding involved is confirmed by feedback.

communication nets The patterns of communication between groups of people.

component A finished good used in the assembly of another good.

concentration ratio A measurement of the extent to which the largest firms in an industry control such things as market share, employment, capital.

conciliation A process of negotiation designed to reconcile the differences between two parties.

conflict The situation generated when interdependent people or organisations have different objectives.

conglomerate A business that produces a wide variety of goods and services.

constraint The limitations experienced by a business in attempting to achieve its objectives.

consumer The final user of a good or service, not necessarily the person who makes the purchase.

consumer panel A carefully selected group of consumers who provide information to a business on a continuous basis about their reactions to a particular product or service.

content theories Theories of motivation which emphasise the factors that might affect motivation rather than the processes experienced by the individual.

contract of employment The contract between the employer and the employee in which the employee agrees to do a certain job, under certain conditions in return for an agreed rate of pay. The Employment Protection (Consolidation) Act of 1978 states that the employee must be given a written copy of the contract within twelve weeks of starting work.

contribution analysis The distinction between the revenue received from selling a product and the variable costs arising directly from that product. The difference is the contribution that product makes to fixed costs.

contribution pricing A method of determining the price of a product by ensuring that the price will cover the direct costs and so make a contribution to fixed costs.

control The systems by which a business checks that its operations and performance are in accordance with its stated objectives and plans which have been formulated to achieve those objectives.

co-operative A business owned by the workforce and operated for their benefit.

cost The amount of money spent to produce a good or service.

cost benefit analysis An inter-disciplinary approach to the evaluation of projects that are likely to incur social costs. All costs are given a monetary value.

cost centre A unit of a business enterprise to which costs of production can be allocated.

costing The process of identifying and allocating the costs associated with the production of a good or service.

craft union A union whose members have all served an apprenticeship to a given trade.

credit The time allowed between the receipt of a good or service by a customer and the final date on which payment is due.

creditor A person or organisation to whom a business owes money.

critical path analysis (CPA) A planning method which shows the interrelationships between the different activities involved in the completion of the project and places them in sequence.

critical path The path through a network that represents the shortest time in which a task may be performed.

cumulative frequency The frequency of a variate plus the frequency of all values of variate lower than it.

current assets Assets which can change considerably within a given accounting period. These usually include stocks, debtors and cash.

current ratios The ratio existing between current assets and current liabilities.

customer The purchaser of the goods and services produced by a business.

customer service The extent to which a business has decided to satisfy the demands of potential customers in terms of supply, quality, after sales service, etc., accepting that perfect service is impossible.

cyclical unemployment Unemployment caused by periodic fluctuations in the level of activity within an economy.

debenture A long-term loan to a company to be redeemed on a future date. The interest is normally paid annually. Debenture is paid before dividends on preference and ordinary shares.

debtors A person or organisation that owes money to a business.

decentralisation A situation in which authority is delegated to lower levels of management.

deciles The values of variate, arranged in order of magnitude, which divide the data into ten equal parts.

decision tree A branching diagram that summarises the options available, over time, in a decision process. Probabilities are allocated to the branches.

deed of partnership A legal document drawn up by people entering into a partnership together and who wish to vary the terms laid down by the Partnership Act of 1890.

deficit budgeting A deliberate policy undertaken by a government in which expenditure is greater than expected revenue. The difference is financed by borrowing.

deflation A reduction in the general level of activity within an economy.

delegation This occurs when a superior gives a subordinate the authority to carry out a specific range of duties.

demarcation The distinction drawn between the roles assigned to different jobs in an organisation.

democratic leader A leader who consults subordinates before taking a decision.

depreciation The amount by which profits are reduced to allow for the decline in the value of fixed assets. The term is also used to describe the fall in the value of a country's currency in relation to foreign currencies.

desk research Any research that relies on the analysis of information already collected, collated and published rather than the collection of raw data by field research.

devaluation Reduction of the official rate of exchange at which a currency can be converted into another.

development areas Geographical regions of the United Kingdom, usually typified by high unemployment, designated as being in need of special economic provision.

deviation (from the mean) The value obtained when the value of the mean is subtracted from the value of the variate.

differentiation of products The use of techniques such as branding and advertising to give similar products a separate identity in the eyes of the consumer.

direct costs Costs which can be clearly allocated to a particular product. Such costs usually vary according to the level of production.

direct taxation Taxes that are tied to a person or company rather than levied on a product or process.

Director General of Fair Trading A civil service post created by the Fair Trading Act of 1973. Among other things the Director is responsible for monitoring and controlling the competition policy of the government.

directors' report The report compiled by the directors of a company and presented to shareholders annually at the general meeting. It is required by law.

discount house A financial institution that buys short-term bills before their maturity date. By this service they increase the liquidity of short-term debt and make it more acceptable.

discounted cash flow (DCF) A method of appraising investments that calculates the present value of the profits the investment is expected to generate.

discriminatory pricing When a business charges different prices for the same product to different customers.

diseconomies of scale Increases in unit costs as a result of increases in scale.

distribution The business function concerned with getting the product to the customer.

diversification The introduction of new products into the product range.

dividend The amount of a company's profits that are distributed to the shareholders.

division of labour The specialisation of labour.

divorce of ownership and control A situation in which the owners of a business delegate their power to representatives and employees.

double entry The standard method of bookkeeping in which all transactions are entered as both a debit and a credit or an adjustment within either classification.

durable consumer good A product which will be used by the final consumer over a period of years.

earliest start time Term used in critical path analysis to denote the earliest time an activity can start given the constraints imposed by other activities.

economic ordering quantity The quantity in which stocks should be ordered to minimise costs and take advantage of discounts for bulk purchasing.

economic sanctions The restriction of international trade as part of a strategy to achieve political objectives.

economies of scale A situation in which an increase in the scale at which a business operates will lead to a reduction in unit cost.

efficiency   A ratio of the input of an operation or process to the output.

emotional motives   Buying decisions made to satisfy the emotional drives of the customer. These are not necessarily limited to the purchase of consumer goods.

employers' associations   Organisations formed to promote the interests of employers either in a particular industry or generally. The Confederation of British Industry (CBI) is an example of the latter.

enterprise   The ability to see a market opportunity combined with the willingness to accept risk in order to exploit it.

entrepreneur   One who sees opportunity, undertakes risk to exploit the opportunity and organises the necessary resources.

environment   The economic, physical, social, political, cultural and ethical conditions within which a business operates.

equity   The value of a company's assets after all liabilities, other than those of shareholders have been allowed. Sometimes used to mean shareholders' funds.

ethics   The fundamental ideas and rules of behaviour that govern the conduct of a society or group of people.

exchange rate   The value of one currency expressed in terms of another.

expected value (of an event)   The probability of the event occurring multiplied by the benefit of such an occurrence to the business.

exploitation   To take economic advantage of a situation, for example in the exploitation of natural resources. It is also used in the sense of taking unfair advantage by the use of economic power.

extension strategies   Plans devised by a business to achieve the objective of extending the life of a product.

factors of production   The resources used in any business activity: land, labour, capital and entrepreneurial ability.

feedback   The response of a receiver to a message. It can be verbal or non-verbal.

FIFO   A method of stock valuation: 'first in first out'.

fixed assets   Assets which are expected to stay in the business for longer than the given accounting period. They are usually assets that the business needs in the long term in order to continue its operations.

fixed capital   Stocks of money, plant and equipment used in a business enterprise.

fixed costs   Costs which stay the same for a given period of time over a given output.

flexible working practices   Methods of work organisation that widen the range of duties which an employee can be asked to perform.

float   A term used in critical path analysis for extra time available for the completion of a particular activity.

floating exchange rate   The situation in which the exchange rate of a country is fixed by market forces and not established by official government policy.

flow production   A method of production organisation in which the work moves from one work station to another as each process is completed.

forecasting   Predicting possible future trends by drawing on statistical and accounting information available on past trends.

formal groups   Groups which exist as part of an organisation.

franchise   A legal agreement giving permission for a business to market a product or service developed by another business.

free collective bargaining   Collective bargaining which is not constrained by law.

free economy   An economy in which allocation decisions are made by the unrestricted operation of the price system.

frequency (of a variate)   The number of times a value of a variate occurs in a distribution. The term is also used for the number of values of variate occurring in a class.

frequency polygon   A polygon formed by joining with straight lines, the mid-points of the tops of the rectangles of a histogram.

frictional unemployment   Unemployment considered unavoidable in a free labour market. Generally assumed to be caused by people registering as unemployed in the short interval between one job and another.

fringe benefits   Additional rewards for employment given in kind.

full employment   Sometimes defined as a maximum unemployment level of 3 per cent. There is considerable debate about the measurement of full employment.

functions of money   Medium of exchange, store of value, unit of account, standard of deferred payment.

gearing ratio   The ratio of loan capital to owners' capital.

General Agreement on Tariff and Trade (GATT)   International agreement to reduce barriers to trade such as tariffs, quotas and subsidies.

general union   A union whose members are engaged in a wide range of activities.

geographic pricing   A pricing strategy which takes into account the geographic area in which the goods are sold.

goodwill   The value a business can command in addition to the value of its tangible assets.

grapevine   Patterns of communication based on the personal relationships rather than the official communication channels.

greenfield site   Business sites on the edges of urban areas.

group norm   The standards of behaviour considered acceptable in a member by a group of people.

Hawthorne effect   The tendency of a group of people to change behaviour when being observed. The name comes from the studies conducted by Elton Mayo at the Hawthorne plant of the Western Electrics Company, Chicago in the 1920s and 1930s.

hierarchy of needs   Concept developed by Maslow that people place their needs in a hierarchy, according to importance. He argued that people satisfied lower level needs before experiencing the drive to higher level needs.

hire purchase   Form of purchase in which a good is bought by instalments but the ownership remains with the vendor until the full price has been paid.

histogram   An illustration of distribution by means of vertical rectangles whose areas are proportional to the frequencies.

historic cost   The valuation of assets at their original cost rather than their current market value.

holding company A company that has a majority shareholding in other companies (subsidiaries). Sometimes referred to as the parent company.

horizontal communication Communication between people on the same level of hierarchy in the business.

horizontal integration A merger or takeover that unites businesses in the same type of production.

hygiene factors Sometimes known as maintenance factors. These refer to the conditions under which people work. They do not act as motivators but, if they reach a satisfactory level, can compensate for the more unpleasant aspects of a job. 'Its boring work but the pay is good.'

incentives Any improvement in working conditions designed to make people work harder or accept changed conditions of work that are likely to prove unpopular.

income elasticity of demand The responsiveness of the demand for a product to changes in income.

index number A method of reducing a set of related figures to a single number to enable convenient comparison over time.

indirect costs Costs which cannot be allocated directly to a named product.

indirect taxation Taxation levied on goods and services, for example Value Added Tax.

induction The introduction of new employees to the way in which an organisation works.

industrial inertia The term used to describe the reluctance of business organisations to relocate.

industrial tribunal Tribunals which deal with disputes concerning unfair dismissal, sexual discrimination, redundancy pay.

industrial union A union that draws all its members from one industry, for example the National Union of Mineworkers.

inflation A general rise in the level of prices.

informal groups A group of people who are drawn together by friendship, interests, etc., rather than by the requirements of an organisation.

information overload A situation in which the amount of information available for decision making is so great that the person making the decision is unable to process it effectively. 'You cannot see the wood for the trees.'

injections Inputs into the circular flow of income of an economy. Investment, exports and government expenditure are the categories usually quoted.

interface The overlap between two systems.

inter-firm comparison The comparison of the performance and profitability of businesses operating in the market using techniques such as ratio analysis. When a similar comparison is made between departments or subsidiaries of the same business it is known as intra-firm comparison.

intermediate areas Geographical regions of the United Kingdom which have some identified economic problems.

International Monetary Fund (IMF) An international financial organisation, established by the Bretton Woods Agreement in 1944 with the objective of encouraging international trade by assisting in the short-term liquidity problems of countries.

inventory Another term for stocks.

investment Commitment of resources to a particular project.

investment appraisal The analysis and evaluation of the profitability of an investment.

job analysis A detailed study and description of the tasks that form part of a job which are then classified in terms of abilities required, responsibility and working conditions.

job description A broad description of the roles and tasks required by a given job in an organisation.

job enlargement An increase in the content of a job in order to reduce boredom levels experienced by workers in routine and monotonous work. The extra tasks are from the same level of hierarchy, that is they carry no additional responsibility.

job enrichment Similar to job enlargement but the increase in tasks involves an increase in responsibility.

job evaluation The systematic analysis and comparison of jobs within an organisation in order to determine the position of one job relative to another in the hierarchy. It is used to establish a pay structure (though not the levels of pay). It is important to remember that job evaluation is concerned with the job not the person who is doing that job.

job production A method of production organisation in which a single product is made from start to finish by one person or group of people.

job rotation A form of job enlargement. Instead of the tasks of a particular job being redefined the employee is moved from task to task.

job satisfaction The degree to which an employee is pleased by the content of the job and the environment in which it is performed.

job specification A detailed statement of the personal, physical and intellectual qualities required for the successful performance of a particular job. It is used in drawing up the recruitment profile.

labour turnover The flow of workers into and out of an organisation in a given period of time.

Laspeyre index A method of calculating index numbers.

latest finishing time A term used in critical path analysis to specify the latest time at which an activity can finish if the established critical path is to be adhered to.

lead time The time elapsing between the placing of an order for stocks and delivery.

leadership The ability to persuade or influence others towards the attainment of established goals.

leasing A contract in which the owner of an asset (the lessor) agrees to hire that asset for a sum of money to another person or organisation (the lessee). The lessor retains ownership but not use of the asset.

levels of hierarchy The defined levels of authority and responsibility within an organisation.

liabilities Money used by an organisation for which it is externally accountable.

LIFO A method of stock valuation: 'last in first out'.

limited company A company which is a separate legal entity and whose shareholders enjoy limited liability.

limited liability Shareholders enjoying limited liability are only responsible for the debts of the company to the limit of the money they have invested in it.

line management The authority relationship between superior and subordinate that follows the chain of command.

linear programming A mathematical technique to determine the best way to allocate scarce resources.

liquid assets Assets which can be converted into money without loss of value.

liquidity The ease with which an asset can be exchanged for money.

maintenance factors *See* hygiene factors.

management An organisational role which involves planning, organising, controlling, communicating and co-ordinating in order to achieve set objectives.

management buy-out A situation in which the existing management of a subsidiary buy it from the parent company. When the majority of the required capital is provided by external loans it is called a leveraged management buy-out.

management by objectives (MBO) The systematic application of leadership, communication and motivation to the management of subordinates.

management science The application of a scientific approach to management problems with the objective of helping managers make better decisions.

manpower plan An outline of the resources and tactics to be employed by a business to ensure it will have the necessary manpower to achieve its objectives.

margin of error The difference between the actual output of a business and its break-even output.

marginal costing A costing method in which fixed costs are separated and the other costs (the marginal costs) are apportioned to products.

market The total number of potential customers for a product that can be identified by certain characteristics, e.g. age, income, geographical area.

market economy An economy in which the allocation of resources is determined by the behaviour of the markets for goods and services.

market niche A sub-group of the market segment. A clearly defined group of customers which a business is intending to please with its product.

market oriented When the activities of a business are ruled by the needs of the market for its products.

market penetration The proportion of the total sales volume of all suppliers of a product that is met by a business in that market.

market research The activities undertaken by a business in order to identify and assess the needs of the market for its products.

market segment Part of the total market for a product defined in terms of similar characteristics of potential customers.

market share The sales of a business in a particular market segment expressed as a percentage of the actual market volume in that segment.

market structure The characteristics of a particular market that determine the relationships between buyers and sellers and the degree of power enjoyed by each. Characteristics include size of businesses, ease of entry, number of buyers, products and their differentiation and the amount of capital employed.

marketing The business activity which aims to satisfy the wants of customers.

marketing mix The major functions of marketing usually given as product, price, promotion and place.

mass production The organisation of specialised labour, machinery and plant to produce large quantities of standardised products.

matrix organisation A method of organisation in which work teams are selected for the relevance of their skills to the task in hand rather than according to functional departments.

maximum stock level The maximum amount of stock it is economic for a business to hold.

mean (of a distribution) The measure of central tendency obtained by dividing the sum of all values of variate by the total frequency.

mean deviation The measure of dispersion obtained by dividing the sum of the absolute values of deviations by the total frequency.

measure of central tendency A number that in some way indicates the middle of a distribution.

measure of dispersion A number that in some way indicates how the values of variate are scattered about the mean.

median The measure of central tendency that is the number for which there are as many values of variate smaller than it as there are greater than it. It is the middle (50 per cent) quartile.

memorandum of association The document outlining the external organisation of a company which must be presented to the Registrar of Companies before a certificate of incorporation can be issued.

merchantable quality The minimum level of quality a product must possess if it is to perform the task for which it is sold. It is a requirement in law.

merger When two companies agree to combine to form a new company.

mid-range The measure of central tendency that is the arithmetic mean of the smallest and largest values of variate.

mixed economy An economy in which some allocation decisions are made by the state and the rest are made by market forces.

mode The measure of central tendency that is the value(s) of variate with the largest frequency.

money income The money value of income as opposed to real income which measures the purchasing power of income.

Monopolies and Mergers Commission A body established by law and reporting to the Department of Trade and Industry. It monitors the degree of competition in the economy by, for example, investigating the extent to which proposed mergers will result in a monopoly or significant reduction in choice for the customer.

monopoly The precise definition is a market in which one business is the sole supplier. In legal terms a monopoly is a market in which at least a quarter is controlled by one supplier.

mortgage A loan secured on property.

motion study The breaking down of the working movements required to complete a task into very small parts so that unnecessary movements can be eliminated and potentially tiring movements can be modified. The aim is to increase the efficiency of operations.

motivate To persuade people to carry out the work allocated to them willingly and effectively.

motivation The processes or drives that cause people to act in a certain way.

motivator Any reward, incentive or circumstance that motivates people.

moving average A technique for short-term forecasting based on past trends. The calculations smooth out fluctuations and update previous calculations.

multinational enterprise A business which produces and sells in more than one country.

multiplier The ratio between an injection into an economy and the increase in national income generated as a result of the injection.

negative cash flow A situation in which the amount of money flowing out of a business is greater than that flowing in.

net current assets Current assets minus current liabilities.

net present value (NPV) The difference between the costs of an investment project and the revenue expected to be generated by it after discounting by the cost of capital.

net profit Gross profit minus expenses such as the costs of marketing, finance and administration.

network A set of interrelated activities.

network analysis A body of techniques, for example critical path analysis, that are used in the planning and controlling of projects consisting of a number of activities with a complex interrelationship.

non-verbal communication The communication of messages using facial expression, actions and stance.

normal distribution A frequency distribution with a symmetrical, bell shaped curve, to which many distributions conform approximately.

objective probability A number, obtained from historical data or experience, which measures the likelihood of an event.

objectives The specific aims to which the activities of an organisation are directed.

ogive The graphical representation of cumulative frequency.

open system A system which interacts with other systems.

opportunity cost The inevitable sacrifice of alternatives when a decision is made.

organisation The division of the overall management task into a number of subordinate roles and the delegation of authority to perform these roles.

organisation chart A diagram showing the structure of a business organisation.

organisational conflict Conflict within an organisation arising from the conflict of functional objectives.

overheads Indirect costs of production.

overtrading When a business has expanded in such a way that it lacks sufficient working capital and so suffers liquidity problems.

owners' capital That part of a business's liabilities which are due to the owners of the business.

Paasche index A method of calculating index numbers.

packaging The use of materials to protect goods and to divide them into suitable quantities. It is also an important part of the promotion of consumer goods.

participation Term used to describe the variety of methods by which employees are encouraged to increase their involvement in the business.

partnership A form of business organisation in which between two and twenty people combine as owners. All partners are responsible for the actions of the other partners and there is unlimited liability. Unless a deed of partnership is drawn up the business is governed by the terms of the Partnership Act of 1890.

patent The right of the inventor of a product or process to have sole use of the invention for a period of years. The invention must be registered with the patents office. The equivalent right for books, records, films is copyright.

payback A method of investment appraisal which calculates the number of years it will take for the revenue of an investment to cover the original cost.

penetration pricing The setting of a very low price in order to capture a large market share.

percentiles The values of variate, arranged in order of magnitude, which divide the data into one hundred equal parts.

perception The way in which people interpret events in their life as a result of past experience.

performance standards The target set by a business in terms of output and quality for the performance of a stated task.

personality The characteristics and qualities displayed by an individual which show little variation over time and can therefore be used to predict behaviour in certain situations.

personnel The business function that is concerned with manpower planning and management.

physiological needs The basic requirements to ensure the survival of the individual. They are usually listed as food, warmth and shelter.

pie chart The diagrammatical representation of a frequency distribution by means of the sectors of a circle whose areas are proportional to the frequencies.

piece rate A method of payment in which an employee is paid according to the amount of work completed.

planned economy *See* command economy.

planning The drawing up of a detailed programme by which stated objectives can be achieved given the level of resources available.

plant layout The organisation of machinery and processes.

point of sale The place in which the purchase of a product is made. Point of sale promotion includes displays, advertising and demonstrations which are designed to boost retail sales of a product. These are particularly useful when research indicates that customers make their buying decisions at this stage.

Poisson distribution A frequency distribution often used in queuing theory.

population The entire group of data involved in a statistical investigation.

preference shares Part of the capital structure of a company. Holders are paid after debenture holders but before ordinary shareholders. The rights of preference shareholders vary from company to company and are laid down in the articles of association.

present value The current value of future cash inflows after discounting.

pressure group A group of people with a common interest who organise to influence public opinion and government policy.

prestige The esteem in which a business is held in the industry and in society generally.

price elasticity of demand The responsiveness of demand for a product to changes in price.

price leader A business that sets the price for the market in that other businesses in the same market tend to raise or lower prices according to the decisions of the leader.

pricing The marketing function that decides on the appropriate price for a given product.

pricing methods The ways in which a business can calculate prices.

pricing strategy The overall relationship a business decides on between its prices and those of its competitors.

primary groups Groups whose members are in regular contact with each other.

primary sector All businesses engaged in farming, fishing, mining, quarrying and drilling.

private company (Ltd) A limited company with share capital that has no statement in the memorandum of association that it is a public company. It cannot advertise share issues to the public, can have a minimum of one director and has no minimum share capital requirements for either registration or trading.

private costs Costs that are borne by the business.

privatisation A general term used to describe the transfer of provision of goods and services from the public to the private sector.

probability A numerical measure of the likelihood of an event occurring.

process theory Motivation theories that emphasise the process of motivation rather than the ways in which it can be achieved.

producer co-operative A co-operative that produces goods.

product The goods and services a business offers for sale.

product launch · The activities necessary to introduce a new product to the market.

product life The period of time over which a product is expected to sell.

product life cycle The pattern of sales in the life of a product usually divided into introduction, growth, maturity, decline.

product line A group of closely related products classified according to customer needs, price, use, markets or distribution channel.

product mix Sometimes called the product range. The combination of products produced by a business.

product planning Deciding on the products necessary to meet the needs of the market in terms of design, quantity and price.

production Any business activity which adds value to existing goods and services.

productivity The ratio between the inputs to a production process and the output.

productivity deal An agreement between employer and employees for improvements in pay and working conditions dependent on improvements in productivity.

profit The surplus generated by business activity.

profit and loss account Accounting statement showing the profit a business has made over a given period of time and the way it has been used.

profit related pay A payment system in which a proportion of total pay depends on the profit made by the business.

programme evaluation and review technique (PERT) A technique used in network analysis.

progressive taxation Taxation which increases as the tax base expands.

promotional discounts Price discounts used as an incentive for people to purchase a product.

public corporation A state owned business incorporated by act of parliament, responsible to a minister of the Crown and which offers goods and services for sale to the public.

public costs Costs incurred by a production process which are not met by the business, for example pollution.

public limited company (plc) A limited company with shareholders having a minimum capital of £50 000 and at least two directors. It can advertise its share issues to the public.

public relations The activities undertaken by a business to influence the views and attitudes of the public.

purchasing The business function concerned with the buying of raw materials and components.

quality control The business function that ensures that products achieve the levels of reliability, safety, etc., laid down in the design specifications.

quality control circle A form of worker participation which aims to make the employees involved with the actual production process by drawing on their direct experience of the job. It emphasises the servicing role of management.

quality target The desired level of quality laid down in the design specifications and aimed at satisfying the needs of the market.

quartile The values of variate, arranged in order of magnitude, which divide the data into four equal parts.

queueing theory A mathematical technique that solves problems caused by waiting lines of people or parts.

quota An agreed limit on production, imports or exports that is lower than possible output.

random sample A selection of data, from a population. Each item in the sample has the same likelihood of selection as every other item in the population.

range The largest value of variate minus the smallest value of variate in a frequency distribution.

ratio analysis An accounting technique to measure the performance and profitability of a business.

raw data The data as originally collected, before being subject to any statistical manipulations.

real income The purchasing power of money income.

recession A downturn in the level of economic activity.

recruitment The personnel function that supplies new employees who have the correct qualifications for a given job.

recruitment profile The list of qualities, personal, physical, mental and intellectual that are needed to perform a given job. It is drawn up on the basis of the job specification.

redeployment The transfer and retraining of an employee from one area of activity to another within the same business.

redundancy Dismissal of an employee because the job performed is no longer required.

regional unemployment A situation in which a particular geographical area suffers higher levels of unemployment than the national average.

registered company A business registered and incorporated through the Registrar of Companies.

Registrar of Companies A civil service function that is responsible for the registration of companies and the issue of certificates of incorporation.

regressive taxation Taxes that remain the same when the tax base expands.

relative frequency The frequency of a variate divided by the total frequency of the distribution.

remuneration All direct and indirect financial payments gained by employment.

resale price maintenance A situation in which the producer fixes the price at which goods and services are retailed to the customer. The terms of the Restrictive Trades Practices Act of 1956, the Resale Prices Act of 1964 and the Fair Trading Act of 1973 have largely abolished this practice. However industries can still fix prices if they can prove that it is in the interests of the final consumer.

research and development (R&D) Scientific and technical research targeted at the discovery and development of new products.

reserves That part of owners' capital which derives from undistributed profits. It is an item on the balance sheet of a company.

residual value The expected value of a fixed asset when it has reached the end of its life.

responsibility The extent to which an individual is accountable to a superior for the performance of a job.

restrictive practices (employee) Any activity by groups of employees designed to control the organisation of production. Demarcation is an example of this.

restrictive practices (trade) Defined by law as a trading agreement which is not in the public interest, for example price fixing.

retained earnings The undistributed profits of a business.

return on investment An accounting ratio that compares profit with the shareholders' funds.

revenue The money received by a business from the sale of goods and services produced.

rights issue An issue of new shares offered by a company to existing shareholders according to their existing holdings.

sales promotion Marketing activities which are not concerned with describing features of the product but offer an advantage to the customer that is not directly related to the product. Examples include holiday competitions, tokens for gifts, etc.

sample Part of a population, used to represent the whole population.

sampling The method by which members of a sample are selected.

sampling bias A defect in the method of sampling which prevents the sample from being truly random.

scheduling The prediction of the time at which a product or group of products will arrive at a given machine. It is an important part of production organisation.

secondary groups Groups whose members do not have frequent contact.

secondary sector Manufacturing and construction industries.

selection The process of choosing from a number of candidates for a job the person who is likely to perform the tasks most effectively.

self-actualising needs Needs that are inherent in the personality of an individual.

separate legal entity The status conferred on a limited liability company by the certificate of incorporation. The company is a separate person in law from the people who own it. It can sue and be sued,

buy and sell property. In the event of criminal actions by the company the directors serve the sentence.

share capital The money raised from investors against the issue of share certificates. In the case of ordinary shares this gives them the right to vote at the annual general meeting. Preference shareholders have rights to payments.

shareholders' funds The money raised from the issue of share capital and retained profits.

shelf life The period of time a finished product can be stored before deterioration and changes in taste make it unsaleable.

simulation The use of mathematical models to represent real life situations. Simulation allows decision makers to test the results of a number of courses of action. When used to evaluate complex projects it is a relatively cheap way of avoiding mistakes.

siting The selection of a suitable place within a locality for a business enterprise.

skimming A pricing policy aimed at maximising the profits received from a product in the shortest possible time.

social costs Costs of business activity which are carried by society rather than the business.

social needs The needs of an individual which are satisfied by the society of others.

socialisation The process by which individuals are encouraged to conform to the norms of society.

sole trader The form of business organisation in which one person is the sole owner and has unlimited liability.

span of control The number of subordinates a manager can effectively control.

specialisation The term used to describe the tendency for people, businesses, regions and countries to concentrate on those areas of activity in which they have a natural advantage.

staff functions Areas of activity in a business where authority and responsibility are based on the possession of expertise.

stagflation An economic situation in which high unemployment is combined with inflation.

standard costing A costing technique in which the costs for defined parts of the process are determined in advance, for example on the basis of work study. Actual costs are then checked against the standard costs. The method provides management with a constant check on changes in costs through variance analysis.

standard deviation The positive square root of the mean of the squares of the deviations from the mean.

standardised values The values to which the values of variate are changed so that the distribution may be approximated by the normal distribution.

statistic Any piece of data or any number which represents some characteristic of a distribution.

statistics The body of knowledge used to extract the relevant characteristics of a distribution.

status The position in society conferred on an individual or organisation by its peers.

status needs The need of an individual to have status confirmed by the behaviour of other people.

stock control The techniques used to ensure that a business holds the optimum level of stock, that is, sufficient for the business to trade without interruption whilst at the same time minimising costs.

stock exchange Central market for the trading in shares of public limited companies that have been accepted for listing.

Stock Exchange Council The body that controls the operation of the London Stock Exchange.

straight line depreciation A method of asset valuation that accounts for the eventual obsolescence of a fixed asset by reducing its value by a fixed amount each year.

strategy The long-term planning of a business designed to achieve its objectives.

structural unemployment Unemployment caused by changes in demand and technology so making existing skills redundant.

subjective probability A number assigned, by an individual, to the likelihood of an event occurring. It represents the degree of belief in such an occurrence.

subsidiary A company in which another company holds the majority of shares and can therefore control its activities.

subsidies Payments made by a government to certain types of business to help improve its competitive position.

sub-system A system which is an integral part of another system.

surplus budgeting The situation when government revenue is in excess of expenditure.

system A collection of interrelated parts in which the behaviour of any one of the parts will have an effect on the other parts.

tactics Short-term plans to support the strategy of a business and so help achieve its objectives.

takeover bid An attempt on the part of one business to buy a majority of shares in another company.

tally sheet A means of recording data as it is collected.

target market The defined market to which a business is aiming its marketing efforts.

technological unemployment Unemployment caused by a change in the technology of an industry.

tertiary sector Businesses which offer services for sale.

test market A representative part of the total market in which a new product is tried before being offered for general sale.

Theory X Douglas MacGregor's proposition that the average person dislikes work, does as little as possible and requires authoritarian leadership.

Theory Y The contrary proposition to Theory X. This states that individuals have a capacity for hard work, responsibility and appreciate participation. Authoritarian management styles act as a barrier to them achieving their full potential.

time rate A remuneration system in which an employee is paid according to the number of hours worked irrespective of the amount of work done.

time series analysis A forecasting technique based entirely on historical data collected over a period of time.

trade discount The money deducted from the selling price by a manufacturer or wholesaler when selling to another dealer. The amount can be adjusted to take into account the amount of goods purchased.

trade exhibitions An important part of the marketing mix for industrial goods. It is an exhibition, usually with a common theme, which gives manufacturers or their agents an opportunity to display their goods.

trade union An organisation representing a group of employees in matters of pay and other conditions of employment.

trademark A symbol that distinguishes the products of a business.

trading account That part of the profit and loss account which calculates gross profit by deducting direct costs from revenue.

training That part of the personnel function which is concerned with developing the knowledge, skills and attitudes essential for the effective performance of a job.

trend A discernible pattern in a set of historical data.

turnover The amount of business transacted in a period of time together with income from other sources.

under-employment A situation in which a person is employed but there is insufficient work to fill the time available. The term is also used to describe a situation in which an employee is over qualified for the work allocated.

unlimited liability When the owners of a business are personally liable for all the debts of the business.

Unlisted Securities Market A market of the London Stock Exchange which trades in the securities of selected businesses which do not possess the financial requirements for a full listing.

value added tax (VAT) A tax levied on the value added by each stage in the chain of production. The tax is levied when exchange takes place.

value analysis A technique used to analyse the design of a product to ensure low cost without sacrificing design competitiveness.

variable costs Costs which vary with the level of production.

variance analysis The comparison of actual with planned results.

variate A symbol representing a quantity that may assume any of a set of values.

vertical communication Communication between different levels of a hierarchy.

weighted average A measure of average in which the relative importance of each item is taken into account.

white collar union A trade union representing non-manual workers.

winding up The process leading to the liquidation of a company. It may be voluntary or involuntary.

withdrawals A term used by economists to describe outflows of money from the economic system. The major three withdrawals are saving, taxation and imports.

working capital Current assets minus current liabilities.

Index